Dick Howard

The PRIMACY *of the* POLITICAL

A HISTORY OF POLITICAL THOUGHT FROM THE GREEKS TO THE FRENCH & AMERICAN REVOLUTIONS

COLUMBIA UNIVERSITY PRESS

NEW YORK

COLUMBIA UNIVERSITY PRESS

Publishers Since 1893

New York Chichester, West Sussex

Library of Congress Cataloging-in-Publication Data

Howard, Dick, 1943–

The primacy of the political : a history of political thought from the Greeks to the French and American revolutions / Dick Howard.

p. cm. — (Columbia studies in political thought / political history)

Includes bibliographical references and index.

ISBN 978-0-231-13594-8 (cloth : alk. paper) — ISBN 978-0-231-13595-5 (pbk. : alk. paper) — ISBN 978-0-231-50975-6 (ebook)

1. Political science—History. I. Title. II. Series.

JA81.H648 2010

320.01—dc22

2010010726

Columbia University Press books are printed on permanent and durable acid-free paper.

This book is printed on paper with recycled content.

Printed in the United States of America

c 10 9 8 7 6 5 4 3 2 1

p 10 9 8 7 6 5 4 3 2

The Primacy *of the* Political

COLUMBIA STUDIES IN

POLITICAL THOUGHT / POLITICAL HISTORY

COLUMBIA STUDIES IN POLITICAL THOUGHT / POLITICAL HISTORY

Dick Howard, General Editor

Columbia Studies in Political Thought / Political History is a series dedicated to exploring the possibilities for democratic initiative and the revitalization of politics in the wake of the exhaustion of twentieth-century ideological "isms." By taking a historical approach to the politics of ideas about power, governance, and the just society, this series seeks to foster and illuminate new political spaces for human action and choice.

PIERRE ROSANVALLON,
Democracy Past and Future, edited by Samuel Moyn (2006)

CLAUDE LEFORT,
Complications: Communism and the Dilemmas of Democracy, translated by Julian Bourg (2007)

BENJAMIN R. BARBER,
The Truth of Power: Intellectual Affairs in the Clinton White House (2008)

ANDREW ARATO,
Constitution Making Under Occupation: The Politics of Imposed Revolution in Iraq (2009)

CONTENTS

A NOTE TO THE READER

BEFORE BEGINNING THIS VOYAGE, the reader will want to know how and why I myself have undertaken the journey. I am convinced that a fateful break in the long history of Western political thought took place at the end of the eighteenth century. The same year that heard the splendid principles of the American Declaration of Independence saw the publication of Adam Smith's *The Wealth of Nations*, arguing that the imperatives of political economy defined the goals of politics. Less than two decades later, the French revolutionaries sought to realize the rights they had declared in 1789 by using the power of the state in what they did not hesitate to call "the Terror." The answer to this new mode of political action was the invention of conservative political thought that turned to the past for its political models. Although each of these late-eighteenth-century developments was a sign that a rupture had taken place in the understanding of the nature and the goals of politics, they can also be seen as marking the culmination of a tendency that has been inherent in the long history of Western political thought. I call that tendency "antipolitics." Its antithesis, I hope to show, is democratic politics.

Antipolitics is the expression of a paradox that is present in all political thought. Political actors claim that their intervention will produce measures that will resolve the age-old task of determining the best way for men and women to live together. But if such political action were to succeed, it would put an end to the need for politics. In this sense, antipolitics is a politics whose goal is the elimination of politics. Providing ultimate answers, it eliminates the need to pose new questions. Solving problems, it reduces the rich complexity of human possibilities. Overcoming conflict, its unspoken intention is to put an end to history. It is a political theory that denies the need for political thought. If we remain with the examples with which we began, the imperatives of a free-market political economy based on the quest for wealth are no more "self-evident" than the Americans' claim that "all men are created equal." The French attempt to impose the reign of virtue by force was no more truly just than the conservative's confidence in the moral lessons of traditional society. To understand the triumph of antipolitics, it is necessary to rethink the history of political thought.

The history of political thought begins with the creation of democracy in Greece. Its basis was the citizens' freedom to participate in the decisions that determined their lives. The life of democratic politics has not been easy. Freedom can be felt as a burden; the responsibility of legitimating the choices we make weighs heavy at times. The individual's freedom in democratic societies is not unlimited; my freedom exists only insofar as yours is recognized as well. Our choices may clash; I may find myself in the minority. But the majority may be wrong, caught up in its own passions, blinded by self-interest, its members having sacrificed their own judgment to the rush of public opinion. Men and women over the ages have been inclined to give in to the temptation of antipolitics. Indeed, for long periods in the previous two and a half millennia of Western political life, antipolitics was the dominant attitude among the population. The history of real democracy has been a series of all too brief and at times tragic episodes because the freedom to choose includes the right to err. But the history of political thought has kept alive the questions that have motivated men and women as they try to invent more just ways of living together.

My claim is that the increasing prevalence of antipolitics during the past two centuries is a threat to the renewal of Western democracy. "Democracy" has become a value that is preached rather than practiced; its virtue is unquestioned, taken for granted, and for that reason misunderstood. As a result, its self-destructive possibilities—which are manifestations of the antipolitical temptation—are ignored. This danger existed in previous moments of political effervescence, but the threat was held in check and the possibility of political renewal kept alive by the fact that the history of political thought remained alive. Today, when antipolitics has incrusted itself deeply in the public's conscience and the politicians' calculations, the chances for renewal seem faint. Even those who feel the need for reform have lost touch with the resources of political thought. It is no surprise that political science has replaced political theory. The unconscious power of antipolitics leads us to look to political science for answers rather than to attempt to understand the questions that have motivated political thinkers since the dawn of Western history. Something more radical is needed. My claim is that the renewal of democracy and the recovery of true freedom as well as social solidarity demand that antipolitics be recognized as a threat to democratic political life. This recognition, in turn, can be achieved only by the retrieval of the history of political thought.

Writing a history of political thought was not something that came naturally to me (any more than democracy is a natural way for people to live together). My instincts and my interests did not point me to the past, but to the present and its problems. My education was pragmatic rather than classical or historical. A decade ago I could not have imagined writing this book. Although I have taught political philosophy for nearly four decades, I have written and spoken mostly about contemporary politics, at home and abroad. When I did turn to the past, I found inspiration in the nineteenth-century tradition of German idealism that began with Kant, was developed by Hegel and Marx, and continued to inspire critical theorizing in the twentieth century. These historical figures interested me because their thought lay at the basis of what I considered the most radical theories and the most critical practices. The public to whom I wanted to speak had similar concerns. That congruence of interests had an unintended consequence, however. My writing became more convoluted, self-referential, and academic. "Doing" theory had become a kind of practical engagement of its own. Criticism became an end in itself. Radicalism was its own reward. It was time to look elsewhere.

Although there is a great deal of often excellent practical debate among political theorists working within the normative framework inspired by John Rawls's path-breaking *Theory of Justice,* my pragmatic interests turned me instead to the study of history. I spent nearly a decade reading and writing about the American Revolution and its French cousin. The unintended consequence of that work was a new appreciation of the traditional questions posed by classical political thought. The revolutionaries, after all, took their inspiration from that history and couched their debates in its conceptual language. They used it against the powers that be, and they radicalized its potential in their struggles against one another. Increasingly interested, I began to teach introductory courses in the history of political theory, learning more with each course, widening my reach while increasing the depth of my interpretation. In the process, I retained the lesson of my turn to history, setting conceptual analysis within its social and political context. This book is the result that process.

I suggested at the outset of this note that the American and French revolutions marked the end of the classical tradition of political thought that began in Athens two and a half millennia ago. For some, political theory has been replaced by political economy; for others, the critical spirit of modernity must be contained by a conservative respect for the limits of human action, whereas their radical opponents want to continue the process of modernization. But neither economic liberalism nor political conservatism nor even the nineteenth-century theories of revolution have shown themselves capable of providing a framework for understanding the New World (dis)order that began with the fall of the Berlin Wall in 1989. Is this incapability a sign of the impotence of the tradition of Western political thought? Why reconstruct what should properly be deconstructed, if not destroyed once and for all? Why not look elsewhere for a model—to the many other ways in which men and women have sought to live together? Why the West to the exclusion of the rest? Is the Western tradition of political thought deservedly dead? Was it built on the domination of others and even of nature itself? Does it unjustly neglect other traditions that might enrich it? Many such objections can be raised against the present project.

There is no doubt that human history in its glorious diversity has produced types of civilization that are astonishing in their beauty and richness, admirable in their depth and complexity, and humane in their respect for others and the natural world. Nor is there any doubt that many civilizations have been able to avoid the injustice, inequity, and inhumanity that have too often marred the history of the West. Nor have women and men passively accepted conditions of alienation, exploitation, or subjugation. Analysis of these examples would repay the modern student with dividends. But it is worth noting that a major virtue of classical political thought is its recognition of the achievements of other civilizations and its criticism of its own. The Greeks, who were the creators of philosophy and democracy, also invented tragic theater and its comedic complement in order to avoid blindness to others' perspectives. Their first great historian, Herodotus, taught them to look at themselves with the eyes of the other, knowing that their achievements were neither permanent nor perfect. That is what made the civilization they inaugurated both critical and self-critical. It differed from others, however admirable and worthy those others might have been, because it could admire them while trying to surpass their achievements.

The critical and self-critical aspect of Western thought points to a second virtue that distinguishes it from other forms of civilization: it has a history—or, more strongly, it *is* a history. Its achievements and its defaults are never complete; they do not stand as monuments, and they are not self-contained. The Greeks inaugurated the analysis of history as more than a simple chronicle of deeds done and facts recounted. For their self-critical civilization, history was never past; it lit the present and carried the potential of a future. The Western civilization that they inaugurated is not univocal or unitary; it tells many stories that compete with one another. It is precisely for this reason that it has survived; its unity is built on difference, competition, and contradiction. Although the Western political tradition is hardly without its faults, it has endured because it has been able to integrate into its self-understanding the criticism of its failures to live up to its own ideals.

But why, then, it might be asked, do I spend so much time on religious thinkers in this book? Aside from the fact that religion (especially but not only in its fundamentalist forms) has come to play an increasing role in contemporary political life, two more theoretical answers to this question can be suggested at the beginning of this study of the long history of political thought. The first is that religious thinkers' concern with the other world only apparently turns them away from this one. In fact, it forces them to pose sharply the fundamental question of political theory: What makes social relations legitimate? The religious appeal to a divine principle of justice makes clear a point that the classical thinkers of Athens and Rome had only presupposed: that power supported only by physical necessity can never be taken for granted; its legitimacy must be demonstrated, and its existing form can be criticized. That is why Saints Augustine and Thomas adapted Plato and Aristotle, respectively, to produce their theories of the necessity of politics.

The second reason to study religious political thought appears with the Protestant Reformation and the Renaissance. The reformers' stress on the believer's conscience is a manifestation of the emerging individualism that is one of the principal characteristics of modernity. Because this Protestant form of individualism retains its referent to a transcendent source of justification, however, it makes clear once again the necessity of political legitimation and makes possible political criticism. But the modern individual is neither a classical hero nor a simple atomic cog in a mechanical world over which he has no control. Nor can he stand alone, outside of and independent from the community. It is no surprise that modern individualist thought seeks that communal support by returning to the classical theories of republicanism, both with Machiavelli at the time of the Renaissance and again with Rousseau in the years prior to the French Revolution.

I have deliberately limited myself to a discussion of the classic texts of Western political theory (even though some of them are less well known today than they were when they contributed to the great storehouse of political thought and political history). I have not tried to define the status of a "classic" and may have omitted some thinkers who deserve consideration here. My selection is based on both practical and theoretical grounds. Concerned to introduce political thought to a general reader, I have often followed the majority opinion expressed in the many anthologies and textbooks in political theory available on the market, but I have also been guided by my own study, whose motivation has been the attempt to understand the nature of political democracy and the conditions for its contemporary renewal. For that reason, this book differs from most available introductions, which present classical texts by means of discussions focusing on contemporary analyses of general problems such as property rights, the nature of justice, and racial and gender relations. The result of the latter approach is that both politics and history are left out of the history of political thought.

I have not sought to enter into debates with my contemporaries. Writing for readers rather than for already-minted scholars, I did not want to make this work into an academic treatise in which every interpretation is footnoted and justified by reference to or criticism of other scholars. Although I have read and learned from many others, my goal is to tell an exciting story that will lead contemporary readers to think afresh for themselves without having to pass through the screen of professional scholarship, which would distract their attention from the great innovators studied here.

In narrating this story of political thought, I have tried to set clearly the stage on which each thinker was also an actor. Thought does not take place in the mind alone; it must take into account both those to whom it is addressed and those against whom it is developed. This integration of the historical context with the theory that tries to address it is one of the book's important contributions. The history that I have chosen to recount is necessarily selective. A professional historian motivated by that false god of pure objectivity might well place the accent differently. My choices were governed by the attempt to understand the relevance of the history of political thought to the challenges facing contemporary democratic politics. Events acquire their significance in part from the way in which thinkers react to them; theories become richer when their context is clarified and their impact weighed. At the outset of each chapter and at the conclusion of subsections, I summarize the results of the preceding arguments and point the reader to some of the issues in the next chapter or section.

The history of political thought manifests continuity as well as change. The heritage of the past is at once always present and always being modified. In recounting the story of political thought, I have tried to avoid the temptation to tell the reader to pay special attention at this point or that to the way in which arguments from Plato or Aristotle are being adapted in order to deal with the new conditions facing a later author. Doing so was not always easy; later thinkers not only draw on their predecessors, but also draw out implications that the earlier thinkers were not aware of. If they didn't mention their predecessors, it was because the force of their own theory had to stand on its own merits.

In avoiding the lure of scholarship in favor of the attempt to explain and illustrate political thought, I am assuming that my reader will see the links that exist even when the chronological distance between two thinkers is great and the problems they faced differ from each other. For example, when the eighteenth-century Frenchman Jean-Jacques Rousseau and Polybius, the historian of republican Rome, make a similar argument concerning the idea of justice, I do not flag the relation. I trust that my presentation of Rousseau's republican goals will have alerted the reader to the probability that he had read his classical forerunner productively. For the same reason, I have not adopted the role of the omniscient narrator who warns the reader that the implications of this or that idea will become fully clear in a later context, as, for example, when Cicero's ideal of the Roman republic is reinterpreted in Saint Augustine's vision of the City of God. The retrospective discovery of discontinuous continuities (Polybius–Rousseau) and of continuous discontinuities (Cicero–Augustine) reflects the oscillation between the stress on unity and the concern with diversity that accompanies the history of political thought as it confronts the ever-present temptation of antipolitics. Fixation on either pole, unity or diversity, can lead to a denial of political legitimacy.

Finally, despite my concern with the present fate of democracy, I have resisted the temptation to draw explicit contemporary analogies to the historical analyses presented here. Again, doing so was not always easy. Plato's mocking criticism of democracy recalls traits of the confused anarchy that at times appears around us. Aristotle's distinction of arithmetic from proportional equality reminds us of arguments used to justify, for example, affirmative action. But Plato's stress on political unity does not make him a "conservative," nor does Aristotle's concern with diversity make him a "liberal." Nor are the "heretics" against whom the Roman Catholic Church sought to affirm its orthodoxy—for example, the Pelagians or the Donatists in the case of Saint Augustine—simply precursors of modern radicalism in the present, despite their similarity. But it is just such similarities between the problems facing the classic theorists and our own problems that explain why we continue to read these authors. Political thought is not a science. Its past is always present, constantly renewed, never finished. If this narration of the history of political thought is successful, its contemporary relevance will prove itself in the connections readers make as they read, but also after they have read and have again returned to the original texts and the antipolitical tendencies of our age.

ACKNOWLEDGMENTS

THE IDEA FOR THIS BOOK was conceived with the enthusiastic help of Peter Dimock, who was then a senior editor at Columbia University Press and originally developed the series of which the book is a part. Wendy Lochner ably took over the reins, encouraging me and nursing the manuscript to its successful conclusion.

I owe a debt to the anonymous readers of the original draft of this manuscript and to those who commented also on its penultimate version, produced after I had used my earlier version as a text in an upper-division and a graduate course at Stony Brook University. These comments were exceedingly helpful in providing the final version of the manuscript. Michael Denneny's philosophical acumen and editorial experience saved the project from sinking under its own weight at one crucial moment.

For the reasons that I explain in the prefatory "Note to the Reader," a number of years ago I began to concentrate my teaching on introductory undergraduate courses in the history of political thought. I owe a debt to the students in these courses, who have shown sufficient interest in my teaching to encourage me to deepen my studies in this area. My greatest debt, however, is to the graduate students at Stony Brook University who have worked with me as teaching assistants during these years. Some have helped during a single semester, others for longer, and still others have worked specifically on the preparation of this manuscript. Among the latter, Michael Roess, who took responsibility for the glossary, deserves first mention; Cara O'Connor and Caroline Arruda have been constant sources of encouragement.

Professional colleagues read and commented on sections of the manuscript according to their specialties. I bent the ears of many other colleagues, including Richard Bernstein, Carol Bernstein, David Carr, Andreas Kalyvas, Lee Miller, and Samuel Moyn, as I became increasingly captivated by my discoveries. One friend in particular, Anthony Kammas of the University of Southern California, read and commented on the entire manuscript, constantly prodding and encouraging me to develop my arguments.

Finally, I thank my family, who sometimes helped, sometimes suffered in silence.

The **Primacy** *of the* **Political**

INTRODUCTION
Democracy and the Renewal of Political Thought

Although the history of democracy began in Greece two and a half millennia ago, its enormous achievements contrast with its brief life. The great early political thinkers who tried to understand it—Plato and Aristotle—wrote after it had fallen prey to its own inner demons. The democratic desire for self-government reappeared in the Roman republic, which went on to conquer the Western world. But success again carried the germ of failure when social conflict led to a violent civil war, which concluded with the creation of an empire whose citizens no longer governed it. As with their Greek predecessors, the great Roman political thinkers who sought to explain republican political ideas—Livy and Cicero—were trying to understand a way of life that had expired. It was only after fifteen long centuries had passed that republicanism, with its potential for a politics of active citizen participation, was renewed in the Italian city-states of the Renaissance, particularly in Florence. And its greatest theorist—Machiavelli—was once again a defeated politician writing after republicanism's moment had passed. It was only three centuries later that democratic political values reemerged in the American and the French revolutions, whose heirs we remain. Yet the achievements of modern democracy have not been unmixed, and its founding principles remain subject to conflicting interpretations.

History makes it clear that democracy is not the natural way men and women have chosen to govern themselves. Indeed, neither the American Revolution nor the French Revolution was made in the name of "democracy." Only in the nineteenth century did democracy gradually come to be perceived as desirable, and it was only in the early twentieth century that Woodrow Wilson could justify America's entry into a world war by claiming that the world would "be made safe for democracy." But the Bolshevik leaders of the 1917 Russian Revolution that took place at the same time as that war claimed that their new state was the realization of a truly *social* democracy that was superior to the merely formal one that existed elsewhere. And in the years that preceded the outbreak of the Second World War, Italian fascism and German Nazism laid their own claim to democratic legitimacy by denouncing the bourgeois domination of Western democracy in the name of popular (or national) sovereignty. With the outbreak of the Cold War, two opposing systems, each claiming to represent the democratic will of the people, stood rigidly against one another, each contesting the other's legitimacy.

At the end of the Second World War, only some 20 percent of the world's nations could be considered democratic. Then the wave of decolonization in the 1960s suddenly created dozens of newly independent nations that claimed to be democratic. In the 1970s, another wave swept away dictatorships in Europe (Spain, Greece, Portugal), Latin America (Argentina, Brazil, Peru), and Asia (Indonesia, South Korea, the Philippines). Finally, in 1989, the wall fell in Berlin, and within two years the Soviet Empire was no more. Democracies were everywhere, it seemed. The twenty-first century is apparently destined to be the realization of what had begun in Greece two and a half millennia ago. History would have the fairy-tale ending for which humanity had waited so long. Indeed, some have gone so far as to talk about "the end of history."

The omnipresence of democracy today has had the unfortunate effect of transforming what should be a question about the rarity of democracy and the difficulty of preserving it into an answer that is assumed to be applicable to any society, regardless of its history, economy, or political culture. This democratic self-certainty has become a trap. It blinds those who are convinced that they enjoy it to the tensions within their own society and to the danger of trying to export what they consider their own virtues. It is well and good, as George W. Bush asserted in his second Inaugural Speech, to have "complete confidence in the eventual triumph of freedom . . . because freedom is the permanent hope of mankind, the hunger in dark places, the longing of the soul." But confidence can breed overconfidence. America's sad experience in Iraq; the North

Atlantic Treaty Organization's difficulties in Afghanistan; the European Union's inability to ensure peace and prosperity among its Balkan neighbors; the slide of Russia and other former Soviet states toward authoritarianism; the spread of religious fundamentalisms—all of these developments point to the necessity of learning to think about politics critically before appealing to truths that only seem to be self-evident. The twenty-first century is not an age for political complacency.

I

The fact that democracy's greatest theorists wrote about it only after it had begun to disappear in their societies suggests that even when it exists, it and its republican cousin are not forms of political life that can be achieved once and for all. As the rule (*kratos*) of the people (*demos*), democracy is restless, active, and self-critical. These characteristics are its virtue, the source of its great achievements, and the root of the richness of democratic life. But democracy can become a threat to itself because it accepts no limits on the aspects of social, individual, and private life that it governs. The threat can be illustrated by looking at one of the basic values held by democratic citizens. Does the equality of all citizens refer only to formal equality before the law? Or does it extend to equal participation in elections to all offices? To the equality of material satisfactions? To equality among ethnic and religious groups? To gender equality? But if equality continues its unlimited expansion, does it begin to threaten the freedom that is also a principle of democratic life? The defense of liberty can lead to the same tendency to limitless growth, to the point that this growth may in turn threaten the principle of equality. This simple set of questions suggests some of the ways in which democracy can become a threat to itself and the reasons why it is such a rare historical phenomenon.

The familiar saying that "the only cure for democracy is more democracy" expresses a self-confidence that blinds democrats to the necessity of thinking about the principles that make democracy possible and how these principles may become a threat to its existence. That is why this book returns to the foundations of the Western political tradition, drawing on materials from the past that will permit the renewal of democratic thought from a democracy that has become so self-certain that it is in danger of losing the ability to criticize its own premises and to recognize its own limits. The rarity, value, and the precariousness of democracy become apparent when set within the broad outlines of the history of political thought. Most of the thinkers studied here were not democrats; they were responding to the political challenges of their own times with the conceptual tools of their times, just as the defenders of democracy sought to reply to their own era. That is why they all belong to the tradition of Western political thought that I am claiming can help renew our own modern democracy.

By the term *political,* I mean simply the way in which people decide to live together and to understand the legitimacy of their social relations. The crucial concept in this preliminary definition is "legitimacy." Some members of the society always possess qualities that make them a dominant force and allow them to control others. If their power is to be more than violence, enforcing sullen obedience from a passive population, other members of the society must recognize and accept it. The latter must see the existing social relations as reflecting what they themselves have willed. They must agree, for example, that physical courage or the experience that comes with age or familial descent or well-schooled rational judgment or election to office by a majority of citizens is a criterion that qualifies a person or a group of people to govern them. At that point, what first appeared as the domination by brute force has become legitimate; it is now accepted as *power,* and the political leaders can rightly be said to have the *authority* needed to rule.

For long periods in Western history, the source of political legitimacy was located in the religious sphere. In one or another way, secular relations were justified as reflecting the sacred order. God's will—however interpreted—provided a framework within which social relations acquired their legitimacy. This schema was effective because God was conceived as a transcendent power whose authority could not be questioned, however grim the social relations of the time might appear. What could be challenged was whether the secular powers—which included the institutional church as well as profane social institutions and the relations among these bodies—were adequate to carry out the divine mission. These institutions could and did change, but whatever secular forms were finally adopted, the source of legitimacy in monotheistic religious societies transcended them. In this way, the transcendent principles of religion created a political framework within which diverse forms of social relations could coexist. The competition of the secular and the sacred did not threaten the basic principle of political legitimacy that ensures the unity of society because it remained separate from and outside of that legitimacy. The long life that was thus guaranteed to religious society contrasts with the brevity of the democratic experience.

Because democracy is a form of *self*-government, it has to discover a principle of legitimacy that is imminent to society. Only in this way can it maintain a balance among the diverse interests that exist within the society while ensuring that this diversity does not prevent the preservation of social unity. In a religiously based political system, the divine is an always present but transcendent guarantor of unity that also permits a (minimal) degree of diversity. In a democratic society, however, there can be no such external source of legitimacy; the existence of such a source would limit the fundamental possibility for humans to govern themselves. That is why the principles of liberty and equality are so important to democratic societies, whose dynamism is maintained by the competition between the two. But the immanence of these two principles explains also why their extension is limitless; there is nothing outside them that can stop their restless advance, which, in turn, may lead them to contradict or conflict with one another. Democratic political institutions' task is to ensure a peaceful coexistence between these two immanent principles. They can do so insofar as citizens recognize these institutions' legitimacy. It is for this reason that democratic politics is the paradigm of successful modern and secular politics.

The democratic paradigm of political legitimacy is not identical with either liberty or equality; it establishes the conceptual (or constitutional) framework that makes their coexistence possible. The danger is that sometimes one and sometimes the other of these two basic values may appear to dominate; or, at still other moments, the two may annul one another. In both of these cases, democracy is then threatened from within. The history of the twentieth century provides a simple illustration. It appears to the capitalist that too much concern for social equality is a threat to the freedom necessary for economic innovation and social progress; as a result, politicians insist on the primacy of freedom while ignoring (or downplaying) the inequalities that result from the blind logic of the market. In reaction, socialists defend a politics that—in its extreme form, communism—uses the power of the state to impose equality with no concern for the individual (or social) liberty that is lost. The political compromise between these two poles is proposed by the welfare state, which Europeans call "social democracy." Some in America see this compromise as producing the worst of both worlds; others identify positively it with the liberalism of the New Deal. In the global world of the twenty-first century, however, it has lost its efficacy as the nation-state loses control of large swaths of its autonomy. No one knows what will replace the seemingly stable political compromise that since the end of the Second World War has preserved the basic principles of democracy.

The problem of democratic legitimacy can be reformulated in terms of the twin values of unity and diversity. Political unity must be able to coexist with social diversity, plurality, and conflict. But unity goes together with universality, whereas diversity entails a concern with particularity. If, for example, the universality of the law is said to create "a government of laws, not of men," are there to be no exceptions that take into account particular circumstances? Or if the appeal to nonpartisanship pretends that differences of opinion are "only political," does this appeal show a disrespect for the right to be different? Does it tell people that their ethnic, sexual, and religious identities are not important and need not be taken seriously? What of the case where the defense of the national interest is said to justify violations of individual rights? Democracy again becomes a threat to itself, when it destroys its own basic values in order to save itself. It becomes an *antipolitics*.

The problem is that unity without diversity becomes either repressive or merely formal; it loses the creativity that arises from the competition of plural interests. That is why the separation of powers has been fundamental to democratic politics. Once again, however, the solution is unstable. The separation can become a rigid division that threatens the state's ability to act decisively. A difficulty may appear when minority groups or defenders of individual rights assert themselves. At first, they may restore a healthy balance of unity and diversity, but when one of the interest groups that make up the diverse society begins to worry that another has gained too great a share of the power that rightfully belongs to the people as a whole, it will then claim that its duty is to reestablish the power of the people. If it succeeds, the power of all of the people will be replaced by the rule of some of them—who claim to act for the good of all, but who do so by excluding the others from participation. Unity will be restored, but democratic principles will have been replaced by another form of *antipolitics*.

It is important to recognize that the threat to democracy comes from within; the same principles of equality and liberty, unity and diversity, universality and particularity that explain democracy's dynamism can become the source of its self-destruction. This threat is based on the fact that modern democracies do not enjoy a stability based on the transcendent guarantees of legitimacy found in religiously organized political societies. But that transcendence of the sacred that protects society from its own worst instincts also puts a limit on what can be accomplished in the secular world. The lack of limits is the source of the attractive power of democracy. Democratic societies are dynamic; their prosperity results from their refusal to rest content with their present achievements. Yet this same perpetual movement can be a source of an anguish that gradually eats at the democratic citizenry's self-confidence. Now a new form of *antipolitics* can appear. What appeared to be a limit—the existence of a transcendent source of legitimacy—may bring comfort to the individual, who fears the loss of meaning in a godless world in which each person is responsible for creating the meaning of his or her life. This desire to be part of a greater whole is another reason that democracy is the rarest and the most threatened form of political life. Although some religious societies may have achieved some greatness that compels admiration, it is only when men and women govern themselves politically that they achieve the true autonomy that is the signal historical measure of democratic humanity.

II

The uniqueness of democratic self-government and the rarity of its historical appearances stand out against the background of the two and a half millennia of Western political history. Although democracy represents the exception within that history, it is also an essential part of it. In particular, the interplay between politics and antipolitics as manifested in the relation between unity and diversity necessary in any society forms a recurrent theme in this book. In the remainder of this introduction, I present a brief overview of philosophies covered in the book and the historical context in which they emerged. The purpose of this sketch is to underline the fact that the unity of political thought not only is defined by men and women's attempt to live together without submitting to arbitrary force, but is also characterized by the diversity of the solutions to this reappearing problem and the constant presence of an antipolitical temptation to find a once-and-for-all solution to it.

Chapter 1 describes the emergence of democracy in Athens and the ideal portrait of it in Pericles' funeral oration. Pericles understood that this democracy was not the expression of the natural way in which men and women (and slaves) had always lived together. He was speaking at the height of Athens's glory, well aware of the way in which a series of complex political choices had gradually led from the heroic Homeric warrior-aristocrats to the participation of all (male and free) citizens in the decisions that governed their society. Yet one of these free decisions would lead to the Peloponnesian War, in which Sparta defeated Athens. Another led to the condemnation of Socrates for the supposed crimes of impiety and the corruption of youth. In this context, it is understandable that Plato's great political theory, *The Republic,* is an attempt to demonstrate the legitimacy of a rational, united polity to replace the instability and impulsiveness that had led to the self-destruction of Athenian democracy. *The Republic* is the first full-fledged theory of antipolitics.

The vast sweep of Plato's unitary theory demanded a response that would give plurality and diversity their proper place. This response was the task of Aristotle, Plato's former student, who recognized that legitimacy could come only from a government in which all the classes of society participated. Aristotle based this proposal on his recognition that equality is not an absolute but a proportional value and that stability can be ensured only by the rule of a "middle class." He knew, however, that his own solution left unresolved a basic political question: Will a good person, one who acts as a moral individual, also be a good citizen (and vice versa)? The source of the difficulty is the fact that individuals belong to many diverse associations, each of which has its own values. Although the political is the highest form of association because it is the most inclusive, the obligations imposed by membership in other associations cannot simply be neglected. Denial of the diversity of spheres of social life would produce an antipolitics.

This opposition between Plato as the theorist of unity based on an absolute and rational standard and Aristotle as the defender of diversity who understood rationality as the application of the proper measure to each particular object forms a recurring theme in the history of political thought. Before a theoretical synthesis between the two could be proposed, the conquests of Alexander the Great destroyed Greek independence. The political thought that had been expressed in the public sphere where all citizens could participate now turned inward; it became a new type of antipolitics. The Cynics denied the force of outside authority; the Epicureans accepted only such external content as pleased them; and finally, the Stoics synthesized these two tendencies. The significance of these three philosophical orientations lies in their rejection of the conflictual public sphere in favor of a unitary moral stance that concerns only the private person. Such moral comfort is a reaction to a situation in which political engagement seems impossible, although it can also be an excuse to avoid the risks of politics. The Stoic synthesis became important in late republican Rome, the stage on which latent democratic values reappeared after Greek independence was lost.

Roman historians' analysis of the sources of Rome's greatness expressed the self-understanding of the Roman republic. Livy, writing after the demise of the republic, which he regretted, reimagined its origins in order to explain the dynamic spirit that had animated it. Recounting the social conflicts that in barely fifty years had led from the abolition of monarchy to the creation of republican institutions, Livy illustrated the way this spirit presided over an institutional creativity that produced a political structure that could at once preserve unity and encourage diversity. He built on Polybius's analysis of the way these institutions actually functioned—an analysis Polybius carried out at the height of republican power in his attempt to understand why Rome had become a world power, whereas his native Greece had remained caught up in the particular and parochial life of its small city-states. Livy pointed to the way that division, plurality, and institutional competition gave the republican spirit an expansive political power as each sector and each institution sought to make itself stronger in order to face others' challenge. This competitive mixture of the institutions of government provided a dynamic that surpassed the more conservative mixing of social classes by which Aristotle had sought to achieve stability. But the new dynamic republic needed a principle of self-limitation, which Cicero, not incidentally the Roman heir to Greek stoicism, proposed nearly a century later.

The problem, however, was that Cicero's republican political synthesis looked to the past, which made it impossible for him to propose realistic solutions to the civil war that engulfed Rome in his time. Theory that built on past glories was no help as Augustus's creation of an empire made possible the Pax Romana that would rule the world for centuries even as it destroyed what remained of the republican desire for self-government. As in the wake of the Greek democratic experience, political thought now turned inward; morality replaced politics and found a home in the soul of the individual—in this case, the Christian. As the Gospel of Luke (2:1–7) recounts, Jesus was born in Bethlehem because his parents had returned there to be counted by census takers of the new Roman Empire. An epochal transformation began thereafter; the source of political legitimacy now lay in a transcendent God who had become immanent in the suffering of the Son before being transformed into the Holy Spirit. "My Kingdom is not of this world," said Jesus (John 18:36), but the church and the believer were indeed of it. Political life continued, and political thought faced a new type of antipolitical challenge.

The task of a properly Christian political thought was to create a framework of meaning to hold together the sacred and the secular worlds. Saint Paul, whose mission to the gentiles began the creation of the church as a political entity, laid the basis for what came to be known as doctrine of the "two swords," according to which the church was charged with the sacred while the state was responsible for the secular. Because God willed each of them, the relation between the two domains remained undetermined. It was only at the beginning of the fifth century that Saint Augustine proposed a theory that tried to establish the relation between the unitary "City of God" and the diverse "City of Man." His use of the term *civitas* (city) and his frequent citation of Cicero underlined his political intent, and his reliance on a Platonic version of Christian theology suggested that his aim was to establish the fundamental unity of the two poles by subordinating the diversity of the secular to the unity of the sacred. But this theoretical solution could not be maintained in practice. How, for example, would the church deal with heretics? Conversely, how would it reply to the accusation that its morality of love and submission was responsible for the Roman Empire's inability to defeat the invading barbarians who sacked Rome in 410?

During the time of the so-called Dark Ages, it was the church, in particular the cloistered monks, that maintained what remained of classical culture. But the secular gradually reclaimed its rights when Charlemagne was crowned Holy Roman emperor in 800. The problem of the "two swords" now became acute as pontiff and emperor clashed repeatedly for political primacy. Their conflict came to a head in the Investiture Struggle of the eleventh century. The papal victory in this conflict had a paradoxical outcome. The church won control of its own institutions, but this same autonomy freed the state from its authority. A new synthesis had to be invented to rejoin what had been sundered. In a Christian society, the emerging secular state still needed the legitimacy offered by religious authority. And on its side, the church's spiritual mission needed secular support. It is no surprise that the first crusade (1096) followed closely on the conclusion of the Investiture Struggle.

The rediscovery of the lost writings of Aristotle made possible the creation of a new theology that seemed capable of facing up to the practical problems of the secular society that was emerging from centuries of stagnation. The excessive weight that had been placed on the unitary Platonic theology had proved too heavy, so Saint Thomas Aquinas proposed an Aristotelian vision of the plural nature of the Creation, each of whose domains has its own proper type of legitimacy. On the secular side, Aquinas developed the stoic idea of natural law; on the religious side, he distinguished what belongs to divine grace from what remains in the power of men and thus subject to secular laws. In this way, he restored the harmony of the two swords. But the Thomist synthesis proved too powerful. It seemed to leave insufficient room for individual piety and the personal experience of the sacred; and its vision of a hierarchical natural world governed by its own inherent lawfulness left insufficient place for human freedom. The theoretical and the religious reaction to Thomas's scholastic theology set the stage for the emergence of modernity inside and outside of the church.

The birth of modernity was slow, painful, unintended, and incomplete, but its effect was radical. Humans' vision of the natural world changed, as did their idea of human nature. In the classical age, men had tried to understand the laws of nature in order to conform their reason to nature's (or a divine creator's) goals. Now it was human reason that had to provide the ends to which nature must be made to conform. This shift, identified with the Reformation and the Renaissance, anticipated the rebirth of democratic political thought. The virtues of the modern individual differed from those that had ennobled the Greek or the Roman citizen; they differed as well from those possessed by a member of the universal Catholic Church. Those premodern individuals were born into membership; the community and its values had priority, and freedom was needed only to do what ought to be done according to values that existed outside of and prior to the individual. In contrast, modern individuality exists prior to and independent of the community. The result of the shift was a modern freedom that brought with it a terrifying alienation from the world and from other men. The challenge for modernity was to conceive of a new political form that would unify individuals who are always in principle free to escape any bonds to which they do not freely consent.

The dilemmas of modernity became acute in both the religious domain and the political domain. In the sphere of religion, Martin Luther rejected the church's doctrinal teaching, which he claimed had become too worldly, arguing that "only faith" and "only Scripture" offer the possibility of salvation. But if the individual's relation to the divine depends on his faith (and God's grace), coupled with his personal interpretation of the holy text, what would hold together the community of believers? Not surprisingly, Luther's theological challenge to authority unleashed a rebellious torrent that threatened the established order, including his own new church. In the end, Luther could only vest power in the secular rulers and lodge the quest for salvation in the private sphere. It became John Calvin's task to rethink the relation of the sacred to the secular. His alternative to Luther's Platonic-Augustinian theology presented a modern, Aristotelian-Thomist theology. Calvin argued that the believer's conscience functions as the mediator between heaven and earth. The Calvinist internalizes the divine commandments, to which he constantly compares his own behavior as he attempts to conform to them. In this way, Calvinist theology offered a template for what counts as legitimate social relations. As opposed to Luther's reliance on the state, the new church would define the relation of the secular and the sacred. The one-sidedness of both arguments provided the foundation of a new type of antipolitics.

In the city-states that began to flourish in Italy in the fifteenth century, the republican desire for self-rule once again breathed the fresh air of the city. But the interlude was short-lived. Driven into exile, Machiavelli sought to understand its demise. He recognized that power must be used to maintain the stability of a society in which the initiative of the individual faced the uncertainties of fortune. But what can make this power legitimate? To many readers, the answer was simple: success. But this answer is an oversimplification. Machiavelli warned against the danger of confusing the way we live with the way we ought to live. Because there is no perfect or final solution to the problems of human coexistence in an uncertain world composed of individuals who are free from transcendent moral or religious rules, the legitimacy of power depends on the ability of those who exercise power to find the most economical use for it. Despite its title, *The Prince* recommends no single form of government; it analyzes a wide range of historical examples in order to understand the logic of political action. A similar concern governs Machiavelli's other great political work, *The Discourses on Livy*, whose secular and republican sympathies make clear that the Florentine was not just a "Machiavellian."

The Reformation challenged the framework of traditional political life. Religious wars broke out, culminating in the Thirty Years' War (1618–1648), which devastated the continent before the Treaty of Westphalia consecrated the secular state's political autonomy. This autonomy faced its most serious challenge in England, where the absolutist monarch's attempts to dictate religious matters provoked a civil war. The Protestant "saints" led by Oliver Cromwell overthrew the Crown and tried and beheaded the monarch before creating a republic, which soon degenerated into one-man rule called a "protectorate" until the old monarchy was restored. These abrupt reversals made it clear that political theorists had to find a new way to think about the unity of a divided society. The theological claims that justified the old absolutism had lost their legitimacy, and the spiritual autonomy that the Reformation had promised did not produce a stable political democracy.

Attention now turned to the implications of the ideal of modern individualism. Political theorists imagined the existence of a "state of nature" in which individual freedom had reigned prior to the creation of institutional social bonds. They assumed that no rational person would enter binding relations with others unless this natural freedom were preserved. This assumption led to the idea of a "social contract" that tries to define the terms on which individuals join together and accept reciprocal obligations established by laws applicable to all of them. The first great application of this idea was Thomas Hobbes's attempt to explain the creation of a unified society governed by a single sovereign power whose absolute rule both guarantees the enforcement of all citizens' equality before the law and preserves their private freedoms. In this way, individual rights and public equality are to be protected. This modern version of a unified society governed by a Platonic philosopher-king seemed to its critics, however, to produce unity at a price that modern individualist society could not accept.

John Locke proposed the equivalent of an Aristotelian response to Hobbes's Platonic vision of politics. Locke's version of the state of nature contained already existing, plural social interests. The political state was needed only as a referee to judge among these interests when they came inevitably into conflict because each individual judged for himself what was right. But Locke's contractual theory protected inequalities that he assumed to be natural and therefore acceptable. It was perfectly consistent with his view that the English Bill of Rights enacted after the Glorious Revolution of 1689 did not guarantee the rights of individuals to social equality or to individual liberty, but rather protected only the liberty of the Parliament. For this reason, the English "revolution" was in fact a confirmation of the existing unequal social order against the usurpation of the restored monarchy. It prevented further development in the direction of a democratic society by restoring the social relations that had been disrupted by both absolutism and the revolution that abolished it.

The development of modern social contract theory concludes with Jean-Jacques Rousseau's republican version that is often said to have been one of the sources of the French Revolution of 1789. Rousseau proposed a synthesis of the two variants of contract theory. His *Social Contract* shares Hobbes's goal of finding a way to impose unity on a society of individuals, but Rousseau argues for the strict rule of law against the potential arbitrariness of a monarch. Yet, like Locke's work, his *Discourse on the Origins of Inequality* recognizes the existence of social plurality. By posing the question of inequality's origins, Rousseau implied that inequality was the unnatural product of the existing political order. In this way, he returned to the classical idea that the political form of society is the cause rather than the effect of the social relations within that society.

But his insistence on equality and on the liberty that it makes possible was a sign of his modernity. The unresolved mixture of these classical and modern political assumptions would clash in the French Revolution. The result would be a form of antipolitics that stepped forward with its own claims to legitimacy rather than remain simply the shadow side of politics.

Social contract theory ultimately failed to integrate the passions and the interests of the modern individual into a political community capable of reconciling equality with liberty, unity with diversity, theory with practice. This failure became evident at the end of the eighteenth century, when democratic political action reappeared on the stage of history. The same year, 1776, that witnessed America's Declaration of Independence saw the publication of Adam Smith's *An Inquiry into the Nature and Causes of the Wealth of Nations.* It would be incorrect to interpret Smith's path-breaking attempt to establish the foundations of a new science of political economy as a reaction to the American events, although both were opposed to the subordination of economic relations to the political demands of English mercantilism. But Smith's coupling of politics with that aspect of life that was for the Greeks the domain of women and slaves and for the Christian the punishment for original sin was not fortuitous. The creation of wealth, on the basis of the increasing division of labor and with the help of an "invisible hand" by which market forces replace political choice, was an unintended result of modern individualism. It seemed to produce social unity without the need to appeal to politics. Now economic science began to replace contract theory as the foundation of a political unity built by blind market forces over which the individual had no control. Rather than reconcile equality and liberty, political economy legitimated a new type of inequality that was seen as the product of ineluctable economic necessity. Politics had no place in this new world; if it sought to interfere, it risked upsetting the market forces' neutral action. The antipolitical implications of this argument are evident.

The quest for republican and democratic institutions reappeared in the years that followed the French Revolution. Although many of the revolution's early protagonists sought to imitate the British model, the revolution itself escaped their grasp and took on a life of its own. After a series of internecine conflicts, a republic was declared in 1792, and further radicalization followed. The leading revolutionaries' goal was to effectuate a social transformation that would eliminate the arbitrariness of politics. They seized state power as a means to remake social relations so that that there would no longer exist a difference between the political state and the society it was to govern. Their ideal can be seen as a modern version of Platonism. Its result would be what I call a "democratic republic," in which republican unity is imposed on society in a way that leaves no room for democratic diversity. The French Revolution became antipolitical as a result. Once the revolutionaries had overthrown the old order, they had no way to set a limit on the equalization of social conditions that they had begun to establish. Where should they stop? If all difference were destroyed, what would remain? As if frightened by their own audacity, they decided that order must be restored. Doing so was the task of "the Terror," led by Maximilien Robespierre. To overcome modern individualism, the Committee on Public Safety sought to impose the classical virtue that had founded ancient republican liberty. Although the Reign of Terror was short-lived, the new French republic—like its Roman ancestor—became a world empire under Napoleon, and the republican desire for self-government disappeared from its political life.

The founder of modern conservatism, Edmund Burke, predicted the failure of the revolution in his 1790 work *Reflections on the Revolution in France*. This new conservatism was a modern way of understanding the political, which represents a third form of antipolitics. Prior to the emergence of the modern individual and the idea that nature is neutral material to be used for ends dictated by humans, there was no need for a holistic, hierarchical, and backward-turned vision of the goals of politics. Although Burke appeared to be defending social plurality against the revolutionaries' attempt to impose an abstract unity on society, his ideal was classical and Aristotelian. He returned repeatedly to the wisdom of tradition amassed through the ages, denouncing the abstract rationalism of the philosophes while showing that their lack of practical experience left them no option but to expand the reach of the state continually because that was the only political tool they understood. Burke rejected the individualist premises of both social contract theory and capitalist economics, arguing that the individual's relation to the state cannot be compared to that of two merchants forming a contract to trade sugar and spices. But his vision of unity and harmony and especially of the power of tradition to bind the present to the past while giving meaning to the future was based on a rejection of the modern individualism that had made conservative theory necessary. This paradox condemns the conservative project. It is a modern theory, but it rejects the individualism that preserves the rights of diversity against the sweeping thrust of political or economic unification.

What unites these three reactions to the rebirth of the democratic and republican desire for self-government—the neutral logic of the market, state terror, and conservative traditionalism —is their rejection of it. Their thought is antipolitical. It is the search for a final solution to the perennial human problem of uniting freedom, order, and power by transcending all secular forms of political accountability. Glimpses of the antipolitical temptation had appeared in classical thought, particularly in the unitary rationalist tradition originated by Plato, which could be adapted to the religious legitimation of another style of antipolitics. But it was only with the emergence of the modern individual and the renewal of the republican and democratic quest for self-government that the antipolitical temptation became explicit as a mode of properly political understanding. As a reaction to the conditions that made modern democracy possible, this temptation argued that there are immanent constraints on citizens' ability to ensure that their government is accountable to those in whose name it operates. For this reason, it was only at the end of the story recounted here that the tacit and latent implications of the steps along the way became clear. But the story was not over; the last die had not been cast.

The American Revolution is the living proof that antipolitics is not the modern answer to the age-old political problem of how men and women can live together under a government that is legitimate. Although Edmund Burke supported the American cause (because he saw it as the assertion of traditional British freedoms against arbitrary political intervention by Parliament), the implications of the colonists' demands for the "rights of an Englishman" became more radical as the conflict deepened. After independence was declared, sovereignty had to be won not only on the battlefield, but by the creation of political institutions that could maintain it. The Articles of Confederation failed. The popular debates about the new constitution of 1787 were given their fullest theoretical formulation in *The Federalist*. Those eighty-five essays, published first in newspapers and then bound as a book, were more than a political polemic; without intending it, they mapped out the political theory of the "republican democracy" toward which the Americans were groping. The power of that political form was confirmed by the election of 1800, which brought Thomas Jefferson to power. For the first time in history, power passed peacefully from one political party to another, a feat whose foundation was the recognition that the republic was at once unified and yet divided. In 1803, the Supreme Court ruled in *Marbury v. Madison* that it was the Constitution rather than the temporary holders of office that represented the sovereign will of the people. This American republican democracy inverted the unitary democratic republic sought by the French. Its political framework protected civil rights, ensuring the competitive coexistence of diverse social interests rather than attempting to collapse them into a unified whole. In this way, it preserved the space for politics.

III

The U.S. Constitution does not represent the final and ultimate form of democratic political institutions. The republican democracy that it brought into being recalled both the greatness of the Roman republic and the glories of Greek democracy, but the American achievement was no more certain to endure than its Greek or Roman ancestors. Just as the Greeks and Romans' successes led both of them to undertake imperial adventures that in the end cost them their freedom, so the Americans, already in the nineteenth century and more powerfully as the twentieth century was ending, had to face the demon that tempts those who are too successful. Other similarities appeared on the home front. For a time, the clash of the interest of freedom with the demand for equality produced a healthy competition that made each of them stronger, extending their reach ever more widely to embrace new domains. But too much of a good thing can become harmful. As Montesquieu, to whom the American founders referred frequently, observed in *The Spirit of the Laws*, even virtue needs to know its limits. An excess of reason, he added, can similarly be undesirable. But how is a people to limit itself if not by political means? And if it does not impose such limits on itself, can this be taken as a sign that antipolitics has come to power?

In recent American history, the faith in unbounded freedom has spread beyond the economic sphere to the broader domains of social relations, culture, and family. At the same time, equality has expanded to encompass class, ethnicity, and gender relations. The first part of the introduction described the logic governing this process. At the same time, American pretensions to virtue have led to attempts to spread American values throughout the globe, by force if need be. Each of these extensions of American ideals may be, for a time and in some cases, a positive achievement. At some point, however, they may come to threaten the very democracy that makes them possible. The difficulty is that we will know we have breached the limit only when it is too late to pull back. Better, then, to learn from the past rather than be blindsided by an onrushing future, as has happened previously in American history—most cruelly with the Civil War, more recently at the time of the Great Depression. The nation was lucky to find political leaders who understood politics and its limits. That luck may one day run out. Antipolitics lurks always in the shadows, disguising itself as political wisdom or practical expediency.

The historical trials and contemporary dilemmas of American democracy are not the direct theme of this book, but I hope that practical and engaged readers will ask themselves, in the words of Vladimir Lenin, "What is to be done" to preserve, improve, and renew the democracy that we have inherited? They will recognize the inadequacy of the definition of politics offered by that Bolshevik leader in the famous aphorism "kto kogo" (who does what to whom). Building from the storehouse of human experience, they will rethink anew the nature of politics. For my part, in the brief conclusion to this volume, I suggest some themes gleaned from the history of political thought that, as I see it, might contribute to a renewal of democracy in the twenty-first century.

№ 1
THE RISE AND FALL OF ATHENIAN DEMOCRACY

A FIRST OVERVIEW of the basic difference between the Platonic and Aristotelian understanding of the tasks of political thought suggests that Plato's philosophical presuppositions incline him toward antipolitics, whereas those of Aristotle lend themselves more easily to properly political thought. But the contrast is not absolute. An historical account of the origins of Athenian democracy and the realization of its ideals at the height of its glory during the Age of Pericles adds nuance to this schematic presentation of two of the basic categories that organize this history of political thought. Beginning with the Greek cultural ideals presented in the poetry of Homer and Hesiod, this background casts light on the improbable process by which Athens gave birth to both democracy and philosophy. The fact that no other civilization produced such an unlikely combination is one reason why Greek political thought stands at the foundation of more than two thousand years of Western civilization.

◆

Plato seeks to define the unequivocally best constitution, whereas Aristotle recognizes the need to take into account the conditions in which ordinary men and women can best live together. As a result, Plato can be said to propose the replacement of politics with political philosophy; his political theory is antipolitical because it eliminates the need for the negotiation and compromises that make political choices legitimate in the eyes of the participants. The attraction of the ideal—the promise of a fully rational society and a theory that encompasses particularity within a universal framework—has reappeared in the many historical renewals of Platonism. This idealism is attractive to the social critic as well. The universality of its claims permits a critique of any particular status quo, denouncing the self-deceptions, illusions, and interests that mislead the citizens. But what may appear to the idealist as self-deception or worse may be in fact a realistic evaluation of the chances available to people attempting to realize their idea of the good life within the constraints of the world as it exists here and now. At this point, Aristotle's philosophy seems to offer a practical political alternative. His recognition of the complexity of political life leads him to undertake comparative empirical analyses that provide a complement to Platonic idealism. In the real world, he seems to suggest, the best may be the enemy of the better. Philosophy cannot replace politics. The task of political thought is to develop the prudence and judgment needed to live in a world peopled by diverse men and women who seek to maintain the unity and legitimacy of their social relations.

This initial opposition between Plato's stress on the ideal and Aristotle's insistence on the real has further political implications. As philosophers, both are searching for truths that are universal. Plato starts from the universally true in order to understand and criticize ever-changing particular experience. This approach leads him to distinguish sharply between appearance and reality, opinion and knowledge, belief and truth. Aristotle takes the opposite tack, beginning from the diversity of particular phenomena in order to generalize toward increasingly universal forms of knowledge. This strategy leads him to try to find reality in the experienced world, to seek knowledge through deliberation, and to take seriously the opinions that motivate humans to act.

The distinction between the two philosophers can be seen in their method of procedure. Plato's reasoning is a priori; its validity does not depend on factual confirmation any more than do the truths of mathematics. And just as mathematical truths apply to the real world, so too Plato's idealism does not mean that his claims are divorced from reality. Aristotle's theory is a posteriori; its validity depends on empirical demonstrations and practical distinctions that support its claims as his argument moves from the particular cases to increasing universality. Although both philosophers seek truths that are universal in scope, these methodological differences have consequences for their political theories. For Plato, truth exists in the domain of absolute ideas to which only philosophers have access; for that reason, philosophers should rule. For Aristotle, truth is to be discovered by reasoning about particular experience; philosophers are thus like ordinary citizens who must convince themselves and others of the legitimacy of their knowledge.

Both Plato and Aristotle seek to understand the principles that make social relations legitimate in the eyes of the participants; in that way, social stability is assured without recourse to force. Plato's concern is to establish the unity of the society, which depends on ensuring that justice is done universally so that all of its members benefit. Individual character and the moral virtues valued by society are ensured by this establishment of social justice, which they then conserve as long as their character remains just. Aristotle begins from the recognition of plurality within society, which means that social stability can be assured only by creating a political structure that renders justice to its members proportionally, taking into account what is due each of them in his particular situation. For this reason, the good man may not always be identical to the good citizen, as Plato's unitary vision implies. This distinction has political consequences. Plato's stress on unity, like his idealism, leaves no space for individual political action; justice is imposed by the philosopher-kings' rational rule. Aristotle's insistence on the diversity of social relations leads him to recognize the uniqueness of the political sphere, which cannot be governed by universal philosophical reason but instead demands its own particular mode of thought. The citizens of Aristotle's society participate in the decisions that affect their destiny.

Despite their differences, both Plato and Aristotle were Greeks. They shared basic assumptions about nature and the world. Most important was their understanding that all things, animate and inanimate, and all actions are determined by what the Greeks called their telos, the end that makes them what they truly are. Whether that end is defined by a priori Platonic reason or is discovered by a posteriori Aristotelian research, it represents the truth of the things that appear to men. The tables and chairs that clutter a room, like the people that inhabit the house, are defined by the end for which they exist; and if they fail to be adequate to that end, they can be criticized. This teleological vision extends to the world itself, which means that the things within it exist in an hierarchical structure that is itself natural. The implication of this Greek teleological worldview is that the individual subject exists only as a part of a whole that is greater than he. It follows that the community has priority over the individual and that politics, which concerns the good of the whole, is the highest form of human activity.[1]

THE ORIGINS OF ATHENIAN DEMOCRACY

Although the opposition between the Platonic and the Aristotelian responses to the challenge of creating legitimate political institutions recurs in the history of political thought, it is important to look closely at the different forms that this opposition has acquired in varying historical conditions. There are constants in human history, but they gain their signification when they encounter another omnipresent aspect of human history: the fact that the present can always change. For that reason, political thought and political history are interdependent; neither makes sense without the other. There is no singular, definitive, and universally valid political theory, and no political institutions can put an end to the possibility of change. It is true that the new may emerge with imperceptible slowness, remaining below the horizon, digging underground like a mole that may emerge unexpectedly; the theorist's eyes may not see the new, but political thought will sense its possibility and try to illuminate it. In this way, the theory that furnished the accepted paradigm for understanding the legitimacy of existing social relations will become inadequate, and the search for a new theoretical paradigm will begin.

The study of political thought can take place only within the horizon of the political history that precedes it and that furnishes the raw material with which it works. But the events that make up this raw material become significant only when political thought draws out the possibility with which they are ripe. The events' signification comes from the way in which they help to clarify both the reach and the limits of the political thought that seeks to explain them. The brief historical sketch that follows highlights some of the stages that led to the flowering of Athenian democracy. It also provides an illustration of the interplay between the quest for unity and universality, on the one hand, and the need to take into account diversity and particularity, on the other.

Plato and Aristotle shared a culture celebrated in myth and poetry. Both cite Homer as an authority, but a long path separated the epic drama of *The Iliad* and *The Odyssey* from the democratic Athens of Pericles. The ruins of Mycenae, from which Agamemnon and his fellow Greeks set out for Troy in the thirteenth century BCE (an abbreviation I do not repeat in the chapter because all dates occur "before the common era"), are the remains of a vast fortress, protected by massive stone walls, seated high above a valley. Because the type of warfare waged by a society influences the form of its political life, the few who could provide their own arms ruled the city. The many, who were peasants and lived outside the walls, counted for nothing. It is no surprise that there is only one scene in the *Iliad* when the voice of a commoner is heard. The speaker is Thersites, "the ugliest man . . . bandy-legged . . . with one foot clubbed, both shoulders humped together . . . his skull warped to a point, sprouting clumps of scraggly, wool hair." His words are "full of obscenities, teeming with rant, all for no good reason." Odysseus beats him mercilessly, earning the approval of the army, which had threatened to abandon the attack on Troy. "Their morale was low, but the men laughed now, good hearty laughter."[2] Authority is legitimated by this use of force against the commoner.

The Homeric warrior ethos identifies might with right and victory as therefore deserved. Greek culture was agonistic; its foundation was conflict, competition, and strife. The rivals striving for victory sought glory for themselves and craved fame in the eyes of those who shared their values. But they also considered their victory to result from the fact that their action conformed to the natural order, which rewards those who are naturally best. As a result, this world of conflict was not without unity. This paradoxical unity based on difference received its full expression in the quadrennial Olympic Games, which were inaugurated in 776, the historical moment when the Homeric poems were finally given a written form. The cession of warfare during the games (where competition was deadly serious) bore witness to a kind of pan-Hellenic political unity that underlay the conflictual diversity celebrated by the games. The basis of this unity was the shared idea that from strife (*eris*) would emerge a justice (*dike*) to whose implacable verdict all must consent.

The poet Hesiod, writing around 750, took the next step toward rationalizing this notion of justice. Whereas wandering bards recited the Homeric rhapsodies at wealthy warriors' well-appointed dwellings, Hesiod explains that the muse found him while he was tending his flock. This difference signals a shift in the understanding of how society is held together. Hesiod's *Theogony* adds to the Homeric mythology the tale of the deeds of Prometheus and Pandora—he who stole fire for the benefit of humankind, and she who opened the jar containing the evils that would afflict humanity, shutting it only just before hope could escape. The same concern with things human is evident in Hesiod's other great poem, *The Works and the Days*. As its title suggests, *Works* reflects the disappearance of the Homeric world of warriors competing for glory according to an ethos that identifies justice with power won on the field of battle.

Hesiod recounts his conflict with his spendthrift brother, Perses, who not only has wasted his half of their inheritance, but is now bribing judges in an attempt to control the remainder of the estate. Hesiod reminds his brother that Zeus protects justice even when earthly judges do not. But unlike Homer, who reproduced the deliberations of the gods, Hesiod insists that no mortal can know the will of Zeus. After he denounces the judges as "bribe-eating" lords, he explains this practice as reflecting the present "Age of Iron," which is the last of the Five Ages of Man that began with the Golden Age. Despite this practice, justice remains possible. Hesiod recalls the fable of the hawk who tells the nightingale he has captured that there is no use in crying, for the strong do as they wish.[3] But he does not interpret this tale as implying that might makes right; rather, he points out that it is only among wild beasts that the stronger devours the weaker, whereas Zeus has given to men justice (*dike*), a virtue greater than force. The poem goes on to demarcate its path.

As its title suggests, *The Works and the Days* seems to suggest that justice can be gained through work. Hesiod insists, for example, that "work's no disgrace: it's idleness that's a disgrace." In another passage, he explains that "it's easy to get all of Wickedness you want. She lives just down the road a piece, and it's a smooth road too. But the gods put Goodness where we have to sweat to get at her. It's a long, uphill pull and rough going at first. But once you reach the top she's as easy to have as she was hard at first."[4] It is important not to read these lines anachronistically. Hesiod remains a Greek; his concern is the way work reflects and affects the workers' character and virtue. The implacable *dike* of the agonistic warrior culture is replaced by the idea that justice is within the reach of a certain type of men. Work is the process by which humanity produces itself as autonomous. Its value is not economic; it is political.

These two great poets seek to construct a sense of order and meaning from a world of conflict ruled by the gods and their arbitrary interventions. In this sense, their work is political, but it is not concerned with the legitimation of political institutions. The first example of that kind of institutional thought took place in Sparta. The novelty of Spartan political thought lay in the fact that its political institutions were not said to be natural. The Spartans claimed that their constitution had been given them by a legendary figure, Lycurgus, who had come to power in the mid–seventh century. Their appeal to a myth of origins was perhaps based on the rulers' fear that if they could give themselves a constitution, others might want to do the same, dislodging them from their positions of power. By claiming that their constitution was given to them by a mythical figure and that it was therefore so perfect that it could never be altered, the Spartans ensured the legitimation of the established order.

The Spartans' political fiction can also be understood as resulting from the fact that the power of their land-locked city was based on its domination over a conquered population, the helots, who made up a majority of the city's inhabitants. As a result, Spartan society was organized by and for warfare; youths were separated from their families, lodging together even after marriage in order to bond and to ensure that courage at war was their first virtue. This militaristic-communitarian upbringing ensured Sparta's power, but the need to control the city's helots meant that Sparta could never pursue overseas conquests. Making a virtue out of necessity, it developed an autarchic economy, reinforcing its isolation by using a simple iron currency that cut it off from commercial relations with other cities to whom such coinage was useless. As a result, it remained apart from the cultural and philosophical developments that would take place elsewhere in Greece. To preserve the unity necessary for its survival, Spartan morality subordinated the individual to the community of peers who dominated the helot population.

Although the Spartan Constitution ensured the rule of an oligarchy, it divided the institutions of governance in order to ensure that no particular group could use them to dominate the others. In this way, legitimacy was preserved by preventing autonomous political activity. For example, there were two royal families, which ruled jointly. Their power was limited to the direction of religious and military affairs. A five-man commission called the Ephorate and a Senate called the Gerousia shared a separate executive power. Each of these institutions had a different basis for its power and a different term in office. The Ephorate was elected by the assembly of citizens for a one-year term, whereas the Gerousia consisted of thirty elders selected for life. There was also an electoral assembly consisting of all male citizens older than thirty who had gone through the rigorous communal-military training program. When important decisions had to be made, the two executive bodies deliberated together with the two kings. In this way, the separation of powers provided a formal structure that ensured political legitimacy by checking the warrior culture's temptation to value individual heroism above social unity.

It is not surprising that Sparta's creativity manifested itself above all on the field of war. The Spartan invention of the phalanx, which dates from roughly 640, reflected the society's political structure. A disciplined army made up of lightly clad warriors carrying their shields on the left arm, their sword (or spear) in the right hand advanced rapidly across the terrain while holding tightly to one another because the shield on the left arm of one's neighbor was the sole protection for each fighter's sword-wielding right side. The communal ethos that had evolved to defend against helot revolts thus became an offensive force. The heroism of the individual Homeric warrior was replaced by a collective battle waged by hoplites, citizens who were able to provide for themselves the light arms needed for (necessarily) short military campaigns.[5] The political implications of the use of hoplite armies are seen most clearly in the history of Athens, which adopted this tactic. Because the decision to go to war is the most important that a city can make, the hoplite citizens who would bear the brunt of the fighting had to be allowed to participate in public deliberations.

In 683, a government of six archons chosen by lot for a one-year term replaced the Athenian monarchy. Although chosen by lot for a limited term, each archon nonetheless supported his tribe's particular interests. To counter this threat to social unity, Dracon, a chief archon, introduced a written legal code in 621. Because it was a written code, it could be posted publicly, defining obligations that applied equally to all. Its universal character meant that justice would be rendered according to fixed principles known by all citizens. This equality before the law meant that the citizen's general obligations took priority over particular tribal or familial bonds. Decisions were now legitimate only insofar as they were in principle universal in scope. Dracon's code was only a first step. Its author's name is remembered today by the adjective *draconian* because the code prescribed the death penalty for nearly all offenses. Nonetheless, blood revenge was now taken by the state, which meant that its administration was in principle egalitarian. This code was thus political progress, however limited.

Developments in Athenian socioeconomic life soon challenged the unforgiving egalitarianism of Dracon's code. New forms of particularism challenged social unity. A new commercial class whose wealth came from increased maritime trade emerged. It had the financial ability to participate in the kind of hoplite army pioneered by Sparta. Its weight made itself felt in 594, when Solon began to create a new political framework. He first ensured himself the support of the peasantry by eliminating debt bondage. He then distinguished four types of property ownership to which he attributed different rights and duties. This definition of rights in terms of personal wealth created social distinctions that were now based on a universal standard (wealth) rather than on particular (tribal) bonds of blood. The same political logic led Solon to create a system of censitary voting that permitted the holders of different forms of wealth to cooperate in the creation of universally valid laws. The legitimacy of these laws now depended on the citizens' participation.

Solon's ability to maneuver between the peasantry and the increasingly powerful commercial forces in the city made his reforms possible, but no institutional arrangement is exempt from misuse. Peisistratos, who came to power in 560, imitated Solon's tactical maneuvers to create a tyranny.[6] Although he lost power in 556, he spent the next decade so successfully cultivating popular support that he was not only returned to power in 546, but was able to pass his rule to his son at his death two decades later. Peisistratos's success illustrates the temptation (on the part of the ruled as well as of the ruler) to institute a social unity that transcends the friction of particular interest. But the denouement of the story shows that particular concerns cannot be ignored. His son, accustomed to absolute rule, refused to recognize any limit to his own desires, expanding his power into the private (in this case, sexual) sphere. This violation of the individual's rights provoked a revolt whose repression turned its leaders into martyrs for freedom. A new spirit of resistance emerged;

regime change became inevitable because political rule had turned into its opposite.

The successful leader of the new regime was Cleisthenes, who came to power in 508. His reforms sought to realize the ideal of isonomy, an equality (*iso*) before the law (*nomos*) that ensures that the universality of the law takes into account the particular case. Cleisthenes divided the population into ten *demes* composed equally of members of the city's agricultural, urban, and commercial strata. In this way, people of different life conditions joined together as equal members of a common political unity and were thus reunited. Although each of the ten *demes* was particular, membership in them was based on citizenship, a quality shared with members of other *demes*. For that reason, although the *demes* could compete with one another (because particular), they could also cooperate and compromise (because made of up citizens).

The conditions of isonomy made other reforms possible. The General Council (the Boule) was opened to broader participation as each of the ten new *demes* sent fifty members to serve annual terms that could be renewed only once. Fifty of the five hundred members of the Boule were selected by monthly rotation to set the agenda for discussion, and one of these fifty was chosen daily to preside over deliberations, whose results were then submitted for popular ratification. A second set of reforms expressed the consequences of isonomy for the individual. Torture was banned, and the condemned were offered the possibility of drinking the hemlock-poisoned chalice, thus affirming their autonomy to the bitter end. Citizens deemed to be dangerous because their popularity represented a threat to the citizens' equality and the city's unity were subjected to ostracism, a temporary expulsion (for ten years, without loss of property).[7] This second series of reforms protected human dignity, taking into account the need to supplement political equality with individual freedom.

External events now accelerated the process of democratization. The Persian king Darius assembled a massive force to strike Greece in the late fifth century. The contest pitted the unity of empire against the plurality of the Greek cities, which united against the external threat without abandoning their own independence. The Greeks defeated the Persians at the battle of Marathon in 490. This defeat of a vast empire by armed citizens fighting to defend their cities' autonomy was a sign of democratic vitality. When Darius's son Xerxes sought to restore what he took to be the natural power of empire a decade later, the Spartans proved their mettle, fighting to the last man at Thermopylae in order to give Athens time to prepare its own defense. In an unprecedented choice, Themistocles convinced the Athenians to abandon their city and to gather their naval forces at the offshore island of Salamis, where their agile navy defeated the heavier Persian fleet. The Greek victory was consummated in 479 on land at Plataea and at sea at Mycale. It remained, however, for the Greek allies to invent political institutions that would preserve the possibility of uniting against any new threat without denying their cities' independence.

The boldness of Themistocles' plan was an expression of the Athenians' political self-confidence. Its citizens recognized that their autonomy did not depend on the possession of particular material things, but on their own political ability to govern themselves. A further growth of democratic participation followed. The ships that fought at Salamis were triremes, whose maneuverability depended on the coordination of their three lines of rowers. Alongside the hoplite marines who boarded an enemy ship when it was rammed, these common seamen were crucial to the victory. And like the hoplite forces, whose military contribution brought them political participation, the rowers had to be given citizen rights. As a result, the powers of the Boule were broadened to include supervision of state finances. The Boule verified all public officials' accounts, with the option to impeach those who violated the public trust. Somewhat later, under Pericles, the Boule's powers were expanded to include judicial functions that had been previously reserved to the aristocratic Areopagus, or supreme tribunal. Jurors were chosen by lot; and the juries were large in order to avoid any possibility of corruption. In order to ensure equal participation, the principle of payment for public service was generalized to include jury duty.

This further democratization of Athenian political life had an unintended effect on the Greek cities, which still had to worry about an eventual Persian threat. In order to pay for its reforms and to equip its military forces, Athens had to pursue a politics of conquest. Although it did not shy away from the use of force, its hegemonic position had to be legitimated in the eyes of both its subject-allies and its own citizens. This is one of the reasons for the erection of the great public works that were the cultural expression of the Periclean Age. Taking control of the treasury of the nearly four hundred allied Greek cities of which it was the leader, Athens created a sort of democratic empire that was both a reflection of its greatness and the eventual root of its demise in the contest with Sparta and Sparta's allies, known as the Peloponnesian War.[8] Both processes are apparent in the speeches that Thucydides (c. 460–395) puts in the mouth of Pericles in his *History of the Peloponnesian War*: the first is the famous funeral oration, the second an often neglected speech warning the Athenians of the cost of their imperial ambitions.[9]

THE IDEAL AND THE REALITY OF ATHENIAN DEMOCRACY: PERICLES' FUNERAL ORATION

Pericles begins his funeral oration by reminding his audience that a funeral ceremony consecrates the shared project that unites the living with the dead; that is why his speech was preceded by the burial of the bones of an "unknown soldier." The eulogy for the dead is also a celebration of the life of the city.[10] Athenian democracy recognizes the need to reconcile liberty and equality by ensuring that the city's affairs are in the hands of the many rather than the few. But although the laws ensure equal justice for all, they do not seek to create full equality in all spheres of life. Social diversity exists, but it is not fixed by tribal or familial lineage. The equal protection under the laws ensures the freedom of those with talent to rise because public life is open to merit. And poverty doesn't prevent a person's political participation because the city pays those who serve. Furthermore, regular rotation of office by drawing lots ensures that everyone has the chance to enter political life regardless of his private fortune. Indeed, this equality is maintained even in death because any personal or private demerits the dead may have had are canceled by the fact that they died as citizens rather than as particular individuals, resisting rather than submitting to blind necessity.

After this praise of political equality, Pericles stresses the fact that each Athenian is free to do as he chooses in the private sphere and that no one takes offense at personal behavior. He admits that this freedom might seem to encourage anarchy, the absence of any rule (*arche*). On the one hand, if all are ruling, then no one, no particular person or group, is ruling; on the other hand, if each is concerned with his own affairs, who is responsible for the community? In order to explain the maintenance of social unity, Pericles points to what he calls a "fear" or a "restraint of reverence" that ensures that the citizens will obey the laws, especially those laws made to help people who have suffered an injustice. Although he says that Athenians also obey the "unwritten laws," by which he means religious codes, the fear or reverence to which he refers is not a guilty conscience in the face of a transcendent deity. What he has in mind is the very Greek and democratic fear of being shamed or disgraced in front of one's peers. In this way, equality of all before the law creates the motivation for private conformity to custom, tradition, and authority. The injustice that Athenians cannot tolerate is not private inequality, but public and political disgrace. If Pericles insists that no one should take offense at private behavior, it is because private behavior has no direct effect on political life. What counts is the esteem of one's political equals, rich and poor, young and old, from all walks of life.

Pericles seems to anticipate the objection that always standing in the public eye will destroy the capacity for individual creativity. He contrasts Athens's democratic unity built on diversity to Sparta's collectivism. Sparta's economy was based on agricultural self-sufficiency, its military force resulted from an ethos of forced socialization, and its rejection of relations to other cities was ensured by an iron coinage that no one wanted to acquire. Such collectivism, notes Pericles, is a sign of weakness due to a lack of confidence in individual freedom. By contrast, the democratic Athenians are able to divert themselves with the elegant furnishings of their homes because the greatness of the city (and its silver money) draws to it products from all of the earth, increasing the free diversity that founds its strength. The self-confidence engendered by the active life that produces this wealth of diversity, Pericles continues, is also manifested in the fact that, although preparing for war, Athens remains open to all; it never expels foreigners in order to prevent them from seeing things that might give advantages to its enemies. Living daily with diversity, the Athenian democracy is justly confident in its ability to meet any enemy.

The comparison with Sparta points to a further virtue of Athenian democracy. Pericles criticizes the Spartans' rigid education, which presupposes that conformity is the precondition of political strength. By contrast, the Athenians are said to exercise nobility with restraint and to acquire wisdom without any softening of character. This pairing of nobility with restraint and wisdom with character expresses the Athenian ideal of a harmony that avoids excess yet retains the ability to integrate diversity. Wealth does not serve private ends but is used for action, which is the only way of gaining that praise that is the only end that counts in democratic societies. For the same reason, poverty in itself is not shameful; what is condemnable is doing nothing to escape it. The quest for others' esteem also explains why citizens involved in public affairs do not neglect their personal welfare: the value of an individual results from his contribution to the public good. And those who remain in the private sphere are nonetheless sufficiently informed about public matters because all take part in deciding (by their vote) what is to be done. Indeed, this participation in public life explains the Athenians' bravery. Ignorance does not make people brave, nor does thinking induce cowardice. Real bravery depends on knowledge of both the risks and the pleasures that result from action taken.

Calling Athens a "lesson for Greece" that needs no Homer to praise its power because its accomplishments are its own monument, Pericles returns to the dead. He stresses once again the interdependence of the public and the private. The fallen are not epic heroes whose singular deeds are to be memorialized; they died as citizens, members of the city, equal to all others. For this reason, this funeral oration not only unites the dead to the living, but also points to a future that enfolds its listeners. The fallen, who valued their city above themselves, have left to the living the obligation to preserve the democracy. Each citizen should consider it his good fortune to draw the lot that leads to a similar glorious end. Because the generations are bound together, the city will ensure the upbringing of the children of the deceased, while those parents who can must produce new offspring. As for the grieving aged, they can glory in the honor won by their children because "the love of honor is the one thing that never grows old," and they will gain happiness "not in gathering wealth (as some say), but in being honored."[11]

This soaring hymn to democracy contrasts with the sober realism of Pericles' final address to his fellow citizens. The first year of war had gone badly, and the next year brought a sweeping plague that would cost many lives. In these conditions, the private rights protected by a democracy can become a threat when its prosperity is challenged. Pericles tries to rally those who would put their own interests above those of the city.

"I believe that if the city is sound as a whole, it does more good to its private citizens than if it benefits them as individuals while faltering as a collective unit. It does not matter whether a man prospers as an individual; if his country is destroyed, he is lost along with it; but if he meets with misfortune he is far safer in a fortunate city than he would be otherwise."[12] Only when a city is a solid whole can it benefit its private citizens; if it puts the particular good above the common good, it will be unable to accomplish what it sets out to do. This may be true, but the realistic Athenian politician knows that more than theory is needed to motivate fearful, self-interested men.

◆

Pericles' theoretical argument is coupled with a realistic warning. Athens will have to face the anger of those whom it has ruled, who will turn against it in the future. As a result, you have no choice, he tells the Athenians: "your empire is really like a tyranny—though it may have been thought unjust to seize, it is now unsafe to surrender."[13] Pericles, who was carried off by the plague, did not live to see Athens become increasingly blind to the effects of its actions on its friends, its enemies, as well as those who sought to remain neutral. Thucydides presents three crucial debates that illustrate the decline in the quality of Athenian democratic deliberation. The first concerned the treatment of the rebellious island of Myteline; in this case, the temporary triumph of demagogy was overcome by a new deliberation. The second decided the fate of the island of Melos, which had sought in vain to retain its neutrality; this time the Athenians abandoned democratic pretence, opting for a realpolitik of pure power. The fatal third confrontation led to the decision to invade Sicily in the quest of private honor and wealth; the result was a disaster that destroyed large parts of Athens's military forces. Although Athens recovered briefly, it succumbed in 403. The Age of Pericles had passed.[14]

PLATO'S PHILOSOPHICAL ANTIPOLITICS

Reflecting on Pericles' role in Athenian political life, Thucydides comments that "what was nominally a democracy became in his hands government by the first citizen." Yet, he continues, after Pericles' death things went from bad to worse, as "successors on a level with each other, and each grasping at supremacy . . . ended up by committing even the conduct of state affairs to the whims of the multitude."[15] Did the equality of democratic citizens lead to the mediocrity of their leaders because they refused to let a single outstanding person stand out? Did equality constrain the freedom of those who were truly gifted? But what then accounts for Pericles' mastery? Could a new Pericles have saved Athens? Or was a different kind of leader needed, one schooled in true philosophy? That is the implication of Plato's (428/27–348/47) political philosophy.[16]

Plato's philosophical opponents were called Sophists. Although the Greek term alludes to a love (*philos*) of wisdom (*sophos*), the term has come to refer to someone who manipulates arguments with specious effectiveness while disregarding their truth. Further, a Sophist is willing to sell his rhetorical ability to any person who can pay his fees. Even if it is admitted that the Sophist does indeed have a kind of skill or technical knowledge that can be taught, such practical know-how that is useful when facing the transient problems of daily life is said to be qualitatively distinct from philosophical truth, which is universal and unchanging. True wisdom, the followers of Plato insist, should not be simply a technical means to reach an arbitrary goal; it must be an end in itself, valuable for what it is rather than for what it can produce. This explains why a Sophist is said to be frivolous, treating serious questions as a game in which victory is valued at all costs. The Sophists are said to reduce deliberation to a technique for winning arguments by forcing their opponents into self-contradiction rather than by demonstrating the truth of their own claims. There is no room for Truth in the excitement of a competition where paradox trumps clarity, seeming is more important than being, and reasoning replaces reason. As a result, the Sophists are accused of destabilizing the community by teaching youths to doubt their ancestors' values and traditions.[17]

Yet each of the negative characteristics attributed to the Sophists can be shown to have a positive value in a democracy. Argumentative skill that doesn't hesitate to engage in thrust and parry in debate implies a respect for others' ability to decide for themselves; it implies that reason is not founded on a Truth that is transcendent but emerges from collective deliberation and judgment. The idea that the rhetorical know-how needed for skillful participation in debate can be taught, sold, and learned by anyone regardless of their personal status makes possible social mobility, dissolves static hierarchy, and implies that people have the right to better themselves. The competition that is intensified when knowledge has become a technique that can be sold is not just a frivolous fight for personal glory; an agonistic society raises the knowledge level of all participants, who can never rest on their laurels. The fact that this technique can be purchased reflects the fact that society has become wealthy and thus has the time and leisure for the free public exercise of political opinions. Knowledge focused on the transient world reflects the needs of a democratic society that must always be open to change and able to exercise its ability to judge in particular instances. Such knowledge is indeed a means, but the ends that it serves are to be determined democratically while always remaining open to further reflection and debate. The fact that the gods of the community may be destabilized by the Sophists' dialectical paradoxes contributes to the vivacity of democratic debate by legitimating the expression of diverse opinions. Indeed, the fondness for dialectical paradoxes, logical puzzles, and the multiple meanings of words is an expression of human freedom unconstrained by external necessity.

Plato's attitude toward democracy was influenced by what appears to be democracy's original sin: the trial and condemnation of Socrates, whom he called "the best man then living." That verdict seems to prove the incompatibility of the philosophical quest for truth with the equal participation of citizens in a democratic city. The 501 jurors who sat in judgment on Socrates had been selected by lot; to ensure that all citizens could participate in the jury system, they were paid for their service. In the end, only 281 of the 501 jurors voted to condemn Socrates; a shift of 31 votes would have changed the verdict. Their judgment may have reflected the uncertainties of the times because democracy had been restored in defeated Athens only four years previously. Some jurors may have been affected by Socrates' role as the teacher of the traitor Alcibiades, whom many considered responsible for the ill-fated invasion of Sicily; others might have resented his friendship with some of the Thirty Tyrants, such as Charmides or Plato's uncle Critias. Whatever the jurors' motives, Plato's retelling of the trial in *The Apology* suggests a different religious simile. Socrates' death is not only democracy's sin; it is a demonstration that Socrates had to die in order that his message of salvation by philosophical reasoning might survive. Socrates would be a martyr to Truth, the first saint of the philosophical calendar, and Plato would be his messenger.[18]

The accusation against Socrates in effect accuses him of being a Sophist. His famous imperative to "know thyself" is not simply an injunction to look inward in searching for truth. Socrates recognizes that a person's character manifests itself fully and truly only in his relations to others. The Socratic dialogues portrayed by Plato were conducted in public; their aim was to break down the self-certainties of Socrates' partners, show their self-contradictory assumptions, and reveal not only their ignorance, but also the vanity that prevents them from questioning themselves and their beliefs. This practice made Socrates popular among the Athenian youth who witnessed it, but it also made him hated by powerful people who felt threatened by his challenge to accepted social beliefs and practices. As a result, he was brought to trial on charges of "impiety." *The Apology* is a vigorous defense of this practice. Socrates does not "apologize" or excuse himself for having done wrong.

The charge of "impiety" was no doubt the expression of a democracy that felt threatened and unsure of its own values. Socrates was accused of not recognizing the gods of the city, of inventing new divine things, and of corrupting the young. His rebuttal of the first charge invokes the authority of the Delphic Oracle in his favor. This wisest of Greek deities had announced that there is no one wiser than he. What could that mean? he wondered. Over time, he came to realize that his "wisdom" consists in the paradoxical fact that he knows that he doesn't know. The "wisdom" of this ignorance is confirmed in his constant questioning of his fellow citizens, from the poets to the craftsmen, who think they possess knowledge but find their certainties melting away as Socrates challenges them. For this reason, he continues, the accusation of inventing new gods is false; he has made no doctrinal claims. Finally, Socrates admits that his search for wisdom draws the interest of the young, but what he in fact shows them is that those who think they possess knowledge are in fact and for just this reason incapable of true knowledge because their supposed wisdom closes them off to the truth; in other words, they don't seek truth because they think they already have it. Surely this way of seeking truth does not corrupt the young.

Socrates is aware that the charges against him resulted from the fact that his practice appears to threaten the taken-for-granted social relations in Athens. He insists that he is not opposed to democracy, and he reminds the jurors that he has done his duties as a soldier and that he served in office when the lot fell to him. But, he argues, citizenship is not expressed only in external duties; it depends also on the individual citizen's character. For that reason, he did not listen to those who warned him that his philosophical activity was putting his life in danger. Recalling Homer's description of Achilles, he explains that he "had a much greater fear of living as a bad man." With this stress on individual character, the argument appears to change course. Socrates asserts that "if he's to survive, the true champion of justice . . . must necessarily confine himself to private life and leave politics alone."[19] That is what he has done, and his poverty bears witness to his spiritual purity (as will his martyrdom), but, he points out, this apparently private virtue has public effects. It is the reason that the young (among whom he mentions Plato) are attracted to him. The fact that private virtue has a political signification suggests the need for a deeper understanding of the nature of politics.

Once the verdict is read, the trial passes to the penalty phase. Socrates refuses to plead for mercy because, as a citizen of democratic Athens, he knows that he cannot accept life in exile or just keep quiet rather than pursue the dialogues that are essential to his character. He reaffirms the maxim that "the unexamined life is not worth living." But this examination of life cannot occur in private, where people convince themselves that they know things of which they prove to be ignorant. The search for knowledge must take place in the sunlight of the marketplace. That is why, in spite of Socrates' praise of private life, he calls himself a "gadfly" whose questioning challenges the Athenians to reflect on their own actions. And, turning the tables on the jury, he asserts that "if you kill me—since I am the person I say I am—you won't harm me more than you harm yourselves." Just as Socrates' dialogue partners learned that they only thought that they were wise, so too Athens will find that it deceives itself if it thinks that its condemnation is just. Instead, warns Socrates, "you'll be notorious and blamed by those who want to revile the city because you've killed Socrates, a wise man—for those who want to hold you in contempt will say that I am in fact wise even if I'm not."[20]

Socrates' last words to the jury proved correct in two very different senses. Athens was reviled for its sin against philosophy, and those who denounced it did indeed stress Socrates' wisdom. Chief among the latter was Plato, whose translation of the living Socratic dialectic into a written text transformed the practical democratic gadfly into a theoretical philosopher professing a distinct and subtle doctrine. Plato's analysis of the nature of justice in *The Republic* is faithful to Socrates' insistence that politics concerns not only institutions, but the citizens' character. In this respect, Plato remained true to his master. The problem is that if this unification of the life of the good man and the life of the good citizen were truly realized, there would be no need or place for politics. There would be no reason for Socratic debate provoked by a critical "gadfly." The rationalist philosopher would replace the active, risk-taking, and pleasure-loving citizen of Periclean Athens. A truly just society in this Platonic sense would have no room for finite humans to seek together what they consider the best life possible. It would produce what I have called an *antipolitics.*

At times, Plato recognized the dilemma. Although he wanted to formulate a politics that would transcend the grubby and self-interested everydayness of politics, he was aware that the absolute vision of a society ruled by the best institutions and inhabited by the best men left no way for him to realize his project. But he persisted, refusing to accept anything less than justice. This dilemma explains the eternal attractiveness of his political thought. He recognized the lure of the ideal, but he knew, too, the deception of the real. The dilemma comes to a head in book VIII of *The Republic,* when Plato admits that his philosopher-kings will not be able to carry through their project because their philosophical certainties are foreign to the everyday world of appearance in which human action takes place. At that point, his perfect republic starts its spiraling descent from timocracy to oligarchy to democracy and finally to tyranny. Plato seems to recognize this impasse in his two later political works, *The Statesman* and *The Laws,* which are no longer animated by the utopian vision. It is not surprising that these two works have had little effect on posterity. Because of its enduring importance, I reconstruct Plato's political philosophy as it is presented in the sometimes meandering dialogue of *The Republic.*[21]

◆

The Republic begins with a charming vignette that serves to distinguish philosophy from traditional values while posing the question of justice.

The ensuing discussion appears at first to be a set of verbal jousts that may lose the first-time reader. Their payoff emerges when Socrates refutes the claim of the Sophist Thrasymachus that justice is simply the interest of the stronger because might makes right. The positive implications of the Socratic method become fully clear, however, only when Plato explains his theory of political education.

At the outset of the dialogue, Socrates and his young followers meet old Cephalus, the father of one of them, who is returning from prayer. The conversation turns to the difficulties of old age, which is often said to bring a loss of the good things that come with bodily vigor. Cephalus replies that in fact he has found instead a new tranquility now that he is freed from the "service of Aphrodite," which was "a raging and savage beast of a master." This opposition of the fleeting passions and changing desires to the fixity of "character" and "temperance" is a variation on the contrast of particularity and universality. But Socrates' friends object that the real reason Cephalus is content is that he's wealthy and thus free from the everyday cares of the world. Cephalus replies that wealth is only a means to gain tranquility of character, which is the greatest good. This claim, however, depends on whether the wealth is gained and put to use in a just manner. For example, is it just to pay one's debts always? Should one repay a person who has gone mad? Or a person who would abuse the money if returned? The point of these questions is that justice is not the unthinking application of the norms of custom and tradition.

Cephalus's son, Polemarchus, tries to reformulate his father's argument in order to take into account particular cases. Justice, he says, is rendering each his due. How does one know what is "due" to another, however? The answer must apply a more specific rule that fits the particular case at hand: friends owe friends some good and no evil. Leaving aside the problem of what "some good" might in fact be, the difficulty with this new rule appears when the corollary question is posed: What do we owe to our enemies (if they too must be given their due)? If the answer is that we should render them evil, the next question is not simply quantitative—"How much?"—but qualitative: How can doing evil, even to one's enemies, be called just? Socrates maintains that it is better to suffer injustice than to be guilty of doing it. The person who does evil has to live with himself, which, no doubt, is a just punishment for his evil behavior, but it does not render justice to the person he has harmed.

To escape from these difficulties, Plato makes a typical philosophical move: he looks for analogies. This procedure is not so straightforward as it might appear. If something is "like" something else, it is also in some way different from it. The difference may not be important at first glance, when the analogy helps to cast the old particular question in a more general light. The difference may play a role only at a later stage in the argument. For example, Socrates asks how the notion of justice is applied to practical arts such as medicine or cooking. One can say that the doctor must find the "right" means to restore the individual to health, just as the cook must season meat in a way that brings out what is "best" in it. The analogy suggests that doing justice to the sick human or to the raw meat brings out its specific virtue, which is the end (telos) for which it exists. This end lies in the nature of the thing; it is not imposed on it, as if the thing were but a means to an external goal such as the satisfaction of a potential customer—which implies that political justice realizes the true nature of social relations.

But how do we know what the proper end of a thing truly is? On the assumption that the world is in principle an organized system of ends, their realization depends on the application of the proper means. These means are a craft or technique (*techne*) that is mastered by experts who determine in particular cases how to realize the natural end of a given being. Just as the doctor decides in the case of medicine, the cook or the pilot of a ship is an expert in a particular art, and expertise in a craft is required to render something its due. But the analogy breaks down when Plato returns to the question of how to render enemies their "due." The expert in harming enemies is the soldier, but his knowledge is useful only in war. What is more, the warrior's craft is only a means to an end decided by others, who may err in deciding to make war in the first place, as did the Athenians when they decided to invade Sicily. What is more, the friend whom I help may only seem worthy, whereas an apparent enemy may in fact be a true friend. As a result, the warrior may injure a good person (the seeming enemy) or benefit a bad one (the false friend)—neither of which is a just act. The attempt to save the traditional formulation of justice as "rendering his due" is thus proven self-contradictory.

At this point, Thrasymachus speaks up, aggressively demanding that Socrates cease his play with analogies and give a definition of justice. Thrasymachus was a well-known Sophist whose brutal cynicism contrasts with Socrates' philosophical sagacity and intellectual probity. Socrates pleads ignorance, turning the tables by suggesting that Thrasymachus give his own definition, pointing out that his behavior suggests that he thinks he knows the answer. The trick works; the Sophist answers bluntly: "the just is nothing but the advantage of the stronger."[22] But some cities are governed by tyrants, others by aristocrats, and still others by the citizens in a democracy; and each of these ruling strata are in fact the strongest forces in their society. They create laws—*nomoi*, conventions—that permit them to keep power and the benefits that it brings. And in order to legitimate their domination over those who do not benefit directly from these laws, they assert that the laws are just.

Socrates accepts the idea that justice must indeed give an advantage. But that leaves two questions unanswered: To whom, and how? If "the stronger" benefit, what is the nature of their strength, and how does justice benefit them? After all, if a friend may only seem to be a friend, is it not conceivable that a ruler, too, might err in judging what is to his advantage? In that case, some laws that were intended to benefit the stronger may in fact serve the interests of the weaker. What the rulers called "just" may turn out not to be to their advantage because the obedience rendered by the weak works to the disadvantage of the stronger.

Thrasymachus doesn't fold his cards after this first hand; he, too, plays the analogy game. Someone who makes errors can no more be called superior than a doctor who errs is truly a doctor or an accountant who miscalculates is worthy of the name. A true craftsman doesn't fall victim to such confusion. For this reason, continues Thrasymachus, Socrates' objections are merely exercises in verbal agility that prove nothing. On this first point—who benefits from justice—neither combatant has yet defeated the other.

A second game ensues. This time Socrates takes the lead. He does not ask whether the stronger (or ruler) is supposed to benefit, but how. He makes use of the fact that an analogy relates things that are alike but also unlike. Because the ends sought by specific types of action define those actions, Socrates asks whether a doctor acts in order to earn a wage or to heal the sick? Does the pilot of a ship rule the sailors for his own ends or to bring the crew safe to port? The doctor's wage and the pilot's rule are clearly justified by their end, which is the good of those on whom they act. As in the examples of medicine and cooking, the arts bring out something essential to the nature of their object. For that reason, the arts must be in some way stronger than their object because their application permits the restoration of its natural state. Socrates concludes, therefore, that the art of ruling practiced by the doctor or the pilot does not work to the advantage of the stronger, but instead benefits the weaker. Because the doctor doesn't heal in exchange for a wage, and the pilot doesn't work for his own benefit, the stronger party profits only insofar as and because the weaker gains from his action.

Thrasymachus replies scornfully to what he sees as the naivety expressed by Socrates' analogy. He proposes a more cynical comparison. The shepherd who fattens his sheep is not acting for the good of the animals. This analogy of the ruler to a shepherd suggests further that the relation of the ruler to the ruled is "simple" and that the ruled are happy to serve. It implies further that the just man is like a sheep, leaving himself at a disadvantage in relation to the unjust, paying taxes in full, working for the public good without benefit, while the unjust man gains material happiness. Thrasymachus adds to his charge the scornful observation that "it is not fear of doing wrong but fear of suffering wrong that calls forth the reproaches of those who revile injustice." The notion of justice is only the feeble self-defense of the weak, who must appeal to the pity of their betters because they cannot fend for themselves. "Thus," concludes Thrasymachus on a note of triumph, "injustice on a sufficiently large scale is a stronger, freer, and more masterful thing than justice."[23]

Socrates' reply applies another argumentative technique, distinguishing facts from norms. He admits that the strong may indeed impose their rule but asks whether Thrasymachus is right to say that this factual power is therefore just. Why does Thrasymachus assume that what is the case ought to be the case? After all, particular conditions can change, whereas norms must be valid universally. More concretely, what is the true normative worth of the material "happiness" gained by Thrasymachus's strong ruler? Is the unjust life truly, universally superior, or is it only a temporary condition that can change?

Socrates finally introduces his winning hand. He leaves the domain of particular facts to propose a thought experiment comparing perfect injustice and perfect justice. He accepts Thrasymachus's scornful description of the just man as a simpleton who does not want to rule or dominate others, but wants only to be left alone. By contrast, it can be said that the unjust person wants to get the better of everyone. Socrates now turns to another analogy. A musician or a doctor is a craftsman, but his mastery concerns his craft and only his craft; even within his own field, he seeks to dominate only over those who are ignorant of the necessary technique. In contrast, it is the mark of the unintelligent person that he overreaches because he has no sense of the limits imposed by the telos of his craft. For this reason, the unintelligent are condemned to failure as a result of their overreaching (*pleonexis*). It follows that Thrasymachus's unjust man does exactly what the ignorant person does; he overreaches, letting himself be ruled by his passions rather than by the reason inherent in the mastery of his craft.

Socrates' second refutation of Thrasymachus's argument has broad implications. In the Greek world, where everything has its proper end, injustice occurs because some individuals are ignorant of their proper place and of the limits imposed on their action by the natural ends of the object of their action. As a result, they overreach, producing disharmony, faction, and civil strife in the city and in themselves as well. As a result, Socrates concludes, the just are not only wiser and more intelligent (because they recognize their own limits, just as Socrates knows his own ignorance), but also and for the same reason more capable of action because their lives are built on harmony, unity, and justice. As a result, contrary to the Sophist's claim, Socrates has shown that injustice does not produce happiness, but rather its opposite. He uses a final analogy. The eyes have their particular function, the ears have theirs, and the two can work together so long as neither overreaches into the other's domain. Similarly, the specific function of what he calls the soul is the management or rule concerned with the good of the whole. To realize its function, the soul must act justly. If it fails, disharmony reigns within the individual, and the city is riven by faction, discord, or anarchy.

Although Socrates has refuted the Sophist's claim that justice is defined by the advantage of the stronger, he has not yet explained positively why a person should be just. Glaucon now raises this question. Granted, being just is something good, but there are different kinds of good, some that serve as means to an end, others that are an end in themselves. This question sets off another round of analysis and analogy, which ultimately fails to define what justice truly is. As a result, Socrates proposes to look instead at the results of justice as they exist in the larger framework of a city composed of just men. Once this ideal of justice writ large has been clarified, it will be possible to return to the nature of the just man, who is of course also a citizen.

The detour is a long one. The question posed here by Glaucon in book II does not find an answer until book IX, when the relation between types of political regime and the forms of the soul that they nurture is examined. The ideal political regime in which justice is "writ large" is not a fact of nature; the philosopher must explain its origin, its further development, and its legitimacy. Political institutions have to be created, and civic education must be organized in order to produce the traits of character that ensure their stability. This political structure—which Socrates calls "our City"—is an ideal that serves as a standard permitting the classification of existing regimes according to their proximity to it. The passage from one type of regime to another—regime change—will depend on the relation between the political institutions and the type of individual character they produce.

◆

The investigation of the nature of the just city begins with an account of its origin. Men join with one another because of their lack of self-sufficiency. They are creatures of need whose quest for satisfaction draws them to others, with whom they at first exchange simple things such as food, clothing, or shelter. Because exchange is based on difference, a division of labor emerges, giving rise to specialization, which both increases the efficiency and wealth of society as a whole and benefits each member individually. This specialization and division of labor are said to be natural because, for a Greek, each individual has his specific virtues. As the city grows, the division of labor and specialization increase; previously latent talents now find a use when, for example, imports and their commercialization begin. At that point, the question of how to distribute the social wealth emerges. Plato suggests using a market, which entails a further division of labor because the craftsmen who produce goods cannot spend their time waiting for customers. Those who are weakest of body will be employed in the market, and those who "in the things of the mind are not altogether worthy of our fellowship, but whose strength of body is sufficient for toil" will be the producers. At this point, Socrates has constructed the ingredients of a simple city oriented to the satisfaction of basic needs.

An unexpected development now occurs. Glaucon denounces what he calls a "city of—or for—pigs." When Socrates asks him what he would put in its place, he proposes to add some of the luxuries that "we" enjoy. Socrates is at first critical of this proposition. He distinguishes the simple life of his healthy city oriented to the satisfaction of needs from the "fevered state" of the luxurious city in which people quest constantly for new satisfactions. As new "needs" continue to emerge, further refinements of the division of labor follow: now poets, rhapsodists, dancers, and even manufacturers of women's adornment find their place. The "needs" multiply, and the division continues because now servants, tutors, and wet and dry nurses appear to be necessary. With a touch of irony, Socrates adds that doctors obviously will be necessary for people living such a feverish life.

Despite Socrates' criticism of the luxurious city by comparison to the ascetic model built around the satisfaction of immediate physical needs rather than the artificial needs that emerge with the ever-expanding division of labor, the next step in the division of labor brings a new perspective. To maintain the wealthy, refined city, territorial expansion is necessary; with that expansion will come wars with neighbors and the cost of raising an army not only to win but thereafter to defend newly won wealth and territory. Plato's reader recognizes in this city made rich by the things that "we today enjoy" the world of Periclean Athens. It illustrates the logic that led to the creation of Athens's democratic empire and to the overreaching that brought its ultimate defeat.

It is important to see that Plato's criticism of wealth and refinement does not lead him to propose a return to the simpler existence governed by sheer necessity. He recognizes that luxury transcends necessity just as reason demands liberation from the enslavement to desire. As the division of labor increases, the sphere of the political emerges. The first step is the creation of military specialists whom Socrates calls "Guardians." Their particular specialization is unique insofar as it concerns the good of the whole city. Although these soldiers are at first selected by natural aptitude, as with other crafts, the basis of war is a kind of knowledge without which simple natural courage would turn into self-destructive folly unaware of its own limits. The Guardians must therefore be given leisure and time for training. They must also be selected with care in order to make sure that they don't use their force against the population. This stipulation calls for a specific kind of education to produce men of worthy character.

The goal of producing a harmony between the senses and reason determines the means by which the Guardians are educated, which Plato describes in detail. More important than the details of this educational program are its political implications, which suggest that Athens's failure was not due to its material wealth (which, in fact, was beneficial because it freed the citizens from the bonds of necessity), but to its inability to produce the kind of enlightened citizenry needed to preserve a just city. This is the ultimate basis of Plato's critique of democracy, which he claims is incapable of producing the kind of citizens needed to maintain its freedoms. But Plato is a philosopher as well as a critic. He proposes as a remedy the replacement of political democracy by the rule of philosopher-kings. In so doing, however, he makes the error for which Socrates criticized Thrasymachus: he conflates what is with what ought to be, facts with norms. The fact that Athenian democracy died does not mean that all democracies must always die. Nevertheless, Plato sets out to discover how his normative vision can be realized and to remedy the defects he attributes to democracy.

The division of labor continues among the military Guardians. Some of those who have learned to be both spirited and brave are taught an additional virtue, which Plato calls "sobriety" or "temperance" (*sophrosune*). This virtue ensures self-mastery by instilling a recognition of limits. Socrates illustrates his point by returning to the analogy of the just man and the just city. Just as the soul has a better and a worst part, and the better (the rational) must rule the worse (the appetites), so in the city the superior should rule the inferior. For this reason, sobriety, which is also called "harmony," is achieved in the city when the educated few rule over "the mob of motley appetites and pleasure and pains one would find chiefly in children and women and slaves and in the base rabble of those who are free men [only] in name."[24] When this kind of mastery exists, the luxurious city has been fully purified, and justice has been established under the guidance of the philosopher-Guardians.

The political implication of Plato's argument is that "justice" is not a "thing" that is added to the city in the same way that "luxury" was brought to the simple city. Justice is not an object that can be possessed, purchased, or earned; it is a relation among members of a society who themselves have achieved a just relation among the parts of their souls. It follows that justice exists both in the society and in its members. Each particular person works for the good of the whole by doing what he is by nature best suited to do, avoiding the overreaching that is characteristic of the unjust man. For this reason, justice is the first and highest principle that organizes the relations among the other elements in a just society—the producers, the soldier-Guardians, and the philosopher-Guardians. At the same time, justice organizes the three elements of the soul: the appetitive (which corresponds to the artisan producers), the spirited (which corresponds to the military Guardians), and the rational (which corresponds to the philosopher-Guardians). In this way, Plato has presented a political theory that ensures the coexistence of the different elements that make up society.

At this point, Glaucon is ready to concede that justice is more worthy than injustice, but Socrates explains that the situation is more complicated. The next phase of the argument (in book V) changes the focus to the education and role of the philosopher-Guardians. This shift in emphasis brings out what I have called the *antipolitical* implications of Plato's political theory.

The weakness of the argument for rule by the philosopher-Guardians is that it implies that justice can be imposed on the soul of the citizens, who are simply passive receptacles on which the rulers act. This view neglects the fact that justice is a relationship. As such, it must ensure the unity of elements that are different from each other. Both parties must see the relation of the rulers to the ruled as legitimate. Socrates' friends push him to describe the lives of the Guardians, the principles of their selection, and the details of their education. For example, can women be Guardians? Why not? answers Socrates. Their exclusion today is due only to convention because there is nothing in their physical differences from men that disqualifies them from ruling. This response, however, leaves as yet unanswered the source of the legitimation of Guardian rule.

The Guardians' lives are organized to ensure what might be called a "communist" unity and universality of their condition. Plato's description recalls Sparta more than it reflects any aspect of the life of Athens. A universal equality among the members subsumes plurality, particularity, and diversity. In this way, the argument suggests, there will be no danger that Guardian rule will be arbitrary. For example, the women who become Guardians are to "be common" to their male colleagues. Private cohabitation is forbidden; all children belong to the community, no parent is allowed to know his or her child, and no child its parent. All of these measures ensure that favoritism will be excluded. Any particular interest is similarly avoided by ensuring that the Guardians have no private possessions (including wives or children). Unity among them is assured by the fact that with the abolition of private property, the Guardians are obliged to live in communal dwellings, to take meals in common, as well as to study and do gymnastics together. And even if "innate necessity" leads to sexual union, there must be sharing so that no one covets what others claim to possess. Universality and equality condition one another among these ideal rulers of society.

Although social equality does not exist outside the elite group, the Guardians must ensure that unity is established in the larger society in order to avoid the injustice that would result from the kind of overreaching (*pleonexis*) that destroys the harmony of society. Plato compares the Guardians' political intervention to the breeding of animals, which ensures not only that like mates with like, but also that like is not overcome by a passion for unlike. In carrying out this task, the Guardians are allowed to "make considerable use of falsehood and deception [because it is] for the benefit of their subjects."[25] For the same reason, the temptation to expand beyond the limits of the city must be avoided by limiting the size of the population. This prescription gives rise to another use of the lie in order to ensure that inferior men (who get either inferior women or no women) will blame chance or fate rather than choices made by their rulers, who, having more access to superior women, will produce better offspring (the inferior ones are secretly eliminated). All of these measures, which work to avoid particularity and conflict are justified by the good of the city; in this city, everyone rejoices and grieves at all births and deaths; and everyone uses the word *mine* to refer to the same things.

To modern eyes, this picture is not attractive, as my description of it as "communist" suggests. Eugenic breeding, systematic lies, and the elimination of private interest are foreign to the contemporary ethos. But it is important to see that what Plato is proposing is a rationalist vision of politics that is not without its intellectual appeal. Because Plato recognizes that justice is not a thing but a relation, he understands that rule must be legitimate in the eyes of the ruled. However, the structure that he portrays is *antipolitical* insofar as it is organized in order to make political action on the part of citizens unnecessary. The virtuous character that real Athenian democracy was unable to maintain would be bred into the population by Plato's ruling Guardians, the philosopher-kings, and would be maintained by their manipulation of opinion. Although the difference between rulers and ruled remains, the principles of equality and universality are maintained within each class. That is why Plato notes that a cobbler who does the work of a carpenter (or vice versa) would not render the society unjust, but if an artisan or money maker tried to use his wealth to enter the class of soldier-Guardians, or a soldier tried to enter the ranks of the philosophers, injustice in the form of overreaching would result. What remains to be explained is the reason for which Plato considers this relation of rulers and ruled legitimate.

At this point, Plato's argument moves toward a synthesis. In the first part of *The Republic*, he had looked for justice in the individual; he then sought it in the political relations established in the city. He must now bring these two poles together by showing that they both participate in philosophical reason. Plato distinguishes four general types of knowledge, the least certain of which is the most fleeting and particular, whereas the most certain is permanent and universal. These types of truth are plotted (proportionally) by the simile of the Divided Line that stretches from the visible to the intelligible world.[26] This leaves open the question of how finite humans gain access to the higher forms of knowledge. Plato's answer is suggested by the Allegory of the Cave. Imagine, says Socrates, that humans live in an underground cave. Behind them is a source of light, the sun; in front of them is a sort of movie screen; and between them and the light is a stage on which real things are present and interact. The humans are said to be physically restricted in a way that permits them only to regard the large screen in front of them. The result is that their knowledge consists simply of the shadows cast by the real objects on the screen; these appearances *are* their reality, and they compete with one another to see who is the most astute in deciphering the nature and meaning of the appearing world. With this allegory, Plato introduces the distinction between appearance and reality that explains why someone might only "seem" like a friend. As always in the use of analogy, however, this distinction presupposes the existence of something shared that also relates the things that are distinguished.

Imagine, the allegory continues, that someone is freed from his bindings and rises to the sunlight, where he is able to see the true nature of the human situation. He now knows that there exists a reality behind the appearances that men take to be real. Imagine further that the former cave-dweller returns with the mission of enlightening the others. They would not believe his wondrous stories about a truer reality than the only one they and their ancestors have known. What is more, the missionary who has returned to the shadows from the blinding sunlight will be temporarily unable to regain his focus in the world of the shadows; he hesitates, stumbles, and generally shows himself incompetent. It is not surprising that public opinion likewise disdains the "philosopher," who appears to be lacking common sense, his head caught up in the clouds, accused, as was Socrates, of rejecting the gods of the city or of inventing new divine things. Yet the philosopher is not claiming special access to a mystical domain reserved for the initiated; the truths he asserts are simple and open to everyone—if only they know where to look.

The political implication that Plato draws from the Allegory of the Cave clashes with the educational theory that it seems to imply. A teacher does not feed facts to empty minds as if he were writing on blank paper; his task is to turn the student in the right direction so that the student means it literally when he says, "I *see* what you mean." That is why the acknowledgment of ignorance that shows the individual that he doesn't know what he thinks he knows is the precondition for a shared voyage of discovery toward the truth. Socrates confirms this interpretation when he insists that the "craft" of "turning around" is not the same as "putting sight" into a person. That "turning around" was the goal of the introductory discussions that, in the first part of *The Republic*, led to understanding that justice is not a thing, but a relation that unifies the diversity of society. The playful chatter that began with the encounter with old Cephalus had an educational role.

But Plato seems to doubt the implications of his allegory. Why, he wonders, would people listen to the philosopher? And why would the philosopher who has risen to the sunlight be willing to return to the cave? Only the philosopher's universal truth can ensure the maintenance of the relation between justice in the city and the harmony in the individual soul. The uneducated are incapable of ruling because there is no single end that guides their actions; they are the slaves of their conflicting passions. But is it just to force philosophers to rule? asks Plato. Would that not force them to live a life beneath their capacities? Plato's answer returns to his critique of the undisciplined Athenian democracy. "We" would be wrong to let the philosophers do as they please; justice as universal is not concerned with the happiness of any one group within society; it concerns the harmony of the whole, to which each—including the philosophers—must contribute what he can. Because the philosophers are philosophers, their rule will *not* be political, concludes Plato. Indeed, "If you can find a way of life that is better than ruling for those who are going to rule, your well-governed city will become a possibility."[27] Then only the truly rich—those for whom wealth is a good and rational life—will be in command.

At this point, the reader will rightly begin to doubt Plato's political realism, and that is just what Plato himself now does. He admits that the ideal city is condemned to decline because the philosopher-kings must rely on mere sense perception to put into practice their eugenic project. They are bound to make mistakes when deciding the allocation of the population to specific functions. A slippery slope ensues as Plato analyzes the successive less-than-ideal regimes that are inexorably transformed, one after the other, from the second best (timocracy) to the worst (tyranny) and passing through the stages of oligarchy and democracy as they spiral downward until the cycle begins anew when tyranny is replaced by a wise monarch. The dynamic that governs this fatal decline results from the rupture of the unity that the philosopher-king sought to establish and ensure between the political institutions and the kind of individuals that are needed to make them function. Both Plato's soaring idealism and his sober realism are apparent in his recognition that even the best political regime cannot survive if the citizens' character is unjust.

The first step in the process of decline occurs when the ideal city is replaced by a timocracy in which rulers are legitimated by their ability to achieve honor through courageous victories that win their fellows' esteem. Their success is due to the domination in their soul of one of its components, the spirited, or thymic, element. This lack of psychological harmony explains why the timocracy, despite its military triumphs, will be unstable. The timocrat who has sacrificed personal well-being for the good of the state and honor in the eyes of its citizens is succeeded by a son who sees that others around him are advancing their own personal welfare, whereas his family has sacrificed its particular welfare to the service of all. This son sees that the sources of political legitimacy have changed; as a result, he begins to behave in a different manner. Honorable service is no longer a justification for rule; the thymic qualities that distinguish a person lose their importance as private benefits come to be valued above the public good. The timocracy will now be replaced by an oligarchy, the rule by the few whose power is justified by their wealth. This oligarchy acquires legitimacy because the superiority of its wealth can be measured objectively in the eyes of all. The virtues of courage and honor, which are personal qualities, are replaced by the skill in the acquisition of wealth, which is quantitative. The transition to the new regime takes place when there is a conflict between the personality type encouraged by the existing regime (courage and honor) and a new set of values that can be satisfied only by new forms of political legitimation (the acquisition of wealth).

The new oligarchic regime will also be plagued by a fundamental instability. Fortunes are inherently fleeting. Unlike the qualities of a person, material wealth is quantitative; it can be won, but it can also be lost. Moreover, money is a only a means; it is a good that is not good in itself, but only for what it can buy. As a result, the sons will again betray their fathers. The appetites of the first generation of oligarchs were restrained by the need to use reason to direct their money making. Their well-born heirs no longer need to discipline their appetites in order to search for wealth; indeed, the habituation to satisfaction deprives them of the spirited thymic aspect of the soul that their oligarchic fathers had inherited but then used to motivate their drive for wealth. These heirs now become slaves to their passions; as a result, their rule becomes erratic, they begin to overreach, and their regime loses its legitimacy. With this loss, the transition to what Plato calls democracy is prepared.

The rule of the people does not arise spontaneously to take the place of the discredited oligarchy. Although its material base is present among the many who had been subjected to an oligarchic government that has lost its legitimacy, the spark that kindles the democratic fire will come from within the oligarchy itself. Material suffering alone does not lead to social change; Plato's account of the transition to democracy is political. There will be some among the oligarchy who have retained positive aspects of the acquisitive spirit; unwilling to live as mere consumers of material goods, they will seek a wider field for the realization of their limitless passions. The only satisfaction that seems worth their efforts is power. But because oligarchic government has lost its legitimacy, their only option is to take the lead of a popular antioligarchic movement that demands satisfaction of its own passions. As a result, their leadership gives political form to a demand for democratic equality of participation. But they will fail to stabilize any power they may gain because the quantitative reason that animated the oligarchic spirit is merely tactical; it does not understand that the democratic demands to which it has given a platform will sweep away its temporary rule.

Plato's description of the democratic rule unintentionally unleashed by the power-seeking oligarchs is biting; democracy is the prelude to the descent into an anarchy in which the idea of legitimate government itself is destroyed. Democracy promises a liberty that frees the appetites from all restraint. The result is a chaos that destroys even the tactical, quantitative reason that remained from the time of oligarchy. Plato mockingly describes this "beautiful polity" as a coat of many colors that appeals to boys and women, people drawn to the superficiality of bright and shiny things. Worse, the principle of absolute freedom means that democrats tolerate a right not to submit to laws with which one doesn't agree, and they accept an individual right not to hold office even if qualified. These weaknesses lead Plato to conclude that democracy will prove to be a "heavenly and delicious entertainment for the time being."[28] But it will not last; the good that democracy values—complete freedom—turns against whatever institutions are established because it can accept nothing less than immediate gratification. So it is that democracy gives way to anarchy; a society where diversity has destroyed any unifying principle leaves no place for rule (*arche*) or government.

The cycle reaches its final point when the threat of an anarchy that dissolves any remnant of social coherence leads to the demand for the creation of a new unity by the intervention of a tyrant. This tyranny is hardly better than the anarchy that preceded it. It simply replaces the chaos of everyone's lawless and arbitrary appetites with rule according to a single person's lawless and arbitrary appetites. The price of new unity is thus steep. The source of the dilemma in the first instance was the thoughtless adoption of democracy by power-hungry revolutionary oligarchs. The claim that all citizens have equal rights and absolute liberty led to the anarchy where no one is allowed any particular rights because that would destroy equality and thereby infringe on liberty. The restored unity imposed by the tyrant is a pale reflection of the ideal city insofar as it replaces the rule of philosophical reason with the arbitrariness of the tyrant's passions. This is Plato's political point. Democracy arose as a result of the absence of philosophical reflection by the oligarchs; tyranny now results from the same absence of philosophical thought. This result leaves open the question whether Plato hopes that the completion of the cycle of degeneration by a new unity will make possible the rule of reason by philosopher-kings, who will find an audience that recognizes the danger of abandoning rational rule. Or does he, like his teacher Socrates in *The Apology*, put his faith in a renewal of the citizen's virtues?

In effect, Plato now turns to the experience of democracy as it exists in the individual citizen's soul. The democratic allergy to any form of rule creates a political climate in which those who obey the rulers are denounced as willing slaves. Meanwhile, both rulers who behave humbly toward their subjects and subjects who behave as if they were rulers are praised for their "democratic" integrity. This love of unrestrained freedom affects private life by destroying all semblance of familial order. The father behaves like a child and fears the judgment of his sons, who for their part act as if they were the father, feeling neither shame nor fear in front of their parents. The young compete with their elders, who act like children for fear of appearing disagreeable or authoritarian. Teachers come to fear their students, whom they feel obliged to flatter, which, of course, only adds to the students' disregard for their teachers. The democratic malady spreads, demanding that the resident alien or foreign visitor be treated as the equal of a citizen. This plague of freedom rolls on, as slaves claim equal rights with their masters and women demand legal equality with men—a point, Socrates remarks ironically, that he almost forgot to mention. Putting the dot on the *i*, he adds that even domestic animals are freer in a democracy because horses and donkeys can roam where they will, bumping into anyone who gets in their way. At this point, he concludes, the citizens' souls have become so sensitive to the allures of freedom that if they find someone who accepts even the slightest restraint, they are offended.

The transition from this democratic anarchy to the tyrannical imposition of unity obeys a political logic that combines the objective account of regime change with the subjective analysis of the types of personality needed by each. Plato's claim is sharp: "tyranny develops out of no other constitution than democracy—from the height of liberty... [results] the fiercest extreme of servitude."[29] The democratic city is composed of three groups: the idle talkers who direct the political life of the city, the well-organized wealthy, and the working people who are willing to participate in politics only if they gain rewards for doing so. This triadic structure is the source of a perverse dynamic in which the third group will perceive any alliance of the other two as a threat to its integrity, which it must match with countermeasures—force, ruse, or other illegitimate means of action—whose aim is to break up the alliance by drawing one or the other of the alliance members to its side. In spite of his antipolitical goals, Plato shows himself here to be a sharp analyst of political dynamics.

The political analyst pushes further his account of the lines of force created when the oligarchs join with the people to produce a democracy. As the source of the "honey" coveted by the other groups, the wealthy know that they are the object of jealousy for both the politicians (who envy their power) and the people (who are jealous of their well-being). They seek to justify the power that comes with wealth, but the radicals accuse them of plotting against the people, whom they want to lure to their own side. The temperature rises; the wealthy whose legitimacy is threatened seek to protect themselves, but they do so by acting like oligarchs, using their wealth to buy support to buttress their power. In order to avoid the potential oligarchic domination, the people unite by choosing one of the politicians as their defender. In this way, the tyrant—who claims to serve the people—is brought onto the stage and given power by popular demand. Once he has the experience of domination, he acquires a taste for it; his soul is corrupted, and the temptation to overreach now assails him. He may bring false charges against potential enemies or may murder or banish others; at the same time, however, he hints to the people that he will cancel debts and redistribute land. The wealthy, who feel threatened, will then begin to plot against him. Their threat leads the tyrant to ask the people to give him a military guard, which they willingly grant because he claims to be their champion, and they therefore worry more about his safety in the present than about their own in the future. At this point, the wealthy will have no choice but to flee. With no more enemies, the leader no longer needs to hide the tyranny that has come to possess his soul by claiming to be the friend of the people; he is now the complete tyrant on whom no limits are exercised. However solid his position appears, though, the tyrant will overreach. The disorder of his soul reflects the anarchic appetites that rule democracy, which are now given free reign by the arbitrary power of tyranny.

Plato's conclusion is stark. The major difference between democracy and tyranny lies simply in the number of persons who rule, and the height of freedom coincides with the depth of servitude. The ground of his argument is his philosophical insistence that nothing but the rule of reason can create power that is legitimate and authority that is just. The strength of this philosophical imperative is shown by his ability to criticize all other forms of political life. This philosophical goal (more than his hatred for the regime that killed Socrates) in the last resort explains Plato's critique of democracy. But his ideal city remains a thought construction; in this sense, it is an antipolitical utopia rather than a positive political form of rule. Plato sets philosophy and democracy, which were born together in Athens, on separate paths that will meet rarely in the course of human history.

◆

Antipolitical though Plato's goals may have been, his understanding of the dynamics of political life in the different, less-than-perfect regimes that he discusses in *The Republic* warns his reader against the temptation to denounce him and the tradition he has founded as an idealism that ignores the exigencies of real life. The delicate structure of his analysis as it moves from the question of justice in the individual's behavior to the existence of justice in the city and then, finally, to the play of the subjective and objective forms of political justice remains a model of political thought. His warning that a regime will be shaken by instability if the individual citizens' character does not correspond to the nature of their political institutions retains its relevance over the course of Western history. From the time of the Roman republic to the days of modern democracy, critics have warned that a politics whose basis is the unprincipled claim that the end justifies the means—one that, for example, condones torture or imperial rapine—will rot the very character of the citizens who brought it to the heights of power, thus preparing its decline and defeat. Perhaps it is necessary to be an idealist in order to see deeply into the self-deceptions that guide the cold realists as they rush for power without principle, apply force without legitimacy, and let their passions define their interests.

Plato seemed to recognize the limits of philosophical reason in his two later political works, *The Statesman* and *The Laws*, which seek to accommodate the pure philosophical reason that governed his earlier antipolitical theory to a finite world. Because these late works have not had the influence of *The Republic*, I do not summarize their claims here.[30] They never fully abandon the idealism of his great work, even though they pour some water into Plato's heady philosophical wine. The modifications resulted from Plato's recognition that the kind of perfectly moral individual citizen needed to realize the ideal city is a philosophical fiction. The philosopher-king cannot change social relations while remaining separate from them; he has to take into account people as they actually exist in the given society. Recognition of the need to account for the world as it is (without neglecting the question of how it ought to be) is implicit in the brilliant accounts of the dynamic relations that lead from one regime type to another. This concern with the particular becomes explicit in the work of Aristotle, whose two decades of study with Plato took place after the idealist theory elaborated in *The Republic* had been composed and while the later, more modest, and therefore more political works were maturing.

ARISTOTLE AND THE PROPERLY POLITICAL

Aristotle (384–322) criticizes explicitly the antipolitical implications of *The Republic* in book II of his *Politics*. Although this discussion follows his own definition of the political in book I, it can serve as an introduction to Aristotle's political thought. Whether Aristotle is true to the spirit of Plato's text or chooses to exaggerate its letter in order to make his own arguments is not important in the present context. Once he has refuted (to his own satisfaction) the tightly structured harmony of Platonic political thought, it is incumbent on him to produce his own synthetic understanding of what counts as properly political and then to demonstrate the value of his definitions by making clear the distinction of legitimate forms of political rule (or governance) from other forms of domination, including his much debated defense of slavery.

◆

At the outset of his discussion, Aristotle asks whether citizens of a community share everything, nothing, or some things. This methodological approach, which he applies in all aspects of his philosophy, is not based simply on formal or logical distinctions; it expresses his recognition that the world itself is plural and diverse. In the present case, because citizens obviously must share something, the next question is whether members of a community must share everything. Aristotle has in mind Plato's claim that women, children, and property should be "in common" among the Guardians. In that case, however, he points out, the unified community resembles a household in which diversity exists only as a means to achieve an end that is external to it: physical self-preservation. As opposed to the household, which is based on the combination of husband and wife (and slaves), a city contains many diverse elements. The unity of the city cannot destroy but must preserve and promote the different types of members who compose it because each of them contributes in its own way to ensuring the self-sufficiency that permits it to set its own goals. The plurality of talents that compose a city permit it to maintain itself when the conditions change. Just as a household is more self-sufficient than a single person, so the city is more self-sufficient than a household. Its diversity ensures the self-sufficiency that guarantees that the city remains a political unity that preserves the freedom of its members. A city is not unified by its walls, but by the political relations among its citizens, who differ from one another in some ways but are equal insofar as they share in the benefits and burdens of ruling.

Aristotle draws further implications from his critique of the unitary Platonic vision. He rejects the idea that unity depends on the fact that everyone says "mine" or "not mine" at the same time and about the same thing. There is a difference between all citizens individually saying that the same thing is mine (as when they all benefit from that thing—for example, justice) and all of them claiming ownership of the thing insofar as they are part of a collective unity (as in Plato's "communist" vision). In the first case, possession is a real benefit; in the second, it is only formal and abstract. If the individual can speak only in the name of the collective, expressing only what he shares with the others, then the diversity needed to ensure political self-sufficiency is lost. When property is held in common and said formally to belong to all, no one is actually held responsible for its maintenance. Because all things belong in principle to all citizens insofar as they are members of such a collective, each individual as an individual can take what he wants without concerning himself with the condition of what remains. Similarly, if the children belong to all members of the community, no single member will give them the care they need because none of them feels a connection to any particular child. For that reason, Aristotle points out that "it is better to have a cousin of one's own than a son in the way Socrates describes."[31] And of course, he adds, it is naive to think that people would not have suspicions about who their brothers, sons, fathers, or mothers are because there are evident familial resemblances. In short, formal unity cannot overcome actual diversity.

Aristotle also rejects the Platonic idea of a unity that, in his words, would "reduce a harmony to a unison, or a rhythm to a single beat."[32] He insists once again that to be self-sufficient, the city must maintain its diversity. Furthermore, the fact that Plato's unity is imposed by the rulers will become a source of conflict because the spirited and warlike members of the Guardians will become jealous of the power of the philosopher-kings. This divisiveness is accentuated by the claim that the rulers will make the whole happy by sacrificing their own happiness because they accept the priority of the communal whole over the choices of the individual parts who compose the community. You cannot ensure the happiness of the whole, Aristotle counters, if that happiness is not present individually in all of the parts, including the Guardians, who, if forced to return to the cave, may take out their bitterness on the public. Thus, the plurality of political life that Plato ignores will come back to haunt the practical realization of his ideal city. It does not follow, however, that political thought can go to the other extreme; empirical analysis of the diversity of social relations cannot abandon the philosophical imperatives of unity, universality, and lawfulness that are the concern of the political.

What, then, is the political for Aristotle? At the most basic level, the political (the polis) is distinguished from the concerns of the household (the *oikos*). The political is the sphere of freedom, where citizens join together to deliberate and decide the nature of the good life, which is distinct from mere biological life. The household is the domain of necessity where women and slaves produce the means that support the citizens' political freedom. The distinction between the two spheres of life is sharp. The political is the stage for action, where individual initiatives can create both cultural and social relations that have never existed before; the household is the place of production, where ends are predetermined and individuals carry them out without question or doubt because they are governed by necessity. For this reason, politics is the expression of freedom and autonomy because it is the citizens themselves who decide the ends that they seek. The household is characterized by necessity and heteronomy because the production carried out within its walls is simply a means to an end that is external to the producers.

These first distinctions are based on the Greek idea that the end (or telos) for which something exists defines its nature, determines its function, and fixes its place among the complex of other activities that make up human societies, ordering its function within a hierarchy of values. This end can also be called the "good" that any given action seeks. There are, of course, different kinds of good, which are realized by different means. What counts as good (or just) in the polis is determined by what Aristotle calls "political rule" as opposed to both "household management" and the rule of the master over his slave. Aristotle's teleological understanding of the natural and social world fits together with the more complicated idea that there is a natural hierarchy among the things and social relations that men encounter. This teleological assumption permits him to propose an empirical analysis that does not abandon the values of unity, universality, and lawfulness on which Plato placed such stress.

Aristotle's descriptive approach begins from the world as it exists, seeking to classify and to distinguish among cases that might appear similar at first glance. The justification of this mode of thinking is seen in a brief discussion in his *Metaphysics* that explains the basic task of philosophy. The passage is significant in the present context because it criticizes Socrates for limiting philosophy to "ethical matters and neglecting the world of nature as a whole." Ethics is concerned with what men in general, all men, should do. It formulates universally applicable judgments by concentrating on definitions. But "the common definition could not be a definition of any sensible thing, as they were always changing. Things of this other sort [i.e., definitions], then, [Plato] called ideas, and sensible things, he said, were all named after these."[33] This description of Plato's theory of Ideas (or Forms), as suggested, for example, in the Allegory of the Cave, makes clear the deeper ground of Aristotle's critique: beginning from the universal forgets that "the relative is prior to the absolute." Aristotle challenges Plato to show "what on earth the Forms contribute to sensible things," criticizing the incoherence of his answers to questions such as whether the Forms "cause" the particular instances, and if so, how such causality works.[34] For his part, beginning from "the relative" is justified because it acquires its full meaning only from the end that it serves. Aristotle's method is thus an empirical or inductive investigation of the hierarchy of ends. As a result, his dogged drawing of distinctions is more pedestrian than Plato's scintillating speculative dialogues. He offers a series of classifications and illustrations that put off the first-time reader. Yet it pays to pursue them with him.

When Aristotle looks at "the relative," he sees it as part of a world that is organized by a natural hierarchy of ends. Ends can be described and classified as higher or lower than other ends insofar, for example, as one is more inclusive than the other. In this way, Aristotle's philosophy can propose an evaluation of the relative worthiness of the different domains that it studies. The polis is a form of association, a type of community that brings together different persons and activities. Individuals belong to many associations, all of which seek some result that they consider good. Some of these "ends" may be only means to other ends, in which case their place in the hierarchy of values is lower. Other associations, such as the family, may be both ends in themselves (to ensure social reproduction and to provide the necessities of life) and means to an end that stands outside of them (to produce citizens to fight wars and deliberate about political choices). At the top of the hierarchy must stand a kind of association that is not a means to some other end, but rather a good in itself. This highest type of association not only is the most valuable, but also offers the criterion that permits putting the others in their place within the natural hierarchy. This criterion is the degree of autonomy attained by the particular association, which Aristotle also calls its universality or its degree of sovereignty. The highest form of association is autonomous, universal, and sovereign in the sense that it includes all of the other lesser types of association. This independence explains why the polis is the place of freedom.

Each type of association is governed or ruled in a specific manner. The three basic types of rule are that of a statesman in a polis, that of a manager of a household, and that of a master over his slaves. Although the latter two forms of association belong within the domain of the *oikos,* where necessity determines behavior, they are nonetheless different from one another. The nature of each form of rule depends on the end for which it exists, which in turn means that, as opposed to the universal Platonic harmony, relations among the members will differ. The most simple association is based on a natural impulse that exists in all animals and even in plants: the need to reproduce the biological species by the pairing of male and female. Reproduction will be the goal of the family, which unites a naturally ruling and a naturally ruled element, creating a unity that is higher than either of them. The ruling element (the man) is said to have the intelligence needed to exercise foresight; the ruled (the woman) represents the bodily power to produce the desired result (the child, who is thus not just the accidental result of the momentary pairing of two independent beings). The governance of the familial unity differs from the mastery exercised over the slave, who is not ruled but dominated. Aristotle illustrates this distinction at first by condemning the "barbarians" for treating women and slaves as if they were identical, which is said to be a sign that their cities are less richly diverse than the Greek democracy.

The two simple associations—the household and the master/slave—come together to form the *oikos,* whose goal or function is to supply the necessities of daily life. At some point, a threshold is surpassed when several associations (families, clans, or villages) come together to become self-sufficient, autonomous, and thus capable of giving themselves their own laws for engaging in activities that go beyond the sphere of necessity. This higher stage of development permits Aristotle to introduce a distinction that is fundamental to his political thought. Although the polis grew from these two simple associations' quest to maintain mere life, the now autonomous polis exists for the sake of the good life. The capacities needed to maintain simple physical existence differ qualitatively from those that contribute to the achievement of a good life. As a result, there may be times when the maintenance of physical life demands the sacrifice of the values essential to the good life. In that case, people may judge that mere life is not worth saving.

Aristotle's categorical distinction of life from the good life has a further implication. Life is maintained by the production of things that are simply a means to an external end (mere living), whereas the good life depends on free activity that defines ends deemed worthy of being sought. That is why Aristotle insists that production and activity differ from one another. Production takes place under the command of necessity; the end sought determines (to a greater or lesser degree) the means that can effectively be used. Activity is a manifestation of creative freedom that is also an appeal for the cooperation with others. Thus, a person cannot act alone, but he can work in solitude. As a result, the management of production must impose preexisting rules on the participants, whereas political activity invents its own rules collectively and is able to transform its previous mode of governance.

The creation of the polis is at once the result of a natural process and the realization of a potential that is inscribed in human nature. This distinction between potentiality and actuality results from Aristotle's insistence in *The Metaphysics*, as noted earlier, that "the relative is prior to the absolute." The ends of nature are not always completely or at every moment fulfilled. Man, says Aristotle, is a "political animal," a being who must live in a polis if he is to actualize his human potential. But the fact that the life in the polis is a goal of nature does not mean that nature imprints a single type of communal life on humans. Nor does it mean that all cities are equivalent; the "barbarians" who were unable to distinguish women and slaves live in less-perfect cities than the Greeks because they have not been able to develop the full potential of the natural instinct to live together. Nonetheless, even an imperfect polis is governed differently than the way a father rules the family or the master dominates the slave. Aristotle and his students analyzed 158 different actualizations of this human potential to create cities in a text of which only fragments remain.[35] The distinctions among them are due to the fact that although nature made both bees and men as gregarious creatures, only men have the capacity for speech, which they can use in debating, disagreeing, and then acting to bring about the conditions of what they consider to be the good life.

The distinction between potentiality and actuality has a further political implication. Although the polis comes into being only after the simple forms of association have been realized, the fact that it is the highest form of human association means that it is a whole whose existence makes possible and gives meaning to the parts of which it is composed. Aristotle illustrates this argument by analogy to the body. Analysis of a foot or a hand that is separated from the body gives limited and not very useful knowledge because the separated organ is simply a mass of lifeless material that can serve whatever ends its possessor decides to seek. By contrast, a body that has lost one or more of its parts may continue to function, however imperfectly, as a human being. The implication of this argument, which is typical of Greek thought, is that the individual is not self-sufficient; he is a part that depends on the whole that is the polis. It provides another reason for the claim that justice belongs to the polis—which, of course, is responsible for defining the nature of the justice that defines the good life.

Aristotle's analysis of slavery underscores the import of the distinction of the polis from the *oikos,* the good life from mere life. He knows that he is dealing with a contested issue, admitting in the *Politics* that "others believe that it is contrary to nature to be a master (for it is by law [*nomos*] that one person is a slave and another free, whereas by nature there is no difference between them), which is why it is not just either; for it involves force."[36] Slavery belongs to the *oikos* insofar as it participates in the sphere of the production of necessities needed to maintain life, but it concerns the polis insofar as the satisfaction of physical need is the precondition for the autonomy and freedom needed to define the good life. As a part of the *oikos,* the slave is a kind of property, and the art of acquiring property belongs to the sphere of production rather than to the political action of free men. To acquire property is an instrumental task; appropriate means to that end must be found. These means can be inanimate (a ship's rudder) or animate (the sailor at the helm), and an animate means (a slave) can use an inanimate one (a hammer) as a means to realize a preassigned end. These means are also a form of property whose characteristic is that it is unfree; it is only a means used for an end that it does not chose.[37] However, the slave is not a hammer, but a human, and so the question of the political (as distinct from an economic) justification of slavery must also be addressed.

Aristotle's political explanation of slavery is based on his conception of the world as naturally hierarchical; the higher justly rules that which is less perfect, and this subordination benefits both parties by realizing their essential nature. There are different kinds of rule because there are different subjects of rule and different levels of perfection. The slave can be said justly to rule the hammer because the animate instrument is superior to the inanimate. Similarly, the soul rules over the body, for the benefit of both. In these two cases, rule is imposed directly; its force faces no resistance. There are also intermediate cases—for example, the domination of the male over the female or the rule of the mind (or understanding) over the appetites (or the desires that are the affective part of the mind). As opposed to the domination of soul over body, where the body clearly needs the soul to continue to exist, in these more complicated cases, the "ruler" must gain the cooperation of the ruled, who is capable of understanding arguments but not of formulating his own. The implication is that the first type of rule exists for the sake of life, whereas the second is a potential ingredient in the good life because the cooperation of the ruled entails at least a minimal element of self-determination. In the first case, the body is thirsty and needs any liquid nourishment to survive; in the second, a person desires a glass of good wine and will abstain from lesser vintages. Those who are governed by their immediate needs and who therefore must be guided toward satisfaction can be said to be naturally slaves; those whose appetites make them at least capable of understanding should in principle or potentially have a different, relatively higher status.

Although Aristotle's claim that some people are slaves "by nature" would be repeated often in Western history, he himself was clearly unsure about its validity, often returning to it. At one point, he admits that although nature tends to make the bodies of slaves and free people different, this is not always the case, and the same applies to the soul of the enslaved, whose relative beauty is even more difficult to judge than that of the body. The political claim finally breaks down in uncertainty. The chapter that follows in the *Politics* (book I, chap. 6) returns to the argument that slavery is based only on conventional law (*nomos*)—for example, in the case of the defeated parties in war. But that means that the enslaved were subdued by force, and their enslavement thus cannot be said to be beneficial to them. To escape the problem, Aristotle again turns to nature, suggesting that the victors must have had some good quality, whereas the defeated lost because of their own defaults: they were "unwilling to be ruled, but naturally suited for it," he concludes.[38] He has to admit, however, that there may be unjust wars whose victims do not deserve their fate. In the end, although he is unable to offer a convincing political argument for slavery, a significant remark in another section of the *Politics* makes clear that its justification cannot lie solely in the economy.[39] When it comes to deciding whether to go to war, explains Aristotle, those who live in the border region and whose households are therefore at risk are not allowed to vote. Political decisions must be made free of the constraint of economic necessity. The implication of this remark is that Athenian democracy was not dependent on the production of its slaves. After all, many other slave societies that were not democracies existed in antiquity. Why did the Athenians rule themselves democratically? And was slavery a threat to this rule of the free over the free?

When Aristotle looks more closely at the kind of knowledge that the master needs in order to rule the slave, he admits that "there is nothing grand or impressive about this science." When the master directs the production process, he is himself governed by the same kind of necessities that rule in the household. Therefore, if he has the resources to do so and if he is wise, he will not let himself be contaminated by learning such slavish pursuits, which should be left to an overseer while he engages in politics or philosophy. Although the master must first devote himself to the acquisition of property (including slaves), this pursuit is not harmful because "the amount of this sort of property that one needs for the self-sufficiency that promotes the good life is not unlimited."[40] The danger incurred in the quest for wealth arises when the exchange of useful things in the form of barter through which all participants benefit by acquiring goods that they need to become self-sufficient is replaced by commercial exchange made possible by the introduction of money. Although money greases the wheels of trade, its accumulation can also become an end in itself. As with Midas in the fable, this kind of wealth may be useless in procuring the natural necessities needed to support the household. Worse still, monetary wealth, by its very nature, has no limit and therefore no end because useful things must be useful for something (and excessive amounts of a useful thing may bring harm or add nothing of real benefit).[41] It follows that those who continue to seek excess wealth have not learned to distinguish between living and living well, and the wealth that they continue to acquire gives gratification only due to its excess, which is an unnatural form of satisfaction.

The upshot of Aristotle's analysis is that not only is there no political justification for slavery, but its existence can become a threat to political life itself if it is not kept in its proper place. It is a form of rule over objects rather than subjects whose agreement would make it legitimate; it is based on a kind of knowledge that is merely instrumental; and it may create in the master a kind of desire that turns him away from his obligations as a citizen. Slavery exists legitimately only within the *oikos*, not in the polis, to which it must remain subordinated; its concern is with production, not with action based on cooperation.

Against this backdrop, Aristotle's account of the nature of properly political rule stands out more sharply. Because a city is composed of a diversity of members, each belonging to several different associations, it is not possible to construct one true, just, and eternal ("Platonic") City. The differing constitutions of present and past cities have to be analyzed, types of political rule distinguished from one another, and the conditions that ensure stability (or that threaten change) clarified. It will then appear that the "best" constitution must be one that can be achieved by fallible humans living in a world that cannot be assumed to have actualized its full natural potential.

Aristotle's relegation of slavery to the *oikos* illuminates his analysis of the citizen. A city is a whole composed of different parts. The nature of the polis—whether it is an oligarchy or a democracy or a mixture of different institutional forms—determines the nature and role of the person who is a part of it. For example, the citizen in an oligarchy must be wealthy enough to pass the censitary threshold for admittance; the citizen in a democracy is someone who takes part in its government on an equal basis with all others. It follows that the citizen in a democracy may not qualify for membership in a city that is oligarchic. Woman, foreigners, those of mixed race, and slaves, because they are unfree, are excluded from the rights and duties of citizenship in all cities. These empirical distinctions imply that citizenship is the basis for action taken together with one's peers (however they are defined). Belonging does not result simply from residing in the city or from a personal contribution to the production of the necessities that make possible this active citizenship. This definition of citizenship entails a distinction between political rights and private rights (for example, to contract, to sue, or to be sued in court). Thus, Aristotle concludes that the citizen is "someone who is eligible to participate in deliberative and judicial office . . . in this *polis*."[42] Within this general framework, what distinguishes one polis from others are the criteria that qualify a person to act as a citizen.

The fact that there are different qualifications for citizenship in different types of poleis poses a crucial problem: Is the good citizen always a good man? What is the relation of politics to morality? For example, an oligarchic constitution that makes wealth into a criterion for citizenship may encourage an accumulation of wealth that becomes a threat to the individual's ability to act as a citizen. A democratic constitution that treats everyone as equal may discourage the quest for excellence that brings to full bloom the individual citizen's potential. Aristotle illustrates this general difficulty with a typical example. Each member of the crew of a boat makes a specific contribution to the collective success of the voyage; and in that sense, each must act as a good man. Yet if they are to arrive safely in port, there must be a shared quality that binds them together in a larger type of association called a crew. There must exist also a similar shared quality that makes different men who are exercising their specific excellence into citizens of the city. A crew member who pursues his task—say, maintaining full sail—without taking into account the conditions necessary to reach the goal of the voyage would not be a good citizen-participant in the crew. He might keep the sails furled when the wind becomes too fierce or the water too shallow. The implication of this analogy is that there is no unique definition of a good citizen; just as there are different constitutions, so there will be different definitions of the good citizen. And the good man may not fulfill that definition because his excellence is that of the private person whose particular virtues make him into a bad citizen who threatens the stability of the whole.

Once again, Aristotle is criticizing the Platonic claim that the best constitution, by its very nature, will produce good citizens who are also good men. Recalling that a city's self-sufficiency and autonomy depends on the contribution of a diversity of individuals and associations, he points out that the achievement of Plato's "best" constitution may in fact prove harmful insofar as the unity it imposes destroys the needed diversity. Just as a living being is composed of multiple organs that have different functions, and just as the soul is composed of reason and appetite (or desires) as well as sensations, so the polis is a composite in which there is no common excellence shared by all individuals. To say that Plato meant that only the rulers must be both good men and good citizens forgets that the ordinary person who is different from the ruler remains a citizen insofar as he accepts the laws as legitimate. The education of the philosopher-kings may give them the knowledge needed to rule, but if they do not also know how to be ruled, they will not be good citizens. Both qualities are necessary, and each requires a specific kind of knowledge. The citizen who "knows" how to be ruled is not servile like the slave, nor is he adapting to necessity like a craftsman. Aristotle has to demonstrate the existence of a kind of shared knowledge that is specifically political, distinct from the management of a household and from the domination of the master over his slaves.

Proper political rule is the art of governing equal persons who are free of the chains of necessity. But how can the free be ruled without losing their freedom? If ruling is a craft that can be learned, how is it learned? Aristotle's answer suggests a process similar to the way that military officers in a democratic regime rise gradually in the ranks. The citizen-soldier learns how to execute commands, whose legitimacy he comes gradually to understand by participating in their success (or failure). In the same way, the citizen who masters the art of political rule acquires a new virtue that is added to the qualities of temperance, justice, and courage required of all citizens. This new virtue is called *phronesis,* which can be translated as "judgment," "prudence," or simply "prudent judgment." The citizen who has mastered this art can be said to have learned when to behave as a good man and when the situation calls for the action of a citizen. This description of the relevant distinction does not as yet explain how *phronesis* is acquired. For that explanation, it is necessary to make a detour to Aristotle's *Nicomachean Ethics.*

Aristotle explains that ethics and politics are coordinate branches of what he calls "practical philosophy," whose basic assumption is that every deliberative action seeks the attainment of some good. As in the *Politics,* that good is the end that determines the specific value of the action. The number and kinds of goods that can be sought is of course immense, and the domains in which they can be realized and thus the means to do so are correspondingly large. Again, some goods may be also means to other, higher goods; making a stirrup permits riding a horse, which is in turn the means to military victory. To avoid an infinite progression from one desire and its frustration to the realization of another, a good that is absolutely good must be found. The task of politics, with the help of the other practical sciences (which include rhetoric, the art of war, and the management of property, called "economics"), is to create conditions in which that highest good can be sought.

The relation of the good man to the good citizen is not a theoretical but a practical question concerning the type of good that is sought. Aristotle points out in the *Nicomachean Ethics* that "even if the good of the community coincides with that of the individual, the good of the community is clearly a greater and more perfect good both to get and to keep."[43] The good of the individual is of course valuable in itself, but that of the city is higher and "more divine." The good of the whole does not nullify the right of the individual parts to seek their own good, however. That is why Aristotle said that politics is charged with creating "conditions" in which the highest good can be sought, not those through which it is imposed. This distinction limits the degree of certainty that can be claimed by political action. That is another reason that the political good does not always trump the good of the individual. Furthermore, Aristotle notes, there are some good things that can have harmful consequences (such as having too much money or too great courage). For this reason, he concludes, "It is the mark of the educated man and a proof of his culture that in every subject he looks for only so much precision as its nature permits."[44] Politics is concerned not with knowing, but with doing, and action requires its own measuring standards, which is where *phronesis* finds its proper place.

Because a goal's goodness can be defined as a mean between the two extremes of too much and too little, individuals must always deliberate before acting. This general maxim for the determination of ethical goodness does not provide answers for specific cases. Self-defense may be called for in some situations, submission in others. The reason that the general maxim is of no practical use is that it applies to conditions that do not change, whereas practical action takes place in variable circumstances whose evaluation demands calculation or deliberation. Practical action differs from work defined as simply a means to carry out a predetermined end, as in the production of an object where success depends on the degree to which the labor produces that end. The goodness of practical action is contained in the act itself. When an act is said to be well (or badly) done, the implication is that it was a good (or bad) act. For example, in the *Politics* Aristotle compares the work of the flute maker who produces an instrument that he need not know how to play with the practical action of a person who knows how to make the instrument sing all the melodies of which it is capable.[45]

Practical action is the domain of *phronesis*. The prudent person does not act well because he obeys predetermined or scientific rules that can be applied to every situation; his action results from his ability to take into account the particularity of the specific conditions in which he finds himself. Prudence gives rise to conduct that is right, fitting, or proper; it is not based on knowledge (which concerns the unchanging), but on deliberation about the action to be undertaken. Aristotle admits that such practical action may be the right way to achieve a goal that is in itself wrong (think of a "gentleman bandit"). He also recognizes that the deliberation cannot go on for too long because prudence is exercised in particular and changing conditions. Nonetheless, if prudence is not ranked as high as philosophical wisdom, it nevertheless has greater authority because—in the hierarchical Greek world—what creates a thing also commands and directs that thing, and prudence does create a kind of wisdom. By analogy, Aristotle concludes, just as a doctor does not directly cure us but tells us how we ourselves can best gain or maintain our health, so with prudence we learn what we ought to do to attain or retain virtue, which in the world of politics means justice.

Although Aristotle has described the uniqueness of *phronesis* and explained what it can and cannot accomplish, he has not yet explained how it is acquired. Learning how to acquire it is the task of education, to which he, like other Greek thinkers, devotes much attention. His great contribution to this discussion lies in his analysis of the role of habit, whose importance he stresses in both the *Nicomachean Ethics* and the *Politics*. Habit is not acquired by theory; it is a practical virtue. In the *Politics,* Aristotle suggests that it is a precondition for the development of reason.[46] In the *Nicomachean Ethics,* he explains that moral virtues are not implanted by nature but are "the child of habit . . . ethics being derived from *ethos,* meaning habit." Although habits are not natural, they are not unnatural, either. Although a stone cannot be trained to fall upward no matter how many times it is thrown toward the sky, the craftsman does learn to make things by making them, and the musician learns by making music. "By a similar process we become just by performing just actions, temperate by performing temperate actions, brave by performing brave actions," concludes Aristotle.[47]

The political implication of this analysis of the role of habit is that the task of legislation is to make men good by making them behave in a good way. And their conduct, in turn, is the measure of the quality of the regime under which they live. Habits lead not only to practical action; they are also responsible for the ability to control the passions and desires. "It is by refraining from pleasures that we become temperate and it is when we have become temperate that we are most able to abstain from pleasures." Although it may be easy to do a right (or a wrong) action, Aristotle recognizes that it is "not easy to acquire a settled habit of performing such actions." Doing something only once, without understanding why, doesn't create a "disposition" that can carry over to other situations.[48] That is why he insists on the role of the laws in fixing habits. The universal character of legislation makes what may have been a spontaneous reaction to a situation into a rational action.

Aristotle is not suggesting that legislation produces habituated individuals who act unthinkingly in unison. He refers to habits as a "second nature" that differs from invariant physical necessity insofar as they can be more easily changed.[49] These habits become "dispositions" that incline a person to act without determining the end to be sought. They provide the conditions for the realization of a kind of goodness whose actualization depends on the exercise of *phronesis*. Like the laws, which impose a type of behavior, habits provide the general rules or maxims for the ordinary circumstances of life. When a novel situation is encountered, however, and the general rules prove inapplicable to the particular conditions, deliberative judgment has to guide the choice of action. "Second nature" no longer seems natural. The individual must create a new mode of action in the same way that the musician draws new possibilities from the instruments that he had used habitually without imagining that other melodies might be created, other harmonies be invented, other rhythms be discovered. The political consequence of this analysis is that the good man who learned the habits of the good citizen may now find himself at odds with the regime that educated him. And the regime, in its turn, is no longer taken for granted as a kind of "second nature." A process of questioning and eventual political transformation may now begin.

Aristotle argues that legitimate regime types need to be analyzed and evaluated in terms of their relative stability. He explicitly rejects Plato's claim that because change is always present in the finite world, there will be a cycle of changes that follows a path of steady degeneration from the best regime to the worst before a renewal occurs. He asks instead why the movement cannot flow in the opposite direction—say, from democracy to oligarchy to rule by a single person. More important, he points out that the usual experience of change does not move from one regime type to its neighbor (from timocracy to oligarchy, for example), but rather passes from one type to its negation. Kingship is transformed into tyranny, aristocracy into oligarchy, and what Aristotle calls "polity" into democracy.[50] In this way, the best regime becomes the worst, the second best the second worst, and the least good into the least bad. From this account, Aristotle concludes that "polity" will be the best regime because it will be the most stable; the excesses to which it may give rise result in the least radical transformation.[51]

It now becomes possible to better understand why Aristotle's attitude toward democracy, although he is not a democrat, is more accommodating than Plato's. As the rule of the *demos* (people), democracy seems to imply the participation of all citizens in their own self-government. More precisely, all citizens share in the "organization of the city's various offices generally but particularly in respect to that particular office which has authority over everything."[52] Although the definition of who counts as a citizen differs in different types of constitution, Aristotle does not return to his earlier discussion of citizenship in this context. He wants to avoid the common misunderstanding that the number of people who participate in government determines the nature of that government. For example, oligarchy is usually said to ensure the rule of the few who are property owners, whereas democracy gives power to the many who make up the poorer segments of society. But one can imagine a case where the majority are well off and yet a small number of persons (such as the Guardians) who are not so wealthy rule by virtue of some capacity that is valued because it is important to realizing the good life. Aristotle's point is that the nature of a regime is not determined by the numbers of those who take part in ruling; the real difference is found in the (kind of) wealth or nonwealth that exercises sovereignty and expresses through this sovereignty a vision of the good life.

In a democracy, rich and poor share the freedom of citizens, yet each of them pursues goals dictated by their economic interests. As citizens, they share a vision of the good life at the same time that in their personal choices they interpret that ideal differently. More precisely, the quarrel between oligarchs and democrats concerns the nature of the equality that makes them citizens. For the democrat, justice means that everyone who is the equal of everyone else must be treated in the same way, whereas for the oligarch justice must take into account inequality of wealth when dealing with those who are in fact unequal. For the democrat, everyone is to be treated identically; for the oligarch, difference counts. The source of their conflict lies in the fact that each judges from his own point of view, which means that each judges badly because he adopts a particular point of view for which he nonetheless claims universal validity. Democrats ignore the inevitable forms of inequality while stressing those qualities that all citizens share; as a result, they assume that unequal treatment in any single facet of life makes men unequal overall. Supporters of oligarchy make the inverse error, generalizing from their own particular difference from other citizens. They assume that if people are treated equally in one sphere of life, then they will automatically be made equal in all aspects, with the result that the significant difference that singled out their own group and legitimated its privileges is lost. Aristotle does not pursue further here the notion of proportional equality and its difference from arithmetic equality, but when he comes to look at the causes of political change, the subject reemerges.

The source of regime change lies in the formation of factions, of which oligarchy and democracy are the two principle variants. Aristotle recognizes that there can be many types and gradations of democracy and oligarchy. The kinds of inequality can differ; wealth can be held in property, commercial goods, or slaves; it may be derived from birth, education, or (reputation for) virtue; it can be translated as military, political, or societal power. The equality that is sought can similarly spread from the political to the social to the economic to the racial or the sexual, perhaps even descending to the riotous multicolored anarchy that Plato so greatly feared.

The varieties of equality and inequality furnish the occasion for the emergence of faction, whose basis is always the demand for equality. In fact, notes Aristotle, this claim is expressed most often as the claim to be treated unequally—that is, to be favored—by those who consider their inequality with the others to represent a form of superiority that should be rewarded. The same opposition is expressed in the competing claims of those who insist on absolute or "arithmetic" equality and those for whom equality must always be based on merit (and thus be proportional to it, however it is defined). For this reason, Aristotle argues that the ever-present demand for equality implies that dissent and the formation of faction within a polis are inevitable. Faction will become a force for revolutionary change whenever a suitable occasion presents itself or when a new variant of the demand for equality emerges or when the unequal demand new types of privilege or when the existing equilibrium is disintegrating on its own.

Just as faction is inevitable, so too is the attempt to overcome its effects by discovering the constitution that is most fitted to protect itself. This constitution will not be the "best" constitution in an idealistic Platonic sense; it will be the one that is best for the majority of cities and men. It will be a regime that is not out of the reach of ordinary men, who, moreover, cannot be expected to have been provided with a special education that fits them for it. Aristotle gives the premises for discovering the nature of this constitution most clearly in the *Nicomachean Ethics*. A truly happy life is a life of goodness lived in freedom from necessity; that is to say, it is autonomous and political. The goodness that is sought is defined as a "mean"—which is not an average or middle point between two predetermined extremes, such as hot and cold, or a compromise by the mediocre or the faint-hearted. The determination of a mean demands the use of prudential or deliberative judgment. As such, the mean does not exclude the two (variable and always particular) poles between which it is established; the status of the mean recalls that of the appetites or desires that Aristotle showed to be amenable to both reason and the pleasures of the senses. Every individual who finds himself making an ethical choice, Aristotle argues, must determine by deliberation what form of virtue (e.g., of bravery, generosity, truth, or temperance) is the appropriate choice in the given situation. Habit joins with *phronesis* in this judgment, which is always particular and never scientific.

Aristotle suggests that the same reasoning should be applied to constitutions, which, after all, are the expression of the way of life of the body of citizens. This application suggests immediately that rich and poor (however they are defined) will form the poles between which a middle class forms the mean. Those at the extremes will be tempted to form factions. The rich, because they are too strong, rich, or handsome, will be tempted to resort to violence, crime, or usurpation. The poor will reply with roguish behavior and a variety of petty offenses that unsettle the polity. What is more, the rich, who are used to luxury, will find it difficult to acquire the habits needed for discipline, whereas the poor, who lack all advantages, will become mean-spirited and recalcitrant. The rich are unable to obey, and the poor can only obey; envy faces contempt, slaves stand against masters. As a result of such reasoning, Aristotle considers a middle-class regime to be superior to even the democracy that he says is the "least worse" of the six forms of government that he analyzes. He describes this middle-class regime positively as "neither a democracy nor an oligarchy but midway between them; it is called a *polity,* since it is made up of those with hoplite weapons."[53]

Aristotle's reference to "those with hoplite weapons" makes clear that his argument in favor of a middle-class polity is not based solely on economic concern with the need to avoid the extremes that lead to factional conflict; it is a political argument as well. Just as the ethical analysis of virtue as a mean has recourse to *phronesis* as the key to the virtues, so too the middle-class regime has to contain a positive element that holds together the poles that exist in any society. This element is what Aristotle calls friendship (*philia*), which he sees as the virtue that ties together his version of the best constitution. Friendship, he points out, can exist only among equals, who, like the middle class, have more security than the poor and therefore do not covet the goods of the rich, while the middling nature of their possessions means that they need not feel defensive against the pretensions of wealth. Because the middle class neither plots nor is plotted against, it can exercise the kind of freedom that is central to friendship, which is a relation in which each participant sees himself and his virtues reflected in the friend whose happiness confirms his own.

Ever resistant to the allure of Platonic ideals, Aristotle admits that most contemporary regimes are either democratic or oligarchic. The most stable of these regimes will be those in which a middle class has sufficient weight to modulate the extremism of one or the other faction. From this point of view, democracies are more stable than oligarchies because they at least establish no hereditary barrier to social mobility. But, Aristotle quickly adds, a radical democracy with no middle class and many poor citizens will speedily ruin itself. However, such generalizations are untypical of his mode of analysis. He quickly turns back to look at the material conditions that can affect the emergence of the conditions of political stability that he is proposing. For example, prosperous artisans may well emerge in a port city with a growing commercial class, whereas an inland agricultural society has a lesser chance of seeing a middle class grow up between wealthy landowners and impoverished peasants.

◆

We need not follow Aristotle further as he examines the institutions that more or less adequately reflect the political divisions whose socioeconomic origin he has explored. He has shown that a middle-class city, a polity, will have the greatest chance of realizing the mixed regime that is the best constitution available for actual men. This last point is worth underlining. In spite of the analytical care with which he distinguishes among the empirical, historical, and hierarchical types of associations in a society in order to define that which is properly political, his definition of the best political regime is restricted, in the last resort, by the social and economic relations among its members. His careful analytical distinction of the polis from the *oikos* and of the forms of legitimate rule in each of them makes possible a practical analysis that looks squarely at the actual forces that make up the society. But Aristotle is not an economic "materialist." As his stress on the role of middle-class friendship suggests, what he opposes to Plato's absolute idealism is a theory of political prudence and practical deliberation. It is the primacy of the political that determines the weight accorded to the economic.

PHILOSOPHY GOES PRIVATE

Although Athenian democracy was restored during the first part of the fourth century bce, the growing power of Macedonia under Philip II (382–336, father of Alexander the Great [356–323]) represented a threat to its independence. Yet the Athenians chose to reinforce their democracy rather than to try to counter the new military threat. They maintained a multitude of political offices that were renewed on a yearly basis; in addition, some six thousand citizens were selected each year for jury duty. The city paid the citizens who occupied these public functions in order to guarantee their independent judgment and to ensure that the political offices were not monopolized by the well-to-do. This participatory democracy was expensive, and the money spent on it could have been used to rebuild the military. In addition, the yearly rotation in office made it difficult to formulate a continuous policy. As a result, John Davies points out, "it was Athens' singular misfortune to have rebuilt the defences of her political society after 403 so as to face in what proved to be the wrong direction. The real disruptive threat came not from a potential tyrant within but from actual rulers without."[54] With Philip's defeat of Athens at the battle of Chaeronea in 338, Athenian autonomy disappeared.

Some voices warned against the danger in their democratic system, notably the long-lived philosopher Isocrates (436–338) and the great orator Demosthenes (384–322). Isocrates, who had been a student of Socrates, called for the formation of an all-Greek federative unity that he called a *sympoliteia*. However, this kind of extensive political entity would have been possible only if the independent cities had abandoned the norm of democratic participation in exchange for the promise that doing so would (somehow) save democracy. Aristotle had foreseen the cost of such a paradoxical strategy, which would in effect sacrifice democracy in the vain hope of saving it. "A city consists not only of a number of people, but of people of different kinds. . . . For a city is different from a military alliance," in which it is the weight of numbers rather than the diversity of the population that counts.[55] A military alliance might serve to preserve the mere physical life of Athens, but it would destroy the political liberty that was for the Athenians the foundation of the good life.

Demosthenes reminded the Athenians that they had previously rallied to defend freedom from imperial conquest by Persia, in spite of the difficulty of gaining a hearing. His fierce diatribes gave rise to the term *philippic* because of their angry denunciation of the Macedonian ruler Philip. When his appeals failed to mobilize his fellow citizens against the threat, Demosthenes himself led an Athenian revolt against Philip's young successor, Alexander. When his revolt was vanquished, the orator was left with no choice but his own suicide, the ultimate expression of the liberty dear to the Athenian democrat. Solon's democratizing reforms had introduced this idea that suicide is the ultimate expression of freedom, and Socrates' choice to drink the hemlock rather than to flee to a false freedom outside of the Athenian polis illustrated its philosophical justification. Demosthenes' demise now closed the cycle.

Did Athens itself commit suicide by insisting that democracy was essential to the good life? How could it have done anything else? Should it have preferred mere life, limping on though history as a city protected by its walls but from which the beating heart had been stripped? Better to die with its ideals intact. But the ideals could survive only if they found a material support that kept them alive, adapting to a new political climate. When democracy disappeared from public life, its spirit sought refuge in the private sphere. But then it would no longer be the same democracy because it was no longer political; the freedom that it guaranteed was limited to the life of the individual, and the autonomy that it ensured was spiritual. In another sense, this privatized democratic spirit remained "political" insofar as it provided a response to the always present need to legitimate existing social relations. For this reason, it has to be seen as a form of antipolitics.

A new historical challenge emerged when Alexander the Great's generals divided his empire after his death in order to legitimate their rule. This challenge is the origin of what came to be called Hellenic thought (derived from the word for Greece, *Hellas*). Although Athens had lost its political independence, its philosophic achievements remained hegemonic, reinforced by the fact that Greek became the lingua franca of the Western world (which extended far into what is now called the Middle East). Greek philosophy, it was hoped, would civilize the vast spaces now held together by brute military force. But the philosophy that became dominant was not based on the vibrant public democratic deliberation that had made for the greatness of Periclean Athens. Thought turned away from the public square, as if the deception of its hopes had left it only an inner sanctum in which it could find a place to rest from what had proven to be fruitless exertions. Philosophy now marched in a direction opposite to Aristotle's claim that politics is a higher kind of knowledge that includes practical questions of ethics and is the prelude to wisdom.

The first of the new philosophers were the Cynics. Their name was derived from the Greek word for "dog" because the movement's leader, Diogenes of Sinope (c. 412/404–323), praised this animal's natural behavior over the conventional values of society, whose hypocrisy he denounced.

This stress on the priority of the natural over the conventional was an old sophistic trick. Dressed in rags, begging in order to maintain himself, Diogenes is said to have walked the streets carrying a lantern, saying that he was "looking for an honest man." There are many anecdotes about this man's unfettered lifestyle; Plato is said to have remarked that he was "a Socrates gone mad."[56] Perhaps the most famous is the story of Alexander the Great stopping to meet him, only to be told to move away because he was blocking Diogenes' sunlight. Freedom, not power, was the virtue that counted most for the Cynics.

Diogenes' turn away from political life can be seen as an inversion of the democratic vision. Turning inward, the philosopher rejects the constraints of the institutions that were previously thought to form the citizen's character. Rather than protecting freedom as a value that is essential for political participation, the Cynics sought to defend freedom from the political sphere, which they saw as an external constraint imposed on naturally free humans. It is important to note that this cynicism, despite its antipolitical orientation, is indeed a philosophy. The freedom that it seeks to protect is universal; it is treated as the highest of goods to be protected against political institutions' particular demands. The difficulty, however, is that this universal freedom is abstract; it has and can have no particular content. If it does defend a particular practice as desirable in the public sphere (for example, Diogenes was said to urinate and masturbate in the agora as a demonstration of the superiority of nature over convention), that defense is accidental, a product of temporary passions rather than the result of rational choice.[57]

The second of the new Hellenistic antipolitical philosophies, epicureanism, sought to go beyond the abstractness of the cynical refusal of all political institutions. Epicurus (341–270) argued that institutions exist in order to preserve an external peace that permits the individual to cultivate his private, personal pleasures (or at least to avoid pain). He did not conclude from this view that philosophers should involve themselves in political life in order to ensure that the best institutions to fulfill this function are created. He argued instead that the quest for pleasure and the avoidance of pain can be achieved only when the individual turns away from all excess and learns moderation and balance within himself in order to produce a state called *ataraxia,* or freedom from all cares. In this way, the Epicureans can be said to add some content to the abstract inner freedom the Cynics sought. But that content remains subjective, particular to each individual, and therefore incapable of formulating a program for public action. The Epicurean's freedom, which is founded on a materialist understanding of the soul as composed simply of atoms to which it returns at death, escapes the emptiness of the Cynic's abstract universalism, but only to plunge into the particularity of subjective satisfactions that are ultimately arbitrary because they are passive and therefore without effect on the external world. The Epicurean can be free of cares regardless of the conditions in which he is constrained to live, despite the fact that some institutions preserve external peace better than others.

The path of Hellenistic thought comes full circle with the emergence of stoicism. Its founder was Zeno of Cittium (334–262). Zeno and his successors recognized what had been lost in the antipolitical turn of Hellenistic thought: the idea of membership or participation in a universe larger than either the Cynic's abstract freedom or the Epicurean's subjective material pleasures. As a result, Zeno argued that all humans are in fact members of a higher and wider world because they all are subject to the laws of nature (or, as it is sometimes put, to the laws of reason, which are considered to be the same thing). These laws express a necessity that has social as well as material consequences. Zeno's principles were illustrated in his own life. When he was unable to pay the resident alien's tax, the Athenians sold him into slavery. He was then purchased by a friend, who freed him. The lesson that he drew from his experience is the need to accept the implacable laws of the universe, to bear up to circumstances rather than to surrender to them passively. This apparently defeatist attitude has positive consequences. The individual's will is strengthened because recognition of the inevitable action of the laws of nature means, for example, that although a person cannot prevent poverty (or wealth), illness (or health), he can meet them on his own rational terms rather than become a slave to them. Such a freedom based on the recognition of necessity is more concrete and potentially less antipolitical then the preceding two forms of Hellenistic philosophy.

The next step in the Stoic argument turns the individual back toward his fellows. In so doing, it makes a vital contribution to the arsenal of human liberty. It develops a radical idea of human rights and obligations to other persons through a series of terse deductions. First of all, the fact that all men are subject to the same laws of nature implies that all men are equal. This proposition involves a shift from the classical Greek understanding of equality as the product of conventions (*nomoi*) that are freely adopted to an understanding of equality as universal subjection to natural law (*physis*). This definition implies that slavery has no justification. The critique of slavery is the first step on the road to an ever-expanding notion of all humans' natural equality. A further implication of the recognition of human beings' natural equality is that men, because they are equal, have duties toward one another that are at once the expression and the actualization of their equality. These duties are not imposed by conventional laws; they are the natural, prepolitical foundations and justification of such laws, which are illegitimate if they do not accord with these natural obligations. In this way, the antipolitical Hellenistic philosophy comes to stand as the court of appeals at which the legitimacy of political institutions is judged.

As a result of these two expressions of the law of nature, all men can be seen as members of what the Stoics called a cosmopolis—literally, a "world polis." At the same time, however, they remain subject to the specific political laws of the city in which they live. A new source of political dynamism thus opens when the laws of the city are seen to clash with the laws of nature. The laws of nature are higher—because more universal—than the laws of any particular city; as a result, the individual citizen is not bound by the laws of his own city if they violate the laws of nature that are expressed by the Golden Rule, which is the affirmation of the equality among all members of the cosmopolis. Formulated in the Stoics' logical language, natural laws must be rational because nothing is greater than the universe, whereas human laws, which express particular aspects of the universe, may or may not be the expression of rational will. Because all men participate in the universe, they have in principle the right to appeal to natural law to correct their particular cities' imperfect laws. In this way, the moral command to do unto others what we would accept as justly done to us turns out to have strong political implications whose full theoretical implications were drawn by the Roman republican Cicero. In practice, however, as will be seen, the Stoics' political theory was unable to prevent the death of that republic.

◆

Taken together, the three stages of the Hellenic forms of antipolitics move from abstract universality to concrete particularity and then to a dynamic unity of the two poles, pointing toward the possibility of a new political synthesis. The Stoics' cosmopolitics can be considered an advance over the narrowness and parochialism of the small Greek cities, which, even in the case of Athens, focused on their own problems while considering the wider world to be the domain of those they disdained as barbarians. Their stubborn refusal to abandon their intensely participatory political life had the vices of its virtues, and it should be no surprise that Greece ultimately lost its independence. But Alexander's substitution of imperial conquest was not the wave of the future, either. A new form of politics was taking shape in the Roman republic, which, coincidentally, had overthrown its last king in 510 BCE, at the same time as the Athenians had eliminated theirs. But whereas Athens had a brief moment of imperial democratic glory before disappearing from the political stage, the Roman republic would go on to become a new kind of empire in which the universality of the law and the benefits of (passive) citizenship made room for the Hellenic antipolitical philosophies, particularly in the form of the Stoic synthesis. Like agonistic Athenian democracy, the Roman republic was born from conflict, which it was able to keep within limits over a long historical period. Its demise was the result of its refusal to admit limits and its desire to eliminate civil conflict in a unified empire that, in its own way, would actualize the stoic cosmopolitan justice in the particular laws of the world city.

№ 2
THE RISE AND FALL OF ROMAN REPUBLICANISM

IF THE GREEKS WERE THE GREAT THEORISTS of political life, the Romans were its practical masters. This chapter analyzes the story of the rise and decline of the Roman republic. It points also to the rise of a new, religious form of social legitimacy with the emergence of Christianity. Of the political thinkers to be studied here, only one—Cicero—developed an independent political theory, and he was better known to his contemporaries as an active man of politics. The other two, Livy and Polybius, developed their political thought in the guise of historical narrations. These works, which aroused the enthusiasm of generations of young readers when they were rediscovered during the Renaissance, have faded from the modern curriculum. They have not done so because of advances in scientific history, but because they are works of political thought, which we moderns have forgotten. That is how I present both them and the emerging Christian religion here.

◆

In the half century after the Romans eliminated their last king, they began to create the republican institutions that would grow to encompass the world. The imperatives of unity and plurality, equality and liberty, universality and particularity that had polarized Athenian political theory were integrated into a practical structure in which particular interests were guaranteed by the rule of law, which in turn ensured the universality of justice. Each of the players was strengthened by their competition, and the law ensured that the rules of the game were respected.

The result was a republican democracy that combined equality before the law with freedom of individual initiative. Many of the institutions invented by the Romans will be familiar to readers today, who will also be aware of this republic's fate when its expansion brought about a seemingly ineluctable civil war that concluded only when the last general standing, Octavian, renamed himself Augustus and instituted imperial rule in 27 BCE. This world-dominating empire was able to maintain the Pax Romana during the four centuries that followed. In so doing, however, it stifled political life.

The puzzle for those living during the imperial seizure of power was to understand how it could have taken place and what might make it legitimate (or convincingly illegitimate). To solve this puzzle, many thinkers turned back to Roman history to analyze the origins of what can be called the republican spirit and the reasons for its decline. They posed a series of questions. How did republican institutions preserve and spread that spirit? Was there a limit to the reach of these institutions or to the expansion of that spirit? If one or the other were weakened, would it be possible to rekindle the spirit or to reform the institutions? Or would political thought again turn inward, as it had after the glories of Athenian democracy were extinguished? If it followed that Athenian precedent, would it at least retain a critical attitude toward the soulless imperial political world? Or would it seek another kingdom in a better world? These questions provide a focus for the study of classical republican political thought.

Titus Livius, the great historian of early republican Rome known to English-speaking readers simply as Livy, presents a vigorous analysis of the origins of the republican spirit, the difficulties it faced, and the institutions through which it triumphed. Himself a witness to the imperial transition, Livy at times adopts a nostalgic tone in his narrative but also animates it with the creative vigor of a man who feels deeply what has been lost. The chronicles that make up his *History of Rome from the Foundation* are intended to recall the virtues of a people for whom political freedom was the ultimate value to which all else must be sacrificed. But the uplifting episodes and moral set pieces that he recounts are also animated by a republican sensibility to political dynamics that are never locked in place. That was the lesson he addressed to his contemporaries, for whom a unitary empire that could ensure peace had replaced the often contentious republican spirit of liberty. That lesson retained its actuality for later republicans, from Machiavelli, who wrote his own commentary on Livy, to the American founding fathers and French revolutionaries, who appealed to his spirit as they borrowed from his story the pseudonyms with which they signed their revolutionary leaflets (as Brutus, Cato, or Scaevola, for example) or denounced enemies (called Tarquin, Cataline, or Caesar, for example). Livy was no revolutionary in this modern sense; his achievement was to maintain the memory of the republican spirit and its achievements.

Livy's account was indebted to an earlier historian, Polybius, who explained at the outset of his own narration, *The Rise of the Roman Empire*, that he wanted "to discover by what means and under what system of government the Romans succeeded in less than fifty-three years [i.e., 220–167 BCE] in bringing under their rule almost the whole of the inhabited world, an achievement which is without parallel in human history." Polybius was a Greek who spent the years from 168 to 152 in Rome. His high birth gained him access to many Roman leaders, whom he later rejoined as a military advisor. On the basis of this experience, he proposed to show that "the supremacy of the Romans did not come about, as certain Greek writers have supposed, either by chance or without the victors knowing what they were doing."[1] The dynamic created by the interplay of the republican spirit with the complex institutional checks on the power of the Senate, the consuls, the people, and their tribunes explains how and why each of them necessarily sought to expand in order to ensure that it could balance the others. This dynamic did not result in a zero-sum solution of only winners and losers; it presented a virtuous rather than a vicious circle. The diversity encouraged by the separation of powers ultimately produced the unitary drive toward world conquest that Polybius admired.

Global domination proved to be a poisoned chalice once there were no more worlds left to conquer and competition among the republican institutions could no longer contain social conflict. The civil wars that were to wrack the republic for nearly a century before finally killing its spirit began in 133 BCE when the tribunes Tiberius Gracchus and his brother Gaius sought to institute a redistribution of land. Although both were assassinated by their aristocratic enemies, the issue continued to fester. As Rome's conquests spread, its citizen-soldiers were replaced by legionnaires, professionals who signed on for campaigns that could take them away from the homeland for decades. While they served, their wages and conditions depended on the booty won in battle; and after their years of service, they were promised a plot of land where they could maintain themselves decently. As a result, their loyalty shifted from the republic to their generals, who sought to use not only the republican glories of victory, but also victory's material benefits to advance their own political fortunes. This advancement in turn gained them still greater riches that they could use to acquire new followers, to pay additional troops, and to bribe less well-placed opponents.

This was the context in which Marcus Tullius Cicero sought to rekindle the flame of republican politics. He telegraphed his political intent by setting the dialogue titled *On the Commonwealth* in the year 129 BCE, just after the assassination of Tiberius Gracchus. He puts his own ideas in the mouth of Scipio Aemilianus, the republican victor over Carthage in the third and final Punic War.[2] The first two books of this dialogue praise the classical republican institutions described by Polybius, to whom Scipio refers as "my friend" and "our friend."[3] But Cicero, as often occurs in his work, then wavers between a call for decisive action and an appeal for moral renewal. An admirer of Plato, whom he translated from the Greek, he seems to dream of a philosopher-king, or perhaps a temporary republican dictator like Cincinnatus, who would restore the old institutions. At other moments, as with Livy, the hope for moral renewal is all that Cicero can offer. Despite the fragmentary state of this manuscript,[4] this hesitation is evident in the most famous part of the dialogue, called the "Dream of Scipio." Scipio tells of meeting his grandfather, the general who had defeated Hannibal in the second Punic War. His glorious ancestor admonishes him: "You will have to restore the commonwealth as dictator . . . [and] for all those who have saved, aided, or increased the fatherland there is a specific place set aside in the sky where they may enjoy eternity in blessedness." But when Scipio asks, "What is that human glory really worth which can last scarcely a fraction of a single year?" he receives the answer, "Do not give yourself to the words of the mob, and do not place your hopes in human rewards: virtue itself by its own allurements should draw you towards true honor."[5] Which will it be: the political or the moral? Or an opportunistic compromise?

Cicero's inability to decide between the institutional renewal or the spiritual restoration of the republic had another source: his attempt to adapt the Stoics' theories to the republic's legacy. Cicero's stoicism differed from the inward turn of the Hellenic philosophers that sought compensation for the loss of political participation. During the intense period in which he wrote *On the Commonwealth,* he produced another dialogue, *On the Laws,* that was intended as its complement. He applies the Stoics' argument that natural law is both prior to conventional laws and serves as the measure of their validity in order to develop an aspect of Roman republican politics that Livy had discussed only briefly and that Polybius neglected: the idea of law as a universal value whose function is to integrate individuals (including those of conquered nations) into the unitary republic. This application of natural law as a critical measure of political legitimacy would have a rich future. For the present, the imperial throne was about to become the de facto source of law. The political spirit would have to migrate again in order to preserve itself.

The formal-legal imperial institutions animated by the decisions of a single man whose will was the sole source of political legitimacy made room for the flowering of spiritual cults that sought private compensation for the loss of public life. The search for meaning in the private sphere replaced the assurances formerly offered by public life in a republic. Stoicism supplied a sense of belonging to members of the upper classes who were co-opted by the offer of Roman citizenship when their lands were conquered, but it was an empty ideology among the meek and the humble. The new mystery cults were spiritual communities of private men—and, notably, women!—that offered an experience of communion that transcended the private sphere. Among them was Christianity, a religion of love and forgiveness that came to represent the polar opposite of the cold commands of imperial law. The challenge faced by the new Christians was how to transform a private cult into a public church in which the particular experience of communion could be shared equally by all the members. How could this religious concern with salvation become a form of political legitimation? What kind of relation between the sacred and the secular would it establish? Saint Paul, the first of Jesus's followers to spread the universal validity of the message when he undertook his mission to the gentiles, took the first steps on this path, which would prove to be long and torturous.

LIVY AND THE ORIGIN OF THE REPUBLICAN SPIRIT

In the introductory remarks in *The Early History of Rome,* Livy (c. 64/59 BCE–17 CE) concludes with both a sigh of regret and a determination to tell the story as it must be told: "bitter comments of this sort are not likely to find favor, even when they have to be made. Let us have no more of them, at least at the beginning of our great story." Although his history would cover seven hundred years, he summarizes its lessons for his contemporaries at the outset:[6] "I invite the reader's attention to the much more serious consideration of the kind of lives our ancestors lived, of who were the men, and what the means both in politics and war by which Rome's power was first acquired and subsequently expanded; I would then have him trace the process of our moral decline, to watch, first, the sinking of the foundations of morality as the old teaching was allowed to lapse, then the rapidly increasing disintegration, then the final collapse of the whole edifice, and the dark dawning of our modern day when we can neither endure our vices nor face the remedies needed to cure them." The passage is eloquent, each phrase marking a stage first of growth, then of decline, and finally of despair. The paradoxical source of the decline was the republic's very successes. Whereas in republican times "poverty, with us, went hand in hand with contentment. Of late years wealth has made us greedy, and self-indulgence has brought us, through every form of sensual excess, to be, if I may so put it, in love with death both individual and collective."[7] The anxiety that too much success contains the seeds of "death both individual and collective" expresses Livy's awareness of the fragility of the republican spirit and the danger that it can be seduced by "sensual excess."

The Rome that Livy idealized was not born as a republic, but the virtues that it had from its origins made it fit to become a republic when its history permitted that possibility.[8] Not all cities, Livy implies, have the virtues needed to become republics, nor will republican virtue always find conditions for its realization. What are these virtues? They are manifested primarily in an ability to transform force into legitimate power. So it was that after Romulus killed his twin brother, Remus, in a struggle for power, he sought to ensure his new position by opening his city to what Livy calls "the rag-tag-and-bobtail from the neighboring peoples: some free, some slaves, and all of them wanting nothing but a fresh start."[9] As opposed to the Greek insistence on the homogeneity of a small body of participating citizens, in Rome individuals could make a new beginning and attract others to their project. But the growing population brought a new problem: women were lacking. No one wanted his daughter to marry the "rag-tags." Romulus once again had to resort to force, which would have to be transformed into legitimate power. A feast was offered to the surrounding population, but at a prearranged sign the Romans took by force what no one had been willing to give. After this "rape of the Sabine women," the Romans followed Romulus's advice to be kind and flattering to their new companions. As a result, when the Sabine men sought to avenge themselves, the women prevented the carnage, insisting that they were now mothers and that their children were the grandchildren of the vengeful attackers. A peace was arranged, and the two populations were joined into a more powerful political unity. This pattern would continue; violence became politically legitimate—for example, by expanding citizenship to the conquered peoples.

Six kings followed Romulus, ruling in coordination with the aristocratic Senate, whose role was to offer advice. Rome was not yet a republic, but its historical moment came when Tarquin the Proud (?–496 BCE) seized the throne by treachery. "Without hope of his subject's affection, he could rule only by fear; and to make himself feared as widely as possible he began the practice of trying capital cases without consultation [of the Senate] and by his own sole authority."[10] But even Tarquin recognized the need to create political legitimacy by acquiring booty through war and using it to construct public works.

What cost Tarquin his throne was a moral violation that sullied the virtuous character of the Roman citizen, who would learn the need for a republic in order to protect that virtue. One of Tarquin's sons coveted the chaste Lucretia, whom he took by force one evening. When Lucretia gathered her family, recounted the rape, and then stabbed herself, her brother Brutus (Lucius Junius) seized the dagger she had used and swore an oath to chase the tyrant forever from Rome. When Lucretia's body was carried into the public square, Brutus urged the population, "like true Romans, to take up arms against the tyrants."[11] And so it came to pass in 509 BCE. With this incident, the Romans resolved to take measures to ensure that no reign of unbridled force could again appear.

Despite the revolutionary role played by the community of "true Romans," Livy explains that Rome wisely avoided the temptations of popular democracy. The Romans did not "set sail on the stormy sea of democratic politics, swayed by the gusts of popular eloquence and quarreling for power . . . before any real sense of community had had time to grow. . . . Premature 'liberty' of this kind would have been a disaster: we should have been torn to pieces by petty squabbles before we had ever reached political maturity."[12] Conflict and diversity had to coexist within a unified political framework. The first step toward the creation of new political institutions was the abolition of the monarchy, which was replaced by two consuls whom the aristocrats of the Senate would select for a one-year term of office. In this way, unity would exist, but divided and controlling itself.

The Senate's selection of the two consuls proved to be an insufficient protection against tyranny. The Tarquins sought to return, enlisting the aid of some young patricians, among them the two sons of Brutus, who had himself been elected consul. The conspiracy was betrayed, however, and its perpetrators condemned to death. Livy describes the "memorable scene" in which republican virtue was again manifested: "the consular office imposed upon a father the duty of exacting the supreme penalty from his sons, so that he who, of all men, should have been spared the sight of their suffering was the one whom fate ordained to enforce it."[13] Brutus did not hesitate, despite his personal anguish. Livy significantly adds that the slave who had informed the authorities of the plot was granted his liberty with full citizen rights as a sign of the value Romans attached to the preservation of the republic.

Shortly thereafter, the Tarquins made another attempt to return to power with the aid of a foreign army, the Etruscans, which provided a further chance to confirm the strength of republican virtues. While Rome was besieged by the Etruscans, Gaius Mucius felt the need to restore the Roman honor that was sullied by its rather passive self-defense. Stealing into the enemy lines to assassinate their royal leader, Mucius mistook the king's secretary for his master and was captured. Refusing to disguise his murderous intentions, he thrust his right hand into the fire, holding it steady and exclaiming, "See how cheap men hold their bodies when they care only for honor!"[14] The astonished Etruscan ruler, vowing to reward such virtue, freed the prisoner and abandoned his alliance with the Tarquins. Mucius came to be honored with the name "Scaevola," meaning "Left-Handed Man." With such examples, Livy portrays the model of republican virtue.

Republican institutions needed to be enriched to fit the new spirit. The two consuls who replaced the monarch were given all the responsibility of a king, but they were elected and were replaced annually. The fact that they were elected meant that their power was not absolute. Able to check one another and replaced annually (because there was in principle no possibility of reelection), the consuls had to take into account the plurality of social interests while their political authority maintained the republic's ability to act as a unity. This early republican freedom had been tested by Tarquin's attempts to regain the throne with the help of outside forces. That threat was finally eliminated, Livy explains, when its enemies came to understand that "Rome was no longer a monarchy; she enjoyed free institutions. The people of Rome would sooner open their gates to an enemy than to a king. There was not a man in the city who did not pray that the end of liberty, should it come, might also be the end of Rome."[15]

These first republican institutions were not yet fully developed. Events continued to affect political thought. Faced with external enemies, the patrician Senate had to call on the plebian population for support, which led to a conflict when some of the returning soldiers who had left their private affairs to serve the republic "were 'bound over' to their creditors for debt. These men complained that while they were fighting in the field to preserve their country's liberty and to extend her power, their own fellow citizens at home had enslaved and oppressed them."[16] Anger boiled over, a mob formed, and when the senators feebly claimed that they legally could do nothing because a quorum was lacking, the crowd was further inflamed because it knew that this claim was only an excuse to avoid corrective action. News of this domestic discontent, of course, encouraged Rome's enemies. But the proudly aristocratic senators felt that to cede in the face of the mob would cost them their legitimacy. Nevertheless, the external threat led to a temporary truce in the name of national unity, permitting Rome to defeat its enemies. But the poor feared that the regained peace would bring new dangers for their freedom. They were right; the Senate not only refused to cede its power, but threatened to use force to maintain it. However, the temporary dictator that it appointed to do its will finally resigned in disgust at this senatorial recalcitrance. On their side, the common soldiers refused to muster for duty. Force had clearly failed both parties to the conflict; politics was needed to make power legitimate.

The negotiations that followed culminated in the creation of a new political institution to counter the senators' power: the people's tribunes. To fulfill their designated function, explains Livy, the tribunes "should be above the law, and their function should be to protect the commons against the consuls. No man of the senatorial class was to be allowed to hold the office."[17] The insistence that the tribunes be above the law was related to the fact that although it was their task to protect the interests of particular persons or groups, the universality of the law allowed for no such particular interventions. What is more, by refusing to admit anyone of senatorial rank to this function and by designing it to protect the plebeians, the Romans were admitting the existence of legitimate but competing and conflictual particular interests within the unitary republic. This institutional innovation was another sign of the Romans' practical political genius.

Not all patricians accepted the new republican institution that was to protect the poor. Some saw a chance to challenge the tribunate when a shortage of grain led to the need for imports and the poor protested against the resulting price increases. Senator Coriolanus insisted that if the people wanted the economic benefit of a return to the old prices, they should give back the political concession that had created the tribunes. The popular reaction was swift; Coriolanus was saved from the mob only by the clever intervention of the tribunes, who issued a summons against him in order to satisfy the popular anger. He reacted haughtily to being saved by an institution for which he had only contempt, but his fellow senators recognized the need to appease the popular anger. When Coriolanus did not appear in court, opinion hardened, support weakened, and he was constrained finally to exile. After this episode, in spite of other occasions for conflict in the next years, the balance seemed to hold, bolstered by the shared republican spirit. The equilibrium was sometimes threatened by passion, as when Volero, finding no support from that year's tribunes for his demand to overrule the consuls, appealed successfully to the people. The next year, however, when he himself was elected tribune, he put the national good above his own desire for vengeance, and the political balance was restored. Livy attributes another restoration to fate, which intervened when a senator, Appius, refused all appeals to reason in his attacks on the popular party but then took ill and died shortly before he was to be brought to trial.[18]

The invention of the tribunes provided only a temporary truce. At the end of book 2, Livy explains that the renewal of peace and plenty was "accompanied, however, by a return of popular discontent, and troubles abroad having ceased fresh causes for them were sought at home. Once more the tribunes injected the familiar poison of agrarian legislation [i.e., land reform] into the body politic; the Senate resisted and again the tribunes did all they could to rouse the commons against them."[19] At the beginning of book 3, Livy describes how the tribunes took the offensive. Gaius Terentilius Arsa began to inveigh against the arrogance of the patricians in the Senate and to denounce the consuls' excessive powers. He proposed the creation of a five-member commission to codify the laws that limit and define the powers of both institutions, leaving them "only the authority granted to them by popular assent, instead of giving the force of law, as they do at present, to their own arbitrary passions." But he finally backed down when the senators reminded him "never to forget that the power you wield [as a tribune] was given you to help individuals where help was needed, not to destroy the commonwealth as a whole. You [tribunes] were appointed not as enemies of the Senate, but as tribunes of the people."[20] This was sage advice, fully in the spirit that had seen the need for the tribunes to be above the law.

The tribunes did not give up on their challenge. When Terentilius's measure was brought up a year later, continues Livy, the climate was "marked by ominous signs: fires blazed in the sky, there was a violent earthquake, and a cow talked—there was a rumor that a cow had talked the previous year, but nobody believed it: this year they did." It seemed that the conflict would come to a violent head. Everyone felt the danger, but it was avoided—"Would you believe it?" exclaims Livy—by a threatened foreign attack. "The old cycle was being repeated," the historian concludes resignedly.[21] But the mistrust among the senators, the tribunes, and the people remained a threat to the republic.

Some senators, seeing that they could not triumph over both tribunes and people, resolved to bring the latter to their side. The tribunes countered by spreading rumors of potential senatorial plots against the people. This configuration of three competitors, each of whom fears the creation of an alliance of the other two against his interest, creates a political dynamic that (in spite of the different factions' intentions) can work to all parties' benefit. Rather than direct competition with a clear enemy, where the result will be victory or defeat, each participant has to learn to take into account a third party—who is, so to speak, outside of his line of vision—in evaluating the situation. In this way, each actor learns to see at once the unity of the political playing field and the plurality of the possible choices available. That is why force without legitimacy cannot solve political problems; the excluded party will always try to win over the temporary ally of the ruler, whose reign is for that reason never sure.

The situation came to a head when a force composed of slaves and exiles seized the capitol building. The tribunes hesitated to call the people to arms because they feared that the senators would convince the now aroused populous to join their cause. The revolt was overcome only with difficulty and at the cost of the life of the consul who led the counterattack. Cincinnatus, who replaced the deceased consul, then defied his senatorial colleagues. He criticized them for their divisive tactic of allowing the reelection of the tribunes who fomented the troubles that divided the republic. When the tribunes were reelected (despite the term limits), the Senate tried to counter this move by returning Cincinnatus to his position as consul. Livy articulates firmly Cincinnatus's explanation of his own refusal to violate the one-term limit. "'Can I be surprised, gentlemen,' he said, 'that you have little authority over the commons? Your own actions nullify it: because the commons ignore a decree of the Senate against the re-election of magistrates, is that a reason for your wishing to do the same? Do you wish to compete with the commons in disregard of principle? . . . You are merely copying the mob—whom no one expects to be politically adult; you are taking your cue in folly from the very people to whom you should be an example of political rectitude.'"[22] This declaration posed the question of the kind of legitimacy that the Senate, a numerical minority, needed to counter the tribunes' demagogic appeal and win over to its side the tribunes' popular supporters.

Cincinnatus's gesture was not forgotten. The next years saw domestic quarrels alternate with military campaigns, and Terentilius's demand for legal codification remained unanswered. A new outside enemy threatened; Roman fortunes were at a low ebb. Hope turned to the virtuous Cincinnatus, to whom the Senate resolved to send a delegation asking him to assume a temporary dictatorship in 458 BCE.[23] Livy's description of the scene that ensued has been heard across the ages. "A mission from the city found him at work on his land—digging a ditch, maybe, or ploughing. Greetings were exchanged, and he was asked—with a prayer for God's blessing on himself and his country—to put on his toga and hear the Senate's instructions. This naturally surprised him. . . . The toga was brought, and wiping the grimy sweat from his hands and face he put it on; at once the envoys from the city saluted him, with congratulations, as Dictator, invited him to enter Rome, and informed him of the terrible danger [facing the republic]."[24] The character of Rome's new chief enflamed its armies' republican spirit; victory followed swiftly, and although he had agreed to serve for six months, Cincinnatus resigned after only fifteen days in office. The state of exception ended, but the old quarrels were soon renewed.

"Finally," Livy writes, "out of sheer disgust and weariness, the whole question was allowed to drop, and the tribunes began to adopt a less provocative attitude." In the same year as Cincinnatus's brief dictatorship, they proposed the nomination of a commission consisting of members from both parties. These delegates were assigned the task of creating a constitution that would overcome the quarrels that threatened the republic. First, as part of the tribunes quest for legitimacy, it was decided that "three representatives . . . were to be sent to Athens with instructions to take down in writing the laws of Solon, and to acquaint themselves with the way of life and the political institutions of other Greek communities." With their return, the creation of a written legal code would begin. A board made up of ten members, and thus called "the Ten," (in Latin, the *decemviri*) was charged with this weighty task; its constituent authority overrode the existing power of both consuls and tribunes. "Thus it happened," concludes Livy, "that 302 years after the foundation of Rome the form of government was for the second time changed; once power had passed from kings to consuls, now it passed from consuls to *decemvirs*."[25]

The first year's constitutional work produced the Ten Tables of the Law, regulating the procedures used in familial, property, and other domains of the law. These tables were presented to the people for discussion and amendment before adoption. Success seemed to be at hand. Yet, because two additional tables were needed to cover legal institutions that had been left aside, the next year's election of the decemvirs was politically important. Because there was not as yet a legitimate constitution, there would still be no check on their constituent power.

The leader of the Ten was Appius, a descendent of the proud senator who had led an earlier conflict with the tribunes. In spite of his patrician sentiments, he had played the populist card. Once reelected, however, he "threw off the mask and showed his true character. At once, even before their term of office began, he set about the task of moulding his colleagues to his own pattern." The right of appeal was taken away, and "little by little the whole weight of the terror began to turn against the commons." Although the senators worried about this arbitrary justice, "they felt at the same time that the commons were getting what they deserved and were in consequence unwilling to help them. Their blind and greedy stampede for liberty had ended in servitude—very well: might it not be best to allow their sufferings to accumulate, till in utter desperation they came to wish the old days back again, with two consuls and everything as it used to be." The senators miscalculated; they had not taken into account Appius's lust for power. They assumed that the completion of the two new tables meant that there would be no need for the continued existence of the decemvirs. But the next election day came—and went. The tyranny was now undisguised. "Rome's spirit was crushed, "comments the historian, "but that was not all, for the nations beyond her borders were now beginning to despise her and to resent the fact that a slave state—as they thought her—should exercise imperial power."[26] With this remark, Livy recognizes that republican freedom not only legitimated Roman power, but also explained why its enemies feared it.

The suppression of freedom also affected military operations under the decemvirs; the common soldiers preferred failure to a temporary success that only confirmed the power of tyrannical leaders. But their sullen discontent found no mouthpiece, until Appius was betrayed by his own lust, just as the tyrannical Tarquins had succumbed to their own moral overreaching. Appius's attempt to use his judicial power to take the humble Verginia while her father was serving in the army recalled the rape of Lucretia; the relation of forces changed as popular virtue now found its voice. The cry went out for the restoration of the tribunate. But the senators' old fears were still alive. The decemvirs, for their part, saw that their only hope lay in abandoning their powers, but the tribunes to whom these powers would pass wanted revenge. This worried the patricians, whose fear of plebian power had increased because the two consuls leading the army had based their success on an appeal to popular opinion. "True moderation in the defense of political liberties is indeed a difficult thing," notes the politically shrewd historian; "pretending to want fair shares for all, every man raises himself by depressing his neighbor; our anxiety to avoid oppression leads us to practice it ourselves; the injustice we repel, we visit in turn on others, as if there were no choice except either to do it or to suffer it."[27] The republic is threatened when this self-interest leaves no room for the pursuit of the common good because each party must always be alert for lawless threats to its own interests.

Rome's enemies now threatened it when they recognized that "Roman discipline was a thing of the past; her people had lost the habit of war, and she was no longer a united nation." At this point, a new consul, Quinctius, intervened. His speech is one of the longest in Livy's *History*, which can only be paraphrased here. "How is it to end? Will the time ever come when we can have a united city, a united country?" You, the plebs, have beaten us; but other enemies now threaten. If they conquer us, you will lose just as we will; your "precious tribunes" can then give you only words, not return your stolen property. When you were soldiers led by us rather than by political agitators manipulated by your tribunes, you did not use your voices for political slogans meant to scare senators but to emit a battle-cry that terrorized the enemy. "Stick as you will to your assemblies and your petty politics, the necessity of military service, which you try to avoid, will pursue you." Do not listen to the flattering demagogues who claim to be disinterested friends of the people. "In an ordered and harmonious society they know they are nothing, and they would rather lead a bad cause than none at all." Livy says that these frank words denouncing the danger of demagogy brought the people to their senses; "seldom had the mob greeted the speech even of a popular tribune with greater enthusiasm."[28] And so it is that book 3 concludes with Roman victories now undisturbed by civil dissension.

We can leave Livy at this point. The historian has portrayed the process through which the Roman republic acquired its republican virtues. How many times, Livy seems to say, was Rome on the verge of failure, military or moral? How often did it neglect the need actively to confront the world around it because it was caught up in its own private and particular quarrels? Yet these quarrels, in the end, strengthened the Romans' confidence in what they came to recognize as the greatest republican virtue: political freedom. This freedom took shape through the repeated conflict of patrician and plebeian, senator and tribune, tyranny and popular rebellion; it gained adherents as it acquired institutional form. This is a second lesson to be drawn from the historical process that began in 509 BCE with the overthrow of the Tarquins and concluded with the adoption of the Twelve Tables in 449: the recognition that political institutions need to be anchored by a legal structure that makes them more than a temporary truce in a constantly renewed battle. In this way, the quarrels don't become deadly because each party fears the uncontrollable action of a third party acting from behind its back. By moderating the play of social interests, the law has the positive effect of encouraging conflict while providing conflict with a framework that makes it legitimate. Laws do not put an end to conflict; they regulate it.

◆

Roman history, of course, continued its forward march. But whereas Livy sought to reclaim a spirit that had disappeared in his own times, Polybius, who had written a century earlier at the acme of Roman power, assumed that political institutions were responsible for the expansive vigor of its republican politics. The Greek historian offers an account of the way in which republican institutions create a remarkable dynamic stability that explains why Roman power would lead to world domination. Both historians take the legitimacy and indeed the desirability of the Roman conquest of other peoples for granted. As with the Greeks, so too for the Romans the higher rules naturally over the lower, the superior over the inferior, virtue over corruption. Although Polybius works from the same historical raw material as Livy, his stress on the institutions that assure stability while encouraging growth makes his account a complement to Livy's concern with the republican spirit. Together, these narratives imply that neither the republican spirit nor republican institutions alone can ensure the maintenance of the political freedom that is the basis of republican political life.

POLYBIUS AND THE STRUCTURE OF REPUBLICAN INSTITUTIONS

Polybius (c. 203–120 BCE) offers his analysis of Rome's institutional structure in book VI of *The Rise of the Roman Empire,* which addresses the general problem of "the forms of states." He explains that he had waited to do so until this point in his narrative, when the armies of Carthage led by Hannibal had put the Romans on the defensive during the second Punic War, because, as with individuals, the true character of states is manifested only when they are truly tested. This is particularly true of republics, which, he insists, are not created to ensure peace and well-being because republican freedom is a mode of life in which nothing is gained if nothing is ventured and whatever has been gained can always be lost again if care is not devoted to its preservation. In a free republic, all social classes and the political institutions through which they express their interests are constantly active; all know that there are always possibilities for gain and threats of loss. The principal danger occurs when the freedom to pursue self-interest becomes a threat to the civic equality. What kind of institutions can maintain this republican freedom without surrendering to anarchy? How can the diversity of interests in society be legitimately represented while political unity is maintained?

The Greek historian begins his account as a philosopher, examining the general origins of political society. Men's natural weakness leads them to join together like animals in herds; and the same natural instinct explains why the most physically strong and courageous among them becomes the ruler. But it does not follow that monarchy is the natural or the best form of government. The notions of goodness and justice, as well as their opposites, must first emerge. Again, this process appears natural. The sexual instinct produces children, who, as they grow, may not show their parents the gratitude that is natural; others who see this, knowing how the parents have toiled for their offspring, are offended. They fear that the same might happen to them. More generally, when people see that someone who has helped another is repaid with injury, they resent it and fear that the same may happen to them in like circumstances. These feelings give rise to the idea of duty, which, says Polybius, is "the beginning and end of justice."[29] Doing one's duty produces results that affect others as well. A person who takes risks for others or who helps them in some way will naturally gain their favor (whereas someone who acts in the opposite manner will receive only contempt). As a result, specific types of conduct will be admired and imitated because of the advantages they bring in relations with others, who will support the projects of the person who acts in accord with his duty.

More generally, continues Polybius, men in society imitate one another and seek their fellows' approbation. This general trait now permits the emergence of political action. A person who recognizes this natural pattern will act in a way that agrees with the majority view concerning behavior that is to be praised or blamed. That person will acquire a power over others that is not the result of fear or force but is legitimated by their agreement with his judgment. Moreover, the people will resist those who might conspire against this person's rule, so that "almost imperceptibly" he will have become truly a king because now "reason [has become] more powerful than ferocity or force." This process will have worked quite well in ancient times, continues Polybius, when monarchs maintained their authority, built fortresses to protect the people, and acquired land to provide for their necessities of life without setting themselves apart in a way that creates envy because they are perceived as living at the expense of others. But difficulties arise for their heirs. They want to assure their power by distinguishing themselves from the population—for example, by distinct modes of dress—and they want to be free to conduct their love affairs, "however lawless these might be." Envy, indignation, and—in the latter case—passionate hatred follow, and with them arise conspiracies that are a real threat because they are mounted not by the worst, but by the most noble and most courageous of men, who reject instinctively their new rulers' overweening insolence. The Roman reader would recognized the historical basis of this apparently abstract narrative.

Polybius's next steps continue his conceptual account of the progress of Roman history. Aristocracy emerges according to the same pattern, winning the adherence of the people to its reasoned judgment while gaining popular gratitude, with the result that its power is exercised by consent without the need for force. Problems again arise for the heirs, who have not had their fathers' experience. Because they were raised in an atmosphere of power and privilege, they do not value the tradition of civic equality and the freedom of speech that accompanied the process that made the aristocracy legitimate. They become avaricious, drinkers or womanizers (or sometimes rapists of boys). With this descent, aristocracy has slid into oligarchy, and popular rebellion is not far behind because "whenever anybody who has observed the hatred and jealousy which are felt by the citizens for tyrants can summon up the courage to speak or act . . . he finds the whole mass of the people ready to support him." But this time the people remember their experience with the previous king, whose power degenerated into force; they realize that their only hope is democracy. Problems will of course emerge in this case as well when a new generation arises that takes equality and freedom of speech for granted. This new generation then becomes possessed by a "senseless craving for prominence," seeking political office by seducing or corrupting the masses with demagogy, flattery, and bribes. The work ethic disappears as people see how wealth is gained by despoiling others. An ambitious and daring leader whose poverty has excluded him from honors will then find popular support for massacring, banishing, or expropriating his overreaching opponents. Although he is now a master, his power has been legitimately acquired; he does not impose his force on the people.

Although Polybius presents this cycle as natural, his theory is exemplified in his narration of the history of Rome's formation, growth, and achievements. Why, he asks, did Rome not succumb to the vicious cycle? The answer lies in its ability to learn from crises by building institutions capable of tacking the stormy seas. The Greek historian suggests that the Romans have borrowed the wisdom of the mythical Spartan lawgiver, Lycurgus, who understood that any constitution based on a single principle will be unstable and liable to degenerate. They thus created a mixed constitution whose goal is to produce "a state of equilibrium thanks to the principle of reciprocity or counteraction." This mixed political constitution differs from Aristotle's mixed society, whose middle class assured political stability. The Roman model joins together the institutional principles of the three constitutional types in a dynamic equilibrium that prevents any one from becoming dominant. Kings are prevented from becoming arrogant by the fact that the people have a share in government. The people, in turn, do not show contempt for the monarch because they fear that the senators' sense of honor will lead them to side with justice if a popular threat endangers the ruler. As for the Senate, Polybius seems to think that the aristocratic character he attributes to the senators nullifies any threat that they might represent. He did not anticipate the social unrest that would burst out during the tribunates of the two Gracchi between 133 and 121 BCE.

Polybius goes on to specify his argument in three stages. The first describes each of the three institutional structures as they came to exist in Rome and the way in which each exercises its power without overreaching its limits. The second turns to their interaction in order to analyze the dynamic produced by their conflict. He then uses this second aspect of the account to explain the Roman republic's ability to learn from its experiences. This ability in turn explains its world-conquering mission, as opposed to the static constitution of Lycurgus's Sparta.

The analysis begins with the consuls, who inherit the powers of a monarch but do not present the threat of a tyranny. They were originally the supreme magistrates, but each consul's power is limited by the veto power of his co-consul and by the fact that he has been chosen for a limited one-year term in office and is not reeligible for the next ten years. The consuls participate in the legislative power by introducing motions in the Senate, but their power was based essentially on their administrative and military role. (Although the tribunes will later be able to introduce motions to the Senate that the consuls cannot veto, the consuls nonetheless will retain sufficient power on their own—for example, in referring urgent matters for discussion in the Senate and in being responsible for executing senatorial decisions.) The consuls also interact with the people through their power to call meetings of the popular assembly, to propose measures for the assembly's consideration, and to put its decisions into practice. The consuls have a role in both foreign and military decisions as well, interpreting treaties with allies and appointing the military tribunes responsible for conscripting soldiers as needed. They command these armies and have the power to spend whatever public monies they need in order to succeed in their campaigns. In this way, as Polybius concludes, they have monarchical powers (imperium), but they are not monarchs because they are limited by the Senate, on the one hand, and by the people (and tribunes), on the other.

The Senate, which had previously been the advisor to the monarch, is the aristocratic element in the republican constitution. Although senatorial rank is for the most part inherited, new men (*novi homines*) of talent and experience can become members. The Senate is the repository of experience and thus of sage advice, but its primary responsibility is financial. It regulates both revenue and expenses (save those incurred by the consuls in their wartime function). It is more than a bookkeeper, though. Its control over the five-year plans for the construction and repair of public facilities gives it real influence over people who seek state aid for their projects or who wish to benefit from state expenditures. The legitimation of this power lies in its capacity as an established and long-serving institution composed of wealthy and admired patricians to look beyond immediate needs and personal political advantage. Polybius assumes that this ability serves to limit any individual senator's ambitions. As a further check, the Senate has jurisdiction over crimes requiring public investigation—such as treason, conspiracy, poisoning, and assassination. For the same reason, the Senate arbitrates disputes among private persons, who can appeal to it rather than leave their fate and honor to the popular courts. Finally, because the Senate's aristocratic character means that it is able to consider the general good rather than particular interests, it is responsible for diplomacy, including the declaration of war, as well as for receiving and responding to foreign delegations.

What role is left for the people? And what are the limits on their action? The populace is the democratic element of the constitution. It maintains the last word in approving or rejecting laws and in ratifying alliances and treaties. But its most important power is exercised through its role as jurors. Supplying the jury pool, explains Polybius, gives it control over rewards and punishments, which are "the only bonds whereby kingdoms, states and human society in general are held together." Polybius assumes that his readers will understand how this power is exercised in a republican society where shame is the worst of punishments and where there exist no public prosecutors. The courts adjudicate actions initiated by private persons against other private persons (who can also be accused of crimes stemming from their abuse of public office). In this way, the law serves a political function, attacking or demeaning enemies or defending one's own honor. A legal career offers a path to popular political influence and power. Unlike a modern jury constrained by rules of evidence, the Roman jurors would listen to competing political (as well as emotional and often circumstantial) arguments frequently focused on the opposing party's character in order to justify (or to invalidate) the plausibility of the accusation. The court is where Polybius's "rewards and punishments" are meted out. The rewards are political, although money is often involved as well. At the same time, the fact that this popular democratic power is exercised by a yes-or-no vote serves as a sufficient limit on its powers.

After this description of the powers and limits of the three political institutions of republican Rome, Polybius turns to their dynamic interaction. His most fundamental insight is that power must grow to meet the challenges of its competitors. For example, the consul who sets off for war seems to have absolute power. In fact, however, he needs the support of both the Senate and the people. The Senate has to approve his request for supplies. It can influence his war plans either by sending a new consul at the end of the year or by permitting him to continue for an additional term. It can magnify a general's successes or minimize them, if it wishes, either by offering further funding or by refusing to fund the public celebrations called "triumphs" that honor him on his return home. The democratic element enters here as well because the people must ratify or reject the treaties that conclude the military action, and, most important, the consuls must account to the people for their actions, whether successes or failures, once they have been completed.

The interplay of the people and the Senate is more complicated and conflictual. The Senate cannot use its power to investigate offenses against the state unless its decree is confirmed by the people in their assembly. Moreover, the tribunes' veto can prevent the Senate from even meeting. But the Senate is able to defend itself by skillfully using its control of contracts for public construction and repairs. Polybius is aware of the potential for abuse of this power. The contracts are "far too numerous to specify," and "there is scarcely a soul . . . who does not have some interest in these contracts and the profits which are derived from them." Moreover, the Senate decides whether extra time for contract fulfillment should be awarded as well as whether a contractor is liable for faulty work. Furthermore, the Senate's judicial role in prosecuting cases of treason and threats to public order means individual citizens have an interest in remaining on its good side, encouraging them to be cautious before deciding to oppose its will. The power of the people is hard; that of the Senate, subtle.

The upshot of this account is that each power must grow to meet the challenge of the other powers. The republic's stability is preserved by maintaining this competition. In Polybius's words, "the whole situation remains in equilibrium since any aggressive impulse is checked and each estate is apprehensive from the outset of censure from the others." Livy seems to have borrowed from Polybius his account of the mutually beneficial political dynamic that results from the triadic relation among the Senate, the tribunes, and the people, which produces in each the fear that the others will form an alliance against its interests.

The occupants of each institution have to take account of the way the others may be evaluating their chances to gain power. In this way, each learns to see at once the republic's unity as well as the plurality of choices available to it. None can expand by force alone; it needs at least the tacit consent of the others, which will be given only if they do not feel threatened by that expansion. But stability and success are never certain; they may even be dangerous. If peace brings affluence and prosperity, there is a danger that the people will be "corrupted by flattery and idleness and become insolent and overbearing," which "happens often enough." One of the three institutional powers then becomes "overambitious and tends to encroach upon the others." But the institutional dynamic means that "the designs of any one can be blocked or impeded by the rest, with the result that none will unduly dominate the others or treat them with contempt."

Polybius develops his insight into the way power can be mobilized by means of a detailed discussion of the Roman military system and through a comparison with other constitutions. The reason that Polybius turns now to this account of the military organization is that it is essentially a political institution. The use of force rather than the extension of formal law to incorporate new citizens must be legitimated. Polybius summarizes this thesis briefly at the end of his dense discussion, when he compares the encampments of the Greeks, who "think above all of the security they can achieve," to those of the Romans, who "aim above all at ease of movement." Military prowess goes together with the republican recognition that freedom is never guaranteed and that its preservation is ensured only by its augmentation. This relationship explains not only why Rome fought so many wars, but also (a point Polybius does not make) why it always claimed that these wars were defensive wars that had to be fought to preserve its liberty (and only incidentally to gain power and wealth).

To complete his picture of the Roman republic's institutional structure, Polybius needs to show its distinction from other constitutions that can be called "republican" insofar as they are commonwealths aimed at the good of all their citizens. He begins with Athens, whose success is said to be due to the greatness of its leaders rather than to its constitution, whose default is that it permits "the masses [to] take all decisions according to their random impulses." As a result, the ship of state is left without a commander. This state of affairs is no problem when the seas are calm, but it leads to divisive conflict when storms arise. As for the "celebrated republic" of Plato, comparing it to existing constitutions would be "like bringing forward some statue and then comparing it with living and breathing men." Although Polybius looks more favorably on Lycurgus's Spartan constitution, he notes that it is "perfectly adequate to its task" only if that task is limited to defense of the city. The Spartans' "almost obsessive concern with military rewards and punishments, and the immense importance which they attach[ed] to both, [explains why] it is not surprising that they emerge[d] with brilliant success from every war in which they engage[d]." But so too do the Romans. What explains why Rome has conquered the world, whereas Sparta quickly disappeared from the world stage?

Polybius recalls that Sparta's defeat of Athens in the Peloponnesian War was the prelude to its own decline and to that of Greece. The source of Sparta's decline was the difference between the moderation of its citizens' private lives and its ambitious quest for domination over its neighbors. The harmony and equality of its domestic political elite promoted the courage and self-discipline that assured its defense against any threat. But the acquisitive politics that it was led to pursue during the war brought out the hidden defect in its constitution. The egalitarian economic policy that prohibited foreign trade and the private pursuit of wealth made it unable to supply its far-flung army. As a result, its attempt to gain domination over Greece turned out to be a threat to its own liberty when it found itself forced to apply to imperial Persia for a loan in order to ensure the final defeat of Athens. Polybius stresses the contrast between Sparta's forced egalitarianism and the Roman encouragement of both individuals and institutions to strengthen themselves. Although competition among these political forces may produce temporary moments of insolent and overbearing strife, he recognizes that it will always encourage new political mobilization. The motor of that competition in the last resort is not just institutional self-defense, but individual self-interest, which the dynamic and conflictual structure of Roman institutions channels toward the good of the republic and thus the good of all of its members. But will this self-interest clash with a republican virtue that is concerned with the general welfare?

Polybius's conclusion to his comparative explanation of Roman greatness shows that he is aware of the risks that accompany its encouragement of self-interest. Rome had come near to defeat in the Punic Wars. Why did it triumph? The secret to its success did not lie simply in its institutions. After all, Carthage also had a mixed constitution. However, Carthage treated the acquisition of wealth as an end that justifies all means, whereas the Romans accepted individual enrichment only by reputable means, as is illustrated by the fact that they made bribery a capital offense. Polybius seems to be aware that the latter is a weak deterrent (as indeed it was). He adds an allusion to Roman religious beliefs that encourage citizens to be scrupulous in performing their duty because they are bound by oaths. What he calls religion's "mysterious terrors" are said to serve to restrain the fickle masses that are filled with lawless desires and drawn by violent passions.[30]

But the historian who argued that the senators' "character" would limit their ambitions and ensure that they looked to the good of the commonwealth cannot hide his doubts. He recognizes that when a state becomes a world power, its life becomes more luxurious, and competition for office becomes "fiercer than it should." Some will be haunted by a feeling of humiliation and obscurity, but ostentation and extravagance by others will usher in "a period of general deterioration." At this point, the masses will either act from grievance against the greed of others or be flattered by demagogues who aspire to office. Rather than the equality of participation in the institutions of the mixed constitution, they will now demand a greater share of the wealth for themselves. "When this happens," Polybius concludes, "the constitution will change its *name* to one that sounds the most imposing of all, that of freedom and democracy, but its *nature* to that which is the worst of all, that is the rule of the mob [*ochlocracy*]" (emphasis in original).[31]

CICERO AND THE MORAL THEORY OF REPUBLICAN POLITICS

Polybius's fears became a reality during the century after he wrote *The Rise of the Roman Empire*. The republican institutions that encouraged an increasingly expansionist state masked social divisions that grew with the enlargement and enrichment of the state. Polybius was naive to think that the Senate's aristocratic ethos meant that it would not accept bribery or illicit forms of money making. His other hope for the preservation of republican virtue—limits imposed by religion—did not maintain its hold. Meanwhile, the Roman constitution increasingly became a formal framework for masking the reality of the struggle for power. It is not surprising that the empire would soon effortlessly adopt these political institutions, maintaining the Senate, the consuls and the tribunes, and other republican institutions, but exercising real power in the unified central office of the emperor. The fact that the republic was engaged in a long civil war that ebbed and flowed during six long decades prior to the imperial seizure of power does not mean that this historical result was inevitable, however. Contemporaries wondered whether the republic was condemned by an inherent flaw.

◆

Marcus Tullius Cicero (106–43 BCE) lived at a turning point when it still seemed possible to save the republic from its own worst instincts. Alas, he, too, had the vices of his virtues. A "new man" lacking familial patronage, he had frequently to compromise his principles in order to win a place among the aristocrats who dominated the Senate. Always unsure of his political power but certain of his intellectual brilliance, Cicero often fell victim to those who knew how to flatter him. He made a reputation as a lawyer and orator, climbing step by step the ladder that eventually brought him election as consul in 63 BCE at the youthful age of forty-three. To achieve this goal, Cicero had at once to prove himself a friend of the people and yet also an ally of the aristocrats who dominated the Senate. In one of his most famous legal cases, he took up the cause of the Sicilians who were being exploited by their governor, Verres. His victory in the trial that he initiated against that wealthy and corrupt aristocrat added to his reputation for republican virtue. He would win other glorious republican trials. But a Roman lawyer-politician who was a *novus homo* needed both political support and economic means. To achieve them, Cicero took up a number of less than salubrious causes, admitting that "it is the greatest possible mistake to suppose that the speeches we barristers have made in court contain our considered and certified opinions; all those speeches reflect the demands of some particular case or emergency." He knew also that a rising lawyer had to be willing to defend the guilty if they were well placed. "Let me tell you," he told a client, "that it was I who produced the necessary darkness in the court to prevent your guilt from being visible to everyone."[32]

During Cicero's year as consul, 64 BCE, he undertook the prosecution of a popular senator who seemed to be using his influence with the plebian classes to encourage a revolt against the Senate. Cicero's decisive intervention against this so-called Cataline conspiracy increased his own fame, earning him the title "father of his country." The question whether Lucius Sergius Catalina (Cataline) had serious intentions or Cicero had merely taken the initiative to preempt the growing power of the two generals—Pompey and Caesar—whose ambitions would finally precipitate the civil war can be left to the historians. The success that the prosecution won for Cicero was short-lived. The republican ideals that he hoped to restore lay already in the past, and he had no positive program for their re-creation. Two political paths were open to him: he could criticize the factions whose competition for power was growing increasingly violent, using his talents as a lawyer, orator, and pamphleteer to appeal both to the public and to his colleagues in the Senate, or he could adopt the role of advisor to an enlightened prince. Cicero could not decide; he oscillated between the two options. His dilemma grew worse; his republican values clashed with his opportunism. He flirted with Pompey, then joined him openly in 49 BCE. But it was Caesar who became dictator the next year. Although opposed to the dictatorship, Cicero did not join the conspiracy that put an end to Caesar's reign in 44. He did denounce the partisans of the dead ruler, in particular Mark Antony, in vitriolic pamphlets that he, ever the admirer of Greek culture, called "philippics." The new rulers took him seriously enough to have him assassinated in December 43, cutting off both his head and his hands, whose display in the public forum signified that republican hopes had definitely come to an end.

Groping for practical principles in the harried years between 54 and 51 BCE, Cicero wrote two political dialogues that have continued to influence posterity. *On the Commonwealth* begins with a sustained argument in favor of the philosopher and the citizen's active engagement. After a survey of constitutional types, it re-creates the history of Rome along the lines suggested by Polybius. Its overarching goal is to define the nature of the moral politician in the troubled times of a republic that has lost its moral compass. But if taken in isolation, *On the Commonwealth* gives too much weight to morality. It must be read together with *On the Laws*, which shows that the Stoic-republican morality Cicero advocated has a practical partner in the legal structure that emerges from the interplay of natural law and positive law. This legal theory provides the implicit framework in which the moral politician acts. The basis of both works is a stoic political theory that, in spite of Cicero's political intent, gives them both an antipolitical orientation. In the first case, the politician is reduced to moral imprecations; in the second, the republic's legal institutions leave no place for the citizen's action.

Rome's worldly power was so great that the explanation of its decline into civil war could lie only in the very heart of the republic itself. Material conditions could not explain it, nor could institutions be blamed for it. That is why book I of *On the Commonwealth* begins with a philosophical inquiry into the origins of political society. Cicero, rejecting what he calls the Epicurean priority on pleasure or the simple satisfaction of needs as the motivation for building a city, argues that "nature has given men such a need for virtue and such a desire to defend the common safety that this force has overcome all the enticements of pleasure and pain." Virtue, he adds, is not something that can be possessed without using it; it exists only insofar as it is put into practice among one's fellow men.[33] A successful politician will know how to encourage others to practice this innate virtue. In other words, the basis of political success is moral rather than material. Politics actualizes the virtue that exists potentially in all men.

At the end of book II, Cicero alludes twice to Plato. He first stresses the importance of unity for gaining political legitimacy. "What musicians call harmony with regard to song is concord in the state, the tightest and best bond of safety in every republic; and that concord can never exist without justice." At this point in the manuscript, however, eleven pages that were no doubt a commentary on this passage are lost. Although this commentary appears to be a restatement of Plato's own argument, there is an important difference in Cicero's reading. The Stoic republican claims that justice is the precondition of harmony, whereas Plato identifies justice with harmony. The second allusion to Plato, announcing the subject for the next day's dialogue, suggests the need to look more closely at the relation between moral and political reform. "We can go no further without establishing not only the falseness of the statement that the commonwealth cannot function without injustice but also the profound truth of the idea that the commonwealth cannot possibly function without justice."[34] Most of book III's argument that injustice is not necessary to the maintenance of a legitimate republic has been lost. The first part of this claim clearly appeals to Socrates' refutation of Thrasymachus in *The Republic*. It shows that the sophistic justification of power politics is self-contradictory and harmful to its proponent and to the city, who fall victim to their own hubris, overreaching, and disharmony. Once again, however, justice is said to be prior to the commonwealth.

It remains to show how the politician creates justice. Just as Plato concluded his quest for justice in *The Republic* by demonstrating that it had been present throughout the inquiry in the form of harmony, so the Stoic Cicero has assumed that the capacity for justice is always present, needing only the moral politician's leadership to make it manifest. In the leader's absence, that capacity lies fallow. In Roman history, this absence has led to the dilemma described at the beginning of book V. "For if the state had not had such morals, then the men would not have existed; nor, if such men had not been in charge, would there have been such morals as to be able to establish or preserve for so long a commonwealth so great and ruling so widely." There is no morality without a republic, and no republic without morality. But the priority of morality is suggested when Cicero goes on to propose that "we must not only render an account of such an evil," but "it is because of our own vices, not because of some bad luck, that we preserve the commonwealth in name alone but have long ago lost the substance."[35] To correct these "vices" that are destroying the republic, they must be recognized as crimes—indeed, as "capital crimes." Moral reform of men who have fallen so far from their own virtuous natures must take place through public action because virtue truly exists only in action. This is where Cicero's legal theory complements his republican political project. It is not the politician who will restore the justice violated by these "capital crimes," but the law.[36]

The Stoic legal theory presented in *On the Laws* offers a complementary interpretation of the degeneration of republican politics. Two steps are involved in the theory. First, "law is the highest reason, rooted in nature, which commands things that must be done and prohibits the opposite." This definition establishes law as objective and independent of the conventions that men establish among themselves. But this transcendent law must be given human form if it is to be binding on men. Hence, second, "when this same reason is secured and established in the human mind, it is law."[37] *On the Commonwealth* suggests the reason for this distinction of the two moments by which law is established as legitimate: "True law is right reason, consonant with nature, spread through all people. It is constant and eternal; it summons to duty by its orders, it deters from crime by its prohibitions." The law and the duties that it imposes are universal; they apply to all persons. However, Cicero goes on to admit that although good people obey this law, "it does not move the wicked [man]," who "will be in exile from himself [for] he scorns his nature as a human being."[38] Natural law thus depends on what Cicero considers to be naturally given human reason for its worldly realization. Such law is defined as right reason in agreement with nature; it instills virtue among the citizenry because virtue is simply "nature perfected and taken to its highest level."[39]

The problem with this chain of deductions from nature is that not all people at all times apply right reason, even though they are in principle capable of doing so. They may not know how to do so; they may let their material desires govern their reason; or they may indeed be wicked evildoers who prefer their particular self-interest to the universal values of reason. Cicero draws a critical political conclusion from this fact, which is not just a moral failing. He suggests in *On the Laws* that "the most stupid thing of all . . . is to consider all things just which have been ratified by a people's institutions or laws. What about the laws of tyrants?" That is why Cicero invokes the law of nature as the measure against which to evaluate merely human laws (which he calls "positive laws").[40] It follows, further, that the law is binding on the individual (or society) not because it is imposed by force, but insofar as it is known through right reason. In other words, human laws are legitimate only insofar as they do not contradict natural law. But that does not mean that all legitimate human laws are identical to natural law; legitimate positive laws apply the universal principles of natural law to the particular circumstances facing a society.

In book II of *On the Laws,* Cicero applies this notion of natural law to the Roman history that he had presented in *On the Commonwealth.* Referring to the rape of Lucretia and its aftermath, he notes that "reason existed, derived from nature, directing people to good conduct and away from crime; it did not begin to be a law only at that moment when it was written down."[41] Indeed, although the healthy Roman reaction to the Tarquins' brutality did not appeal to positive, written law, it was universally felt to be right and thus lawful. But because not all men will always use their right reason when moral instinct fails, it is not wise to expect the spontaneous exercise of this kind of moral virtue. Legislation is needed; laws have to be written and made public. But different peoples will interpret the natural law differently. As the Romans conquered new lands whose laws differed from those of Rome, they faced a dilemma. How could these different codes be made compatible with one another and with the law of Rome, their overlord?

This expansion of Roman power across the globe provided the context in which the theory of natural law proved its practical value. Conventional or positive laws are the attempt to adapt natural law to particular circumstances. But natural law is by its nature universal; it must be applicable always and everywhere. The implication is that conventional laws, at best, can be shown not to contradict natural law. As long as they do not, they must be considered legitimate. Thus, Cicero formulates the relation between the two types of law in a terse phrase at the beginning of book III in *On the Laws*: "it can truly be said that a magistrate is a law that speaks, and a law is a silent magistrate." The judge expresses the natural law, which sits in silent judgment until it is given voice in the form of a conventional or positive law.[42] Because the magistrate gives only a particular manifestation of the universal law of nature, Cicero points out that the Romans had learned that "judgments are given with the proviso that there is a right of appeal to the people," who can correct the judicial failure to apply right reason.[43] In other words, this two-sided procedure shows that conventional positive law is the application of natural law in a world that is open to historical change, whereas natural law serves as a standard against which both the legislator and the citizen measure the validity of the existing positive laws (and eventually any new laws that replace them).

On the Laws is incomplete, but its theory of natural law suggests an interpretation of the way in which the empire so easily adopted republican institutions. Just as the Greek cities committed suicide rather than renounce the intense democratic participation characteristic of their political life, the republican Rome described by Polybius and idealized by Cicero was built on what might be called juridical participation. Livy describes this structure in the young republic's decision after the rape of the Sabine women to extend to their neighbors the rights of Roman citizenship. This extension meant giving to the others the laws of Rome even when practical difficulties (such as the distance from Rome) meant that participation in establishing them was purely formal. As the years and centuries went on and the republic stretched its boundaries, this practice continued. The reality of Roman domination could be legitimated by the Stoic idea of a natural law in which everyone participates, in principle, through the use of right reason. The result is a nonpolitical type of membership, which can explain the decline of republican morality that Cicero recognized as the ultimate cause of the political miseries of his times.

Cicero did not have the vices of his virtues only as a practical politician; as a political thinker, he was too much the philosopher to see the antipolitical implications of his own theory. The premise that "since there is nothing better than reason, and it is found both in humans and in god, reason forms the first bond between humans and god" leads him to the still more far-reaching claim that "those who share reason also share right reason; and since that is the law . . . those who share law also share the procedures of justice; and those who have these things in common must be considered members of the same state, all the more so if they obey the same commands and authorities. Moreover, they do obey this celestial order, the divine mind and the all-powerful god, so that this whole cosmos must be considered to be the common state of gods and humans."[44] With these lapidary phrases, Cicero demonstrates the attractiveness of the Stoic cosmopolis in a world where the Greek city had lost its ability to integrate its citizens and Roman politicians were more interested in their own wealth and power than in the good of the commonwealth. The Stoic is reconciled with his lot, but the powerful continue to dominate.

THE EMPIRE TURNS INWARD: THE EMERGENCE OF PAULINE CHRISTIANITY

There is of course no reason to blame Stoic theory for the institutionally smooth but politically violent path that led from the republic to the empire. But it could and did serve as a justification of the imperial monopolization of power, both for the slave Epictetus and for the emperor Marcus Aurelius, the two great Stoic thinkers of imperial Rome. The citizens of the empire were offered other compensations, from the cultural glories of the Augustan Age to the material benefits that financed the great public works that communicated to the citizens a pride in belonging to the civilization of the imperium. They benefited also from the shared citizenship defined by Roman law to whose universality individuals could appeal against the arbitrary domination of particular local potentates. Roman public law also made possible the development of protected private rights. For example, the law of contracts set out general rules that had to be obeyed by the parties to the contract, but at the same time it left them free to make whatever particular arrangements each partner took to be beneficial. This last example of the benefits of imperial citizenship illustrates poignantly the cost that was paid for them. The shared benefits of living under common laws is passive, whether these laws are justified by Stoic philosophy, material benefit, the reflected glory of Roman civilization, or the preservation of private rights. The universality of the law is formal, abstract, and external to the individual; its legitimacy comes from its usefulness to private affairs—or from the force to which Rome did not hesitate to resort against opposition when it seemed necessary.

This is the context in which Christianity—along with other mystery cults—emerged to offer meaning where public life itself was stripped of significance. Rome had its panoply of pagan gods and public rituals by which they were honored. Indeed, this panoply was regularly enriched by the addition of deities adopted from one or another newly conquered people. The pagan gods were not jealous; they belonged to all Romans. The mystery cults, however, differed from this customary religion insofar as they were private sources of meaning that united a particular community defined by their personal participation in something that was greater than themselves. These two qualities of the mystery cults were a challenge to the lawful, public universality ensured by Roman citizenship. The new communities' attraction lay in their ability to supply shared communal meaning in a world where public life had lost its legitimacy.

Christianity enters into the history of political thought at this point. The story of Jesus's birth in the manger in Bethlehem is symbolic. The Gospel of Luke (2:1) explains that Mary and Joseph had to return to their home city to be registered by the Roman imperial census. The private religion of love, forgiveness, and hope would soon oppose this imposition of legal universalism in which individuals were simply numbers to be counted. World dominion was vast but empty; the conquerors, as Tacitus put it in a famous phrase, "make a desert and call it peace."[45] Although the Pax Romana would last for another four centuries, and its decline can be explained by its material overreach, the new religion opposed to its abstract universal laws an equally universal—in Greek, *catholic*—stress on the experience of the individual subject that would produce a new kind of community. The communion of believers would replace the Roman republic and the Greek polis.

The emergence of Christianity as a political force that would survive (or, some would claim, cause) the fall of the Roman Empire is illustrated in both the life and the teaching of Saint Paul. While on the road to Damascus, Saul of Tarsus (died c. 64–65 CE), a free Roman citizen of Jewish faith and a well-known enemy of the new sect, was seized by a vision of Jesus, who demanded to know why he persecuted the true believers. This mystical experience transformed Saul into Paul. But Paul's reputation among the followers of Jesus could not be so easily erased; the leaders in the Jerusalem community had known the living Jesus, which was the source of their legitimacy. Like Jesus, however, they had never quite broken with the Jewish faith, whose philistinism they sought to reform. This uncertain legitimacy provided the opening that Paul proceeded to enlarge. He identified Judaism as the dry religion of the law, to which he opposed the warm faith of the heart. He developed this opposition of private to public, spirit to letter, and heart to mind as his mission widened and his theology adapted to his greater activity. But the Pauline religiosity did not exist only within the private sphere or outside of Roman history.

Paul's stress on the spirit over the letter of the law, his certainty that without God's grace mortals can undertake nothing good, and the role that he accorded to experience as central to the faith can be seen as projections of Paul's own position as the representative of a new generation among the faithful. These devotees refused any reformist options within a Judaism that was prey to the same religious ferment that was sweeping the empire. When the first Jewish revolt against the Romans (66–73 CE) was crushed, the reformers as well as the Jews themselves were discredited. It was at this point, shortly after Paul's death, that Christians generally began to think of themselves as establishing a new religion. Paul's letters (epistles) to the Philippians, Colossians, Romans, Corinthians,

Ephesians—all of them congregations that he had established as he took advantage of the Roman imperial system of communication—now served a political function in organizing the new community. They could perform this task because Paul had recognized the need to ensure the external and ritual unity among believers bound together only by a subjective experience that he had opposed to the Judaic legalism that he identified with the abstract universality of Roman imperial law. Although it would take centuries before the separate congregations of the new church acquired their universal institutional system of ritual and belief, Paul's work stands at the origins of this new stage of political organization.

Paul's Roman citizenship permitted him to undertake the missionary work that spread the new faith. His was explicitly a mission to the gentiles. As such, the claims of the new religion were universal in nature. For example, despite the traditional attitude of some of the early believers, Paul refused to distinguish man and woman, circumcised and noncircumcised, slave and free. This stress on the universal validity of the new faith had a political consequence. Rome had accepted the Jewish religion in spite of its monotheistic refusal to worship the pantheon of pagan gods; the Jews were considered an ethnic nation with their own customs, bound to Rome only by the formality of a treaty. The Hebrew God did not compete with the Roman gods because the Jews, as God's Chosen People, left it to God to convert others. The Christians' claim to universality necessarily brought them into conflict with Rome, which made it necessary for Paul to define the relation of church and state. How should the intensely spiritual and private Pauline religiosity relate to secular institutions? To say that the sacred and the profane worlds were both expressions of the divine leaves unanswered the question of their relation. Was the secular appointed to transmit or even to enforce the sacred? Is the institutional church part of the sacred world or the secular world? Is it to guide or to legitimate the actions of the state? Does the church's action fulfill the task Plato attributed to the Guardians: the creation of a priesthood charged with actualizing a transcendent truth in the secular world?

The first two paragraphs from the Letter to the Romans (13:1–6) suggest the complexity of the problems facing Paul and left to his successors. He needs to define the source and nature of the authority by which the state governs its citizens. He begins by asserting that "there is no authority but by act of God," which he immediately interprets as implying that "the existing authorities are instituted by him." Paul does not consider the possibility that these authorities might be exercising arbitrary force rather than legitimate power. He simply concludes that "anyone who rebels against authority is resisting a divine institution, and those who so resist have themselves to thank for the punishment they will receive. For government, [which is] a terror to crime, has no terrors for good behavior." This claim follows from Paul's identification of the existing authorities as divinely instituted. In effect, rulers are not a threat to those who obey the rules, but only to those who break them. Good behavior is simply obedience by a person who does not (and need not) reason for himself or seek the best life together with other members of the city. For this reason, Christianity is no threat to any government. But Paul's thought is more complex than this; the Christian is not subject only to the existing laws of the land.

The passage from Romans goes on to elaborate what Paul means by obedience. "You wish to have no fear of the authorities. Then continue to do right and you will have their approval, for they are God's agents working for your good. But if you are doing wrong, then you will have cause to fear them; it is not for nothing that they hold the power of the sword, for they are God's agents of punishment, for retribution on the offender. That is why you are obliged to submit." Paul appears to be saying once again that obedience is an obligation that results from the fact that "they [the authorities] hold the power of the sword," which they wield as legitimate agents of the divine. But the very next sentence adds a significant qualification. Obedience "is an obligation imposed not merely by fear of retribution but by conscience. That is also why you pay taxes." In this version of the argument, obligation is not made legitimate by God's consecration of the secular powers; obedience is instead rooted in the conscience of the individual who has interiorized the divine imperative. At first, the difference seems minimal; the divine imperative that is internalized still commands obedience to the secular powers. The individual's behavior will be the same in either case. But the legitimation of that behavior in the first case comes from God's authorization of the secular government; in the second case, the individual conscience is bound by the divine command. The difference between these two political claims would come to a head only centuries later, when the Protestant Reformation sought to renew the original Pauline spirituality. Martin Luther developed the first option, John Calvin the second.

The unique position that Paul was trying to stake out contrasts with the classical vision of the political virtues, as is evident in the brief Letter to Philemon. Philemon's slave, Onesimus, had stolen some money from his master in order to travel to Rome to join Paul and his church. In the letter, Paul explains that he is returning Onesimus to his master, offering also to make good the stolen money, and hoping that Philemon will treat the former fugitive with decency. He does not ask that Onesimus be liberated. As in Romans, in Philemon Paul treats slavery as an earthly institution consecrated by God; acceptance of it is obedience to God's will. But Paul adds an admonition to Philemon, who should see his slave "no longer as a slave, but as more than a slave—as a dear brother, very dear indeed to me and how much dearer to you, both as a man and as a Christian." This injunction to treat Onesimus as "more than a slave" suggests that earthly bonds are unimportant. It implies that Christian brotherhood dissolves the reality of public institutions, be they personal slavery or political subordination to the powers that be. During their time together, Paul presumably also convinced Onesimus to accept the fact that although he is a slave in this world, he will be "more than a slave" in another world.

Paul died before any of the Gospels was written and before the Acts of the Apostles, in which he figures prominently, were produced. His letters have remained the source of fruitful controversy because they were pastoral missives that sought to organize particular communities that were attempting to remain Christian while also negotiating their place within the secular Roman Empire. He had to maintain the priority of the spiritual among the believers at the same time that he convinced them that the secular authorities were to be obeyed. Could the church mediate between the profane and the spiritual world by virtue of the fact that it existed as an institution among other secular institutions, yet at the same time follow its true spiritual vocation? Would it be contaminated by the sinful world of the flesh? Or would its otherworldly spirituality make it incapable of consecrating the secular institutions that were a manifestation of the divine will? Its spiritual inwardness inclined the new religion toward an antipolitical self-understanding that was reinforced by its affinities with a transcendent Platonic vision of truth. But in a secular world where politics had lost its legitimacy, Christianity as the source of a new kind of legitimacy was drawn almost in spite of itself to take its place within the world.

◆

How could Christian political thought assert its secular validity when it presupposed that the evils of original sin had made men prisoners of their earthly passions in a world that was the purveyor of the temptations from which the pure soul must flee? Yet this world (and its human inhabitants), as God's creation, had to be understood as at least meant to serve God's purpose, which must be good. Would the same principles of governance apply to the church as to a secular institution? The difficulty arises from the fact that politics and political thought for the classical world were concerned with the ways in which men came to understand their social relations as legitimate. In this case, the source of the authority of political institutions was this-worldly. With the introduction of a creator God, the terms of the political equation changed; the source of the legitimacy of secular relations was now transcendent to them, the object of belief rather than of knowledge, of revelation rather than of reason. Although the church claimed to be God's representative in the profane world, its authority could never be absolute because it was an institution within the fallen world where it and the believers could never fully know the divine will.

Despite its transcendent source of legitimacy, Christian political thought mobilized the legacy of classical political theory as it sought to overcome the Pauline split between the spirit and the letter of the law, which came to be called the "two swords" by which God ruled men and the world. Saint Augustine used Plato and Cicero's conceptual arsenal in order to delimit the legitimate domains of the City of God and the City of Man. As a bishop, however, Augustine had to face two spiritualist movements, the Pelagians and the Donatists, whose refusal of the secular world reflected a challenge to the institutional church at Rome. Centuries later, the "new piety" movement would capture the papacy shortly after the turn of the millennium, creating the conditions for a conflict with the secular ruler of the Holy Roman Empire. The church won this so-called Investiture Struggle, but its victory had the unintended effect of liberating the secular powers to pursue their worldly goals. Political life began to be renewed, acquiring a dignity of its own. It fell to Saint Thomas Aquinas to propose a new synthesis of the sacred and the secular on the basis of the newly rediscovered works of Aristotle. But this synthesis, in turn, was challenged by another mutation of the recurring spiritualism that was part of the legacy of the Pauline foundation of the church. By insisting on the sharp difference between the spiritual and the temporal, the new theology began to prepare the path toward the creation of a modern secular world that would invert the priority previously accorded to the spiritual.

№ 3
THE CONFLICT OF THE SACRED AND THE SECULAR

THE PREVIOUS CHAPTER showed the conditions in which the Catholic church could emerge as an autonomous institution through which people organized their social relations, which in turn changed the conditions in which politics could take place. The relation between church and state cannot be studied in the abstract; they may at times collaborate, at others conflict with one another. External conditions affect their own self-conception. The source of their power or their relative weakness may be sacred or profane, but it cannot be reduced to force or unthinking submission. As in any social relation, the authority of both the church and the state depends on their legitimacy. This authority is not natural; it must be acquired and maintained. Once the church has become autonomous, it must defend its authority over both its members and secular life. The state must similarly preserve its authority over both its citizens and over their religious behavior. As each seeks to legitimate its authority, a conflict of the sacred and the secular occurs. But the triumph of the secular over the sacred or the inverse is only a pyrrhic victory. The church destroys itself if it assumes secular functions, just as the state cannot provide the solace that religion offers. The conflict must continue. That is the lesson this chapter offers.

◆

The first great Christian attempt to interpret the relation of the new religion to the political world was Saint Augustine of Hippo's *City of God*. Augustine[1] explains at the outset that he will refute those who claimed that the adoption of Christianity had weakened the virile fiber of the empire, permitting the marauding Germanic tribes to sack Rome in 410. His systematic justification of the claims of the faith tries to show that Christianity is the true heir to the virtues that had made Rome great. Indeed, he argues that Christian meekness was not responsible for the fall of the empire, but that pagan religious beliefs destroyed the true source of Roman virtue. His ammunition comes particularly from Cicero, whom he cites as having seen the true problem. "But our own time," argued Cicero, "having inherited the commonwealth like a wonderful picture that had faded over time, not only has failed to renew its colors but has not even taken the trouble to preserve at least its shape and outlines. . . . It is because of our own vices, not because of some bad luck, that we preserve the republic in name alone but have long ago lost the substance."[2] This praise of republican values is no accident. Augustine claims that the "City of God" represents the higher and true realization of Rome's secular republic.

The City of God lays claim to more than the republican political heritage; Augustine builds his theology by integrating Plato's unitary philosophical legacy. His Christian version of Plato's *Republic* unites the epochs of all human history, passing from the Creation to the Apocalypse. Eden was the heavenly city, but since the Fall, it has been on a "pilgrimage" that can end only with a return to the City of God. This pilgrimage is secular and political even though its end is spiritual. Although the secular city cannot realize man's ultimate destiny, earthly life and rational thought are not therefore without value. They are, however, limited by the fact of human sin. The relative value of each of the stages reached by the pilgrimage is judged by its closeness to the achievement of the ultimate goal. Finally, in books XXI and XXII, Augustine comes to the Last Judgment, when the wicked will be sent to an eternal hell, and the saints will be resurrected. This conclusion unintentionally puts into question the pilgrimage's secular value, providing potential ammunition for the pagan critics of Christian otherworldliness.

THE TWO CITIES IN THEORY AND PRACTICE

To understand the Christian's obligations in the secular world, it is necessary to see how that believer understands his own faith. Saint Augustine (354–430 CE) explains in his autobiography, *The Confessions*, that his faith is more than just a faith; it is a gift of grace. He records his many failed efforts to find faith. Faith is not the result of a pure will or pious action or of how much one desires it, nor is it an end for which adequate means—provided by the church and its sacraments or by intellectual study—can be found. Faith can come only as a gift given by God's unprovoked grace. That is why, unlike a modern autobiography, *The Confessions* do not glorify Augustine's own unique personality, nor, like the epic poems, does it describe great deeds illustrating the citizen's virtues. Augustine describes his life as that of a sinner lost in a world whose meaning he could not grasp. In this way, his account is the story of God's power and mercy. The experiences he analyzes are not valued for their uniqueness, but as exemplary of the human condition.

The sense of human sinfulness pervades *The Confessions*. In his infancy, when his desires were unsatisfied because what he wanted was not good for him or because he was incapable of making himself understood, Augustine would take his revenge by loud and insistent crying. As a student, he was lazy and hated being forced to read books. Yet he admits, too, that he learned nothing unless compelled. But he also knew that no one who acts against his will, even for a good end, can truly succeed. This realization set up a paradox that he could not understand. The order imposed on him permitted him to develop the curiosity that then led him to learn Latin without the threat of punishment. How could it be that compulsion could produce the desire to learn? The only possible answer, he concluded, is that the discipline imposed is the expression of God's will. "By your laws we are disciplined, from the canes of schoolmasters to the ordeals of martyrs."[3] But God does not always intervene; after all, it was our first parents' disobedience that caused humankind to be forever afflicted by sin.

Augustine did not yet understand God's gift; his life of sin continued. An event from this period seems typical to the older Augustine. With some friends, he climbed into a pear orchard, from which he stole "a huge load" of the fruit. What troubled him is that there was no reason for the theft, no end that could justify it, because he was not even hungry. Clearly, it was the pleasure of doing something wrong—"not the object for which I had fallen but my fall itself." Somewhat later, as a student in Carthage, he would fall in love with love, only to pollute "the spring water of friendship with the filth of concupiscence." When he found a love that was returned, it became only another chain as he was "flogged with the red hot iron rods of jealousy, suspicion, fear, anger, and contention." He was drawn to the theater but had to recognize the "amazing folly" of being part of an audience that is "excited not to offer help, but invited only to grieve" at the spectacle of human suffering placed before it. Then, while continuing his study of rhetoric (where success comes from "deceiving people"), he read "a book by a certain Cicero," the *Hortensius*. The experience "changed my feelings. It altered my prayers, Lord, to be towards you yourself. It gave me different values and priorities." Nevertheless, he continued to teach the liberal arts and remained a Manichean in religion, and he remained also with his mistress, to whom, he adds, he was faithful.[4]

Augustine's career led him next to Rome and then to a better post in Milan. By this time, he had abandoned his Manichean faith, but he still desired "honors, money, marriage." His unhappiness grew, and the Lord made him aware of the depth to which he had fallen when, as he was preparing to deliver a political oration, he came across a drunken beggar with whose "carefree cheerfulness" he compared his own state. "True joy he had not. But my quest to fulfill my ambitions was much falser. . . . [H]e was happy and I racked with anxiety. He had no worries, I was frenetic." His life of sin still continued, though. When his mistress, by whom he had a son, returned to Africa, he found a new one because he was "not a lover of marriage but a slave of lust." He knew that he wanted to believe; he felt close to the decision, but the will to believe could not bring about belief. Finally, the "struggle of myself against myself" came to a head in a garden outside of Milan; the pain was too great, he was moved to tears, and his repeated prayers seemed to find no answer. Through his tears, he heard a voice saying again and again: "Pick up and read, pick up and read."[5] When he obeyed, his eyes fell on a passage from Paul's Letter to the Romans (13:13–14): "Not in riots and drunken parties, not in eroticism and indecencies, not in strife and rivalry, but put on the Lord Jesus Christ and make no provision for the flesh in its lusts." He read no further; his doubt was gone.

This stark contrast between a world without intrinsic meaning that is a trap for the sinful and a church to which the faithful can be called only by divine grace recalls an earlier church father, Tertullian (c. 160–c. 220 CE), who remains famous for his affirmation "Credo quia absurdum" (I believe it because it is absurd). His point was that true religious belief is not susceptible to rational proof; if it were, it would not be belief. This lapidary logic has a corollary: only the believer can receive God's grace, which is not imposed but freely given and freely received. If grace were imposed, there would be no room for human freedom and for the sin it makes possible. This paradoxical logic of faith led Tertullian to ask: "What has Athens to do with Jerusalem?" Do philosophy and religion, reason and faith represent two irreconcilable poles of human life? Is it plausible that a Christian version of the Ciceronian republican political ideal could maintain one foot in Athens, the other in Jerusalem? The title of Augustine's attempt to answer this question, *The City of God*, suggests that the city (*civitas*) is the place where the citizen realizes his virtues. Is God's will to be realized in a city? What kind of city can be a mediator between Athens and Jerusalem?

The Christian in politics faces a fundamental dilemma. Nothing can be expected from the profane world of sinful, feckless men who, left to their own devices, would ruin themselves as well as all those who depend on them. Yet this world is God's creation; the Creator must have envisaged some purpose, some universal and rational end, for His creation that transcends its particular and transitory existence. The believer cannot know this divine telos, but as a political thinker he may wonder whether it is not the end implied by the commandment to "love one's neighbor." How then does the Christian obey that obligation, which is owed to God and not to those he is commanded to love?

With the advent of Christ, the nature of nature changed. For the Greeks, nature was an eternally present, cyclically recurring being whose lawfulness defines the ends for which particular beings, including humans, exist. For the Christian, there exists the promise of a kingdom to come, the notion of a future that will break with the present and a second Creation (or Resurrection) that will be the fulfillment of the divine promise. Two attitudes toward this "Christianized" nature are possible. Either the world has been fundamentally corrupted by sin, in which case the promise can be realized only outside it, in a holy city of the purified believers who have been saved, or this profane world is part of a divine plan in which the believer can find the guidelines for a meaningful life here on earth. The implication of the first vision is that the City of God and the City of Man are incompatible. But what if the neighbor whom the Christian is commanded to love finds himself in need of the healthy benefits of discipline "from the canes of schoolmasters to the ordeals of martyrs," whose benefits Augustine recognized in *The Confessions*? It would seem that secular politics are as necessary in the sinful world as they are useless in the heavenly kingdom.

The citizens of Augustine's two cities are distinguished by their choice to live either by the flesh or by the spirit; in other words, they can live according to human law or God's law. To choose the human law means to accept a world of conflict, envy, and jealousy; it entails division rather than unity; it gives priority to the particular over the universal; and it is always tempted to overreach because it can never achieve a peaceful harmony. To live according to God's law means to love your neighbor not as you would love another person, but to love him in God's way, universally, as a human being. This divine type of love is expressed also by punishing the sinner, disciplining the lazy student, or prosecuting the criminal. Augustine does not recognize that this rigorously universal punitive love can be exercised legitimately only by those who are certain that they have been touched by grace, yet his own experience showed that a person may wish to live according to God's ways but be unable to realize that desire. Nonetheless, the distinction between the two ways of living and loving suggests that obligations that are accepted in particular situations that are subject to change are less truly binding than those obligations that attempt to fulfill the divine command, which is universal and unchanging.

Despite his sharp distinction between the two cities, Augustine is a sober realist and the inventor of the theory of just war. Original sin means that most people will be condemned to the earthly city where strife rules and war is the always present horizon. Life among men is a "hell," but that does not mean that all secular action is equivalent. For example, in *The Confessions,* he distinguishes the discipline that worked on his flesh (e.g., beatings by his teachers) from the erotic lust enjoyed by that same flesh. In *The City of God,* he distinguishes between Jerusalem and Babylon, where God shattered the original unity of humankind because of its proud attempt to scale its tower to the heavens.[6] As a result, secular philosophers speaking different tongues edify theories of desirable earthly goods that are incompatible with one another and incomprehensible to others. The good sought by each is peace, but war is the inevitable result. Yet not all wars are equivalent; in addition to social and civil wars, there are wars like those waged by the Roman Empire. Their effect was "to impose on subject nations not only her yoke, but her language, as a bond of peace." These imperial wars, concludes Augustine, can then be called "just wars," even though they are nonetheless to be "lamented."[7] Christian politics is not a pacifism that simply turns the other cheek as the barbarians advance.

The idea of a just war implies that there are some types of earthly city that can be said to be "good of their kind," even when they are not wholly and truly good. Augustine argues that peace is the good sought by all earthly beings. Peace is the secular city's highest aim. It is the end sought by war, but also by robber bands as well as by the father who imposes harsh discipline on his household. Even the evil man seeks a kind of peace "in that solitary den, the floor of which, as Virgil says, was always reeking with recent slaughter." What, then, is the relation of the earthly city, where peace is based on "the well-ordered concord of civic obedience and rule," to the heavenly city, "or rather the part of it which sojourns on earth and lives by faith"? This heavenly city is "in a state of pilgrimage" during which it makes use of this earthly peace "only because it must, until this mortal condition which necessitates it shall pass away."[8] That is why Augustine justifies the existence of diverse types of earthly city, so long as they ensure peace and do not prohibit worship of the true God.

At this point, Augustine says that he is ready to "fulfill the promise" made in to prove to "our adversaries" that Christianity is not to blame for the fall of Rome.[9] To do so, he will demonstrate the superiority of the heavenly city to even the greatest, because most peaceful, earthly city. He had already pointed out that the pagan gods "never took any steps to prevent the republic from being ruined by immorality." He now recalls the classic Roman definition of a republic—the one Scipio uses in Cicero's *On the Commonwealth*—before going on to demonstrate that Rome had never lived up to those standards. A people whose common "weal" is served by a true republic is not an accidental assembly of people who inhabit a shared place enclosed by walls. To be a people, they must be united by a shared end. In Scipio's words, a people is "an assemblage associated by a common acknowledgement of right and by a community of interests." The shared "right" that binds them can only be justice, to which all other rights are subordinate. "Where, therefore, there is no true justice there can be no right."[10] And where right is absent there can be no people, and hence no republic that secures their "weal."

Thus, concludes Augustine, although Rome may have ensured peace, the wars that gave it power may have been just, and it can even be said to have been good "of its kind," it was not a true republic because all of its citizens were not pursuing a shared end. In this way, Augustine's vision of the heavenly city as the true republic not only appropriates the classical definition of a republic, but it is also Platonic. It condemns the diversity and conflict that Livy and Polybius had seen as the basis of Rome's greatness. Lack of a shared sense of justice, not Christianity, was the source of Rome's fall.

How then does the heavenly city attain its unity? How does it overcome the divisive forces of the earthly city? Augustine returns to his earlier argument that Rome's rule over its provinces was good because it prevented lawless men from doing harm. He now adds that "they became worse and worse so long as they were free, [whereas now] they will improve by subjection." Their servitude is just and right in the same way that God rules man, the soul rules the body, and reason rules the passions. The higher should govern the lower, universality is superior to particularity, and unity must be imposed on diversity. Augustine now adds a Christian qualification to this classical logic, arguing that servitude is useful only "to some." The few who benefit from it are those who aspire to live by the spirit but are unable to realize their desire without supranatural help. Left to their own devices, their freedom has cast them adrift in the world of sin because only the soul that serves God can exercise a right control over the body. If justice is lacking in individuals, "certainly there can be none in a community composed of such persons."[11] That is why the heavenly city is in fact the true republic. Its citizens are selfless servants of a religious truth, just as the Guardians in Plato's *Republic* served philosophical truth.

What is to become of the City of Man? On the one hand, Augustine accepts the distinction between the two swords, each ruling its own sphere as a direct representative of the divine will. On the other hand, his recognition that some secular states are superior to others because they preserve peace (or make only just wars) apparently opens the possibility of a Christian—or at least a just—politics within the secular city. This engagement with the profane political world is paradoxically made possible because of Augustine's faith that only the City of God can be the true city. The implication is that a Christian should not expect that the secular state can or ought to make men just. As a result, the Christian cannot denounce the state for not doing what it was never intended to do; rather, expecting nothing from the secular world, he should look at the state coolly, remembering that peace is the most that it can ensure, and judge that it is good as it is. And when his love of his neighbor demands that he agree that the state must punish that neighbor, he does so both from a love of God and for the good of his neighbor. The punishment that is imposed will have a deterrent effect, preventing crime and thus serving peace. In this way, secular politics and religious obligation overlap in that "pilgrimage" during which the heavenly city sojourns in the profane world.

◆

Augustine's political theology maintains the distinction between the secular and the sacred in order to motivate the active participation of the faithful in the earthly pilgrimage. The appearance of two radical movements within the church threatened the creative tension between the two cities. The Pelagians argued that original sin did not prevent men from exercising their will to choose freely the means to their salvation. This view not only undermined the mystery of divine grace, but also challenged the separation of the secular and the sacred on which Augustine's politics was based. The second movement, the Donatists, was unwilling to accept the Augustinian idea that there could be a religious justification for action in the profane world, and they challenged the purity of church representatives, arguing that their compromises made them unfit to exercise their sacral role. Augustine replied to both movements repeatedly in pamphlets and sermons. Although the church declared the two movements heretical, the questions they raised have returned repeatedly in the history of political thought.

The Pelagian criticism challenged the legitimacy of the church's doctrinal rule over the congregation. At a practical level, it asked how converts could be recruited (and members retained) if God's mysterious grace alone held the keys to heaven. The church needed to be able to offer a reward for the efforts made to follow its doctrine. The believers needed to be assured that their faithful practice would have real results. Augustine's complicated argument that faith was needed to recognize God's grace, but that true faith was found only by means of God's grace seemed either self-contradictory or absurd. His assertions that grace cannot be earned because man's finite and sinful understanding can never know the mind of God and that man's reason is too weak and corrupted to understand the divine will left no role for the participants in the body of the church. To be legitimate, the church would have to promise that men can use their reason to pass beyond the rational to the supernatural, beyond the secular to the sacred, and beyond their finite lives to eternal salvation. There would be no need for God's mysterious grace in a world that He had created but left to humans and their rational capacities.

Augustine's critique of the Pelagian theology accuses it of falling victim to the sin of pride. How can finite men think that they can understand the infinite, that the creature can understand the purposes of the Creator, and that the individual can know more than all of biblical revelation and the body of teachings of the church universal? Further, this theology denies both the consequences of Adam's fall and the lesson of Jesus's suffering. The power it attributes to reason denies that humans' capacities are affected by original sin, and it does not understand that only the resurrection of the suffering son can wipe away that sin. What is more, the Donatists' doctrine of a free will that can be used not just for evil but also for good is a form of self-deception that is heretical because it would make the church into a mere means to salvation, prescribing the rituals to be accomplished by the faithful in order to reach an end that transcends it.

There is, however, a slippage in the last part of Augustine's refutation. If the church is not to be simply a means to achieve a goal that is supernatural, does the church itself become an end? Is it the "true republic" that stands opposed to all of the earthly kingdoms that can only be good of their kind? The difficulty is that if faith is the criterion that distinguishes the believer, and if only God's grace can confer such faith, what is to hold together the church during its pilgrimage? How are the individual believers to be united? Despite these problems in his argument, Augustine was able to convince a church council at Carthage to condemn Pelagianism. He could apply the political logic that he had used in his justification of the subordination of the provinces to Roman power because "as they became worse and worse so long as they were free . . . they will improve by subjection." Now the needed subjection was to be exercised by the institutional church over those who were deemed heretics because their free use of reason flattered the creature while denying the Creator. This reasoning implies that the church, like Rome, is an end that is "good of its kind"—in other words, that its function is in itself also political.

The spark that lighted the fires of the Donatist controversy was more directly political. Although Constantine legalized Christianity in 313, it remained one religion among many in a vast empire, where it suffered periodic bouts of persecution. As a result of this persecution, some priests or bishops left the church or conformed outwardly while maintaining their private faith. When Theodosius finally made Christianity the state religion in 391, upper-class people began to join or return to the church to gain the worldly benefits conferred by membership. Many a well-born Roman who might previously have sought a career in politics could now rise in the church hierarchy, gaining status as well as wealth. Those concerned with salvation and who sought to live by the spirit rather than the flesh were scandalized by this activity The many clear cases of hypocrisy were the impetus behind Donatism. The problem for Augustine was that the mysteries of faith and grace meant that it was impossible to know who was truly saved and who was truly a hypocrite conforming only ritually..

This political background explains the simplicity of the Donatist faith. Both the church and the empire represented claims to universality to which the Donatists opposed the subjective purity of their own belief. They denied the legitimacy of any churchman who was not truly pure and uncompromised. This insistence on the purity of the priesthood implied that a sacrament delivered by an unworthy priest was itself invalid. It followed that the priests who had been consecrated by bishops who had denied their faith under persecution or those who had compromised themselves with the empire were illegitimate. The Donatist attack didn't stop at the apex of the hierarchy; it argued that anyone who had been baptized by such priests was also to be excluded from the church's communion. As a result, the Donatists denounced as illegitimate the whole church as it presently existed and stoked the resentment of potential followers by adding to the stress on their own purity the pressure to join a campaign to uncover hypocrisy in the church and to denounce its alliance with an alien power infringing on the rights of the simple people. The Donatists did not hesitate to use violence and unleash terror: a Roman minister was assassinated, priests were killed, people were blinded by acid while wavering, and followers of the sect were threatened with harm if they left the group.[12]

Augustine's reply to the Donatists is both theological and political. Because no man can read into the soul of another, the accusation of hypocrisy is at best a two-edged sword. How can the accuser know that he himself is not guilty of hypocrisy? He pretends to be truly pious, but has he actually received the divine grace without which his gestures and rituals are only illusory? Can he not be deceiving himself? As Saint Paul reminded the Romans (Romans 12:19), "Vengeance is mine, I will repay, saith the Lord." To this religious refutation, Augustine adds an important political argument. The distinction between the two cities implies that any particular priest officiating during the pilgrimage through the earthly city is administering a sacrament whose efficacy comes from Christ. The particular occupant of an official function is merely the temporary embodiment of the office; he belongs to the office, not the office to him. The office is universal; the priest is its particular occupant whose power comes from its authority and not from himself. Along with Augustine's theory of just war, this political concept of "office" makes clear that the difference between the two cities does not make them independent of each other.

At the outset of the Donatist conflict, Augustine had appealed to logical argument and examples from Scripture. But as the violence continued, the bishop of Hippo began to reconsider. The duty of secular power, after all, is to preserve peace; that is the only justice that can be rendered here on earth. It follows that the state should intervene in order to restore peaceful relations even within the church insofar as the church is also an institution within the secular world. But if it does interfere in church matters, how will that change the autonomy of both partners, church and state, in their relation with one another?

To justify the state's intervention in matters that concerned the church, it was necessary to show that the state would be acting at the behest of the church, which in that way maintained its autonomy. Perhaps thinking of experiences described in the *Confessions,* Augustine distinguished between a punishment that prevents a person from doing harm to himself or to others and a punishment that compels a person to do good. Consistent with his theology, he recognized that it is not possible to force a person to believe, but he saw that there are types of punishment that can lead that person to reflect on the reason he is being punished. State action against the heretics would seem to fit that criteria. In this case, the church defines the heretical beliefs, the state acts against the heretics, and the hoped for result is that the individual decides to abandon the heretical belief. So it was that the Donatists were outlawed within the empire, and the Roman Church reaffirmed its supremacy. But Augustine's justification of state intervention in church affairs soon led to new conflicts.

THE CONFLICT OF THE TWO CITIES BECOMES A REALITY

The idea of a "dark age" in European history that began after the final fall of Rome in the mid–sixth century is an ideological invention. Protestant reformers of the sixteenth century used the idea in order to claim that the Reformation was bringing the renewal of an authentic Christianity that had been degraded by centuries of papal corruption. At about this same time, the humanists of the Renaissance who were rediscovering classical civilization contended that they too were overcoming a time of stagnation during which the human spirit had lost its way. The modern scientific worldview that wanted to study nature as it truly was in order to use it for human purposes rather otherworldly ends began to emerge during this same time period. Each of these innovative projects hid from itself its radical newness by linking itself to a glorious past, which gave it a source of legitimacy that transcended the conflictual tensions from which it had emerged. Yet the millennium called the "Dark Age," from around 500 to 1500 CE, was not simply a period of stagnation; it was a span of time when conflicts were ripening, institutions were forming, and social life was being recomposed. Although it is impossible to do more than sketch some of the turning points during this long gestation, it is important to mark at least some of the moments at which political thought and political history produced new combinations.

Imperial Rome had never truly conquered the Germanic tribes, who began to spill back across the Rhine. A year after Augustine's death, the Vandals conquered Hippo in northern Africa. Two decades later, the hordes of Attila the Hun took Rome. Wars of conquest and plunder continued, sometimes accompanied by a patina of theological justification, although it was rarely the decisive motivation. Some sort of legitimating power was needed to impart a sense of social order. Pope Gelasius I (died 496, served 492–496) tried to establish the church's superiority over the state by appropriating for religious usage the classical Roman distinction between *auctoritas* (the authority located in the Senate, which the church now claimed) and *potestas* (the power delegated by the people, which the church now attributed to the state). Although Gelasius's intent was to keep the state out of church affairs, his use of these classical republican concepts to justify the church's authority over the merely delegated power held by temporal authorities was a reaffirmation of the Augustinian argument that it was the church's task to direct for its own purposes the state's activities. Gelasius's theory lived on in the political and theological arsenal of the papacy, which used it to fend off repeated challenges from the secular powers.

Rome's great rival, Constantinople, developed another interpretation of the relation between church and state. This city, created by the emperor who gave it its name, stood at the head of the wealthier and more civilized Eastern Empire, which included Greece and Asia Minor. Located on the trade route between Europe to Asia and linking the Mediterranean to the Black Sea, the city had long enjoyed commercial prosperity, and its geographical site had protected it from marauding armies (until it fell finally to the Ottomans in 1453). The government of the Byzantine Empire (as the Eastern Empire came to be called) was built on the unity of church and state, both of which were understood as expressing one of the equal persons of the Trinity, none of which competed with the other.[13] Under the long rule of Justinian from 527 to 585, the economically prosperous Eastern Empire undertook a vast legal reform. Because the emperor was considered the representative of God on earth, whereas the church was confined to the spiritual domain, the Justinian Code (as these laws came to be known) treated the ruler as the source of law, its maker, and its interpreter at once. When the West discovered this code in the eleventh century, it used the code's centralizing structure at first to strengthen the papacy. It was not long, however, before the emerging secular states began to apply the logic of the code to reinforce the monarch's power over his feudal retainers, eventually contributing to the creation of the modern centralized state.

Meanwhile, in the desolate West, where politics had no public stage to play on because urban life had disappeared, the only community that reflected Aristotle's distinction between the physical world of necessity and the autonomy of the good life was the monastery. Although the monastic instinct was not specific to Christianity, and the earliest Christian monks were solitary seekers, their action acquired an unintended political role. Often from well-to-do families, educated, and cultivated, the monks felt the need for a simpler, more spiritual existence. The experience of Saint Anthony (c. 251–356), considered the founder of eremitic monasticism, is illustrative. He withdrew from society in pursuit of a contemplative life, but his reputation as a holy man spread. Pilgrims were drawn to his place of retreat, begging him to give them instruction. He accepted this charge as a task of love, but the contradiction between the responsibility to his fellow Christians and his personal quest led him to withdraw still farther into the desert. Others shared Anthony's dilemma and opted for the lonely search for spiritual fulfillment. It eventually became clear, though, that the path of solitary salvation was not possible; the lonely quest could lead to forms of psychological derangement as the believer sank ever deeper into his particular spiritual devotion. Some sort of sociality had to be provided as a check on idiosyncratic experiences that could be a form of self-deception, if not the work of the devil himself!

The great founder of the cenobitic monastic movement, Saint Benedict of Nursia (480–547), had himself attempted the path of solitary spirituality before realizing the harm that could arise from extreme asceticism. Benedict accepted the need for collective life, establishing a monastery at Monte Cassino in the early sixth century. The detailed rules for the Benedictine Order that he founded regulated the life of its members by a code of discipline and authority. No variation was allowed; the day was divided into regular periods of work and worship; meals were taken in silence while religious texts were read. This regularity of obedience and devotion was a reflection of the spiritual harmony and purification that the monk imposed on himself. The Benedictine rules served also as a check on the eccentric forms of solitary spirituality, providing the kind of universality promised by the Christian message of salvation.

The success of the monastic experience contained the seeds of difficulties that threatened its foundation. The monks' spirituality, which permeated their daily work and prayer, created a religious aura that gave the still superstitious population the impression that these holy men were in closer contact with the deity than they themselves. The monastic communities seemed to be earthly manifestations of a heavenly city (which is one reason why monks were called "regular clergy" as distinct from the secular priests who worked and lived among the people). Kings and nobles endowed the monasteries with lands and even with indentured laborers in the expectation that monastic mediation would affect the future of their souls. In time, the monasteries became wealthy, and their fortunes were multiplied still further by their regular and efficient mode of living. Abbots became local powers who were gradually drawn into the society around them as it was beginning to emerge from its desolate status. The monks themselves began to use their monopoly of learning to assume administrative roles in the emerging political institutions. Contrary to what Benedict had intended, his "black monks," whose dark robes were a sign of humility, came slowly to play a central role in the emerging political order between 550 and 1150.[14]

At the outset of this period, Europe was a field of war. The continent had been severely depopulated and left with few military forces; it stood as an open invitation to energetic peoples seeking new territories. After the death of Mohammed in 632, Islam began a triumphant century of conquests. These victories, which left Islam the dominant force in the wealthy eastern Mediterranean, destroyed what was left of the urban cultural base of the Roman Empire. Then the isolated landed estates that remained in the West became easy prey for the marauding Vikings from Scandinavia, who were joined by fierce Celtic warriors seeking booty. By the eighth century, the Germanic tribes, in particular the Franks, became the dominant force in the West, but their reach was limited because their domination was based only on force. In order to establish themselves, these warriors needed more than their arms and the administrative aid of some literate monks. They needed spiritual legitimacy, which could come only from the papacy.

The crucial moment came during the long reign of Charlemagne (742–814), who ruled from 768 to 814. The grandson of Charles Martel (c. 688–741), whose armies had stopped the Islamic advance at Tours in 732, Charlemagne had an ancestral political legitimacy. His conquest of most of Europe established his material power, but it needed to be reinforced by the acquisition of spiritual authority. So it was that on the morning of Christmas Day in 800 the pope crowned him *imperator romanorum*. Charlemagne may have promised to support the pontiff against his enemies in exchange for this benediction, or the pope may have seen the benediction as a reaffirmation of the Gelasian doctrine of papal supremacy, bestowing the crown as an affirmation that the church is the source of the *auctoritas* to which the *potestas* of the state remains subordinate. Whatever the intent, Charles was now the Holy Roman emperor, but the existence of this new role did not put an end to the conflict of the two swords that had confronted Christianity since the time of Saint Paul.

The opposition between emperor and pope continued for centuries as each sought signs of weakness in the other's position. The emperor's secular power was limited by the lack of unity among the nobility on whose force he was dependent, and the pope's religious authority was challenged by clergy who found his worldly ambitions to be in contradiction with his spiritual role. The decisive moment in this conflict was announced by the emergence of a movement called the "new piety" that not only challenged the rot at the top of the church, but demanded a broader moral reform, focusing, for example, on the priestly failure to observe the obligation of celibacy. The election of a new pope, Gregory VII (c. 1015/1029–1085, served 1073–1085), crowned the movement's success. Riding this wave of reform, Gregory was confident in his own strength and ready to challenge the emperor's writ. The issue that he chose for the decisive battle was the investiture of church officers. Would the church control nominations (and thus free itself from the corruption and worldliness that had called forth the reform), or would the state—in the person of the Holy Roman emperor, whose authority was consecrated by God—have that responsibility? Both sides called on their theologians and assembled their arguments. The problem that had not been resolved when Saint Augustine appealed for state support against the heretics and to which the Gelasian theory asserted rather than enforced a response could no longer be finessed. Theory was no help; the test of force had arrived.

The story of the papal victory in this struggle regarding investiture is well known. Emperor Henry IV (reigned 1084–1105) claimed that it was his obligation to defend the church by naming the replacement of the bishop of Milan, an important and well-funded administrative post. Gregory denounced this claim as an illegitimate political intervention into church affairs. He threatened Henry with excommunication if he did not withdraw his nominee. Henry, who felt strong after his recent defeat of his own rebellious barons, replied with a defiant threat. Gregory took up the gauntlet, sending agents to Germany to stir up the defeated nobility and their peasant supporters. At the same time, he threatened to excommunicate the German clergy if they backed Henry. These two measures had the desired effect: support for Henry dried up rapidly. What was he to do? Gregory was moving north, threatening to convene an assembly of the nobility to remove the excommunicated emperor. Henry had but one choice: he needed to gain papal absolution, so he set out on the road to Canossa in 1077, the castle where Gregory had stopped on his move north. The proud ruler is said to have waited three days in the snow before the pope—who was bound by church doctrine to accord absolution to any sincere penitent—agreed to receive and pardon him. Henry retained his throne, but Gregory now controlled the church.

Gregory's victory in the Investiture Struggle brought unintended consequences. Having won control over itself, the church began to apply the recently rediscovered Justinian Code to create the canon law rules needed to establish its self-governance. This application ensured the primacy of the Roman pontiff, who ruled the church as the emperor had ruled his domains. But the same argument by which the church defended its right to govern itself according to its own laws free from interference from the secular world put into question its ability to continue to exercise authority over the political state. The purity that the church had fought to achieve prohibited it from soiling or compromising itself by intervening in secular life. Of course, the distinction between church and state was not fixed or rigid. The last gasp of the "new piety" came in 1095, when Pope Urban II (served 1088–1099) called on the forces of Christendom to undertake the First Crusade to push back the threat of Islam and to retake Jerusalem.

From his side, the emperor (and other secular rulers) began to use the Justinian Code for secular purposes by creating legal institutions over which the emerging state could reign supreme. A trained bureaucracy was needed to realize this project. It was in this context that universities began to be created (at Bologna in 1088, then in Paris and a bit later at Oxford). Their major function was to teach the law, which both secular and religious rulers used. Legal institutions created universal rules that could break down the chain of personal loyalties characteristic of feudal society. But the creation of universities produced also an unintended effect: they not only broke the monopoly of the monasteries on the provision of administrative staff, but also became a place for critical debate that injected a dynamism into what had still been a traditional society fixed in its old ways. With the rediscovery of the works of Aristotle at this time, the Platonic theology that had devalued the temporal world as merely a passing stage on the pilgrimage to the heavenly city was challenged. The Aristotelian distinction among types of rule made it impossible to accept the Augustinian idea that secular rule was merely "good of its kind" because it ensured peace. New standards of legitimacy were therefore needed. For the moment, these new standards had to operate within a Christian theological framework, but their effect would transform the inherited idea of the relation between the secular and the sacred. Like their Donatist ancestors, the adherents of the new piety would not disappear from history, and, as will be seen, their Franciscan heirs threatened the new synthesis between the secular and the sacred established by Saint Thomas Aquinas's integration of Aristotle into Christian theology.

◆

In the twelfth and thirteenth centuries, however, the secular state's autonomy still lay in the future. Although Aristotle's political theory distinguished among types of rule, his hierarchical vision of the natural world led him to argue that the most inclusive type of rule was its highest form and that this type of rule should dominate over the lower, less-inclusive forms. Thomas Aquinas used this presupposition to justify the priority of the papacy over the secular ruler in his essay *On Kingship*. Thomas explains that "those who are responsible for intermediate ends should be subject to the one who is responsible for the ultimate end, and be directed by his command." Under what he calls the Old Law, he admits that "priests were subject to kings," but the New Law brings "a higher priesthood that leads men to the joys of heaven, so that under the law of Christ, kings should be subject to priests."[15] Although Thomas continued to defend the authority of the papacy, the grand theory of his *Summa theologica* can be seen as providing the common ground that would for the moment overcome the conflict between the secular and the sacred, clearing the path for the emancipation of the secular state.

NATURAL LAW AND THE DYNAMIC INTEGRATION OF THE TWO CITIES

The century that followed the Investiture Struggle is often called the "Renaissance of the Twelfth Century."[16] It was the time of the great Gothic cathedrals that crowned the renewal of commercial trade and urban life. It was the age during which recognizable nation states began to take shape in England and France. For its part, the church sought to introduce new rigor and regularity in the work of its secular clergy, codifying the sacraments (specifically marriage and the obligation of regular confession), exercising greater control over the priests in the parishes, and, as a result, interfering increasingly in parishioners' daily lives. As is often the case, the rapid social change and new prosperity called forth a spiritual reaction in the church, which was the moral arbiter that people were accustomed to consult. The reformers denounced the rituals imposed by the new sacramental order as formal and lifeless. If salvation depended on a faith that was crowned by grace, the reformers asked, what need did the sacraments fill (other than creating revenue for the clergy)? Indeed, some went further, asking what need the church itself satisfied. The prestige and power of the regular clergy cloistered in monastic orders only increased an unease felt particularly in the lower orders of society, which had not benefited from the new prosperity.

In response to the challenge to the church, the pope approved the creation of two new religious orders, the Dominicans and the Franciscans, at the beginning of the thirteenth century. Not cloistered, these orders were mendicant and preaching communities sent into the world to do the work of the Lord. Although Saints Dominick and Francis were known principally as preachers, the great names among their followers were teachers as the Dominicans came to dominate the University of Paris, and the Franciscans became anchored at Oxford. The difference between the two orders is seen in their attitude toward property. The critical Franciscans stressed the virtues of poverty, but the Dominicans argued that property is morally neutral, its value depending on its use because poverty itself does not make a person holy. This contrast illustrates the Franciscans' greater emphasis on spirituality as they led the critics of the rationalism propounded by the Dominican Thomas Aquinas (1225–1274).

The universities established to train the administrators of both church and state became battlegrounds where critical thought and religious tradition clashed. The fact that professors were paid by their students, who were free to attend the courses they chose, introduced a competitive climate that both encouraged excellence and created jealousies that could poison the wells of learning. The major bone of contention was the newly recovered works of Aristotle, which challenged the traditional Platonic worldview as it had been adapted to the needs of Christian theology. Aristotle had no idea of a creator god and no notion of original sin. For him, the soul gave form only to this particular body, which meant that there is no possibility of its resurrection. The world as he envisioned it is regulated by cause and effect, which leaves no possibility of miracles. And because the good life can be created in the polis, there is no need to search for a heavenly city. It should therefore be no surprise to learn that the University of Paris banned Aristotle's work in 1210, again in 1215, and yet again in 1231. Yet the very fact that it had to be banned three times in such a short period underlines its attractive power to inquiring minds.

Thomas Aquinas's task was to make Aristotle, to whom he refers simply as "the Philosopher," safe for the church. Thomas had proven his dedication to the church by his decision to join the Dominicans in their combat against the antisacerdotal reformers. His wealthy and politically influential family had finally accepted his choice to serve the church but assumed that he would join the wealthy and politically influential Benedictine Order. Thomas persisted in his choice, however, fleeing to Paris, where he studied with Albert the Great, the leading Dominican intellectual, who arranged a university post for him. The man who set out to refute the subjectivism and mysticism of the potentially schismatic church reformers went on to produce a high-powered synthesis that is justly titled the *Summa theologica* (Summary of Theology)—a reconciliation of philosophy and theology, the secular and the sacred, the City of Man and the City of God. This opus is divided into 512 questions, which are in turn subdivided into 2,669 articles or theses, themselves broken down into 10,000 objections and replies to these objections. Yet the author of this demonstration of the Catholic faith's rationality is said to have had a mystical experience near the end of his life, crying out that "all that I have written now seems like straw." Indeed, the final part of the work remained incomplete at his death.

Thomas's reconciliation of the Philosopher and Christian theology is illustrated by his attempt to recognize the secular state's increasing autonomy without abandoning the church's superior mission. The improvement of social conditions challenged Augustine's description of the state as a glorified band of robbers that, by preserving peace regardless of its institutional form, was said to be "good of its kind." The new secular states were using their capacity to frame laws to regulate relations among people. What made these regulations legitimate? They could not be simply the expression of the absolute monarch's will, nor could they be treated as the direct expression of the divine will. The ruler could not be said to be answerable to his people, but as God's representative in the secular world he was responsible for them. As a result, a new legal theory was necessary to weave together the sacred and the secular. In Thomas's formulation, the sacred is expressed in both the universal form called eternal law and in the particular revelations of divine law; the secular is governed by universal natural law as expressed in the particular forms of human law.

The general status of the law has first to be distinguished from the particular legal systems regulating feudal, canon, Roman, royal, and commercial law. To give systematic structure to this diversity, Thomas poses four general questions. The first is whether law is the expression of reason rather than the arbitrary result of force, accident, or even divine providence. The second question analyzes the end sought by the law because the telos, or goal, for which a thing exists gives it meaning and distinguishes it from apparently similar things. The third concerns the legitimacy of the makers of the law because the relation between the reasons for the law and the ends sought by that law cannot be arbitrary, accidental, or providential. Finally, criticizing implicitly the new piety's appeal to unwritten laws in the heart of all humans, Thomas asks whether laws must be promulgated to ensure that they have a public and universal rather than a private or particular character.

This first set of questions is only the beginning of the process; answers to them can be found by a careful reader of Cicero. The proposed definition of law is both too general and too secular. Thomas has to show further how the sacred joins with the secular to produce a specifically Christian understanding of law, which is what ultimately assures its legitimacy. To realize this task, he has to distinguish the kinds of law that belong to the sacred from those that are applicable only to the secular domain. His theory will then have to meet a double test: it will have to show its capacity to formulate just laws in the profane world, and it will have to demonstrate the limits of secular law by defining the place left for grace. In this way, the laws can be said to be both legitimate and yet limited in their reach.

Thomas, like Aristotle, begins by defining his concepts. A law is a rule or guideline for action, which it either commands or forbids. It may lead you to pay a debt, or it may forbid you from killing your neighbor or coveting his wife. The fact that the term *lex* (law) is a cognate of the word *ligare* (to bind) suggests that the law acts by binding all those whom it governs. If it is truly to bind, it must do so in a way that is universal because law cannot be obeyed simply as a matter of habit, the result of constraint, or simple external necessity, all of which are particular and need not exist. That is why Thomas goes on to insist that the law binds because it is an expression of reason. Reason governs action doubly: it sets ends, and once they are set, it again intervenes to determine the proper means to attain those ends. All acts of will are thus intentional: they are self-motivated, and they are guided by reason. This dual use of reason—to determine the end sought by action and then to discover the proper means to reach that end—is called "right reason." The force of this claim is seen in Thomas's reply to the sophistic argument that law is simply "what pleases the ruler." That claim is valid only when the ruler's will is defined by reason, not when it imposes its law by the force of arms.

These definitions imply that the end sought by a law guided by reason must be universal, which implies further that the law seeks the common good rather than any particular gain. It might be objected that because it is individuals who act, their actions are always concerned with particular matters. It might also be said that individuals acting for their particular ends use reason only in order to find the best means to reach those ends. Thomas admits these objections but also recalls Aristotle's insistence that individuals are parts of a whole to which they relate as the imperfect to the perfect. Because the part cannot exist without the whole, the whole is more perfect because more encompassing. On this basis, he can reply to the objections. The law affects the individual insofar as he is a part of the community and does so because it is concerned with the community's happiness, which is the common good. If the laws were not concerned with what is good for all individual members of the community—the common good—there would be no way to ensure that all of them will obey it. But this point leads to a new problem. If it is admitted that each individual seeks his own particular good, who is it that can determine the good that will be valid for the entire community? How is the lawgiver to know the common good?

Knowing that the entire community must benefit from law does not explain how the lawmaker functions. The regulation of the common good must logically fall either to the whole people or to someone who can represent the whole people because "the directing of anything to the end concerns him to whom the end belongs."[17] Thomas defends the representative function of monarchy, whose justification is based on the idea that the part depends on the whole, which is represented by the monarch. The defense of monarchy is not, however, his main concern here; he is not presenting a theory of how government works, but rather an analysis of what makes it legitimate. His concern is also to refute the antisacerdotal heirs to the new piety who deny the church's representative role, oppose the spirit of the laws to their letter, and appeal to a law of nature inscribed in the hearts of men. He cites and refutes several of their arguments. For example, to the objection that if the law is to lead men to virtue, then anyone—not just church or state authorities—can help a friend achieve this goal, Thomas replies that private persons can only give advice, which may or may not lead to virtue; they cannot make laws that regulate virtue universally. For this reason, not only must the lawgiver represent the community, but the laws, to be legitimate, must also be promulgated publicly and be knowable by all.

After this definition of the nature of law, Thomas turns to the distinction among the types of law, each of which is determined by the different ends for which it exists. In order to reconcile the Greek view of the natural world as eternal with the Christian vision of a creator, he distinguishes between eternal law and divine law. Eternal law can be said to be God's thought before the Creation. The universe bears silent witness to the divine reason imprinted in it. But men, who have been created, are lesser beings than their creator. As a result, they are not governed directly by eternal law; they have to use their finite reason to try to understand the will of God. In this way, men discover what Thomas calls "natural law," whose universality has then to be adapted to particular cases by means of human law. But the finitude of reason means that there will be instances that defy human lawmaking capacity. That is the place of divine law, which is the expression of God's love and mercy in the revelations of religion, whose truth lies beyond all human capacity. The interrelation of these four types of law apparently permits Thomas to overcome the distinction between the secular and the sacred.

The first three types of law lie within the reach of finite human reason. Although the created world is finite, human reason reflects the fact that men still have a spark of the divine in them. Their reason permits them to interpret the eternal law, which they cannot know directly. The result of their reasoning is natural law, which thus participates in the eternal law even though it is not identical with it. Natural law expresses men's finite understanding of what the order of the universe reveals about God's eternal laws. The problem is that natural laws—for example, the command to worship God because we owe devotion to that which is superior to us or the interdiction to murder because the life of another person belongs to God—are universal rules that come with no instruction manual for their application to particular cases. This is where human law, although limited by divine law, enters the Thomist legal architecture.

How can rules made by finite and fallible, particular and sinful humans have the quality of law? How can human reason, which itself was created, claim to create a world of laws by which to govern itself? Thomas applies the logic of Aristotle to these questions. Just as humans use their naturally given reason to understand the natural law, so too can they use that reason to move "from general and indemonstrable principles [of natural law] . . . to certain particular determinations of the laws."[18] Doing so will produce human laws that are valid only in the particular conditions for which they are formulated. Although they are laws, they don't have the degree of universality of a natural law and still less that of eternal law. As laws, human laws apply universally, but only to the particular conditions for which they were made. That means that they are subject to change.[19] Although the interaction of natural law with its formulation in terms of human law would later become fundamental to the West's legal and the political dynamic, Thomas's concern with the reconciliation of the two cities leads him to stress a different problem: the way in which the human law relates to the divine law.

Divine law expresses the rules by which men must act in order to achieve their final end, which is salvation. Because unaided human reason cannot perform this function, it must be supplemented by revelation. Revealed truth is needed also because human laws developed to deal with the variety of particular and contingent matters that face men in their everyday existence will themselves be diverse and perhaps contradictory, leaving men uncertain of the proper rules to be followed in particular cases. Furthermore, humans can err, whereas the divine does not. Recalling the need for laws to be promulgated, Thomas adds that human laws concern things that can be judged by others, who have to apply the laws. But that means that human laws regulate only external behavior, not private thoughts and intentions. As a result, human law is limited to the public sphere; the rest of man's existence—for the Christian, no doubt the most important part—remains the province of divine law.

This limitation that divine law imposes on human law has an important positive implication that illustrates the relation of legitimation and limitation. Thomas's argument here recalls Aristotle's critique of Plato's Guardians. If human law tries to punish or prohibit all evil actions, it will also inevitably eliminate many good things, whatever its intentions. By overreaching in that way, human law violates the very definition of law, which is said to exist for the common good of society. The Christian lawgiver can accept this limitation because he knows that sin will not go unpunished because divine law promises that God's judgment, although merciful, will also be just. By accepting this limit, human law ensures its own legitimacy, avoiding the temptation to overreach.

This general philosophical theory has practical political implications. Thomas applies it, for example, to the question of the justification and limits of private property, which divided the Franciscan and Dominican orders. He begins from the most simple definition—property is an external thing—and moves to more complex and contested issues. As a thing, property is God's creation and therefore not subject to human disposition, but it exists also for the use—that is, for the ends—of humans, who, as the Bible says, are to have "dominion" over "the fishes of the sea . . . and over every creeping thing that creepeth upon the earth" (Genesis 1:26). What is more, the use of external things is perfectly natural because, as the Philosopher says, the imperfect is there for the more perfect—that is, dumb material is there for rational human use. But this is only a first step in the analysis; a further step takes into consideration that the things of the world are not there for arbitrary usage. What uses are legitimate? And what makes them legitimate?

The first question to ask when evaluating the rules that regulate the procurement and the distribution of the things that can become property is whether all property should be private, or are some things to be held by the community? After all, the individual monks who took a vow of poverty benefit from their order's wealth. Aquinas first offers three justifications of private property that develop Aristotle's critique of Plato's "communism." People take more care of what belongs to them than they do of things that are shared by the community. Also, if they know that the work that needs to be done will be for the community, they are less inclined to do it themselves. Second, when one person is given responsibility for a particular thing or task, the work will be done in a more orderly way; knowing who is responsible for what ensures that each person will take care of his assigned duty. Third, when each person has his own property, he will tend to be content with what he has, knowing that it is and will remain his own.

This justification of private property is put into question by the general analysis of the legitimate uses of external things.[20] It would seem that their benefits should go to the collectivity in order to ensure that those in need share in the goods that result from using these creations of God. In this sense, natural law seems to prescribe common possession and to oppose private property. That was also the monastic model. But Thomas has given three solid practical reasons that not only support the usefulness of private property to humankind, but show also the costs of collective ownership. To escape this dilemma, he asks whether there is another way to realize the imperatives of natural law. Can there be human laws that establish and regulate the nature and limits of private property in a way that is not opposed to natural law, but is instead an addition to it made by human reason?

The dynamic interplay of human and natural law begins from the premise that human law cannot violate natural (or divine) law, but also that it is not identical with either of them. This premise implies that although human law can protect some private property, its protection is not guaranteed by a natural law. Not every external object can become private property. Unlimited accumulation may not serve real needs, but instead selfish, private greed, and there are some things that serve only collective rather than individual needs. Human laws that regulate private property are the product of specific circumstances, which can change. For example, one benefit of private property is that each individual will work harder and take more responsibility for what is his own property. In this way, the human law brings rewards that the natural law of sharing fails to offer. But this success has unintended consequences. Those working for their own benefit may acquire a surplus of goods, whereas others are left in a state of poverty. In this case, natural law commands that some of the private wealth be used to aid the poor. Although Thomas doesn't explain what human laws would actually put that natural law into practice, he does affirm that if the "need be so manifest and urgent . . . then it is lawful for a man to succor his own need by means of another's property, by taking it either openly or secretly, nor is this properly speaking theft or robbery."[21]

This same process is seen in Thomas's consideration of the political problem of legitimating profit made by selling a good for a higher price than was paid for it.[22] He appeals to the Philosopher's distinction of two kinds of exchange. The first is natural; it is seeks to satisfy the basic needs of life. Because this natural trade is concerned with life's necessities, it belongs to the household, which exists outside of the public sphere where human laws are applicable. That exchange of necessities differs from the work of the merchant engaged in commerce; his activity is public, subject to regulation by human law. It seems at first that the commercial exchange of commodities for money is a violation of natural law because it satisfies no natural need, but rather results from greed. Because the quest for profit is quantitative, it has no limit and therefore no end that can be satisfied. As a result, it debases the person pursuing it. In spite of these criticisms, however, Thomas insists that because commercial activity belongs to the public sphere, a human law can transform it into something virtuous, perhaps by ensuring that the profit be taxed to aid the needy or for the good of the public.

Thomas's account of usury offers another illustration of the place of human law. Although the Philosopher had shown that the natural use of money in the exchange of necessities is just, the use of money to make money violates money's useful quality. Such activity cannot be virtuous because it has no limit and therefore serves no end. But human law may nonetheless permit this unnatural use of money even though this use does not aid in realizing the ends of natural law. Its justification is based on the fact that human law must leave some things unpunished both because human reason is imperfect and because it would be impractical to try forbid all sins. Hence, although usury may be permitted by human law, that does not mean it is just; it is something that may (but need not) work to the benefit of some (but not all) men. Moreover, the believer knows that divine law will ensure that justice is done and evil punished.

This final example of the interrelation among the types of law illuminates Thomas's broader goal of overcoming the difference between the secular and the sacred. He asks what ends can be achieved through the law. In particular, can the law make men good? In principle, a just legislator aims at the true good, and a Christian legislator is governed by principles of divine justice, which produces good men. But Thomas had learned from Aristotle that actual rulers may aim only to produce what is useful or pleasant for men. In that case, the law makes men good only relative to a particular city, an earthly city. Nonetheless, the citizen of such a city will be good in terms of the city's values. Although this good man uses the proper means to achieve his end, that end will not be universal. Nonetheless, the fact that the Philosopher argued that "lawgivers make men good by habituating them to good works" implies that even the laws of the City of Man have a positive value; they infuse the habits of lawful behavior that prepare the individual for the gift (or grace) of insight. That is why Thomas says that even a "tyrannical law"—which is not, strictly speaking, a law, but rather its perversion—has something of the nature of a law in that it aims at the citizens' being good, even if this means only good with respect to their government.[23] Secular rule thus ensures more than just the peace needed for the Augustinian pilgrimage to the holy city; it creates habits of obedience and the recognition that laws are necessary. It is not an end in itself, however.

Human laws are needed because men's natural aptitude for virtuous action is rarely actualized without outside help. Parental discipline or personal inclination may suffice in some cases, persuasion or teachers in others. But some men cannot be moved; they must be prevented from doing evil by force and fear; they have to learn to do voluntarily what they did first from fear. Again, however, as the idea of divine law teaches, this state of affairs does not mean that the law should repress all vices. Children may be permitted behavior that is forbidden to adults; less-virtuous women are permitted what is not tolerated in the virtuous.[24] As in Aristotle's ethics of the mean, human law is concerned with the many who are not perfectly virtuous. Hence, it should forbid only those vices from which the majority can abstain, particularly those that harm other people or society. Human laws, after all, are made to govern secular society.

In spite of this stress on human law, Thomas does not conceive of the City of Man as radically opposed to the City of God. Because the ends sought by an action determine the action's value, Thomas distinguishes those spheres of life in which man needs grace to exercise what he calls "supernatural virtue" and those where man's finite nature suffices. Before the Fall, natural man was able to achieve by means of his "acquired virtue" those goods that were human, yet even in that state of human perfection he still could not on his own do the good deeds that can be the result only of the "infused virtue" granted by grace. After the Fall, man is still able to do some good things (such as building houses, planting fields, and the like), but he now needs grace to do even the good that is natural to humans as God's creatures. In this way, although divine law, as the expression of God's mysterious nature, plays a role in secular life, it points also to the godly grace that transcends everyday life while remaining compatible with it. In opposition to the idea that original sin separated mankind forever from the divine, Thomas argues that without God's presence in the secular world, sin would have made human society impossible. Corrupted human nature cannot function without the presence of the divinity. Therefore, God must necessarily be present in the secular world.

◆

Although it was not his intention, Thomas gives new weight to the political in the shaping of a just world. His political theology overcomes the Augustinian pessimism. The dynamic interrelation of the four types of law legitimates political action as long as it does not violate natural law, and the creative use of human law—as limited by divine law—encourages the expectation that this action will work for the common good. The political state's authority gains a legitimacy that permits the state to stand as an equal to the church without being accused of a violation of the Gelasian doctrine of the primacy of the spiritual. But Thomas's invocation of grace as necessary in both the secular and the sacred spheres appeared to Franciscan spiritualists as merely a compensatory gesture by a worldly philosopher who felt no need for spiritual autonomy. Thomas seemed to have logically proven too much. His critics would turn his rationalism against him, but their criticism had other implications than they intended. Thomism would prove to be the last great synthesis of the classical worldview that began with the Greeks. Its destruction would reveal the need for a new kind of politics made by what can only be called a new kind of man in a new secular world that men would try to mold for their own purposes.

PIETY, THEOLOGY, AND THE BIRTH OF MODERN MAN

Thomas's philosophical reconciliation of reason with both the created world and its creator seems too good to be true. It is often said that he opened the way to a truly scientific worldview freed from the Platonic-Christian dichotomy between the Idea and its profane appearance in the secular world. Like Aristotle, he sought truth in the empirical world, taking account of its diversity while seeking to discover its unity. The Creator was not separated from but immanent within the creation. On this basis, the dynamic integration of natural law with the various forms of human law can be understood as giving potential new space and dignity to political action. The play of the universality of natural law with the particularity of human law seems to invite a renewal of political judgment (and potentially of political action) in the attempt to discover the best way for human law to realize the good life. In fact, however, neither of these claims can be maintained because the theological framework within which Thomas was operating meant that he could conceptualize neither the idea of an autonomous science for which nature is neutral material that men use to achieve their own goals nor the idea of a self-governing society in which men are free to live their own lives and determine their own laws. The modern conception of science and the modern understanding of politics were foreign to Thomas's essentially reflexive philosophical mind.

The world whose harmony Thomas revealed was closer to the universe of Aristotle than to the modern world. Although Thomas added a Christian creationism to the classical idea of a naturally lawful, hierarchical universe, his world remained teleological. All things, including humans, are determined by a natural end toward which they strive, and although men can understand these ends, they are still obliged to live with them. This world differs from the world of science, where the laws of nature are used for ends that humans will impose on the world. The rehabilitation of politics suggested by the flexibility of human law is similarly illusory insofar as the ruler is obliged to remain within the preexisting boundaries set on the one hand by natural law and on the other by divine law. The implication is that the ruler is responsible *for* the people rather than being answerable *to* their will. Human law is only a means; it cannot define the ends of the political community, which are given by natural law. In politics as in science, Thomism is the completion of the classical vision of the world and of man's place in it.

The failure of the Thomist synthesis was apparent to his contemporary theological critics, who challenged its rationalism. As is frequently the case in political history, the complete victory of one camp—be it Athenian democracy, republican Rome, or the church in the Investiture Struggle—calls forth a reaction from the other side that eventually transforms triumph into defeat because of its refusal to recognize limits. What then occurs is not the victory of the previously vanquished party, but the emergence of a new historical moment. In the case of Thomas's *Summa,* its reach seemed to rob religion of what is most essential to it: the experience of belief, the faith that warms the heart and gives meaning to individual existence.

The Franciscans took the lead in challenging Thomas, stressing the subjective side of religion, praising spirituality, but depreciating the material world of property, power, and institutions. Although both the Franciscan and the Dominican orders had been founded to oppose the pietistic antisacerdotal movement, the Franciscans tended to fight fire with fire, faith with faith, whereas their Dominican competitors sought to use reason to douse the flames. It was paradoxically this spiritual critique of Thomist rationalism that would overcome the classical universe, allowing the passage, as a twentieth-century historian of science put in a famous phrase, "from the closed world to the infinite universe."[25] We need to examine this paradox in order to see both what was lost and what then emerged as the horizon of modernity.

Although it is not possible to enter deeply into the properly philosophical logic that underlay the attacks against Thomism, it is important to sketch some of its major points and to name its leading proponents in order to make it clear that they were not simply opposing the spirit to the letter, the subjective experience of faith to the objective demonstration of reason, or the force of belief to the power of orthodoxy. Two Franciscan logicians, John Duns Scotus (c. 1266–1308), who taught at Oxford, and William of Ockham (c. 1288–c. 1348), who studied there, made the first dents in the rationalist edifice. A contemporary of William, Marsilius of Padua (c. 1275–c. 1342), proposed some of the preliminary steps that would lead beyond the Gelasian insistence that political life must be subordinate to the dictates of the papal church.

The critics of Thomism were not reacting to the imposing scholastic architecture of the *Summa*, but to its overarching vision. What bothered Scotus was a contradiction that was both logical and theological. The idea of an eternal law through which the Creator endows the world with a rational structure had the paradoxical effect of robbing God of the essential freedom in and through which His majesty expressed itself. Scotus insisted that God is and must remain always free, which means that everything that God does is contingent, independent of the so-called laws of nature, freely chosen. This theological argument had a secular consequence that clashed with the classical worldview. If God's freedom means that He can change the world as He wishes, it follows that the supposed laws of science are themselves only provisional and fallible, probable rather than certain, particular rather than universal. The Thomist understanding of causality as inherent in the world could thus no longer be taken for granted. Scotus did not yet draw the conclusion that humans, too, can posit ends, changing nature to realize their desires. It sufficed simply to show that God's unquenchable freedom renews the thirst of the faithful, who no longer simply have to follow unthinkingly the inherited ritual and religion of the past.

William of Ockham radicalized what Scotus initiated, elaborating the idea of divine freedom in the form of a nominalist logic that denies the reality of claims of universality, such as those of Platonic Ideas or Thomist essences. Nominalism argues simply that the name given to a thing or a type of social relations is the result of humans choosing to impose an identity on them. What appear to be lawlike or causal relations among events in the world are simply the result of men's agreeing tacitly or explicitly to impose a shared pattern on them. The laws of science are thus not understood as having existed in God's mind before the creation; they are the fruit of human reason. With this shift, the grounds for the invention of modern science were laid. On the basis of what is called "Ockham's razor," the nominalist asserted that science need not postulate the existence of some ultimate and unknowable cause of the world's being as it is. More than three centuries later, Isaac Newton appealed to this nominalist insight in his reply to the question regarding what lay behind his famous laws of gravity: "hypotheses non fingo" (I do not invent hypotheses).

Ockham, of course, did not develop nominalism in order to found modern science. He expected that the loss of divine sanction for the acceptance of world as it is would liberate the individual from the idea that the church and its rituals were the only path to salvation. If what is thought to be divine being can be known by finite humans in the same way that profane things are known, it is not divine after all because finite thought cannot understand the infinite. But this limitation on human reason clears the way for a deeper, truer, and more direct experience of the divine because God can be known only in a mystical experience whose intensity is due to the fact that it results not from man's efforts, but from God's freely given grace. In this way, nominalism led its followers into the antisacerdotal camp that was perceived as a threat to the order established by the church. Ockham was accused of heresy and summoned before the papal court at Avignon. He refused to back down. Stressing God's full and unlimited freedom, he argued provocatively that although God chose to become human in order to save humanity, He could well have saved mankind by other means—for example, by becoming a stone, a tree, or an ass. His power over the natural world is such that He could make two objects occupy the same place at the same time. The same divine freedom, added Ockham (perhaps thinking of his own situation), means that God may even condemn the innocent. In short, God doesn't say that things are good because they are good; they are good because He decides that they are so.

Ockham was aware of the probable consequences of his provocation, but he most likely didn't imagine that his nominalist logic would contribute to the emergence of a basic assumption of modern political thought. Fleeing papal condemnation, he sought the protection of Holy Roman emperor Louis IV of Bavaria, who welcomed Ockham's typically Franciscan condemnation of the corrupting influence of the church's material wealth. Although the story may be apocryphal, Ockham is reported to have told the emperor, "I will defend you with my pen if you will defend me with your sword." Whether this anecdote is true or not, Ockham devoted his last years to skirmishes with the church orthodoxy. Nonetheless, he remained a faithful Franciscan, insisting that the church return to the "gospel of poverty" that was Saint Francis's original message. Others would draw alternative political conclusions from his radicalism.

Translated into the logic of political theory, Ockham's nominalism ruled out the idea of a natural law to which political relations must ultimately conform. His spiritual individualism led him to the idea that each person has a right and must therefore have the power to assure his own subsistence. To achieve that subsistence, he must acquire property and create a legal framework for its preservation. This defense of property differs from the one that Thomas offered; it argues that property is necessary to preserve the individual's rights. This idea of the rights of an individual rather than of the citizen who is part of the whole opened the horizon of modernity. It implies that the institutions of secular life are expressions of human freedom that do not depend on divine or ecclesiastical legitimation. Although Ockham never developed these fragmentary political insights, the nominalist logic in later years became the dominant curriculum of many of the new European universities, including the one at Erfurt, Germany, where Martin Luther would study. This program was significantly called the *via moderna* in order to distinguish it from its classical predecessor.

Ockham's exile was shared with other dissidents, including Marsilius of Padua. As his name indicates, Marsilius was a citizen of one of the rising Italian cities that sought to maintain their autonomy from the pope's designs and the emperor's reach. Marsilius's major work, *The Defender of the Peace*, sought secular means to institute a peace that would be more than the resigned Augustinian absence of war during the "pilgrimage" to the City of God here on earth. True peace would be realized only by the creation of a government that ensures that conflict can have no basis because the lawgiver has political legitimacy. Like Aristotle, Marsilius assumes that man is a social animal who naturally seeks community in order to gain the self-sufficiency necessary to attain the good life. But he insists that legislation is legitimate insofar as it expresses the "will of the community, or the greater part thereof." The contrast with the Thomist idea that a ruler is responsible for his people rather than answering to them is obvious. Law as the expression of the popular will is a modern, nonteleological idea.

Marsilius's search for a governmental form that ensures true peace went further. He seeks to combine the constraining unitary force of imperial legislation (*regnum*) with a modernized republican procedure by which the laws are made into the expression of the popular will (*civitas*). The authority of such laws would result neither from the fact that they are essentially or naturally good nor from the claim that they express the divine will, but simply because they have been decided by the proper procedure. Proceduralism was the institutional consequence of the nominalist logic developed by Marsilius's fellow exile, William of Ockham. The laws are conventional names decided by a publically defined and regulated procedure. And just as God's will can change, the laws can be altered when the will of the people chooses to do so.

The complicated story of Marsilius's relations with Emperor Louis IV, who supported him during his exile while encouraging his denunciations of the "tyranny" of the papacy, as well as his defense of secular power, need not be recounted further. The emperor deposed the reigning pope, John XXII (served 1316–1334), whom he replaced with a politically pliant and devoutly spiritual Franciscan. To ensure his power, he applied his own version of political nominalism to convince the prince-electors that there was no longer a need for the pope to consecrate the imperial government as long as they, as "the greater part," followed the proper procedures in the designation of the new ruler. In this way, the nominalist refusal of higher authority meant that proceduralism simply legitimated the existing secular power relations. Within the church, however, the nominalist political logic supported rebellion among those who argued that the pope's authority was neither absolute nor the expression of the divine will. This rebellion gave rise to what is called the Conciliar Movement, a forerunner of the Protestant Reformation, to which we come in the next chapter.

◆

The conflict of the sacred and the secular analyzed in this chapter was rekindled at the end of the fifteenth century. The paradoxical advent of modernity as a result of the critique by religious piety of the Thomist synthesis had effects that were similar to the emergence of the secular state as the unintended result of the church's victory in the Investiture Struggle. Modernity and the secular state transformed but did not eliminate the Platonic and Aristotelian emphases on unity and plurality, universality and particularity, power and authority. The Platonic Ideas were now seen as incarnated in the inward purity of the individual's subjective experience; the Aristotelian quest for a truth found within the given world emigrated to the domain of social institutions (including science) that produced social legitimacy by integrating the subject into a world of other subjects. Martin Luther developed the modern form of religious "Platonism," and John Calvin shaped its "Aristotelian" counterpart. The relation of the two types of reformed religion recalls at first the opposition of the new piety to the theological synthesis, but the context had changed. According to these two reformations, the believer is now an individual whose individualism separates him from both the natural world, which he seeks to fashion for his own ends, and the political community, from which he expects the protection of his rights. This separation frees up the sphere of politics as an arena that has to create its own rules and institutions. This sphere is not identical to the space in which Machiavelli, the Italian contemporary of the Reformation, tried to invent a pure logic of political action, but the renewal of the urban republican spirit justifies considering him within this broader framework.

№ 4
FACING THE CHALLENGE OF MODERNITY

THE TWO GREAT INTELLECTUAL and political moments called the Renaissance and the Reformation are usually considered distinct chapters in the process of modernization. On the surface, the difference between the two lies in the fact that the Renaissance was a largely secular movement, whereas the Reformation sought a spiritual renewal. Art and literature, science and philosophy, courtly manners and the renewal of civic life are associated with the Renaissance, whereas the Reformation focused on a life of prayerful self-discipline in churches from which art and ornamentation were excluded to encourage directness of manners and frankness of expression among the believers. That simple opposition is static, however. It suggests that the Renaissance was a political movement, whereas the Reformation was antipolitical, but the two movements actually shared a common search for renewal of a purer past—the Renaissance looking to classical civilization, the Reformation to primitive Christianity.

This shared belief in a past free from corruption suggests a way to interpret their contribution to the history of political thought. The anti-Scholastic alliance between the adepts of subjective piety and the nominalist logicians of the *via moderna* opened the way for the creation of modern science, while consecrating the new individualism that arose at the beginning of the sixteenth century. It became evident that the synthesis of the sacred and the secular, the ecclesial and the political, the salvation of the individual soul and the creation of communal justice was impossible. The three great political thinkers of the age—Martin Luther, John Calvin, and Niccolò Machiavelli—sought to understand their world by absolutizing the value of their basic premise. All three of them were political thinkers because they shared the premise that the legitimacy of men's relations to one another (and to God) was to be sought in their behavior in this world. Luther developed the logic of the individual quest for salvation (soteriology); Calvin sought to create a church that would make its congregants able to receive God's inexplicable judgments (ecclesiology); and Machiavelli demonstrated the capacity of politics, in the figure of the republican prince, to preserve human freedom. Each was also searching for a "pure" theory, unalloyed by compromise and capable of enfolding its opposite in its own unitary web.

◆

The historical context illustrates the radical nature of the new political thought. Challenges to the late medieval church came from without as well as from within. The emerging secular states sought to influence the election of popes (who controlled large swaths of Italian territory as well as ecclesial powers), which produced a schism in the late fourteenth century as one pope ruled in Rome, another in Avignon. To re-create unity, a council representing the diverse currents composing the church assembled at Constance in 1414. Although the invitation to deliberate was a concession to diversity within the church, orthodoxy was forcefully reasserted when the assembly condemned Jan Hus (1369–1415) to death at the stake. The Czech reformer, who espoused the spiritual virtue of poverty, had not only criticized church corruption, but also, more threatening still, defended the authority of the national state over its church. As rector of the university in Prague, he expressed an emerging nationalist sentiment. His last words are said to have been that "in one hundred years, God will raise up a man whose calls for reform cannot be suppressed." This prediction erred by only two years; Luther nailed his *Ninety-five Theses* to the church door in Wittenberg in 1517, and his most fervent supporters were defenders of Teutonic independence from the Roman writ.

Hus's death did not silence the proponents of diversity and deliberation. For them, the council represented a mode of governance that renewed the church's original foundations. Conciliar government was seen as an instrument that could prevent recurrence of the corruption that had brought the church to the brink of self-destruction. The council participants declared in 1415 that "the general council, legitimately assembled in the Holy Spirit and representing the Catholic Church Militant . . . [decrees] that all men, of every rank and position, including even the pope himself, are bound to obey it in those matters that pertain to the faith . . . and to the reformation of the said Church in head and members." Two years later, they added a decree imposing on the pope the obligation to convene general councils at regular intervals. This affirmation of conciliar authority implied that the pope was a constitutional rather than an absolute ruler to whom the community had only delegated its power while retaining its residual authority in case he exceeded his mandate. It even suggested that the council had the possibility of deposing a pope. This foreshadowing of constitutional government should not be overestimated. The supporters of the council were mainly delegates of the secular states that were trying to defend their own national interests.

The cosmopolitan universalism of the movement called "humanism" contrasted with both the particular interests of the new secular states and the resentful or stubborn pride among Hus and other reformers' followers. This movement promoted a modern, potentially rival creed that took root among the intellectual and political leaders of society. Its central tenant put man at the center of the universe. Erasmus of Rotterdam (1466–1536) was its most influential voice. His worldview developed the idea of a "renaissance"—literally a rebirth, whose basis was the return to the original human experience that inspired the great works of the past. Humanism's concerns were both secular and sacred. One of Erasmus's great achievements was an edition of the original Greek version of the New Testament, which had been lost during the centuries when the Latin Vulgate had been canonical. His goal was to recapture the original presence of Jesus the man and to retell the story of his mission on earth. He applied to the Bible the same editorial methods applied to classical texts, deconstructing encrusted interpretations so that the reader could breathe the pure air of the original. He was deeply conscious of the importance of history, so his humanism sought at the same time to escape history's corrupting effects by going back to its true human origins.

The limits of humanism as a guide to either political or ecclesial reform became evident in its inability to propose institutional change. Erasmus's best-selling satire *In Praise of Folly* illustrated the dangers of self-deception and the follies of superstitious abuses of church doctrine. But when he turned his attention to politics, his treatise *On the Education of a Christian Prince* simply assumed that a just ruler will reign happily over a good people whom he must be educated to serve. As always, Erasmus placed his faith in educational reform in secular as well as in spiritual matters. He was unaware of the changes that troubled his near contemporary Machiavelli, who was a participant in the Italian branch of the Renaissance. Meanwhile, Luther, despite Erasmus's early support for his attack on scholasticism, turned against the humanists' vision of the life of Jesus as the true model for human behavior and rejected its infatuation with secular classic texts, insisting that the holy text is the only access to the Word. Provoked by Luther, Erasmus finally put pen to paper to address their essential difference in his essay *On the Freedom of the Will*. In his reply, the treatise *On the Bondage of the Will*, Luther denounced the humanist's faith in man, developing Augustine's argument (as noted in chapter 3) that "subjection" can be salutary for "some" who "became worse and worse so long as they were free." Only God's mysterious grace, not the efforts of man, can redeem a sinful humanity.

A final figure rounds out the historical context. Thomas More (1478–1535), to whom Erasmus dedicated *In Praise of Folly*, expressed the ambiguity of political life in a small book called *Utopia*. More's title is a play on words. The Greek term *topos* means "place," but the prefix *u-* means "no," implying that utopia exists "nowhere" and that pursuit of it is as futile as was Plato's quest for an ideal republic. Another prefix, pronounced in the same manner, *eu-*, signifies "good," however, suggesting that the social relations described in *Utopia* may be meant as a model for reforming rulers to follow. Both interpretations are plausible. Which of these readings would best convey the humanist's intentions? The one leans toward a Platonic politics; the other points toward Aristotle.

More's story itself is ambiguous. His narrator was apparently traveling to the newly discovered America when he found the marvelous island whose social institutions he then describes. This storyline suggests that the good place does exist and that it can provide a model for human betterment. The island's natural environment seems to have been organized for the benefit of humans, its well-situated rivers permitting the creation of geometrically organized cities, which in turn encourage the common ownership of property and rotation of types of work. It seems to be a rationalist utopia beyond the ken of finite humans. That may be why in *Utopia* More designates trained scholars as the rulers and priests. He leaves room, however, for other options between the poles of "nowhere" and "the good place." For example, his insistence that gold is used only for common objects such as chamber pots and the chains of slaves suggests that his intention is to denounce the follies of contemporary life. For the same reason, religious tolerance is practiced, priests are allowed to marry, and divorce is permitted (but premarital sex is punished by the imposition of lifelong celibacy).

The traces of these four currents of contemporary thought that appear in the work of Luther, Calvin, and Machiavelli are unimportant. The context merely serves to emphasize the originality of their contributions, which I evaluate on their own merits. When I move on to an analysis of modern individualism and the question of political obligation in chapter 5, the questions of national interest, conciliar or procedural legitimation, liberal humanism, and the ambiguous promise of utopia reemerge.

LUTHER'S SOTERIOLOGICAL POLITICS: SPIRITUAL DEMOCRACY OR POLITICAL SERVITUDE

The fact that Martin Luther (1483–1546) chose to join the Augustinian Order rather than any of the other twenty-two monastic orders present in Germany was an early signal of the direction of his mind. He was attracted by the Augustinian-Platonic quest for purity rather than by the more intellectual Thomist-Aristotelian search for a synthesis of religion and the world. He was also moved by a concern that seemed to turn him away from the political world: the unity of his thought was built on the quest for salvation. This unitary foundation would in fact bring the young monk into a tormented relation with both his church and his world. Following the path that led him to confront the established order takes us to his interpretation of the relation between the sacred and the secular. Although only three of the fifty-five volumes in the recent English-language edition of his works treat political questions,[1] the world into which he launched his reform was in political as well as spiritual turmoil. Despite the soteriological concern that animated his life and work, Luther was drawn into the secular arena by some of his radical democratic followers, whose reforms he ultimately renounced in order to save the purity of his new church. Because that purity remained spiritual, however, believers had to accept political subordination as its price.

◆

The eastern region of Germany where Luther was born was thinly populated and relatively undeveloped, but the curriculum of the Erfurt university where he studied was modern. Luther knew the work of the humanists, and he was trained in the *via moderna* elaborated by William of Ockham's successors. Some say that his religious illumination was the result of the doubt produced by nominalism; others claim that his peasant feeling of unworthiness led him repeatedly to the confessional, where he seemed able to find new sins daily. His own explanation was more literally Augustinian: just as the saint's vision in the garden commanded him to "take it [the Bible] and read," so when Luther heard the same call, his Bible opened to Romans 1:17, where he read, "The righteous shall live by faith." This statement became the first tenant of Luther's creed: *sola fides*, only faith can bring salvation. Luther's faith would be tested, its affirmations would be challenged, and he would be abused by his enemies and misused by friends. Although doubt would recur, the faith that he needed to overcome that doubt was reinforced by the constant conflict that surrounded his life's work. Through it all, the purity of his originary vision provided a unity to Luther's thought and action. Nothing less was needed for the great undertaking that was to create a new church and a found new religion.

The familiar story of Luther's first open confrontation with the Catholic Church reflects the religious themes of his future mission, but it also bears the stamp of the secular conditions that would affect his ability to realize his aims. The young monk had been appointed professor of biblical studies at the recently created university in the small town of Wittenberg. In spite of the backwardness of Saxony, its ruler had the status of an "elector" in the Holy Roman Empire, which gave him the power to defend his subjects against the reigning emperor. It also encouraged him to seek to control the church in his own lands. The pope, Leo X (served 1513–1521) had sent a plenipotentiary to Germany with the task of selling indulgences to pay for the rebuilding of St. Peter's Cathedral in Rome. He expected to find ready buyers in the highly religious German society, where nearly one hundred feast days were celebrated. In protest to this directive, on October 31, 1517, Luther affixed to the door of the Wittenberg church his *Ninety-five Theses,* which articulated the need for and steps toward reform of the church. Luther did not propose a theological critique of indulgences in the Pelagianist vein. His message was more simple and direct—and, for that reason, it was more widely heard. Although his *Theses* proposed church reforms, the power of his message came from its ability to combine institutional reform with a salvific message.

The foundation for the reforms proposed in the *Theses* lay in the second article of his faith: *sola scriptorum*. Because only the Bible can rightly guide the believer, and there is nothing in the holy book that justifies the issuance of papal pardons, the papal initiative violates the church's divine ordinance. The church also had to be reformed more generally because it had lost the purity of its biblical foundation. On this point, Luther agreed with the humanists' stress on returning to the originary experience in order to find the truth of tradition, but the practical problem that had next to be addressed was determining who would initiate and who could carry out this reform. Could the impulse come from within the church? The conciliar reforms presented at Constance in 1414 might have provided a model. Or if relief did not come from within the church, might a truly faithful secular ruler overthrow the papal "tyranny"? That kind of intervention had led to the papal schism that was finally overcome at Constance. Should the community of believers assume this heavy responsibility? This approach might lead to the emergence of a new wave of Donatist rebels. How then could the purity of Luther's mission be achieved without entering a compromising alliance with one or another political actor?

Luther's *Ninety-five Theses* fell on receptive soil; the church was forced to react to what might have been a minor academic controversy in a remote small town. Luther was not the first to protest against the indulgences, but his academic training and, more important, his fluid vernacular German gave his message added weight among the public. The Saxon ruler Frederick the Wise refused to turn against a critic whose popular support could strengthen his own hand in imperial politics. Agitation grew. Finally, a public debate was organized at the prestigious University of Leipzig in 1519 in the hope that the upstart monk would be put in his place. His orthodox opponents provoked Luther into radicalizing the implications of his biblical faith. Holy Scripture, he now maintained, has no place for a pope; as a result, the papacy cannot claim to be divinely ordained. Nor could the papal office have been established by Saint Peter, as Erasmus and the humanist critics had shown. Luther went on to attack the rationalism of Scholastic philosophy that had no place for the reality of original sin. Luther's self-defense turned into a further radicalization of his offensive against the corruption of the institution that was supposed to offer men the path to salvation.

The results of the Leipzig debate were a clear indication that whatever hopes Luther may have had that the church could reform itself were merely pious wishes. In the years that followed, the reformers would try repeatedly to knit together the divided shards of Christendom, but this unity could not to be created by the book or won by the sword. After decades of often violent clashes, a temporary truce was achieved when the Peace of Augsburg in 1555 adopted the famous compromise *cuis regio, ejus religio*, "who rules the state decides its religion." By then, Luther was dead, and his faith had become a church. The story of the birth of this new church has to be told before its relation to the secular political world can be analyzed.

Unforeseeable accidents can affect the course of history. Luther's rejection of the authority of the papacy was a challenge to the Gelasian doctrine that established the authority of the church over the state. For that reason, the emperor might have supported Luther's arguments because they offered a vehicle to assert his own autonomy. But Charles V had been elected only recently; although he was a Habsburg, his knowledge of German politics and even the German language was limited because the core of his ancestral lands was Spain. As a result, he needed Rome's support against the German princes who had elected him as a compromise candidate whom they intended to manipulate. In this context, Luther was summoned before the imperial diet at Worms in 1521, where he was to answer to a papal bull threatening him with excommunication. Luther published four widely reprinted pamphlets in his self-defense, the most important of which was *Appeal to the German Nobility*. If the church could not reform itself, Luther suggested, the nobility must assume the task. Although Luther did not say it explicitly, he was appealing to the self-interest of princes, who wanted to be free not only of church interference in the secular realm, but also of their imperial overlord. This would not be the first time that Luther would wonder whether the agent of ecclesial reform could be of sufficient purity to bring about the ends sought. Can worldly power reform a sacred institution?

The image of Luther nailing his *Ninety-five Theses* on the church door is coupled with the picture of his defiant appearance at the Diet of Worms. Traveling under an imperial order of protection, accompanied by the elector Frederick the Wise, Luther was met along the way by popular festivities that reflected an early nationalist feeling. For Charles V, the diet represented a test of his authority. The fact that it took place in an unfamiliar language and a fragile political context led the emperor to refuse all compromise. Luther equally stood his ground, although his critics raised questions whose pertinence was hard to deny. Did Luther think that everyone else was in error? Was the long tradition of the church based solely on ignorance? Might he not be leading into damnation the followers who had flocked to him? Luther responded that his arguments were not based on his personal judgment. His famous peroration staked his claim clearly: "Unless I am proved wrong by the testimony of Scriptures or by evident reason, I am bound in conscience to hold fast to the Word of God. . . . [T]herefore I cannot and will not retract anything. . . . God help me. Amen."[2] As he had argued against Erasmus, his conscience was "bound" by the Word, whose salvific power was the foundation of his faith. He would not retract because he could not; to do so would not violate his own conscience, but the will of the Lord. His soteriological view meant that individual existence is simply a pilgrimage on the way to salvation.

Despite this famous peroration, whose religious force Luther developed in the coming years, his appearance at Worms was a political affair, unlike the Leipzig theological debate. A papal bull confirmed the imperial decree of excommunication issued at the debate's climax, which meant that any of the faithful could kill Luther without fear of punishment, temporal or spiritual. Luther's reply was defiant; back at Wittenberg, surrounded by his supporters, he burned the Roman document at a public rally. His fame spread, and he became the focal point of a nascent but still labile movement, drawing not only followers such as Philip Melanchton (1497–1560), but also critics who wanted to push him to more radical measures, such as the future Anabaptist leader Thomas Müntzer (c. 1488–1525).

The elector Frederick of Saxony saw the secular advantages to be gained from the rebellious monk's popularity. To ensure Luther's protection, he arranged a fake kidnapping, hiding him in a castle on the Wartburg, where, during ten feverish weeks, Luther worked on his German translation of the New Testament, which was published in 1522. The holy text was now no longer the monopoly of the church; even the illiterate, who joined collective Bible readings, could form their own understanding of the divine will and its manifestation in the life of Jesus. Luther would later introduce other reforms that lessened the separation between priesthood and laity, reduced the number of sacraments from seven to three,[3] and abolished priestly celibacy (which drew to his cause energetic leaders eager to quit the constraints of the celibate priesthood). His doctrine of the "priesthood of all the believers" more generally implied the replacement of ecclesiastical hierarchy by a self-governing congregation—although Luther himself did not suggest conciliarist political implications of what was for him a strictly soteriological thesis.

The reforming spirit acquired its own momentum. The danger that it faced came from its own overreaching. By insisting on its purity, it could not recognize the legitimacy of any particular practices outside its reach. The movement was popularized by a flood of pamphlets produced by entrepreneurs who had by now acquired the new printing technology and were eager to satisfy rising demand. By 1523, there were some thirteen hundred different editions of tracts by Luther, amounting to a total of nearly one million copies that were not only read in private, but discussed orally in public meetings. This outpouring of written texts (not all of which came from Luther's pen) had an unintended effect on its popular audiences, however. Because there was no longer an accepted authority to interpret the Word, each individual had to form his own opinion. The universality of the "catholic" church gave way to a multitude of particular sects, each following its own lights. Should one follow Erasmus's reading of the New Testament, which saw in Jesus a model for moral humanity? Or did Jesus turn away from the secular world to create a community of true believers? Was that not the message of the Sermon on the Mount? The message of reform threatened to escape the reformer's control.

Although secular rulers asserting their autonomy could appropriate Luther's criticism of the church, its appeal was deeper and more emotional at the bottom of society. The Sermon on the Mount seemed to confirm the peasants' hatred of the wealthy, their scorn for hypocritical priests, and their resentment of monastic wealth. The peasants were ready to put their faith to the test. Thomas Müntzer, who had been drawn to Luther's teaching but became critical of its social timidity, became the leader of a revolt that spread across the land. Many of the rebels' arguments were reformulations of theses that Luther had himself defended. For example, the "priesthood of all the believers" was interpreted to mean that all of them are equal. Their spiritual purity could abide no hierarchy, rejecting even the sacrament of infant baptism as a violation of the freedom of the earthly saints to choose their own way.[4] This idea of an original purity guided by an inner light brought the rebels uncomfortably close to Luther's own stress on God's unfathomable grace, but Luther could not accept Müntzer's apocalyptic-messianic appeal to a coming Kingdom of God that would eliminate all earthly kingdoms. He rejected this fusion of soteriological yearning with resentment of social exploitation. On the one hand, was this fusion not a return of the Donatist heresy? On the other, had he not defended himself at Worms by appealing to God's will? Why should not others act from an inner conscience inspired by faith?

The aroused peasants became an army, and the princes began to worry. They took to arms to put down the rebels in bloody battles made more brutal by the clash of the fear aroused at the top of society and the hopes kindled at its base. Luther hesitated but then sided with the princes in a polemical pamphlet, *Against the Robbing and Murdering Hordes of Peasants*. Although the repression of the peasants is harsh, he argued, the rebels deserve no mercy for three reasons. First, they are challenging the existing authorities despite the injunction of Romans 13:1–2, "there is no authority except that which God has established. . . . Consequently, he who rebels against the authority is rebelling against what God has instituted, and those who do so will bring judgment on themselves." Second, the rebels who have robbed and pillaged are like a "mad dog" who must be killed before he kills others. Third, the peasants' claim is based on only "the outward appearance of the Gospel," which proves that they are in fact tools of the devil, who is using them for his own purposes. As a result, concludes Luther, a ruler who "can punish [them] and does not . . . becomes guilty of all the murder and all the evil that these fellows commit. For by deliberately disregarding God's command he permits such rascals to go about their wicked business, even though he was able to prevent it and it was his duty to do so."[5]

This encouragement of the use of force against the rebellious peasants utilizes the logic Augustine applied in the battle against the Donatists. Because the peasants cannot be won over by reason (which is another proof of their manipulation by the devil), the threat of violence against them will bring them to their senses. Luther's pamphlet shocked many of his followers, however, in part because it appeared in the very month in which the peasant army was brutally massacred in a final battle. As a result, Luther felt obliged to publish *An Open Letter on the Hard Book Against the Peasants—Introduction* in the same year in order to set the balance aright. In this letter, he doesn't recant his criticism of the Anabaptist rebellion, but he recognizes that the spiritual task he has given the secular princes is fraught with difficulty. In the end, however, he could see no other way of dealing with the rebellion.

How, his friends ask, can a Christian show no mercy? Did the adherents of a pure religion of salvation have to massacre those who thought otherwise? In his self-defense, Luther cites biblical examples of God's wrath, asking why rulers should be limited when God again and again shows no mercy to sinners. On the contrary, he suggests, it is the devil who "tries to deck himself out in a reputation for mercy." In that way, evil is able to spread. Why, continues Luther, blame me for what others have called down on themselves by their rebellious actions? It is the evil-doers who have caused their own ruin; the rulers have punished only what demanded punishment. As he nears the end of his self-defense, however, he admits that his wrath was one-sided. "It was not my intention," he writes, "either to strengthen the raging tyrants, or to praise their raving." He does not mean that "a man can earn heaven with slaughter and bloodshed." He denounces "the furious, raving, senseless tyrants, who even after the battle cannot get their fill of blood, and in all their lives ask scarcely a question about Christ." His friends must understand that his goal was to "quiet the peasants, and instruct the lords." Hell fire, he insists, awaits the latter if they do not repent and learn from his instructions.[6]

Luther does not explain the "instructions" that he wanted to give the secular rulers in order to prevent their overreaching. He had faced a similar political difficulty just prior to the final break at Worms. His *Appeal to the German Nobility* had called on the nobles to support his battle because he assumed that they were indeed truly Christian princes. He had accepted the protection of his religious reforms by the secular authorities in Saxony, but he had not yet reflected on the costs that might have to be paid for this support. His noble protectors may well have been Christians, but they were also princes whose duty was to defend their own secular interests. Luther addressed this difficulty in his definitive political essay *On Secular Authority: How Far Does the Obedience Owed to It Extend?* written in 1523, when radical political rebellion had appeared as a threat to the spiritual reforms he was preaching.[7]

Luther's systematic reflection on political life has to explain both the limits of secular authority and the positive reasons for which a Christian should obey temporal power. He begins from a basic opposition that confronts all believers. On the one hand, Saint Paul had argued, most forcefully in Romans (13:1), that all secular authority exists by the will of God; on the other hand, the Sermon on the Mount (Matthew 5:39) tells the believers to "turn the other cheek," caring not for the blandishments of this world. This opposition is a version of what Augustine had referred to as the conflict between the City of Man and the City of God. But it says nothing about either the limits on secular authority or the positive reasons that a Christian should obey that authority.

It would seem that a true Christian who agrees with Christ's declaration to Pilate that "My kingdom is not of this world" (John 18:36) has no need for temporal law. It is true that if the whole world were composed of real Christians, there would be no need for princes, laws, or swords. That is why Paul explained that the law does not exist for the sake of the just, who do good without its constraint; the law exists for the sake of the lawless, to whom it shows the path of righteousness. An Augustinian realist, Luther knew that lawless men exist and will continue to exist in this world haunted by original sin, where men are always prey to Satan's temptations. There will always be inhabitants of the earthly city who are not true Christians. Secular law exists for their sake. It binds their restless will, directs their unruly spirit, lights their unseeing eyes.

Not only are there few true believers in the secular city, but even those who believe may at times find it difficult to live a life based neither on resisting evil (i.e., turning the other cheek) nor on doing evil (i.e., exceeding the limits of secular authority). Luther's two pamphlets on the Peasant War, *Against the Robbing and Murdering Hordes* and *An Open Letter on the*

Hard Book Against the Peasants, illustrate the difficulty in obeying this obligation. In the first, he argues that the Christian princes had a positive duty to resist the evil deeds of the peasants, but in the second he expresses his fear that his support of the princes had justified the overreaching that resulted in evil by the "furious, raving, senseless tyrants." If even those who consider themselves true Christians find it difficult to act according to the Word, it follows that the sword will always be needed in the secular world. It has a double task: it must prevent injustice, and then, when evil inevitably occurs, it must be there to punish evil. Luther explains himself by a classical analogy. It is naive to think that a savage beast and a tame animal can coexist peacefully. The former must be restrained if the latter is to live in peace. The analogy implies that without laws the true Christian is in danger in the secular world. Without laws, no one would take care of wife and child, let alone serve God. That is why God has created two governments, a spiritual one for the just and a temporal one for the wicked, who will always exist.

Luther's praise of secular law explains his rejection of the Anabaptists' claim that among true Christians, only the Word of the Gospel counts as law. Those who make this claim argue that evil in a truly Christian world comes from unjust human laws that protect inequality and encourage exploitation, which justifies their rebellion. But what Luther calls his "wounds" have convinced him of the existence of wicked persons who argue that just because they are true Christians, they should be excused from obedience to the secular laws that protect property, the sanctity of marriage bonds, and the repayment of debts. The "wounds" that have resulted from his confrontations with false faith tell Luther that there are many who are not the true Christians they claim to be. Baptism doesn't make the Christian; no external sacrament can do that. Only God's grace can redeem original sin. Because that grace cannot be earned, no one can know that another person has truly been saved. To deny this truth is to make the error of the naive shepherd who puts together wolves, lions, eagles, and sheep, commanding them to be peaceful among themselves. The sheep that follow the command will not live long thereafter.

In *On Secular Authority,* after Luther has shown that secular law is necessary in a world where not everyone is a true Christian, he turns to the question of how the true Christian should relate to the secular state. He argues that Christians must use secular law rather than simply turning the other cheek and ignoring the affairs of the world. The two cities seek different kinds of good. The church is concerned with spiritual righteousness, whereas the secular rulers are responsible for ensuring external peace and preventing evil deeds. Because men are both spiritual and temporal beings, both types of good are necessary, and neither is sufficient without the other. If only secular government existed, hypocrisy would be inevitable even when behavior conforms to God's commands because without the Holy Spirit no one can be truly righteous no matter how fine his works. God's grace, not men's works, is the foundation of justice. But the spiritual law (and divine grace) that rules true Christian souls is not sufficient on its own because it has no effect on earthly wickedness, which would be left to pursue freely its self-interest unhindered by the spiritual law that applies to Christians. That is why the Christian needs secular law to prevent the spread of evil deeds.[8] The two cities complement rather than contradict one another.

Luther has now prepared the reader of *On Secular Authority* for his crucial argument concerning the obligation that binds the true Christian to the secular state. He introduces a third party between the individual and the law. Those who want to live without law in a community of saints forget that the true believer is commanded to live not for himself, but for his neighbor, who may not be a true Christian. Because the sword is beneficial insofar as it preserves peace, punishes sin, and restrains the wicked, the Christian must accept it. He pays taxes, honors authority, and works to help it function, but the crucial point is that he does not do all these things for himself. Indeed, he does nothing for himself! When visiting the sick, he doesn't expect himself to be healed; when feeding others, he doesn't expect to be fed. Obeying the secular law and ensuring that it fulfills its functions, the Christian obeys the divine command to love his neighbor. He himself doesn't need government, but others need its protection. He sacrifices nothing when he works for the secular government; he doesn't harm himself (that is, as long as the government is just), and he benefits the world. Indeed, not to serve would be unchristian, a denial of aid to others who are in need. Finally, Luther adds, not to aid the state would set a bad example, bringing the Gospel into disrepute by making it appear to teach insurrection or by producing self-centered people unwilling to serve others. This remark is a sign of Luther's political shrewdness; he knew that his religious movement could appear as a threat to the secular government.

Luther goes a step farther in his argument that the true Christian must serve the secular state. As opposed to the pacifist claim that the Christian is forbidden to use or to serve the sword, he argues that the faithful are obliged to use the secular powers for the good of those who have not yet attained true Christianity (because their faith becomes true only by God's grace). Luther, of course, knew that the secular powers cannot impose conversions or control the mind of the heretical. To dispel any illusions left from his earlier *Appeal to the German Nobility*, the second part of *On Secular Authority* stresses the distinction of the two cities and emphasizes the limits on the authority of the secular government that the believers are obliged to serve. Force can compel the body, but not the spirit. If force overreaches, it will constrain only those with weak consciences, whom it makes into hypocrites who say one thing while their hearts believe another. The true Christian has a firm conscience, permitting him to turn the other cheek when evil is done to him, knowing that his suffering is God's will. That is why he can and must serve secular authority. Indeed, if the government needs hangmen, constables, or judges, and the Christian individual is qualified, he must volunteer to serve because he is not seeking vengeance or returning evil for evil; he is enforcing peace for the sake of his neighbor. In this way, it is not for his own salvation that he resists evil (punishes wrong-doers, serves as hangman, and so on); it is for the sake of his secular neighbor.

Luther still has not answered the question, "How far does the obedience owed to secular authority extend?" Must the Christian serve any and every secular state? Must he apply the law rigorously across the board, or is there room for the kind of mercy that Luther had refused to the peasant rebels? Are there limits on the Christian's obligations? If so, can he be expected to resist (as Luther resisted the authority of a corrupt church)? In that case, what kind of resistance is permitted? And if resistance is permitted, is it obligatory in all cases? Must the faithful scour the secular world for the barest signs of injustice?

These questions bring Luther to what he calls the "main part of this sermon." He repeats the claim that secular government rules the body, whereas the soul can submit only to God. Only God, not the church, has authority over the souls of the faithful because the state's use of the force to constrain belief would violate the separation of the two cities. Even heretics cannot be punished by the government because that would prevent one evil by doing another, and worse, evil. If the ruler commands the believer to accept some false belief, the Christian's strong faith will permit him to resist. But this resistance will be only a stubborn but passive refusal that says, "Command me in what lies within your authority, and I will obey, but your command cannot affect my belief." Should you (the believer) be punished for this refusal, continues Luther, should your goods be taken from you, "then blessed are you, and you should thank God for counting you worthy to suffer for the sake of the Word." Evil, he insists, "is not to be resisted but suffered."[9]

Despite this limitation of government's reach, Luther turns finally to the proper manner for a Christian prince to exercise his authority. He admits that he knows nothing about the political world other than the fact that there are plenty of law books to give everyday guidance. All he can offer is advice on how a ruler should "dispose his heart" with regard to their use.[10] He had earlier warned against the overreaching entailed by the claim that the Christian should use the power of the sword to uproot evil. Success would be a "miracle" that is "unusual and dangerous" because no one can know that this person is really a true Christian. Luther advises the faithful prince that if his aim is to attain heaven, he must count on his faith rather than on his deeds. He more concretely warns the prince to be especially careful of advisors who claim to be true Christians, recalling that Lucifer, too, was once an angel. Luther advises that rather than use the power of government to impose rigid lawfulness, the prince should apply mercy in the meting out of justice. He recalls the popular saying that "a person who can't wink at faults, doesn't know how to govern."[11] Finally, in a remark that reflects the humanist education of the *via moderna*, he cites Augustine's denunciation of those who do not recognize that the source of all laws (God) should not be held captive to the stream (of laws) that flows from that source. In other words, the existing laws do not bind the freedom of the lawgiver.

The same flexibility that Luther offers to the prince in the application of the law to particular cases seems to be granted also to the Christian people. But this gift is a Trojan horse. Are the people obliged to obey the prince when he is in the wrong? The immediate response is that, of course, no one has a duty to act unjustly. Luther had already argued that the believer has a right to resist unjust laws, even if only passively, "with words," but he now makes a concession, asserting that if the subjects of a prince are not aware of his injustice, "they may obey without danger to their souls."[12] This odd claim makes sense only when considered in its historical context. It suggests that the purity of belief that constituted the force of the reformers blinds them to the realities of the secular world and its injustices. Because what counts is salvation, which is spiritual, the "injustice" of which the Christian is unaware must be secular. With this claim, Luther has prepared the subordination of the church that he founded to the secular power of the state, justifying Christian obedience to that power as long as the latter stays out of the spiritual domain. At the beginning of his career, Luther had used the state's protection to preserve his reformist activities, but he finds at the culmination of his mission that the princes have cleverly used his spiritual project to turn the faithful away from the world as a means to protect the princes' own secular power. Whereas he sought to legitimate politics among the faithful, absolutist princes turned that justification into a crude and sometimes arbitrary antipolitics.[13]

Luther's encouragement of the faithful to act as Christians within the secular world in order to realize their obligations to their neighbor is a brilliant demonstration of the interdependence of the secular and the sacred. In the end, however, his church was willing to sacrifice that secular world to the governance of the prince in order to preserve its own soteriological mission. The paradoxical political implication is that the Christian is obliged to obey the secular prince in order to live as a true Christian. The result was the development in the German lands of a particular kind of (anti)political power that was not legitimated by its actions, but by its simple existence. Its citizens did not obey it because it rendered justice; rather, obedience was an obligation due to a higher, sacred authority. Luther's great reforms were essentially over by 1526. The further history of the peculiar kind of secular political life that his soteriological theology justified need not concern us here. Its mark would be long felt in Germany, which stood for centuries on the threshold between the old order and modernity.

◆

Luther's great French successor, John Calvin, turned his efforts to the other pole of reform: ecclesiology, or the institutions and self-government of the church. But just as Luther's concern with the soul led unintentionally to the subordination of the individual to the state, Calvin's focus on the church's autonomy led him to expand the reach of ecclesial power to the state itself. Calvin's *Institutes of the Christian Religion,* which he revised repeatedly in the light of his practical experiences between 1536 and 1560, prescribes a form of church-state relation that led to Geneva's being called the "New Rome." The label is in fact ambiguous because it could refer not only to the Rome of the Catholic Church, but also to a renewal of Roman republicanism.

CALVIN'S POLITICAL ECCLESIOLOGY: CONSERVATIVE REPUBLICANISM

Luther did not make the Reformation by himself. The spark struck in Wittenberg fell on combustible soil. It was modified as it spread south to Switzerland, west toward France, and north to Sweden, England, and Scotland. Leaders emerged, corresponded, debated, and sometimes attacked one another in polemics that enriched the movement. But the same process expressed also the difficulty of maintaining the unity of a movement that reflected the emergence of the modern individual with a right to the free exercise of his conscience. Secular interests were involved, but the legitimacy of their claims had to be established in theological terms. For a time, the reformers were held together in their response to the force of the Catholic counteroffensive, whose military might was given theological arms by Ignatius of Loyola's creation of the Jesuit Order in 1540.

The ecclesiology of John Calvin (Jean Cauvin, 1509–1564) acquired its political role when the Council of Trent (1545–1563) reaffirmed the traditional Catholic doctrine, signifying that hope for the reconciliation of Christendom had ended. As opposed to Luther's Platonist vision that insisted on purity as the condition of unity, Calvin's reformed church recognized the need to take into account the diversity among the believers—although not that of their beliefs—in order to create a different kind of unity. By adapting the Aristotelian idea of mixed government, Calvin's church acquired power within the state without appealing to the Gelasian theory that the spiritual authority should rule over the temporal powers. The Calvinist remained a citizen; he did not accept the Lutheran subordination to the temporal powers for protection of the faith. Although Calvin never held political office, his Geneva was a republic based on a civic religion whose values were the presupposition and foundation of its political life. As Calvin put it concisely, the secular magistrate's obligations "extend to both Tables of the Decalogue"; the magistrate owes duties to both God and his fellow citizens.[14] This attribution of both spiritual and secular power to government has contributed to Calvin's reputation as the advocate of an all-powerful theocracy. In fact, his theory is more subtle, although in the last resort his conservative ecclesial instincts prevailed over the political prospects of republican renewal.

As a young man, Calvin studied law and humanism. His religious conversion seems not to have involved the titanic inner drama, doubt, and despair that had brought Luther to his faith. Where the German had to contend with the still solid structures of medieval theology, the twenty-six years that separated his birth from that of the French reformer had created a nearly unrecognizable religious world. Although the reform was not dominant in Paris, and Calvin had to flee after his conversion, the focus of his attention was less on the polemic with the Roman Church than on the knitting together of the new religious edifice. Luther had preserved the spiritual purity and ecclesial unity of his new church by giving power to the secular rulers, but the unintended result was that the German state was without a soul: there was no way to impose limits on its action or even to define the proper ends that would justify it. Its action was necessary for Christians, but it was itself not necessarily Christian. Calvin's theology was built around an ecclesiology that legitimated the reformed church as the mediator between the divine and the profane, the sacred and the secular. In this way, it replaced the one-sidedness of the Lutheran understanding of the political but opened itself to the danger that the Calvinist church would destroy the autonomy of political life by enfolding it in ecclesial life.

Calvin's theology seems at first to integrate humanism with the basic tenants of Luther's reform, but it quickly takes a harsher turn. As a humanist trained in the law, Calvin begins from the Ciceronian idea of natural theology based on the claim that human knowledge and God's wisdom share a common characteristic. The divine truth expressed in the Creation comes to be known in men's conscience by the use of right reason. In this way, man is enjoined—and knows himself to be enjoined—to ethical behavior as well as to religious belief. But because human reason is affected by sin, God must reveal himself in Scripture, enlightening the minds of those who can use the humanists' interpretative techniques to understand this revealed truth. Calvin is at one with Luther in rejecting any version of the Pelagian idea that men can earn salvation or even attain true faith by the force of their own will. But his idea of this unmerited divine intervention has a more radical foundation than Luther's. In Calvin's view, an omniscient and omnipotent God must have already dictated at creation each and every human being's destiny, which leads to Calvin's idea of predestination. This harsh doctrine apparently leaves no place for politics.

Taken literally, predestination leaves no role even for the church because God chose at the beginning of time both those who are to be saved and those who are to be damned. Looked at more closely, this double predestination in fact explains the role of the church and its relation to the world. Because no finite human can know the will of God, who has designated the elect, the true church is invisible. At the same time, however, the church is also visible wherever men publicly worship the one true God who has revealed Himself both in Scripture and through the Redeemer's sacrifice. Among the believers, there will also be some who have not been saved (even though they cannot know this). As a result, the organization of the visible church must not only ensure the administration of the sacraments, but also deal with the relations among the different members of the church (who are distinguished, as by Aristotle, according to the ends they pursue). In this way, the organization of the visible church is reflected in the City of Man, whose diversity must be accepted at the same time that its unity is maintained by the shared recognition of the one true God (who may or may not save the individual citizen).

Calvin's theological concept of predestination thus leads him to formulate an ecclesiology that explains why and how the believer is obligated by the church to specific types of behavior in both the spiritual and the secular worlds. As opposed to Luther's pessimistic nominalism, which suggests that God's freely given grace can also be lost, Calvin's predestinatarian theology argues that once God chose, the choice was to be for all eternity; the elect do not lose their status because of temporary lapses. As a result, the Calvinist's relation to the secular world differs from the Lutheran's in that the latter, in spite of his obligation to his neighbor, leaves the political world to the care of the secular state. The Calvinist interprets his place by analogy to that of the Jewish people, who, although chosen, are not made perfect and remain liable to error. They may violate their side of the contract, the Prophets may take them to task for their failings, God may inflict the trials of Job on them, but the covenant between them and God cannot be undone. This doctrine of election gives to the Calvinist, who hopes that he is among the chosen, the courage to go out into the world. He may become a missionary seeking converts, be active in political affairs, or become a leader in the new world economic system called capitalism.[15] And his success (or his tribulations) in the world will seem to him to confirm (or deny) his election.

The political implications of Calvin's ecclesiology are developed in his brief discussion of "civil government" at the conclusion to the *Institutes of the Christian Religion.* The higher dignity of the sacred does not mean that Christians must avoid the secular. As a worldly institution, the church permits us "in this mortal and evanescent life . . . some foretaste of immortal and incorruptible blessedness."[16] But this, and no more, is all that it can offer, insists Calvin, who, like Luther, had to take precautions against radicals' desire to realize heaven on earth. Secular government has the legitimate task to foster the worship of God, defend the pure doctrine, and ensure the church's autonomy during mankind's "pilgrimage" on earth. By encouraging but not defining religious practice, government preserves the unity of a plural society in which no one can know whether he has been chosen. The idea that this secular power should be abolished is "barbaric"; government is as beneficial as bread, water, sun, and the air we breathe—and its dignity is far greater. Not only does it make life possible, but the end that it seeks makes possible the good life by preserving "the public form of religion amongst Christians," which fosters peace, guarantees property, and maintains "humanity amongst men."[17]

The powers that Calvin grants to secular government are real but limited. He distinguishes three distinct actors involved in politics: the magistrates, who are the guardians of the law; the laws themselves; and the people, who are governed by the laws but whose obedience to them must not conflict with their obligations to God. Although the magistrates' role appears to repeat the Pauline doctrine that all powers are from God, Calvin's account in fact opens the path toward a theory of representative government. He rejects the unitary Platonic absolutism of Pauline theory in favor of an argument similar to the idea of mixed government in Cicero's reading of Polybius or in Aristotle's mixed polity.[18] On this basis, he develops the notion of natural law (as "equity"). When he turns to the role of the people, he thus takes the first steps toward the idea of a right to resist tyrannical power. Each of these steps, which John Locke would develop more fully in seventeenth-century England, needs to be examined separately in order to show the originality of Calvin's political theory.

The magistrates are to act from conscience, knowing that their office has been established to carry out God's will. The notion of conscience is fundamental to Calvin's attempt to overcome Luther's rigid distinction of these two domains as complementary but radically different from each other. Calvin accepts the traditional view that men are divided beings whose spiritual and material natures are at war with one another. The possibility of sin is thus constantly present, which is why the believers must keep constant watch over themselves, living a methodical life, keeping diaries, looking for signs of weakness that may reflect a turning away from God. The paradoxical result of the Calvinist sense of the omnipresence of sin is a recognition of the existence of a higher law that binds the individual, who knows that if he does not accept that higher law, he is a sinner. Conscience is thus the internalization of God's will, and conscientious action is the realization of the divine command. That is why the secular magistrate, too, is bound by his conscience. For the same reason, the Calvinist magistrate is responsible for "both Tables of the Decalogue." This account shows that the magistrate himself is bound by earthly as well as heavenly law rather than granted unlimited or arbitrary power.

Although Calvin calls the magistrature a "holy ministry" (in the Latin text) and a "vocation" or "calling" (in the French), he takes care to explain that this does not mean that only the monarch has been given the authority to rule. Unity is not imposed from the top down; it arises from diversity. He analyzes the advantages and disadvantages of the "three forms of government which philosophers refer to," concluding that "it is not easy to decide which is the most beneficial." Each has advantages, depending on circumstances. Calvin draws the lesson that "the vices and defects of mankind . . . make it safer and more tolerable that several persons should govern [jointly], all of them assisting, instructing and admonishing one another, so that if one of them arrogates more to himself than he is entitled to do, there will be others to act as his censors and masters, to curb his license." The result will be the kind of checks and balances defended by Polybius's republican political theory. Calvin's goal is the creation of a government "in which liberty and the right degree of restraint are reconciled."[19] Like Aristotle, he is not seeking to create the absolutely best society, which explains why he warns that his theory does not propose the replacement of monarchy by mixed government. Appealing again to circumstances, he instead argues that God institutes different regimes in different conditions.

At this point in Calvin's account, an ambiguity appears that is lifted only when he turns to the discussion of the people's duties. He seems to forget the republican overtones of his account. He says that his analysis of magistrates' duties is intended "not so much to teach magistrates themselves, as rather to teach others what magistrates are and why God established them." More precisely, he seeks to explain the individual's obligation to obey. For example, despite the prohibition against killing, the magistrate is authorized to apply this extreme measure because he is realizing God's will when he punishes trespasses (although he does so with "clemency").[20] When the magistrate decides to make war, it not only must have a justified end (peace), but must also make use of legitimate means (to avoid the excesses of human passion). Taxes are also justified, even if they are used to maintain the splendor of the magistrate's house because that house is linked to the dignity of high office (but this use of taxes is illegitimate if the dwelling is treated as his private property). In short, private persons should not "rashly revile" princes, who are indeed the delegates of God on earth. But because the will of God cannot be known, and because the magistrate is supposed to apply the law in the exercise of his office, Calvin's analysis turns to the nature of the law, which serves to limit magisterial arbitrariness.

In its broad outlines, Calvin's legal theory belongs to the natural-law tradition of Cicero or to its modified form in Aquinas, but his justification of it is significantly different. The Old Testament distinguishes three kinds of law: the moral law, which inclines men to worship God and love their neighbors; ceremonial law, which is a tool for educating the young Jewish people; and judicial law, which preserves the civil order, justice, and equity. The first type includes laws of the heart, which are given a positive form in habits acquired through the second type of law, ceremonial practice. As in Aristotle, these habits create the attitudes and expectations that make the acceptance of the third type, judicial law, a matter of reason rather than force. Although the three kinds of law differ in form, their content is identical because each furthers the mutual love among men. Calvin goes a step farther, asserting that the same principle holds for the diverse forms of law among peoples: "all these laws must be measured against the law of love." This shared content is itself the basis of a higher law that Calvin calls "equity." "Equity," he explains, "in as much as it is natural, must be the same for all, and therefore all laws ought to make it their purpose, although accommodated to the particular object with which they deal."[21] The need to apply the principle of equity to particular conditions makes room for political discretion, as well as for legal progress.

On the basis of this theory of equity as a kind of "measure" of all other laws, Calvin returns to the problem of both the church's and the private individual's obligation to the laws. He recalls the passage in Romans 13:5 where Paul explains that we must obey magistrates "not only for wrath, but also for conscience sake." Obligation cannot be based on fear ("wrath"); its legitimation lies in the individual's conscience, which mediates between the divine and the human by internalizing the idea of a higher law. The private citizen obeys the magistrate because he knows that the office is delegated by God. Although Calvin doesn't stress the point, the magistrate is in this sense a representative, but what he represents is the divine, which is why Calvin defines the magistrate as the living or external form of each individual Christian's inner conscience. Obedience, therefore, is due not to the person who holds the office, but to God, whose representative the magistrate is.

Calvin's theory of office differs from Augustine's insofar as he insists that one should not act toward magistrates "as if the dignity of the office could mask their stupidity, villainy or cruelty, their immorality of life and viciousness." Although Calvin is writing at the outset of the age of the modern individual, he quickly steps back from the implication that disobedience, if not resistance, would be justified in such a case. "If there is something in need of correction in the public order, private men are not to create disturbances or take matters into their own hands." The key phrase here is "private men," whom Calvin had previously warned not to "rashly revile" the magistrates. If conditions worsen, the aggrieved parties "should submit the matter to the cognizance of the magistrate." He adds, however, that they may act if a "superior"—that is, another magistrate—lends them his authority.[22] This remark needs further explication.

Calvin knows that the portrait of the magistrate with which his essay began is an ideal and that "we find in almost every age another sort of prince." He also admits that mankind has "an innate hatred and detestation of tyrants, just as it loves and venerates lawful kings." But his concern is not mankind's opinion; his ecclesiology is intended to explain the need for subordination. Yet after several pages of biblical citation to demonstrate that this obligation is owed to the Creator (not to the magistrate), Calvin concedes, "You will reply, superiors in their turn reciprocally owe duties to their subjects. I have already acknowledged it."[23] This affirmation marks a new direction.

Calvin expresses the kind of duty owed to subjects with an analogy. Husbands and wives, parents and children owe each other mutual duties, but what if they don't perform them or do so in a manner that provokes anger or is stupidly executed? The duty is still owed, says Calvin, but this obligation is not based on a contract with the other party. Rather, each individual is concerned only with his own duties, not with the actions of the other party (who may have reasons for not carrying out the bargain that are not immediately evident). Each should therefore ask only about what is in his power. Is it his fault that the other has defaulted? Are his sins the reason that he himself is suffering? "It is not for us to remedy such evils; all that is left to us is to implore the help of the Lord, for the hearts of princes and alterations of kingdoms are in his hands." But the passive subordination that Calvin recommends here is not his final word. His analogy compares political obligations with private duties whose nonperformance may be the fault of the person who now suffers; for example, the person's wife or family no longer show love and affection because of the way he has treated them. The fact that these duties and obligations are analogous to public duties and obligations does not mean that they are identical.[24]

Returning to the problem of tyranny, Calvin sees a testimony to God's goodness and power in the fact that "sometimes he raises up avengers from amongst his servants, designated and commanded by him to punish the tyranny of vicious men."[25] Calvin does not say whether these are private men or magistrates, but, whatever the case, they play a public role. And the fact that God calls them forth implies that they are his representatives or a sort of prophetic magistrate. The difficulty is that they fulfill no secular office; if they were to call for assistance, there is no way for them to "lend their authority" to oblige others to join in their mission. The prophet may remain a lone voice in the wilderness.

Calvin's goal is to ensure that the magistrates do not overstep their bounds. His examples of divine vengeance are a caution: "Let princes hear and be afraid." But what are they to fear? Calvin repeats that private men can do nothing against the magistrates. "All that has been assigned to us is to obey and suffer." But the former humanist shows his unease when he turns from Scripture to political history. He recalls the Spartan ephors and the Roman tribunes, but they were magistrates who could legitimately command obedience. Calvin wonders whether the authority of the three "estates" of the kingdom can represent a similar type of office when they meet together. After all, when the legitimate ruler becomes a tyrant, he can no longer claim the authority of his office, which is instituted for the public good. He has made himself a private person who is seeking particular goals, so not only may he be resisted by other private persons whom he tries to oppress, but his office may also be assumed by any other public power that can claim divine sanction. That is why Calvin suggests that a private person can act against a magistrate if another magistrate lends him his authority. But Calvin goes no further in this line of questioning, which in the religious wars between his French Huguenot followers and the established Catholic state authorities would give rise to rich debates over the logic and justification of tyrannicide. Calvin's conclusion in *On Civil Government* is ambiguous. He repeats his ecclesiological thesis that "we must never allow ourselves to be diverted from our obedience to the one to whose will the desires of every king must be subjected. . . . Would it not be an absurdity to give contentment to [mere] men [by obeying them], but thereby to incur the wrath of him on whose account [any human being at all] must be obeyed?" An unjust magistrate could have been set over the people only to punish their trespasses or to test their faith or perhaps because they are damned for all eternity (which could not be true of an entire people, though). His best hope for overcoming injustice is the "fear" in the hearts of tyrants, whom the elect, designated by God as "avengers," will punish.[26]

◆

Although Calvin's French Huguenot followers, the Monarchomachs, would draw the antiabsolutist political implication of his theory of the natural law of equity as the "measure" of the legitimacy of all laws, justifying resistance to tyranny, Calvin's own ecclesiological politics forbid any challenge to the reformed church's claim to be the external representative of the individual conscience that legitimates obligation by mediating between the secular and the sacred. If Calvin's Geneva was a "new Rome," it was not a revival of the republic, but the creation of a church that, for all its differences, was as absolute in its claims as its Catholic forbearer. The liberation of politics from the weight of the sacred was not yet realized. That would be Machiavelli's task.

MACHIAVELLI'S POLITICAL REALISM: THE ILLUSIONS OF THE REPUBLICAN PRINCE

Although Niccolò Machiavelli (1469–1527) benefited from a humanistic education, he was not a scholar, but an active politician who held high offices in Florence during its republican period from 1498 to 1512. He led diplomatic missions to France, Germany, and Switzerland, becoming chief assistant to the head of state, the *galfoniere*. When the republic was overthrown, he was driven from office, briefly tortured, and finally banished to the countryside. It was there that he began to write the political essays that made him both famous and infamous. His name soon became an adjective describing a ruthless, amoral politics for which the ends justify whatever means seem necessary. This assessment is true insofar as, for Machiavelli, political ends are no longer natural or divinely prescribed, but rather set by men in their quest for power. This view in turn lends a certain plausibility to the accusation of amoralism because it implies that politics is the unique source of the legitimacy of social relations. That is why the discussion of Machiavelli belongs in this chapter, which examines the search for a "pure theory." In order to develop his insight into the primacy of politics, Machiavelli had to change the traditional understanding of the nature and function of the political.

Machiavelli's reputation rests on his two major works, *The Prince* and *The Discourses on the First Ten Books of Titus Livy*.[27] The first is apparently a guidebook for a ruler seeking to conquer and maintain power by any and all means. A lazy reader, unfamiliar with the history of political thought, may focus on chapter titles such as "How a Prince Should Keep His Word," (chapter 18), "How a Prince Should Act to Acquire Esteem" (chapter 21), and "How Flatterers Are to Be Avoided" (chapter 23). Better-read critics may denounce Machiavelli as heir to Sophists such as Thrasymachus, but the Florentine politician was familiar with the classics. He knew that there is a difference between household management and political rule and that power is not a thing that can be wielded like a club or exercised by a master on a slave. Power differs from force insofar as it must be legitimate in the eyes of its subjects. In the emerging modern world, the need for political legitimation meant that power had to preserve the individual's freedom. This insight, which emerges from a closer reading of *The Prince*, becomes explicit in *The Discourses*, whose republican spirit was evident already in the choice of Livy as Machiavelli's conversation partner.

A more sophisticated analysis of Machiavelli's political theory has to begin from the fact that modern social relations are no longer regulated by the natural ends taken for granted by classical and Christian thinkers. As a result, Machiavelli tries to develop the idea of an "economy of violence" that attempts to limit the effects of the inevitable conflicts that emerge in political life. Modern freedom without limits necessarily produces social frictions that can never be wholly overcome because their complete elimination would destroy the liberty that defines the modern individual. When each individual's freedom comes to clash with others' freedom, the best that the politician can do is to seek the most "economical," least costly, or least oppressive way to hold together a society of self-seeking individuals who want to protect their personal freedom. This idea explains much of what disturbs readers who see *The Prince* as a manual for tyrants.

Two illustrations of the economy of violence suggest its attractiveness. Chapter 3 of *The Prince* examines the position held by the ruler of a new territory.[28] Many of the territory's inhabitants may at first be willing to accept him because he appears to offer them the chance to better their lot, but the measures that he must impose in order to unify the new territory with his own may disappoint them. Now the prince will face two rebelling enemies, the friends of the old order and his disappointed former allies. When he puts down the ensuing rebellion, he will have to take stern measures because "one must either pamper or do away with men, because they will avenge themselves for minor offences while for more serious ones they cannot; so that any harm done to a man must be the kind that removes any fear of revenge." Because mild punishment might encourage further resistance, the sterner measure economizes the possibility of renewed violence. Thus, in chapter 8, which treats princes who come to power by wickedness, Machiavelli explains that the effectiveness of cruelty depends on whether it is "well or badly used." But he adds that "well used are those cruelties (if it is permitted to speak well of evil) that are carried out in a single stroke, done out of necessity to protect oneself, and are not continued but instead converted into the greatest possible benefits for the subjects."[29] The parenthetical caution suggests that although his theory is independent of moral values, it is not for that reason indifferent to them.

The problem with this idea of an economy of violence is that it treats politics as the action of a subject, the prince,[30] using an instrument, violence, to subdue a (relatively) passive object, the population. For example, the passage from chapter 8 explaining the proper use of cruelty is followed by the explanation that "injuries, therefore, should be inflicted all at the same time, for the less they are tasted, the less they offend; and benefits should be distributed a bit at a time in order that they may be savored fully." But by reducing political thought to social psychology, the argument neglects the need to show how force becomes legitimate power by gaining the assent of the governed. Although psychology has a role to play in political thought, it is not in itself an explanation of properly political behavior. Among other things, it neglects the dynamic structure of history and the difference between its classical and modern forms. Machiavelli's use of historical example differs from the humanists' search for experiences to be imitated. He stresses the dynamic tension produced by the interplay of *virtù* and *fortuna*, neither of which can exist without the other.[31] That is why, in the introductory pages of both *The Prince* and *The Discourses*, Machiavelli warns the reader to pay attention to this tension.

◆

The Prince, written while Machiavelli was in exile in 1513, begins with a dedicatory letter to Lorenzo di Medici, who had overthrown the republic the previous year. Its flattering tone has contributed to the idea that Machiavelli was currying favor, vaunting his qualifications for a new job in the government. Machiavelli is treated as being without scruples, ready to abandon his prior beliefs in exchange for power and to recommend to the new ruler similar behavior. This interpretation seems confirmed insofar as his failure in achieving a position led him to adopt a republican perspective in *The Discourses,* which he addressed to politically engaged aristocratic youth meeting at the Rucellai gardens and dedicated to the gardens' owner. He calls attention to the fact that this dedication differs "from the usual practice of authors, which has always been to dedicate their works to some prince, and, blinded by ambition and avarice, to praise him for all his virtuous qualities when they ought to have blamed him for all manner of shameful deeds." Was Machiavelli so machiavellian? If so, his thought would be at best of historical interest.

The dedicatory letter to Lorenzo illustrates the interplay of historical example and practical politics that has made reading Machiavelli so difficult. His phrasing is lightly ironic, noting that traditionally those who seek to win favor from a prince give him material things that they know will please him, such as horses, arms, and precious stones, all of which pay tribute to his majesty. Machiavelli can offer only what he himself most values: "the knowledge of the deeds of great men, which I have learned from a long experience in modern affairs and a continuous study of antiquity." Machiavelli is suggesting that the same kind of knowledge will be useful to Lorenzo. Experience of the present directs attention to aspects of the past that were unnoticed or undervalued at the time; study of the past conversely ensures the ability to resist the pressure of immediate events by situating today's needs within a broader context. This knowledge, the letter continues, results from the study of the actions taken by particular individuals, which despite being specific cast light on universal virtues. This play of the particular and the universal is the first expression of Machiavelli's historical dialectics, which is concerned with "great deeds" and heroic action capable of seizing the high tide.

The next paragraph of the dedicatory letter makes it clear that Machiavelli is not presenting a handbook for tyrants, but rather a political theory. The light irony is maintained. Although he is unable to offer precious material gifts, he is "sure that your humanity will move you to accept [this gift]." He does not use flowery phrases to add surface appeal but counts on the variety of his subject manner and seriousness of his analysis to gain favor. Is it presumptuous, he asks, for a man of "low and inferior station" to debate the role of princes? Comparing his work to that of an artist, he points out that "just as those who paint landscapes place themselves in a low position on the plain in order to consider the nature of the mountains and the high places and place themselves high atop mountains in order to study the plains, in like manner, to know well the nature of the people one must be a prince, and to know well the nature of princes one must be of the people." Aristotle had already insisted that the just ruler must know not only how to rule, but how to be ruled. To work for the common good, a prince must know the people because their support is necessary for him to maintain his power. The corollary, that one must be "of the people" to know the nature of the prince, implies that political knowledge is not reserved to the elite; the people "know" the prince because they experience him directly, for good or ill.

The letter's final paragraph has to be read in the context of the concluding chapter of *The Prince*. Machiavelli flatters Lorenzo, hoping that his "little gift" will achieve his own "heartfelt desire that you may attain that greatness which fortune and all your own capacities promise you." This flattery of the ruler who overthrew the republic and sent Machiavelli himself into exile returns in the concluding chapter of *The Prince*, titled "An Exhortation to Liberate Italy from the Barbarians." But now Machiavelli speaks as an Italian patriot. Suffering Italy finds no one "in whom she can have more hope than in your illustrious house." Your task will be made easier, continues Machiavelli, "if only you will use the institutions of those men I have proposed as your target." The "institutions" to which Machiavelli refers are republican, as he indicates by stressing that "it is necessary before all else, as a true basis for every undertaking, to provide yourself with your own native troops." The citizen militia had been the foundation of Rome's might; its use now would make Lorenzo truly powerful. "What doors will be closed to him? Which people will deny him obedience? What jealousy could oppose him?"

The republicanism that is only implicit in *The Prince* becomes explicit in the preface to book I of *The Discourses*. As he did in *The Prince*, in *The Discourses* Machiavelli promises to present "what I have arrived at by comparing ancient with modern events . . . so that those who read what I have to say may the more easily draw those practical lessons which one should seek to obtain from the study of history."[32] He insists that history is not just a chronicle of events lost in the past. History is concerned with deeds and actions; it is not an object for contemplation. His contemporaries "lack a proper appreciation of history." They take pleasure in the stories they hear, "but [they] never think of imitating" the deeds they recite. They honor antiquity but tend to overvalue it, treating it like an old statue that was purchased at a high price rather than learning to practice the virtuous actions of the generals, citizens, or legislators who served their country. The history revered by the humanists thus serves only to justify the present or to regret its values rather than to challenge them. This use of history is conservative, even if it criticizes the present for not living up to the values of the past, because its certainty that the values of the past are the only true values directs attention away from the challenges in the present.

In *The Discourses,* Machiavelli again insists on the uniqueness of his own vision of history, and its political implications. "I have decided to enter upon a new way, as yet untrodden by anyone else." Rather than treat Livy like an honorable old statue, he will use him critically to demystify the accepted values and virtues that constitute the storehouse of wisdom of the Florentine status quo. He will challenge Livy. He will portray neither a virtuous Roman republic corrupted by self-interested politicians nor a harmonious system of checks and balances among honorable senators, upright tribunes, and a freedom-loving people. If such virtue and harmony had actually reigned, the Romans would not have needed to invent politics. Although Machiavelli never states it explicitly, this basic insight guides his thought: politics is necessary because society is never fully reconciled with itself, harmony is never permanent, unity cannot be total. That is why he does not offer political advice to actual or potential rulers, but instead warns against political illusions that blind the rulers or the people to the existence of conflict, passions, and interests. Because of his concern with demystifying illusions, his political theory may be called *amoral,* but it is not for that reason *immoral.*

◆

The foundations of a properly political form of rule begins to be laid in chapter 6 of *The Prince,* when Machiavelli asks how a ruler can acquire new lands by his own arms and skill. The ruler's success is described as a dialectic between *fortuna* and his own *virtù*. Fortune, accident, or simply good luck provides the occasion that permits a prince to use his skill, cunning, and ability to impose form on the material world around him. Machiavelli stresses the interaction between these two variables. The prince's virtues and abilities would have had no effect on the world had not the fortunate chance provided the conditions needed to actualize them. Without the opportunity provided by luck or good fortune, those qualities would be for all practical purposes nonexistent; their reality exists only insofar as they affect the world. But it is equally true that without those skills, the opportunity presented by fortune would not be perceived or acted upon. In that case, the occasion that in retrospect seems so propitious would, in effect, have not existed. In short, without the conditions provided by fortune, the abilities and skill go to waste; without these virtues, the chance is not recognized, and the occasion is missed. This political dialectic cannot be reduced to psychology, nor does it simply apply the calculating economy of violence. The difficulty is that this dialectic between *fortuna* and *virtù* can be recognized only in retrospect.

Machiavelli elaborates the prospective implications of his political dialectic in chapter 9 to explain what he calls the "civil principality" in which political rule by a private citizen depends on the favor of his fellow citizens. Such a ruler is a republican prince. The way that his power becomes legitimate shows why conflict and violence are inherent in modern politics. Machiavelli assumes that there is a basic opposition inherent in every city between the rulers and the ruled, the nobility or aristocracy and the people. Their conflicting desires create the basic dynamic of political life. The republican prince can come to power with the support of either the people or the aristocracy. By their very nature, the aristocrats want to rule, whereas the people wish only to avoid oppression. The republican prince will have to judge when the relation between these two forces and the conflict of their respective interests make his rise to power possible. Machiavelli analyzes the configurations that lead to success and the dangers that face a republican prince who depends on one or the other of these social forces to legitimate his power.

The civil principality can arise in two different ways. The nobility may recognize that they cannot stand up against the power of the people; they decide, therefore, to designate one of their own as prince. Although his power is justified as representing the unity of the society as a whole, the aristocrat who is made prince is expected by his peers to carry out their particular projects and interests. But doing so would threaten his legitimacy because he is then clearly representing particular interests. The second possibility for the creation of a civil principality emerges when the people understand that they cannot resist oppression by the nobility. Machiavelli assumes that although the people are incapable of ruling directly, they can designate one of the aristocrats to rule, raising him to power in order to gain protection against the other nobles. In this way, the common good sought by the republican prince benefits the popular interest. It would seem that the rule of such a prince, whose support comes from the people, will bring legitimacy and stability to the state, but it is not so easy to overcome social conflict and eliminate the threat of violence.

Machiavelli compares the risks and benefits of the two types of republican prince. If the prince depends on the nobility, he will face difficulties in gaining legitimacy due to the fact that he is surrounded by people who think they are his equals, who are used to giving orders rather than obeying them, and who will not willingly obey his commands or accede to his wishes. On the contrary, a person raised to power by the people will have little difficulty in obtaining its assent because he is in effect carrying out their will. The contrast goes further. On the one hand, the aristocrats on whom the prince depends will not be satisfied if he acts fairly and avoids injuring others, whereas the people, who want simply to avoid oppression, are content with such equitable behavior. On the other hand, the popular prince's situation is not completely secure; he is not free to act as he wills. He has to beware of a threat that arises from the hostility of the people, whose numbers can overwhelm him. This possible outcome suggests that he should therefore not bank on popular support but seek that of the aristocrats because he need not worry about the anger of a few nobles. This solution, in turn, is no more certain, however, because the few hostile aristocrats may be more cunning, have more foresight, and thus be more dangerous in the long run. Is there a way out of this rondo of conflict and instability?

Machiavelli suggests what appears to be a solution to the dilemma. Brought to power by the aristocrats who want to use him for their own purposes, the republican prince may escape their grip by turning to the people for support. Doing so will be easy because the people want only to be protected from oppression. Moreover, they will be well disposed toward someone whom they previously feared if he now brings them benefits instead of harm. Although Machiavelli stresses that this approach refutes the "trite proverb" that to build on the people is to build on sand, he is no democrat. Immediately after this praise of the people, he notes that popular support is not certain in times of adversity, when the people no longer find it in their interest to aid the prince and instead throw their support to a domestic or foreign rival. Faced with the possibility of such an unexpected turn of events, "a wise prince should think of a method by which his citizens at all times and in every circumstance, will need the assistance of the state and of himself; and then they will always be loyal to him." In short, permanent stability cannot be ensured by any form of political rule; conflict and violence lie always on the horizon, and so, in the last resort, the wise prince must avoid the illusion that he has overcome them. Although Machiavelli does not use the term *illusion*, that state of being is the foundation of antipolitics.

Machiavelli's recognition of the instability of political legitimacy explains some of the "Machiavellian" behavior that he recommends to the prince. On each occasion, the prince's goal is to avoid antipolitical illusions, to take account of the always-latent conflict, and to recognize that violence has to be controlled even though it cannot be eliminated. A crucial illustration is found in chapter 15 of *The Prince*, which considers "those things for which men, and particularly princes, are praised or blamed." A famous phrase contrasts "how one lives and how one ought to live." Machiavelli explains that "anyone who abandons what is done for what ought to be done learns his ruin rather than his preservation." The political consequence is that a prince must not only know how not to be good, but be able "to use this knowledge or not to use it according to necessity." This "knowledge" is derived from opinion, which in politics is not the opposite of truth, but rather a source of stability because it is universal, shared by everyone. The successful prince recognizes these values and knows how to appear to have the expected virtues even when, in reality, he does not. This knowledge is still no guarantee of political success, though. The values cherished by opinion may have harmful political effects. Thus, chapter 16 notes that although the public praises generosity and dislikes miserliness, a prince who is generous in spending public funds in order to win popularity may lack the support needed to raise taxes in times of need. Miserliness in spending state revenues may conversely permit the ruler to store up the means that permit later acts of generosity while alienating the affections of only a few of his subjects in the present.

The question of force returns in chapter 17 because the politics of opinion proves unable to assure stability. Machiavelli repeats his argument that a few acts of well-placed cruelty can prevent potential rebellions. The implication is that it is safer for a prince to be feared than to be loved. Because men are generally ungrateful and self-seeking, they will give their affection to a ruler from whom they expect benefits. But a ruler should have no illusions about his popularity, which will last only until a crisis comes onto the horizon. He should realize that friendship based on mutual gain is "purchased but not owned." A ruler who wants to maintain his power can rely only on "fear . . . sustained by a dread of punishment." In short, although a prince cannot command his people's love, he can instill the fear that holds them in their place. But government based on force proves to be unstable as well. Fear can become hatred, which is a passion that threatens civil peace. This shift occurs when fear of the severity with which the law is exercised becomes hatred of the prince because he is perceived as tyrannical and arbitrary. A greater danger, analyzed in chapter 18, is that the hated prince will come to be despised because he is "considered changeable, frivolous, effeminate, cowardly, irresolute." The hatred that seeks revenge will now find support from both popular opinion and formerly loyal supporters. If the prince senses the difficulty, he will take preemptive action, but that action now makes his rule truly and openly tyrannical, and the ensuing revolt will be still more inevitable.

The reader who thought that *The Prince* was a guide to the seizure and use of power has by now learned that each method for doing so proves to be illusory. No one can put an end to the conflict that is inherent in any society because there will always be rulers who are distinct in one or another way from the people whom they rule. If they were not different, they would have no claim to rule. The three types of civil principality ruled by a republican prince have also shown themselves to be liable to instability and conflict. A republican prince can no more rely on aristocratic support than he can on popular support. The ruler who knows how and when to take account of opinion in order to give the appearance of conformity with social expectations will find that fear is a more permanent source of power than the people's affection, but also that the line between fear and hatred is difficult to maintain and that the latter can turn into the disdain that encourages rebellion. All forms of rule are fragile and threatened by the unexpected. Machiavelli's guide for the perplexed prince consists ultimately in a series of warnings against the antipolitical illusion that conflict can be overcome, stability achieved, and social unity finally established once and for all.

As Machiavelli comes to the end of *The Prince,* he returns to the idea, invoked briefly in chapter 6, that political thought depends on the dialectical relation between *fortuna* and *virtù.* In the penultimate chapter, he opposes the antipolitical view that because this world is controlled "by fortune and by God," humans cannot affect its course and should let well enough alone. Machiavelli has nothing to say about God. His concern is human freedom. He is willing to admit "that fortune is the arbiter of one half of our actions," but he adds immediately that "she still leaves the control of the other half, or almost that, to us." The very existence of fortune—in the guise of indetermination, uncertainty, or just accident or luck—is the guarantor of human freedom. It assures that human affairs are not governed by external necessity. The implication, however, is not that "man" is absolutely free; Machiavelli is not a metaphysician, but rather a political thinker for whom freedom is a human possibility to be conquered and defended. He offers a simile to explain his perspective. He compares fortune to a raging river whose flood tide sweeps everything before it. But when the weather is calm, it is possible to prepare for the next onslaught by building dikes, dams, or embankments. In this context, freedom will be ready to meet fortune in a fair struggle.

Fortune can no more be completely mastered than the republican prince can ensure the elimination of conflict. The political weather is rarely calm; dikes may flood, dams weaken, embankments crumble. Fortune changes continually, whereas the ways of men are governed mostly by habit, and the danger is that men will not recognize the need for innovation. If fortune rules easily over men dominated by opinion, that bridle on liberty must be removed by recovering the *virtù* essential to freedom. Machiavelli has no recipe to offer; *The Prince* is a warning against the idea that there can be a simple solution. All he can do is insist that "it is better to be impetuous than cautious, because fortune is a woman" who prefers men who are bold to those who make calculated advances. And, "being a woman, she is always the friend of young men, for they are less cautious, more aggressive, and they command her with more audacity."[33] Machiavelli goes no further. His readers knew that Fortuna was a pagan goddess who could give only signs and smiles, but no guarantees of her favors. Machiavelli's concluding description of Italy's misery was meant to signal that the times were ripe, but that such signs were visible only to those who had the *virtù* to act on them. When Lorenzo proved that he was not up to the task, Machiavelli turned to the "young men" in whose company he elaborated *The Discourses*.

◆

The Discourses can be read as a dialogue between classical and modern theories of republican politics. In the place of the illusory quest for a republican prince who could unify a divided society, freedom is now to be both the cause and the effect of republican politics. The goal is no longer the transcendence of conflict to achieve a stable harmony. In the first chapter of book I, Machiavelli rejects the classical idea that the founders of cities should build them in a barren place to guarantee that the citizens "would have to be industrious and less given to idleness, and so would be more united because, owing to the poor situation, there would be less occasion for discord." That kind of passive, externally imposed unity is neither desirable nor stable. It neglects men's desire to dominate others, which is why "security for man is impossible unless it be conjoined with power." Power is not the enemy of freedom, but its guarantor. Freedom is also the foundation of any power sufficiently vital to ensure its own preservation. Freedom is the source of the legitimacy of a modern republic, which does not depend on harmony among material interests. Rather, the support of free men gives government its political power, and they will give it their trust so long as it realizes its promise to protect their freedom.

After a brief summary in book I, chapter 2, of Polybius's account of the institutions by which a mixed government apparently guaranteed Roman freedom, Machiavelli sets out to illustrate his thesis that political freedom was Rome's legislator. The task is not simple; "freedom" is not a subject acting on an object that it can transform at will. The conflict between those who rule and those who are ruled both limits the reach of freedom and preserves its effectiveness. From this perspective, Machiavelli retraces Livy's account of the overthrow of the monarchy that led to the creation of the consuls; the senators' arrogant behavior that led to the invention of the tribunes; and the omnipresence of the people, who express their demands in the street. In this process, freedom appears negative at first insofar as the conflicts are the result of the suspicion "that all men are wicked and that they will always give vent to the malignity that is in their minds when opportunity arises" (chapter 3). Positive effects then follow. "To me," says Machiavelli, "those who condemn the quarrels between the nobles and the plebs, seem to be caviling at the very things that were the primary cause of Rome's retaining her freedom. . . . [T]hey pay more attention to the noise and clamor resulting from such commotions than to what resulted from them, i.e. to the good effects which they produced" (chapter 4). These "good effects" are the reaffirmation of freedom against the imperious action of rulers who identify their own particular good with the general welfare.

Machiavelli's stress on the positive function of conflict is a criticism of the conservatism of his humanist contemporaries, whose abuse of historical examples he had criticized in the preface to book I of *The Discourses*. His interpretation of history in a "new way, as yet untrodden by anyone else," reflects the same "long experience in modern affairs and a continuous study of antiquity" stressed in the dedicatory letter in *The Prince*. Despite these similarities, *The Discourses* go beyond the earlier work's critique of political illusions.[34] Because Machiavelli does not follow either historical chronology or Livy's text, the thrust of his argument can be sketched briefly without doing violence to the subtlety of his dialogue with Livy's text, which he at once praises and challenges, refusing to treat it as merely a valuable "statue" incarnating eternal values.

The greatness of a republic is measured by its ability to permit and at the same time to contain the effects of conflict, to maintain unity while ensuring diversity. Thus, Machiavelli recalls that "in every republic there are two different dispositions, that of the populace and that of the upper class, and . . . all legislation favorable to liberty is brought about by the clash between them." Rather than repress the conflict in an impossible search for unity, "every city should provide ways and means whereby the ambitions of the populace may find an outlet, especially a city which proposes to avail itself of the populace in important undertakings" (chapter 4). The demands of a free people are rarely harmful to freedom because they result either from political oppression or from a suspicion that such oppression is being prepared. Thus, despite the claims that the public indictments of political enemies were a cause of Rome's decline (and thus, by implication, a threat to civil peace in Florence), Machiavelli defends the practice of indictment in general (chapter 7) and asks the reader to imagine what would have been said of Caesar had the freedom that permitted Cicero's denunciation of Catalina continued to exist in Rome (chapter 10). The "false semblance of renown" that surrounded the victorious general would have been challenged by those for whom freedom is more important than material rewards, political honors, or imperial expansion. Ruling classes, be they in Rome or Florence, always prefer peace and unity to conflict and division because the former ensure and perpetuate their domination.

The need for both conflict and its containment can be seen in two examples from book III of *The Discourses*, which presents a series of reflections on the nature of Roman heroes. In the first example (chapter 9), Machiavelli underlines the need to adapt to changing times in order to continue to enjoy the favors of fortune. The Roman general Fabius Maximus, whose cautious tactics permitted him to defend against Hannibal's offensive, refused to pass to the attack once the relation of forces changed. Had he been a monarch able to impose his policies without opposition, Rome would never have had the chance later to conquer Carthage. "For this reason," Machiavelli concludes, "a republic has a fuller life and enjoys good fortune for a longer time than a principality [i.e., a monarchy], since it is better able to adapt itself to diverse circumstances owing to the diversity found among its citizens than a prince can do." This diversity results neither from Polybian institutions nor from an Aristotelian mixed society; it arises from and is maintained by the free exercise of political criticism like that which led to the condemnation of Catalina but failed to act against the threat posed by Caesar.

When the containment of conflict leaves no more room for the diversity through which criticism is renewed, freedom may be lost. The history of Florence illustrates this danger. Tired by four years of rule by the radical priest Savanarola and fearing a return of the Medicis, Florentine leaders sought to ensure the republic's stability by making Piero Soderini *galfoniere* for life in 1498. Machiavelli, who had served as Soderini's chief secretary, praises his firm character and notes that his good nature and patience had served him well in a series of successes. But when the Medicis formed an alliance with Spain, Soderini did not react with sufficient vigor to the challenge. Machiavelli asks how this failure by such a proven politician can be explained. "There are two reasons why we cannot change our ways," he suggests. "First it is impossible to go against what nature inclines us to. Secondly, having got on well by adopting a certain line of conduct, it is impossible to persuade men that they can get on well by acting otherwise. It thus comes about that a man's fortune changes, for she changes his circumstances but does not change his ways." Why did Soderini lack the *virtù* needed to face *fortuna* by striking out on a new course? The fact that he had been named *galfoniere* for life meant that he did not have to subject himself to the conflicts inherent in republican politics.

These two examples from book III pose the question why the classical republic succeeded, whereas its modern form failed. One explanation is suggested at the outset of book II (in chapter 2) when Machiavelli wonders whether the peoples of old were more fond of liberty because of differences in education, in particular "the difference between our religion and the religion of those days." He contrasts the terrible virility of the pagan faiths with the fact that "our religion has glorified humble and contemplative men, rather than men of action. It has assigned as man's highest good humility, abnegation, and contempt for mundane things." The only strength that Christianity praises is the ability to endure suffering. But rather than blame "our" religion for the absence of republican virtues, Machiavelli notes that it was the Roman republic itself that snuffed out the pagan virtues of the peoples that it conquered, which helps explain the values adopted by Christianity, its concern with paradise rather than with the present, and its willingness to bear rather than to avenge injuries. Yet Machiavelli adds without further explanation, "religion permits us to exalt and defend the fatherland," and "it also wishes us to love and honor it, and to train ourselves to be such that we may defend it." Was Machiavelli referring to Christianity? Or did he have a different kind of religion in mind? What did he mean by "religion"?

The title of chapter 29 in book II of *The Discourses*, "Fortune blinds Men's Minds when she does not wish them to obstruct her design," is taken from Livy's account of Rome's defeat by the Gauls in 386 BCE. The historian suggests that this shameful defeat was the result of *fortuna*'s cunning. The pagan goddess had chosen to make Rome great by first punishing her, as if adversity were needed to reawaken the republican virtues that maintained its freedom. In *The Prince,* Machiavelli refused to identify *fortuna* with providence, fate, or destiny. He now argues that although men cannot oppose her or ignore her power, "they should never give up, because there is always hope, though they know not the end and move towards it along roads which cross one another and as yet are unexplored; and since there is hope, they should not despair, no matter what fortune brings or in what travail they find themselves." These "unexplored" roads echo the "new seas and unknown lands" that the preface to *The Discourses* promised to explore. Machiavelli is speaking to his contemporaries when he recounts Roman history. What are they to hope for? How can their earthly "hope" avoid the otherworldly values of the Christian faith?

The first chapter of book III reformulates this question, beginning with a reminder that although all worldly things are finite, "composite bodies, such as are states and religious institutions," can combat their inevitable decline by a return to their origins. This return or renewal (*ricorso*) is a reaffirmation of human freedom. It can be religious as well as secular or political. Although Machiavelli finds its origins in Livy's Rome, it is central to his idea of modern republicanism. The Romans' invention of a politics that would develop the freedom that regenerated the conflicts that ensured Rome's dynamism acquires its modern complement in the idea of the *ricorso,* which is called upon when politics can no longer play its designated role.

The *ricorso* is distinct from the humanist attempt to rediscover the original irenic human experience: the latter is private, imaginative, and contemplative, whereas the former is public, active, and political. The *ricorso* may be encouraged by special institutions, or a society may seize on unlikely events produced by the whims of *fortuna.* Machiavelli illustrates both possibilities. He explains that prior to the terrible defeat by the Gauls, the tribunes had observed no religious ceremony, and the people had rewarded rather than punished the Fabii brothers' disobedience. The disgraceful defeat made it clear that Roman religion and Roman law, which were the products and the protectors of its republican spirit, had to be renewed if Rome were to conserve its freedom. A different illustration of a *ricorso* is seen within modern Christianity in the case of Saints Francis and

Dominick, who showed the way to live the life of Christ and thereby "prevented the depravity of prelates and of religious heads." This same principle of a return to origins can be found within secular political institutions as well. After praising the judicial "parlements" of France for preventing royal abuse, Machiavelli warns that "should [the parlements] at any time let an offence remain unpunished and should offences begin to multiply, the result would unquestionably be either that they would have to be corrected to the accompaniment of grievous disorders or that the kingdom would disintegrate." And so it would come to pass in France in 1789.

This idea that a periodic return to origins is needed to keep freedom alive is one of the great contributions of *The Discourses*. Although Machiavelli claims to find it in Livy's history, the concept in fact emerges from Machiavelli's "new way" of looking to the past to explain the present and of using the present to interpret the past. Two further examples of the *ricorso* from the final chapter of book III illustrate his method. The chapter's lengthy title refers explicitly to the need for renewal: "A Republic that would preserve its Freedom, ought daily to make Fresh Provisions to this end." Machiavelli describes first the severe Roman practice of "decimation." It took place when the large number of soldiers who neglected their duty made punishment impossible (because punishing some would have been unfair to others, but at the same time those who remained unpunished might have been encouraged to commit further crimes). In order to restore discipline to an army of free, republican citizen-soldiers, the Romans chose by lot one man from every ten who would be killed. In this way, each soldier was forced to recall his duties because he knew that, on the next occasion of transgression, the lot might fall to him. As a result, the individual regains the sense of his particular function in the maintenance of the republic.

A second brief and apparently minor illustration makes explicit the political aim of Machiavelli's argument. The final clause in this chapter's long title claims that Machiavelli will illustrate how a republic can make provisions to preserve its freedom by showing "what Quintus Fabius did to earn for himself the title Maximus." Machiavelli explains that granting citizenship to a large number of foreigners according to the model established after the rape of the Sabine women had the unintended effect of tilting elections away from the classic republican candidates. To restore republican values, Quintus Fabius proposed to create four new tribes that would integrate the newer citizens into the old Roman institutions and values while revitalizing these institutions with new energies. In this way, the newcomers became active participants in the republic, both imbibing and energizing its values. Significantly, the foreigners were integrated and the republic renewed "without changing the constitution." This qualification makes it clear that a *ricorso* is not a simple return to the past; it is a renewal of the institutional spirit that animates republican freedom. That is why the chapter's title insists that the republic must "daily" make provisions for its renewal. No institution can ensure its perpetuation; that task is the repeated challenge of politics.

After his critique of political illusions in *The Prince*, the author of *The Discourses* is suggesting that the republican ideal must itself be renewed in modern times. That is how it can become the religion that Machiavelli claims "permits us to exalt and defend the fatherland" and "also wishes us to love and honor it, and to train ourselves to be such that we may defend it." Roman republicanism was a civic religion. The title of chapter 12 in book I of *The Discourses*, "How Important it is to take Account of Religion, and how Italy has been ruined for lack of it, thanks to the Roman Church," contrasts the classical role of Rome's civic religion to the dangerous political impotence of the modern church. The title suggests the need to renew the old republican faith. Machiavelli does not blame the religion of Christ; the error is political. That is why he goes on, in chapter 13, to give examples of "what use the Romans made of religion in reorganizing the city, in prosecuting their enterprises, and in composing tumults." Machiavelli is describing the functions that a modern civic religion should fulfill. He is asking whether a type of "republican religion" (rather than a republican prince, as in *The Prince*) can renew the spirit of freedom that founds legitimate political power in a republic.

◆

Machiavelli is not simply a theorist of realpolitik, let alone of modern office politics. Many interpretations of his work have been offered. Some read him from the left, seeing him as a republican, even a revolutionary, and others from the right, seeing him as a supporter of strong government against the tumult of liberty. Such ideological interpretations are antipolitical, reducing this critical theorist to the proponent of a unifying thesis that he is said to have recommended as the path to a just society. This antipolitical view, whether from the left or the right, rejects Machiavelli's own way of reading the past with the aim of preserving rather than overcoming the challenge of politics. In *The Prince*, he warns against the dangers of self-delusion, the snares of ideology, and the importance of what the philosophers deride as mere opinion. He also stresses the omnipresence of conflict in any human society from which the basic distinction between rulers and the ruled can never be eliminated. From *The Discourses*, which underline the conflict that was the source of Rome's freedom and greatness, readers learn to be alert for those events, occasions, or institutions that permit or encourage the *ricorso* that announces the renewal of a tired political society whose mortal fatigue is manifested in its stubborn quest for stability, certainty, and unity as a remedy for the conflict, doubt, and diversity that are inherent in modern individualism.

The political tendencies distinguished at the outset of this chapter—nationalism, proceduralism, liberal humanism, and ambiguous utopianism—would emerge in seventeenth-century England as well, but none of them could prevent the outbreak of civil war. The two major political thinkers whose work went to the heart of the conflict were Thomas Hobbes and John Locke. The former continued the Platonic-unitary thought that Luther had reinvigorated; the latter developed the Aristotelian-pluralist approach that Calvin had brought to the threshold of modern political thought. Nearly a century later, in France, Jean-Jacques Rousseau returned to Machiavelli's republican theories to reinterpret critically the liberal individualism underlying his own English predecessors' social contract theories. He realized that the legitimacy of political obligation cannot be explained by the idea that rights-bearing individuals contract with one another to create a state that legislates for them. A renewed, modern civil religion has to complement the social contract.

№ 5

MODERN INDIVIDUALISM AND POLITICAL OBLIGATION

MODERN INDIVIDUALISM MARKED a rupture with the classical and Christian worldviews in which the whole precedes the part and the source of political obligation transcends the domain of individual experience. Classical and Christian liberty consists in a person's ability to satisfy a preexisting ideal of moral and political justice discovered by the use of right reason. The precondition for this liberty is the existence of a just community, to whose reproduction individual freedom in turn contributes. Modern liberty, in contrast, frees the individual from the external constraint of natural or divine norms. Liberation from external obligation produces freedom for the creation of new ideals and norms. But limitless freedom can also lead to anarchy, overreaching, and self-destruction. To avoid this danger, the moderns had to find a way to replace the classical and Christian idea of objective natural law. They invented the idea of a subjective natural law, the foundation of which is the free individual whose liberty is preserved by social institutions that can claim legitimacy. They replaced the transcendent foundation of objective natural law with obligations that are immanent to the way in which naturally free individuals bind themselves to obey the law without giving up their essential freedom. Thomas Hobbes developed the Platonic tradition; John Locke fell into the Aristotelian lineage; and Jean-Jacques Rousseau attempted to combine these approaches in a modern republican synthesis.

◆

The seventeenth century brought rapid changes to traditional life patterns. The new age recognized its own demons in Machiavelli's ruthless analysis of the ineradicable place of conflict and violence in human relations. The traditional barriers against self-seeking egoism were losing their hold. Men seemed to have lost the humility that befits finite creatures in an infinite universe. The Renaissance humanism that looked to the past for models gave way to a worldview centered on individuals who posited their own goals and followed their own desires. The upholders of order and tradition were scandalized. As the fear of eternal damnation that had restrained the passions began to weaken, critical questioning of religious and moral values grew. The church could no longer justify punishment of free thinkers by claiming that it was saving them from eternal torment. The importance of individual conscience led to an attitude in which the present took priority over the past, the earth held precedence over the heavens, and novelty was prized above tradition. Toleration of nontraditional modes of life and thought challenged the idea that there was only one just and moral way to live together with others in a world where cities were acquiring an importance that they had not had since the fall of Rome. But what in retrospect was the stirring of democracy appeared to many as the threat of anarchy.

If neither religion nor reason could hold in check the passions lurking in the depths of humanity, three other options were available: to find a new means of repression; to apply the theory of mixed government to the passions so that the positive benefits of each checks the negative force of the others; or to find one passion that is in fact rational and that should therefore become the guide to a new politics. The first option was impossible; the use of force against free persons is legitimate only if they themselves agree to it. The second was too general to be practically useful because the passions are particular and idiosyncratic; the recipe for mixing them today would need to be changed on the morrow. The third option seemed the most practical choice. Machiavelli had demonstrated that (self-) interest is not only the strongest force motivating individual action, but also in principle a rational, calculating mode of behavior that patiently uses the relations among men to generate power. Interest trumps morality as a guide to practice and provides a political guarantee against the arbitrariness of government because the prince too obeys his self-interest just as do all other members of society. But this solution had to face the modern form of the classical problem of the relation between the public interest (of the citizen) and the private interest (of the individual man). Which interest trumped the other? Which one imposed weightier obligations?

The seventeenth century was also the age in which modern science came into its own. Its great leaps forward obliged the thinking public to try to explain the principles that made possible such advances in knowledge and extensions of man's power over nature. Two philosophical orientations competed with one another. Rationalism reformulated Platonic idealism to describe a world in which nature is composed solely of neutral bodies in motion. It applied the techniques of mathematics to plot the warp and woof of a world that in itself had no inherent ends; it formulated general laws to which the particular cases were shown to conform. In contrast, empiricism revised the Aristotelian worldview to take account of the fact that there were no preexisting wholes to give meaning to the parts. The empirical view of science began from particular cases and sought to find general laws that formed a common denominator to which all the single instances conformed. Neither approach succeeded in refuting the other; as in the clash of the sacred with the secular, both rationalism and empiricism benefited from their competition.

The conflict between the rationalist and the empiricist philosophies of science affected political thought. Thomas Hobbes developed the rationalist perspective, whereas John Locke stood with the empiricists. Both explained political obligation as the result of a "social contract" to which individuals freely consented, but each proposed different explanations of the nature and limits of this consent. For Hobbes, the result of the contract was a modern version of Plato's Guardians in the form of an absolute monarchy; for Locke's more Aristotelian theory, political legitimacy resided in the Parliament, where monarchy, aristocracy, and a modern middle class deliberated together. Although Locke's theory became a reality with the Glorious Revolution of 1689, considered a model by progressive thinkers across Europe, the heritage of rationalist, absolutism remained strong in France, the other great power of the times. It was there, nearly a century later, that Jean-Jacques Rousseau combined social contract theory with a classical republican vision that accorded absolute power to the sovereign people rather than to a monarch ruling by divine right. Rousseau's theory opened a new, but ambivalent, era in political thought.

HOBBES'S LIBERAL ABSOLUTISM

Born while England was fearfully awaiting the invasion of the Spanish Armada, Thomas Hobbes (1588–1679) said of his mother that "she brought twins to birth, myself and fear at the same time." The family was poor, but an uncle sent Thomas to the university at Oxford. Along with his ability in foreign languages, this education qualified him for employment by the aristocratic Cavendish family, to whom he was attached for most of his long life. Although this position meant that he could never afford to marry, it permitted Hobbes to visit with national and international luminaries as he accompanied the sons of his patron (and later their sons) on their obligatory grand tour of cultural and political Europe. At the age of forty, he discovered Euclid's *Elements*, whose rationalist certitudes and rigorous logical demonstrations captivated his searching mind. This kind of a priori certainty provided an antidote for his fears. Further studies of mathematics and optics—a science widely pursued by the European intelligentsia eager to avoid illusions—led to his earliest systematic work, *De corpore* (On the Body). This publication is noteworthy because it shows that this heir to Platonic rationalism was also a radical materialist. The implications of this combination of rationalism and materialism reappear in his political theory.

The fear to which Hobbes referred as his "twin" was not fear of the threat of foreign conquest, but of the danger of religious and civil war, which finally broke out in 1641. The war's roots were both religious and political, opposing a Protestant-dominated Parliament to a monarchy whose claim to absolute power was feared to be the prelude to the reintroduction of Catholicism. The king, Charles I, who had sought to rule without calling Parliament, was forced by financial exigency to call it to session. When Parliament then asserted its rights, the king "raised the standard" in 1642, using this traditional means of calling his feudal dependents to fight for his cause. These aristocratic Cavaliers, riding their horses and doing heroic deeds for individual glory, were defeated by the bourgeois Roundheads, a self-disciplined army of Calvinists staunch in their religious calling. The king was captured in 1646. While negotiations for a political settlement remained unsettled, the more radical members of the parliamentary forces organized a public airing of their views in the so-called Putney Debates in 1647. The Levelers, at times allied with other radicals known as the Diggers, raised democratic and egalitarian demands. The king was finally brought to trial in 1649. After he thrice invoked his absolute power, refusing to testify in his own behalf, he was condemned and beheaded. Meanwhile, radicals and moderates battled in Parliament, which had shriveled to a "rump" of seventy-five members in 1653, until army commander Oliver Cromwell dissolved it and declared himself Lord Protector. When his son was unable after his death to maintain this power, the restored Parliament voted in 1660 to recall the son of the former king from his French exile.

Hobbes was one of the earliest Royalists to return to England. Why did he return in 1651, however, while Cromwell was still in power? His support for monarchy was based on the simple argument that the people had granted sovereign power to the king through a contract that could not be broken at will. As in a marriage, the two parties had become a unity that could not be dissolved even if the bonds of affection that had united them were shattered. This contract legitimated the ruler's absolute power; no popular remonstrance could justly challenge it. But Hobbes's perspective seems to have changed as the exiled king proved to be indecisive, always searching for compromise, unable to follow a constant strategy to end the civil war. Hobbes seems also to have been affected by the arguments of the radicals at Putney, who refused the idea of a limited constitutional monarchy, recognizing their democratic demands as more absolute than those of the partisans of monarchy. As a result, he may have thought that he could capture the radicals' claim for his own purposes when he decided to publish his *Leviathan* in 1651.[1] Incorporating democracy into the unitary power of an absolute monarch, Hobbes would make democracy safe from itself, overcoming his fear of civil war by ensuring the state's absolute power. Whether this was his actual motive or not, this interpretation explains why Hobbes's absolutism can also provide support for a modern theory of individual rights.

Hobbes's biblical title seems to be a provocation, and the frontispiece of the *Leviathan* confirms that first impression. A huge human figure looks out over a peaceful hillside landscape that descends gradually to an orderly, walled town dominated by an imposing, large church. This is the Leviathan, wielding a sword in his right hand and a bishop's crosier in his left, signaling that the sovereign rules over both church and state. Yet a closer look reveals that the Leviathan's body is composed of many small bodies—the individual citizens. The implication, confirmed by Hobbes's definition of power in chapter 10, is that the sovereign's absolute power is made up of the citizens' powers, whose unity the sovereign incarnates and whose individuality he also preserves. This sovereign ensures the peace of the landscape and the order of the city that lie beneath his gaze. Although the sovereign is absolute, sovereignty is not arbitrary or tyrannical. The clearly delineated figures who make up the sovereign imply that his absolute power does not eliminate but rather protects the individual's rights.

At the end of *Leviathan,* Hobbes admits that he knows "how different this doctrine is from the practice of the greatest part of the world, and especially of these western parts, that have received their moral learning from Rome and Athens."[2] To show that he is not defending any arbitrary power, it is necessary to follow closely the logic of his argument. In the process, the modern idea of natural law as immanent and subjective becomes clearer.

Rather than imitate nature, Hobbes exhibits the enthusiasm of his times for the power of science over nature. He explains in his introduction that just as God has made and now governs the world, so man can use science to create an artificial being, which he describes by means of a series of analogies to the fabrication of a watch. The heart is like a spring, the nerves are so many strings, and the joints are the wheels that gives motion to the whole body. In the same way, man can create the great Leviathan, a commonwealth. This state is an artificial man whose functioning is described by another series of analogies to the natural body. Sovereignty is an artificial soul giving life and motion to the whole: the magistrates are its joints, reward and punishment are its nerves, wealth and riches its strength, and the public safety its business. What joins together the parts of this artificial body are "pacts and covenants" that resemble the "fiat" that God pronounced at the Creation. Men constructed this state with the aid of science, and they can control, organize, and master it.

The power of modern science over nature is made possible by the fact that there is no natural hierarchy of transcendent values in a material world composed simply of bodies in motion. The political philosopher has to explain what it is about the nature of man that distinguishes him from other objects in their shared space. He has to show how these men understand themselves and their world and how they relate to and communicate with one another. This is the subject matter of part I, "Of Man." As Hobbes explains in his introduction, "he that is to govern a whole nation must read in himself, not this or that particular man, but mankind."[3] To do so, it is necessary to start with a human being's most basic material properties, the senses and the imagination, and to study their development first in a single, generic man, an ideal type, then to examine the way men coexist in their natural state and finally the way they come to understand the natural laws that ought to govern their behavior. Only then does Hobbes turn, in part II, to the political analysis he calls "Of Commonwealth."

In a world of bodies in motion, indifferent to one another, the relation of the words that men speak to the objects of which they speak is arbitrary. How then do people understand one another? This question is the nominalists' dilemma reformulated by modern science. Hobbes presents a materialist account in chapter 6, explaining that their passions lead men to distinguish what they consider good from what they take to be evil or contemptible. In the most simple case, individual men are attracted to some things and averse to others, so there remains the questions how and why different people in different situations agree on what they mean by the words that they use. "For these words of good, evil, and contemptible are ever used with relation to the person that useth them, there being nothing simply and absolutely so, nor any common rule of good and evil to be taken from the nature of the objects themselves." The only possible solution to this problem, concludes Hobbes, is that definitions come "from the man (where there is no commonwealth), or (in a commonwealth) from the person that representeth it, or from an arbitrator or judge whom men disagreeing shall by consent set up, and make his sentence the rule thereof."[4] With this claim, Hobbes has anticipated what he will now have to prove: that the existence of the uniquely powerful Leviathan is necessary to ensure linguistic unity and a human community.

Hobbes begins his demonstration in chapter 13 by describing what he calls the "natural condition of mankind." His picture of what is generally called the "state of nature" has been as often misunderstood as it has been criticized. The difficulty is increased by the fact Hobbes was not the only seventeenth-century philosopher to appeal to this concept, but he was no doubt the most radical. His argument makes it clear that for modern thought, nature has no pregiven ends. When it comes to establishing what is called "natural law," the modern vision is the inverse of the classical and Christian worldviews. The modern laws of nature are those that are imposed on it by men, but these laws are not therefore arbitrary. Once they are established, modern natural law, like its classical antecedent, will be elaborated in the form of positive laws, which in turn enter into a dynamic interaction with the norms of natural law. Through this process, the Leviathan-state becomes the "artificial" creation of men who in its production have used their knowledge of the norms furnished by modern natural law. If the state derogates from these laws, the positive measures that it legislates are invalid; worse, they can lead to the state's demise.

In their natural state, all men are equal in one important sense. Their differences in body and mind, which Hobbes does not deny, are not so great that any one of them can be certain that he can hold permanently an object that another might desire. For the materialist, there is no preestablished harmony among individuals, which means that two persons can desire the same object. At that point, each becomes a threat to the other, yet their equality means that neither can take permanent possession of it. If one party seizes the object, his competitor may take it from him when his back is turned or he falls asleep, or an alliance of weaker men may despoil him of his possession. The distinction introduced later (in chapter 18) between possession and property captures the implication of Hobbes's account here. A possession is held immediately and physically; when it is put down or lost, possession has ceased. A possession is similar to the (unreserved) seat that a person takes in a theater or to one's place in a line waiting to buy tickets to that show. If the person leaves that seat or place, another may take it. At the other extreme, property is guaranteed by a legal claim whose validity is recognized by other members of the same society and that can, if necessary, be enforced. This comparison points to the fact that the existence of property depends on positive laws that are enforceable by the state. Such laws do not exist in the natural condition, where all men are free to take whatever they desire.

The result of the natural equality that permits any person to satisfy his desire by taking possession of anything that he considers to be a good is paradoxical. All persons' equal ability means that each has an equal hope of achieving his end because all have an equal power. Thus, as noted, if two people desire the same thing, they become de facto enemies; each is an impediment to the other's attempt to realize his desire. It follows that in order to achieve his end, each will seek to eliminate the potential competitor. The result is what Hobbes calls "diffidence of one another," a fear that the other will act first, which generates the more general fear that no one can be secure in his possessions. As a result, each person will be led to take preemptive action, seizing what he might want in the future before another's action rules out that possibility. Hobbes insists that this preemptive action will occur even though in this natural state individuals seek only what is needed for their conservation. This qualification is important. Hobbes is not positing that humans are by nature self-seeking or greedy; he shows that in the state of nature it is rational for men to show diffidence and to act preemptively. Each individual must attempt to increase constantly his own power in order simply to protect what he already has. As opposed to the Aristotelian view of men as naturally social animals, Hobbes concludes that "men have no pleasure, but on the contrary a great deal of grief, in keeping company." But, he adds, this is true only "where there is no power able to over-awe them all." That power will be the Leviathan-state that transforms possession to property and puts an end to what Hobbes calls "the war of all against all." But the Leviathan does not exist in the state of nature; it is an artificial, human creation.[5]

Because man is a creature of passions, the state of nature is marked by constant "war" in which men battle one another as their attempt to satisfy their desires leads them to compete for the same things. The fact that they have an equal chance of realizing these desires leads to that diffidence or fear that makes them think that the best defense is a good offense. In these conditions, human industry will not develop because its fruits are uncertain; today's investment may turn up tomorrow in someone else's pocket. There is no cultivation of the earth, no navigation, no importing of commodities, no development of arts, letters, and social graces. There are only fear and the danger of violent death. Summing up his materialist vision of the human condition in a famous phrase, Hobbes concludes that the life of man in his natural state is "solitary, poor, nasty, brutish, and short." And so it remains, as men must be always on the alert for threats from others even when the state exists to enforce justice. Hobbes grants that actions based on the passions "accuse mankind." In the state of nature, however, nothing can be forbidden because there is no law regulating relations among the material "bodies in motion" that inhabit it.[6]

The challenge is to find some aspect of the state of nature that will permit men to escape its unhappy consequences. Hobbes looks first to the passions and then to reason. In a state of war, force and fraud are virtues, possessions are under constant siege, and the fruits of individual initiative are uncertain. Yet fear of death, the desire for the things needed for "commodious" living, and the hope of attaining them by individual effort incline men to peace. This desire for self-preservation and the hope of doing so are passions. It is these passions—rather than the classical appeal to reason—that offer the first step beyond the natural state. They create a willingness to listen to the voice of reason when it proposes articles for a kind of peace treaty. These "articles" are based on "laws of nature" deduced from the nature of modern man as a creature of passions. Such laws of nature are distinct from what Hobbes calls "rights" of nature, which men possess naturally. Those rights are exercised by the individual, but they are private, others are not obliged to respect them. Obligation is based on laws, which bind universally. Private rights can be given up or exchanged—for example, by means of a contract—but as long as men remain in their natural state, such a contract cannot exist; the words that are spoken (or written) by the two parties may not have the same meaning to each of them, and there is no recognized authority that can enforce the contractual promise by "overawing" the parties.

Hobbes specifies the conditions for overcoming the state of nature in chapter 14, which explains "the first and second Natural Laws" as well as the way that valid contracts make use of private individual rights to bind men together. The basic right of all men is the freedom to use their power to preserve their physical being. This right entails logically the right to do whatever a person judges to be conducive to the preservation of his physical life. Reason translates this right into a "law of nature" based on the nature of man. That law says that men are forbidden to do what is destructive to their life or to the means for preserving their life. This law of nature is the expression in a universal form of the right that all men have as men. But it is not self-enforcing; an individual has the right to drink himself to death or to fail to take measures to preserve his life. Although reason tells men that they should strive to escape from the natural war of all against all by striving for peace, it adds an important qualification that leads to the next step: men should seek peace as long as they have a hope of obtaining it. They should not naively think that sheep and wolves can naturally live together peacefully. Hence, although the "first law of nature" expresses a natural human right in a normative form, its corollary is that men still retain the right to use all means to defend their lives.

If the right of self-defense is not to lead back to the state of war, the first law of nature needs to be supplemented by a second law, which says that each person should be willing, so long as the others also are willing, to abandon his natural right to all things and be content with as much liberty against others as he would allow those others against himself. Formulated more concretely, this second law develops the idea of a contract by means of which two individuals at once bind themselves while remaining free from and independent of one another. In the state of nature, where everyone has a right to everything, a person can renounce his right to something, or he can exchange that right for some other good. Such a contract can be executed immediately in the form of barter; it can be based on a promise to pay or to perform later; and even a gift can be understood as one person's giving up a possession in the hope that he will be rewarded by friendship, a reputation for generosity, or even a heavenly reward. The problem, however, is that the promise to pay, to perform, or to reward the gift is not obligatory in the state of nature. There is always a reasonable suspicion that the other will not deliver because words are too weak to hold in check the passions of greed, ambition, and anger. Therefore, the duty to seek peace expressed by the first law of nature is not yet made binding by the second law of nature; there is no assurance that the others will cooperate, which leads to the next step.

The second law of nature explains only how a contract becomes possible. Hobbes's desire to maintain the individual's rights leads him to admit that there are cases in which breaking a contract is rational. No one can make a contract not to defend himself when force is used against him. The right to life is nontransferable. Even if a contract stipulated that nonperformance is punishable by death, a person retains the right to resist the attempt to execute that penalty. But this right threatens the harmony between opposed interests that is established by the contract: What is to hinder someone from breaking the contract when it serves a less vital interest, one based only on a temporary passion? Some might say that the reason that contracts are not violated is that men desire to earn a reputation for keeping their promises. But that expression of classical virtue is not to be expected from modern men living by their passions in the state of nature. Rather, it is the fear of the results of breaking an oath that will prove to be the binding force that ensures that contracts are executed. This fear is different from the fear for one's physical being that exists in the state of nature. It is a civilized fear—fear of the artificial Leviathan—that replaces natural diffidence in the face of others.

The additional set of natural laws that Hobbes deduces in chapter 15 make clear the paradox that the goal sought by these laws is to escape from the state of nature. In each case, these laws contribute to the overcoming of the war of all against all while preserving individual rights. For example, the third law of nature says that a person should transfer his rights to another if retention of these rights hinders the peace sought by the contract. This law implies that justice is simply the performance of contracts because failure to do so returns the parties to a condition of conflict. Yet how can a person be sure that others will use their reason to come to the same definition of justice? This question leads to the fourth law of nature, which tells the individual that when he receives a gift, he should react in a way that ensures that the giver will not regret his good will. Not to repay a freely given gift destroys trust and mutual help among men. This reciprocity is still not enforceable, however, which is why a sixth natural law says that we should pardon those who repent their ill deeds, and a seventh says that if revenge is taken, it should not be justified by the past evil, but by the good it will contribute to peaceful relations among men. The end that justifies the laws of nature is the establishment of peace. Further examples of these laws—such as the need to acknowledge others as equal so as not to offend their self-esteem or to condemn pride as a threat to peace—makes clear that they are not self-enforcing.

At the outset of part II of *Leviathan,* Hobbes's materialist individualism guides his explanation of the kind of "final cause, end, or design of men (who naturally love liberty and dominion over others)" that can explain their acceptance of the restraints needed to live together in a commonwealth.[7] Hobbes asserts that men seek their own preservation by escaping from the condition of war that exists when there is no visible power to "keep them in awe." It is this material power rather than a quasi-religious awe that produces the civilized fear that they will be punished if they do not keep their covenants and faithfully obey the laws of nature that reason dictates. This fear differs from the individual fear of their fellows that haunts men in the state of nature; it is a political fear, one that is focused on a unique third party that stands above them all. Like God, the Leviathan is a unique, omniscient, and omnipotent power. And like the

God of Israel, this "mortal god" gives its people their unity and their identity. But the analogy does not mean that the people are the passive recipients of an unearned favor; it is they, not Jehovah, who construct the covenant by political means. That is why this power is a "mortal god."

When the appeal to a teleological nature or to a transcendent God is no longer available, and men are free to follow their own desires, the only justification for the obligation to obey lies in the fact that each individual himself has freely imposed that commitment upon himself. Hobbes knows, of course, that force may be used, but he pointed out earlier that men retain the natural right to self-preservation and that they may assert this right by disobeying arbitrary orders. But the problem is not yet solved. A promise made to oneself is not yet self-enforcing; other passions may annul that resolution, which explains Hobbes's radical solution. Each man must agree voluntarily with all other men that together they will make a contract that confers all power "upon one man, or upon one assembly of men," who, in exchange for all men's abandonment of their natural rights, will enforce the peace needed to preserve their lives and to relieve them of their natural fear.[8] In this way, unity replaces the unstable competitive anarchy that exists in the state of nature when no power "overawes" desiring men. The will of the unique sovereign is now recognized as the expression of the will of each of the participants in the contract, who would not otherwise be bound by it. Now, for example, payment of taxes or military service appear as voluntary; they express the citizen's will, not the state's external force.

Hobbes insists that this contract produces "more than consent, or concord; it is a real unity of them all, in one and the same person, made by the covenant of every man with every man." The creation of the sovereign is not a vertical contract made between the people and the already existing state. A vertical contract would impose limits on the exercise of sovereignty, as in the constitutional monarchy that some proposed as a solution to the civil war. The fact that there exists no state in the state of nature means that Hobbes is prescribing a horizontal compact in which each individual says to each and every other individual, in an oath that Hobbes prints in italics, "*I authorize and give up my right of governing myself to this man, or to this assembly of men, on this condition, that thou give up thy right to him, and authorize all his actions in like manner.*"[9] That is why the Leviathan is said to incarnate an absolute and universal authority given to it by every particular member of the commonwealth. It is, of course, difficult to imagine this exchange of mutual promises actually taking place, but Hobbes's concern is normative; he is explaining what each person must presuppose in order to justify his obedience to the sovereign. For obedience to be legitimate, each individual must suppose himself to be the author of the acts of the sovereign, whose goal is to ensure peace and defend the realm. In so doing, the citizen imagines that he is obeying only himself.

Hobbes's theory is not yet complete. His materialist psychology implies that men are creatures of passion whose imagination may outrace their reason. As a result, he has to show that a properly constructed commonwealth excludes the possibility that the individual's private freedom that is protected by the state does not turn against the state. As Hobbes turns his attention to the actual construction of the Leviathan, he has to remember that it is a "mortal god" that can degenerate as a result of what he describes as "birth defects."

The powers given to the absolute state are determined by its task of imposing peace and ensuring the execution of contracts. They can be briefly summarized. The most important power concerns the definition of property. By transforming possessions into property, the state limits the grounds for quarrel among men. Hobbes spends little time explaining the exercise of this sovereign right. Because his concern is the protection of lives rather than institution of the good life, he need not show the benefits that can be produced by private property nor distinguish among kinds of property and among the laws regulating them. The sovereign establishes property rights, which entails the fact that it is the judge in all controversies that arise concerning the distribution of property in order to ensure their peaceful resolution. The obligation to protect the lives and property of its citizens means further that the state decides when to make war or peace. For the same reason, it can also raise troops to fight and impose taxes to pay for the fighting. When peace has returned, the sovereign must appoint all of the magistrates who administer the realm because their allegiance to a private employer would destroy the unity of the state. Two final powers take account of the problems posed by Hobbes's materialist psychology: the awarding of riches or honors and the denial of such benefits. Men naturally demand respect and are not inclined to respect others, which means that the sovereign must accord these precious tokens in order to avoid quarrels. In this matter, as in all other matters, Hobbes insists that the sovereign's power must be exercised according to the law. If there is no existing law, then the sovereign has the final word, judging according to what is best for the commonwealth—for example, in pardoning duly convicted criminals.

The power of pardon that is an exception to the rule of law appears to pave the way for arbitrariness in Hobbes's absolutism. That impression is strengthened when he takes sides in contemporary controversies. For example, he criticizes those who stress the right of conscience against the state's claims. No one, he insists, can justify disobedience to the sovereign by claiming to be bound by a previous contract (with a feudal overlord or any other master). And those who claim a higher obligation to their God forget that because you cannot know whether God accepts the bargain, you cannot claim to have made a contract with Him. Moreover, when each individual made the covenant that creates the sovereign, he was acting freely; the claim of allegiance to another power would destroy the foundation of the sovereignty, which is needed to protect any covenant—including the one that is said to justify disobedience. The same logic implies that a person who is punished for breaking the law cannot say that the state is punishing him because he himself has brought down the punishment by disobeying. Alluding to the Calvinist justification of disobedience when the government fails to fulfill its office, Hobbes points out that because the sovereign was not a party to the contract, he can never be accused of violating it. The accusation that the state has been unjust brings only a return to the (undesirable) state of nature because there is then no longer an agreed-upon judge in controversies. Finally, although a minority may have preferred to give its rights not to one man, but to "an assembly of men," that minority is nonetheless bound because it has entered what Hobbes calls "the congregation" and, by so doing, has "tacitly covenanted" to accept the majority's decision. If that minority still refuses, it has in effect returned to a state of nature, where it can be destroyed without any injustice being done (because there is no justice in the state of nature).

Despite these examples that appear to condemn Hobbes's absolutism, the construction of the Leviathan itself reflects the image on the frontispiece of the book. The sovereign instituted by the contract is made sufficiently powerful to protect citizens' lives by ensuring peace. But

Hobbes takes care to ensure that its absolute power does not violate the citizens' natural rights and freedom. For example, if the sovereign claims new powers simply by saying that they are necessary to protect citizens' lives, he has confused the temporary occupants of power (the government) with the true sovereign. Even in a monarchy, the government can be changed if it appears to the people whose contract with one another has established the sovereign that the government is not effectively performing its function as sovereign. For this reason, the sovereign's absolute powers are limited to the performance of its obligation to preserve peace; and if a government were to overreach and acquire power over the lives and liberties that it is obliged to protect, this arbitrariness would disqualify it. The paradoxical implication of Hobbes's argument is that the stronger the state, the greater the freedoms guaranteed to the individual. As the certainty grows that peace will be maintained, the space in which individuals can exercise their natural private freedom grows without appearing to others as a threat against which they must defend themselves. In this way, Hobbes can be said to defend a modern "liberalism," as the details of the Leviathan's powers show.[10]

After Hobbes has constructed the Leviathan, he returns to the natural right of freedom in chapter 21. He had earlier defined liberty materially as simply the lack of external opposition to a body's motion. Water, for example, will spread freely if it is not caged in by dikes. There may also be internal limits to freedom, as when a stone does not roll downhill because it is flat or when a person who is sick cannot act. But these limits are not constraints on the stone's or the person's freedom; they are only restrictions of its or his power. Hobbes thus rejects the idea of freedom of the will because it is not the "will" but a person who is able (or unable) to act as he likes. The political implication of this materialist account of freedom is a rejection of any theory of innate liberties that limit the covenant that has created the sovereign. In particular, Hobbes criticizes those who appeal to classical ideas of individual virtue as preferable to the absolute state that ensures the execution of contracts by means of fear rather than the promise of a positive form of the good life. For example, a merchant who in a stormy sea chooses to throw his goods overboard in order to save the ship from sinking is acting freely despite his fear for his life; there is no contraction between fear and freedom. Similarly, a person freely chooses to pay a debt because of his fear of being jailed if he does not repay his creditor. Fear does not bind the individual's action; it only "inclines him" toward a decision.

Where, then, is political freedom experienced? Truly human (as distinct from natural) liberty appears only with the creation of the commonwealth, which develops "artificial chains" called civil laws in order to preserve itself. This achievement is paradoxical: freedom manifests itself by creating laws that bind it. Hobbes's justification of this claim begins from the fact that it is impossible for the sovereign to regulate every detail of citizens' speech and action. In those areas that are not regulated by law, men are free to do whatever their reason or their passions tells them is most profitable for themselves. This stress on what is "profitable" to the individual suggests that freedom is a private experience concerned with what Hobbes earlier called "commodious living." The upshot of his argument is that men are wrong to demand that the state grant them a liberty that they already enjoy precisely because the state's laws ensure peace. The subject's true liberty concerns only those things that the sovereign has permitted, such as the rights to buy and sell, to make contracts, to choose their home, their diet, or their field of work, and to educate their children. Hobbes knows that this type of freedom will not satisfy the adepts of classical political thought who are beguiled by "the specious name of liberty," but he replies rightly that the liberty practiced in Greece and Rome was that of the commonwealth as opposed to the modern individual's right to put his own opinions in the place of the common good.

These considerations lead Hobbes to reformulate his political question. What rights are given up and which liberties are abandoned when a person enters the commonwealth? Are there things that the contracting parties cannot sacrifice? The paradox of the Leviathan is that the contract with each of the others by which all individually accept submission to the sovereign ensures both obligation and true liberty. Hobbes is consistent: obligation can result only from free action by which individuals explicitly or implicitly authorize the sovereign's power. The liberal element of Hobbes's absolutism appears in this context. He recalls his earlier argument that a person who is justly condemned cannot be commanded to kill or even to maim himself, nor can his right to resist punishment be restricted. More important and more radical, in Hobbes's day, when confession under torture was accepted practice, even if a person has committed a crime, he cannot be forced to testify against himself. In addition, although the sovereign may intervene when there is no preexisting law, if it does not, the individual is free to act according to his own lights because no law exists to limit its freedom. Finally, if the sovereign is unable to protect the peace, the covenant is void, and the citizens regain the individual freedoms that they had in the state of nature—along, of course, with the conflict and uncertainty that their passions, guided by the reason that deciphered the laws of nature, sought to overcome. This possibility brings Hobbes to his final argument in favor of absolutism.

Hobbes seems to leave his modern reader with a choice between full freedom in the state of nature, which leads inevitably to the war of all against all, where life is "solitary, poor, nasty, brutish, and short," and a merely private freedom guaranteed by a strong state. His argument that freedom exists in those areas that are not regulated by the state implies that the defense of private liberty depends on the existence of a strong state. That is why he turns to examine "those things that weaken, or tend to the dissolution of a commonwealth."[11] Although nothing made by mortals can be truly immortal, Hobbes proposes several precautions to avoid what he calls the state's "imperfect institution." The first and the most serious danger arises from the lack of absolute power. This danger had turned Hobbes against the compromise solution of a constitutional monarchy to end the English civil war. Like Machiavelli, he criticizes those who, wanting to obtain a kingdom, might accept less power than is truly needed, only to find that when a crisis arises, it is too late to demand new powers. The second weakness arises from the acceptance of seditious doctrines, in particular the secularized Protestant idea that every private man is the judge of what counts as good or evil actions. The latter assumption holds only in a state of nature or for private life when there exist no laws that limit that particular freedom. In all other cases, the individual's judgment is bound by the law. Similarly, the idea that acting against one's conscience is a sin weakens the sovereign because the individual conscience can err, whereas the law stands as the "public conscience" accepted by all. Finally, the obligation to obey the law must not extend to the sovereign, who in an emergency must be able to annul a law whose obedience would condemn the state to perish.

The force of Hobbes's liberalism fades as his criticism of the concessions that weaken the absolute state continues. Although a right to private property exists, the very fact that property is private means that it is not absolute. Others cannot interfere with it, but the sovereign, who has created it, can justly violate it when necessary in fulfilling the state's function—for example, by raising taxes to defend the peace. Another threat to sovereignty comes from its division, as in the case of mixed government. The competition among sources of power weakens the state's ability to act. Hobbes remarks ironically that the kingdom of God may be composed of three separate persons who are united, but that condition is supernatural rather than human. Similarly, the opposition of canon law to civil government must be avoided; as suggested by the image on the book's frontispiece, the same authority must hold the sword and the crosier. This rejection of any division of authority haunts the analysis in *Leviathan* to the point that Hobbes goes on to warn against economic monopoly as well. The imperative of unity is seen also in his willingness to accept democratic government as legitimate if it is absolute and in his worry that the popularity of a Caesar may weaken the Leviathan's unitary power. For the same reason, the "immoderate greatness of a town" can become a pole of attraction that weakens the unity of the sovereign.[12]

The power of Hobbes's Leviathan, like his materialist conception of freedom, is based on the elimination of all obstacles to its action. But this absolutism becomes a source of weakness. His theory of obligation is based on self-interest, but this passion cannot be taken for granted when conditions change and a threat emerges. Although Hobbes recognized the problem, his materialist understanding of political power as simply the absence of impediments cannot provide a positive remedy. The Leviathan's power cannot be converted into an authority that replaces the classical or Christian forms of political legitimacy. The paradox according to which the individual's (private) freedom increases as the state grows more powerful has an antipolitical corollary: because the state's power grows with the leveling of obstacles, its ability to mobilize its citizens in the face of unexpected difficulties decreases at the same time. The more private freedom and material comfort the individual acquires, the less his self-interest will incline him to participate in the public sphere. The situation only worsens when the sovereign can no longer guarantee the fulfillment of contracts, which are nothing but the material form of the promises by which modern men commit themselves—without appeal to natural or divine laws—to one another.

◆

Hobbes's *Leviathan* belongs to the unitary Platonic tradition that is subject to the antipolitical temptation to eliminate the threat of human diversity. Hobbes's liberalism makes room for plural interests only insofar as they are limited to the private sphere. Although parts III and IV, which are longer than the first two, explore the nature of "a Christian commonwealth" and "the kingdom of darkness," it is fair to say that *Leviathan* is a materialist complement to Luther's political theory. In both cases, the moral is separated from the political, the private from the public. But Luther's absolutism was justified by appeal to the sacred, whereas Hobbes's is based on secular concerns. It is no surprise that, just as Calvin proposed an ecclesial remedy to Luther's soteriological politics, Locke will propose a tolerant, pluralist societal corrective to Hobbes's absolutist, state-centered theory of political obligation.

LOCKE'S CONSTITUTIONAL LIBERALISM

Like Hobbes, John Locke (1632–1704) came from a family of modest circumstances, but because his father had fought on the side of the revolution, he was allowed to pursue his studies at Oxford. Recognizing the limits of his scientific gifts, he turned to medicine in order to keep in touch with the experimental spirit of the times. He became the personal physician to the earl of Shaftesbury, who rose to the highest positions in government before dying in political exile in Holland. As with Hobbes, this connection to political and intellectual elites at home and abroad was reflected in Locke's political theory, but in his case it produced a recognition of the need for political institutions to tolerate diversity rather than impose unity from above. As he put it in the introduction to his great philosophical work *An Essay Concerning Human Understanding* (1690), he was not a "master builder," but simply an "under-labourer in clearing ground a little, and removing some of the rubbish, that lies in the way of knowledge."[13] Similarly, he explains in his *Second Treatise on Government* (1689) that it is only the "inconveniences" of the state of nature that need to be remedied by the creation of a social contract. Despite this modesty, Locke was an active participant in the events that led to the Glorious Revolution of 1689. Like many participants in such semilegal actions, he unfortunately destroyed as much of the evidence implicating himself as he could.[14]

As opposed to Hobbes, Locke was deeply involved in the economic life of the emerging commercial society that was challenging the traditional aristocratic economy based on landed wealth. For a time, his sympathies seemed to lie with the old order. As secretary to the proprietors of the American colony of Carolina, he proposed a constitution creating a manorial system in which the nobility would always have sufficient votes to control the common people (and slaves). But when Shaftesbury became head of the Treasury, Locke changed sides, writing economic treatises that showed, for example, that because a moneylender and an investor provide different services, it is an error to condemn all high profits as usury. After the Glorious Revolution, Locke was involved in the creation of the Bank of England and was a member of the Board of Trade that regulated domestic and foreign commerce in the growing empire. His new allegiance went so far as to blame poverty on a lack of discipline and corrupt manners rather than on scarcity of provisions or lack of employment; his proposed solutions included the closing of brandy shops, forced work at lower wages, and the placement of poor children in work schools at age three. These thoughts should not be condemned anachronistically; what they show is that Locke was intimately aware of the new world emerging around him.

The changes that accompanied the new commercial society were radical. Free trade, which meant the freedom both to buy and to sell, rejected the traditional ideas of justice, equity, and natural law. Traditional society would never have approved, for example, the freedom to exploit juvenile labor or the right to sell foodstuffs abroad while famine raged at home. It would not tolerate the creation of speculative wealth that brought inflation that wiped out the old landed estates. It could not accept the fact that new rights not accompanied by new duties made possible an unlimited freedom that could become a threat to itself. These modern developments confronted political thought with a paradox. The traditional state was apparently more just even though it left less room for freedom, innovation, and individualism. Freeing the individual from the weight of tradition opened space for creativity that could overcome the crushing burden of work that resulted from the low levels of productivity. At the early stages of this process, the winners were not only the emerging industrial and commercial interests, but also peasants freed to work in the growing urban markets. Wages could rise, although that same new liberty would permit them to fall below subsistence level. The losers were the old aristocracy, whose power depended either on their status (awarded by the Crown) or on long-term fixed rents from their inherited agricultural estates. As with other ruling classes, they did not give up without a struggle.

These new socioeconomic relations were not the immediate cause of the revolution that overthrew the restored British monarchy less than three decades after its return from exile. Religion provided the catalyst. Charles II, the son of the beheaded Charles I, had spent his long exile in Catholic France, but the Parliament that returned him to power after Cromwell's son Richard failed to maintain the inherited Protectorate included a moderate Protestant majority called Whigs and was led by Shaftesbury. Fearing royal arbitrariness, the Whigs passed the Habeas Corpus Act of 1679, establishing a basic right of all men, although their intention was more narrowly partisan. This victory did not calm their fears of a Catholic restoration, which would also have led to replacement of Dutch commercial ties with a French alliance. Parliament's attempt to prevent this shift led the king to dismiss Parliament, sending Shaftesbury to exile in Holland. James II, an avowed Catholic who now succeeded his brother, increased repression and purged the army, the administration, and the universities. This repression stoked tensions because it was both a sign of his fear and an expression of his weakness. The Whigs, who denounced these abuses as tyranny sought Dutch support for their claim that Mary, wife of the Protestant William of Orange and daughter of Charles II, was the legitimate ruler. In 1688, Locke returned from exile with the Dutch army that ensured the installation of this new regime.

The Glorious Revolution made England into a constitutional monarchy capable of integrating the diversity of new forces emerging in society. The "people" to whom the Whigs appealed for support were not the majority of the population, who were still peasants, but the urban and commercial interests represented in Parliament. The Declaration of Rights that was the condition imposed on the new monarch was an act of Parliament, not a decree from the throne. Known as the Bill of Rights, this declaration denied the absolutist motto "A deo rex, a rege lex" (From God comes the king, from the king comes the law), making Parliament the source of the laws whose just administration was the basis of governmental legitimacy. The "rights" that it guaranteed were the liberties that the Parliament needed in order to play its assigned role. The task of Locke's political theory was to justify the primacy of Parliament.[15]

◆

The fact that the Glorious Revolution represented the political culmination of a socioeconomic rupture with the past is illustrated by Locke's decision to publish his two separate and quite different treatises on government in a single volume. Although Locke wrote them (and members of his political faction read them) before the revolution took place, he published them only after the new government was in place, in 1689. He explains in the preface that he hoped that his book would "establish the throne of our great restorer, our present King William, to make good his title in the consent of the people." The philosophical argument for parliamentary sovereignty and popular consent is found principally in the *Second Treatise*. Explaining the more polemical *First Treatise*, Locke says that "I should not have written against Sir Robert Filmer . . . were there not men amongst us who, by crying up his books and espousing his doctrine, save me from the reproach of writing against a dead adversary."[16] Although Filmer, a strong defender of the divine right of kings, died in 1653, Locke needed to put this premodern theory finally to rest in order to legitimate for a modern public a political theory based on the rights of the individual.

The posthumous manuscript of Filmer's *Patriarchia* had been published to great acclaim by the Royalists in 1679, the year that Charles II had asserted his absolute power by proroguing the Parliament. As indicated by the manuscript's title, Filmer's theory justifies royalty by invoking the analogy between the traditional paternal power over the family and the relation of the monarch to his subjects. The avatar of the father is said to be none other than Adam himself. His sovereignty is portrayed as the result of a donation (from God), which is attested by the subjection of Eve and confirmed by Adam's role as father of the race. Monarchs are said to be the direct heirs of Adam, the royal lineage incarnating the unity of humankind. Royal absolutism is thus justified not only by analogy to paternal authority, but also by the grace of the divine will certified by holy Scripture as well as by absolutism's role in unifying the diversity of the human species.

Why did Locke choose to attack what seems a rather simplistic theory? Although he knew Hobbes's work, he had no political reason to attack it directly. Hobbes's materialism and his justification of absolute sovereignty by fear and self-interest had no influence on the aristocratic supporters of monarchy, whereas Filmer's theory appealed to the nobler aspects of human nature that people like to believe are the true motives of their action. This explanation is only a partial one. Locke also explains in his preface to the *Two Treatises on Government* that he was offended because Filmer "boasts and pretends to build on Scripture-proofs." Locke, the author of an essay titled *The Reasonableness of Christianity, as Delivered in the Scriptures,* was not an atheist. He demonstrates that Filmer truncated his biblical citations to make them fit his theory of royal absolutism, indicating that a proper political theory cannot be built on the evidence of divine revelation. Locke's *Second Treatise* offers a political demonstration that the protection of the human rights that he calls "god given" is the task of government. If government fails to fulfill this obligation, it can be legitimately replaced.

The *Second Treatise*'s theoretical ambitions are expressed in its lengthy subtitle, which declares that after "overthrowing [Filmer's] false principles," Locke will treat "the true original, extent, and end, of civil government." At the outset of chapter 1, he explains that a theory like his is needed to prove that "government is not the product only of force and violence."[17] His critique of Filmer had showed already that political power is distinct from other forms of power, such as that of father over children, master over servant, husband over wife. Although this distinction draws on Aristotle, the modernity of Locke's theory is seen in his definition of political power as the right to make laws that include the death penalty and for that same reason the right to make all lesser laws, including those that regulate and preserve property. Although these laws must work for the public good, this definition of power implies that its legitimacy depends on government's ability to preserve the individual's life and the property needed to maintain it. In order to distinguish such political power from arbitrary force and to ensure that the ends that it sets are legitimate, Locke proposes to return to the "state of nature," which he defines as a condition of perfect freedom, in order to show why individuals would consent rationally to give up their natural independence to a government that will preserve their individual rights and freedom precisely because it is of limited extent.

Locke's picture of the state of nature differs from Hobbes's. In it, men are free to "dispose of their possessions and persons, as they think fit."[18] This freedom is limited only by "the law of nature," which dictates that men remain independent of the will of any other person. In this respect, all men are equal. This equality, in turn, is the basis of their mutual recognition of duties owed to one another. As a result, men have both the natural ability and the obligation to make and to keep their promises. For these reasons, Locke replaces Hobbes's "diffidence" with a natural sociability based on both freedom and equality. This idea is confirmed by natural law, whose first command is that no one has the right to destroy himself or any other creature in his possession. This natural law is known by reason, which teaches those "who will but consult it" that all men are equally creatures of God, who alone can destroy or use his creatures.[19] Each individual is thus obliged to preserve himself and to preserve so far as possible the rest of mankind. In this Lockean state of nature, the power to redress violations is left to every individual. How could it be otherwise? Equality forbids giving this power to another person or group, and there is no government in the natural state. But what happens when an individual exercises this right of redress without adequate consultation of his reason?

In the state of nature, there are two grounds for punishment. If a person violates the law of nature, his action is a de facto declaration that he lives under rules that are different from those of reason and equity, which makes him a danger to all mankind and requires that he therefore be restrained or even destroyed. Execution of the sentence belongs to each individual because all are equal and thus are free to execute the law of nature. But when harm is done to a specific person, the injured person has a right to demand reparation from the criminal. The first case is based on a natural law written in the heart of man; Locke cites Cain's cry, "Everyone that findeth me, shall slay me," to illustrate his point. The second case demands a remedy that is proportional to the harm that was done. Although there are differences in the particular "municipal laws of countries," what makes them just is that they conform to the laws of nature. In this way, the first type of punishment serves as a restraint on crime in general, and the second type justifies restoration for crimes that are actually committed. But the determination of the compensation may be distorted by an injured person's self-love, since he acts as both judge and party to his own case. At this point, confusion and disorder are introduced into natural society. That is why, Locke argues, God institutes government. Its task is not to decide what counts as the good life for the society, but simply to restrain human partiality in order to protect the equal rights of the individual, who, as God's creature, is the end that defines the just society.

The threat that individuals may act in their own interest in deciding the proportionality of punishment is the first example of what Locke calls "the inconveniences of the state of nature." It represents a deviation from mankind's natural sociability. The same unnatural partiality is seen in the action of an absolute monarch, whose very existence violates the principle that all men are equal and thus independent of any other person's will. Free and equal men can only bind themselves by an act of their own will. What Locke calls "promises and bargains for truck" between two men on a desert island or between a Swiss and an Indian in the American wilderness are binding for the simple reason that "truth and keeping of faith belongs to men, as men, and not as members of society."[20] Promises do not need the sword to ensure their execution. There is no need for an absolute monarch to incarnate the unity of society or to resolve conflicts among unforgiving interests. But, as Locke admits, "inconveniences" do exist in the natural state.

Although the state of nature does not exclude all conflicts, what Locke calls a "state of war" is not the result of natural passions or hasty decision, but rather expresses "a sedate settled design upon another man's life."[21] When war is declared in this way, self-defense is a natural right because the aggressor is seeking an arbitrary power that denies the individual his freedom without his consent. Locke's argument is directed against rule by an absolute monarch, but he illustrates it by the action of a thief who uses unjust force against an individual who, in the state of nature, therefore has a right to kill the robber. His point is that the thief's illegal act is responsible for the thief's death. Every theft may not deserve the ultimate penalty, however. That decision, which is left to the victim, is another "inconvenience," but Locke is not willing to avoid that difficulty by appealing to an absolute monarch to judge in the place of the individual who has been harmed. He has to find a natural way to escape the inconveniences of the state of nature without sacrificing natural human rights and liberties.

Locke's analyses of slavery and property in chapters 4 and 5 of the *Second Treatise* elaborate the preconditions for the creation of a social contract. His claim that both of these institutions exist already in the state of nature is based on the modern assertions that the individual has a right to himself (which, paradoxically, will justify his acceptance of slavery) and that, as a consequence, not only is he his own property, but he can invest "himself" in the creation of more property by working (but not working himself to death). This idea that a person is his own property would have shocked a classical or Christian theorist, but Locke does not shrink from the implications of this modern individualist society, which he describes as the natural state of humankind.

Locke's justification of slavery reiterates his insistence that in the state of nature, all men are free, and, as subject only to the law of nature, they all are equal. It follows that the classical explanation of slavery as the expression of a natural hierarchy is invalid. Moreover, a person cannot give someone else more power than he has over himself, and only God has the power to dispose of the life of a person. In spite of these points, Locke still attempts to justify slavery. The victim of a criminal act has a natural right to kill its perpetrator, but he can also accept a reparation in place of that ultimate punishment by making the criminal his servant. No injustice is done to the criminal, who has brought the punishment on himself; and if the servitude proves to be too hard, he may resist, bringing about the death he already deserved. The negotiation between the lawbreaker and the victim produces a kind of contract based on a promise that accords a limited power to one party and a similarly limited obedience to the other party. If the master is too harsh or the servant too recalcitrant, the pact is broken, and the natural law is applied to its fullest.

This explanation of slavery foreshadows Locke's theory of the wage contract by which a propertyless person exchanges his labor for the means of subsistence needed for himself and his family. Locke never developed his justification of slavery, perhaps because his work on the Board of Trade surely showed him that his argument did not fit the conditions of African enslavement prevalent in the Americas. Rather than embroil himself in controversy, he simply moved on to his explanation of why private property is the expression of man's natural liberty.

Locke assumes in the *Second Treatise* that in the state of nature men are free to dispose of their "possessions" as they see fit. He now has to explain the origin of this right to ownership. He begins from a modern version of the Thomist argument that although God gave the world to men to share in common, He also gave them reason, which they must use to find the best ways to appropriate this shared world. Each individual asks how he can best appropriate his part of what is given to humankind as a whole. In a society based on individual rights, the use of a part of the natural world depends on ownership of it. For something to become the property of an individual in a state of nature, it must become a part of him. This incorporation of the world into the man is the result of the process of labor. "The labor of his body, and the work of his hands, we may say, are properly his," Locke states. "Whatsoever then he removes out of the state that nature hath provided . . . he hath mixed his labor with, and joined to it something that is his own, and thereby makes it his property . . . [and] no man but he can have a right to what that is once joined to."[22] Private property is thus the expression of natural human freedom.

Locke adds an important proviso to his claim that "no man can have a right" to this property that an individual has acquired by his own labor." He stipulates that a person can continue to appropriate "at least where there is enough, and as good, left in common for others."[23] This limit is imposed by the natural law that guarantees not only freedom, but also equality. For example, when water is drunk from a river, one person's quenching his thirst does not limit another's equal chance to do the same. Diverting the course of the waterway for private gain, however, would be a violation of the law of nature. The guarantee that equality will be maintained leaves Locke with a new question. When, he asks, do the acorns gathered under the oak or the apples plucked from a tree become truly mine? After listing the possible answers—when the acorns or apples are digested or cooked or brought to my home or already when first picked—he concludes that something becomes my property as soon as my labor is added to it. Indeed, he adds that when my horse eats grass or my slave cuts turfs or I myself dig ore, these things become mine. But the natural-law proviso that insists that there must be "enough, and as good, left" for others implies, at first, that accumulation is not without limits—although in some conditions these natural limits may be legitimately abrogated.

Because property is acquired in the state of nature, prior to the social contract, there is no need for consent from others whose needs or wishes might set limits to the amount of property that a person might acquire. Although some may work harder or exploit themselves more, the laws of nature that ensured a right to property do in fact impose a limit on how much a person may acquire. However, because God did not make the world to be spoiled or wasted, each may take only as much as he can use, but no more. The same principle limits a person who contrives to acquire more land than others. The law of nature permits owning only as much of the earth as a person can till, plant, improve, and cultivate by his own labor. Others' consent is not needed as long as there is "still enough, and as good, left." Identifying the law of nature with God's will, Locke claims that by "subduing or cultivating the earth," the labor that makes a part of the world into private property also fulfills God's intention that the world be shared by the industrious and the rational (like the new commercial classes) rather than by the covetous, quarrelsome, and contentious (like the old nobility). In this way, just as during "the first ages of the world," so too today, "as full as the world seems" the same natural law applies because of "the vacant places of America" that ensure that "enough and as good" still exist for all.[24]

Although Locke ignores the existence of the native inhabitants of America, he sees that a problem emerges within the state of nature when "a little piece of yellow metal" is agreed to be worth "a great piece of flesh, or a whole heap of corn." With this agreement, "the desire of having more than man needed [has] altered the intrinsic value of things," which is normally determined by their usefulness for human life. Locke does not explain the origin of this new desire, but he knows full well its consequences. "Thus in the beginning all the world was America, and more so than it is now, for no such thing as money was known." But, he continues, "find out something that hath both the use and value of money amongst his neighbors, you shall see the same man will begin presently to enlarge his possessions." The result will be "a disproportionate and unequal possession of the earth."[25] How did this inequality come about? What can make it legitimate? Locke admits that on a desert island where there is no commerce and plenty of food, no one would want to expand his property beyond what is needed for private consumption. What, then, is the origin of the desire for accumulation? Is it more than another "inconvenience"?

The key to the transformation is the introduction of money, which is a practical development based on the laws of nature. When one person finds himself producing more of a specific product than he can consume, he will bargain with someone who has an excess of a different product. Neither partner violates the law of nature. This barter depends on particular conditions that may not always exist. It becomes universal only with the emergence of commercial society. Now an individual will be able regularly to exchange his wine or cheese for a piece of golden metal, which can in turn purchase a needed commodity. No one appears to be harmed in this process, which does not waste the bounties of nature. But this commercial society results in an "inconvenience" that leads men to abandon their natural state to create what Locke calls "political or civil society." The existence of money means that accumulation is no longer limited by natural spoilage because gold does not decay. To take the sting from this threat to natural equality, Locke points to the benefits of the desire to accumulate wealth for mankind as a whole. For example, a cultivated acre will produce ten times the yield of a fallow field, as is evident in the contrast between the wilds of America and the tilled lands of Devonshire. But this increased social prosperity does not compensate for the loss of natural equality. It makes possible an arbitrariness that threatens the individual's natural freedom and the private property that is its expression. The state of nature has to be replaced by a political society that can preserve natural freedom and equality without the danger that arbitrariness and partiality threaten.

Locke's describes political society in the *Second Treatise* (chapter 7) before explaining its origin (chapter 8) and analyzing the ends that it seeks (chapter 9). His initial description in fact already contains a prescription. A political society is a community that can appeal to a legitimate umpire to enforce laws neutrally, permitting disputes to be decided by fixed rules and punishment to be imposed only by laws that are universal. This configuration implies that the members have given up their natural "executive power" to a third party whose task is to eliminate the uncertainty that arises when each individual is both judge and party to disputes. This third party is not an absolute sovereign; he is (or they are) bound by a contract with men who have surrendered their natural freedom in exchange for his protection. Locke does not yet say how that contract comes into being or describe its terms. His point here is that a person not subject to the community's lawful authority has de facto returned to the state of nature. Absolute monarchy is not a legitimate political regime, and a ruler who exceeds his legitimate powers has returned society to the state of nature, freeing his former subjects from their obligations and permitting them to chose a new ruler. Written before the Glorious Revolution, the *Second Treatise* clearly anticipates it, but Locke's text is more than a partisan political pamphlet—it is a theory of political legitimation.

To understand the origin of a legitimate political community made up of naturally free individuals, Locke asks, What would motivate a person to leave the state of nature? What would lead a free subject to submit to an external umpire rather than exercise his natural "executive power"? Because the individual's life and property are the expression of his freedom, the only reason that would justify surrendering them is the more certain maintenance of that same life and property. The origin of political society must therefore lie in the desire to protect these natural goods in the face of the "inconveniences" of the state of nature.

Unity cannot be imposed on a modern political society from above—for instance, by the force of absolute monarchy; political unity is instead represented by the will of the majority as it emerges from the interplay of the diverse interests arising from the coexistence of different kinds of property in the state of nature. As in a parallelogram of forces, the stronger and weaker forces work together to move an object (or a decision) in a direction that is determined by their joint effort. Because a minority that disagrees with the result is free to return to the state of nature, and because actual consent to every law is impossible, Locke argues that the minority gives its "tacit consent" to the majority's decisions. Indeed, anyone holding property tacitly agrees to abide by the majority's laws; even the traveler passing in a foreign country consents tacitly to obey its laws. This consent does not infringe on the individual's freedom because he can always sell the property or not visit the country in question. To be subject to a society's laws does not make a person a full member of that society, however. Citizenship is based on "express consent," which results not from material interest, but from the political concern to protect natural freedom and property.

What leads natural men to give their explicit consent to join a political society? They ask themselves what they gain from membership and what they must give up in exchange. In the state of nature, where freedom was the rule, equality was ensured, and ownership of oneself and of one's possessions existed. But most men are "no strict observers of equity and justice"; natural equality in fact means that everyone's rights are uncertain. As a result, when men join together, the end that they seek is "the mutual preservation of their lives, liberties and estates, which I call by the general name, property."[26] The "inconveniences" existing in the state of nature must be remedied by the creation of a legal institutions to which common consent is given. This consent gives the laws their legitimate authority. In addition, a neutral judge must administer these laws in order to avoid the partiality that exists when each individual judges in his own case. Finally, the laws must have also the power to punish those who violate them. The first of these remedies is ensured by the constitution;[27] the second is accorded to the legislative function of political society; the third belongs to the executive. It remains to see what natural rights or liberties must be given up and to whom they are given.

A contract is an exchange of rights that unites two parties who remain distinct from one another. Although the exchange is equal, each party must benefit from it; he gives up something that he does not need in order to get something that he finds more useful. Such are the barter relations in the state of nature. By analogy, the social contract is based on the exchange of a natural right that is uncertain for a political assurance that the contract will indeed be guaranteed. The legal institutions of political society furnish this assurance. This is the "vertical" aspect of Locke's social contract: the society of free men enters into a contract with the political state. The individual participants in this political contract give up two rights: the right to do whatever they see fit to ensure their self-preservation and the right to punish violations of the law of nature. The right to self-preservation, which is limited only by the law of nature common to all men, is exchanged for laws made by political society. These laws preserve and protect the freedom of the individual and his property. These political laws have also a second function, which compensates for the abandonment of the individual right to punish crimes. They preserve political society itself by ensuring that justice, like the law, will be universal. This second aspect of the political contract is directed against the pretensions of an absolute monarch.

The relation between Locke's political antiabsolutism, on the one hand, and his identification of natural rights and individual freedom with the preservation of private property, on the other, needs to be clarified. According to his contract theory, no rational creature would enter into an exchange that makes his condition worse. It follows that the political society must guarantee all of its members' natural rights to remain both free and equal to one another. But if the introduction of money into the state of nature puts an end to equality, how then does the social contract realize the common good? The answer makes clear the difference between Locke and classical political theorists, who sought a substantive definition of justice. Locke's modern institutions need only to impose formal legal rules and to act as a neutral umpire among competing interests. The common good consists in the preservation of the individual's rights and liberties. Political society is only a means; its end is the protection of both private property and the inequality that it introduces into the state of nature. "Inequality," however, is only a negative way of describing social diversity in a pluralist society. The actual political revolution justified by Locke's theory rejected the temptation to impose social unity by the creation of absolute government. The antipolitical lure of unity did not disappear, however. Locke had to reconcile the natural diversity of the state of nature with unitary political society.

A constitution, which Locke calls the "first and fundamental positive law," establishes the legislative power whose activity is guided by the most fundamental of natural laws, which is to preserve the society and, "as far as will consist with the public good,"[28] every person in it. This legislative power's actions and those of the subordinate powers it establishes cannot arbitrarily violate natural rights. Although it is absolute, it will ensure the common good insofar as its basis is the people's (explicit or tacit) consent. This dependence on popular consent imposes limits on its action. To ensure that the laws are valid for both rich and poor, they must be publicly promulgated. Taxation without consent is forbidden; it would be a violation of the rights of property, which political society must protect. The power to make laws cannot be delegated to a non-elected body because that would lead to the arbitrariness that arises when particular interests are both judge and party to a decision. The legislators must not give in to the temptation to unite in their own hands the power to make and to execute the laws because that would exempt them from the obligation to obey the laws, which is a violation of equality before the law. It follows that the executive must be independent and that its role must be limited to enforcement of the laws. Finally, Locke proposes the creation of a separate "federative" function to deal with the powers to make war and peace because these questions are too particular for legislative action, yet they demand the kind of political prudence that cannot be expected from a mere executive.

The ultimate legitimation of Locke's vertical social contract is presented at the outset of chapter 13 in the *Second Treatise*. The supremacy of the legislative branch is based on the fact that it represents the will of the majority, which gives it a "fiduciary power to act for certain ends."[29] Its authority comes from its function as a representative. In principle, therefore, power remains always in the hands of the people. Just as an individual retains ultimate power to fire or replace a lawyer who does not do his bidding, so too the legislative can be removed if it violates the trust bestowed on it by the majority. In that case, like the criminal in the state of nature, it is responsible for its own destitution. In the normal case, the end for which power is given serves also to limit the use of that power. If that limit is violated, the fiduciary power is de facto dissolved; its authority reverts to its original source, the majority, who may designate a new representative. This picture makes clear the importance of Locke's positive depiction of the state of nature (in spite of the "inconveniences" that lead men to leave it). Unlike Hobbes's atomized state of nature whose unity depends on an absolute sovereign, Locke's plural natural community retains its power because it existed prior to the social contract. It has the right to preserve itself both from external enemies and (especially) from excesses by its own legislators. The questions that remain to be answered are when, how, and why the normal contractual relations may be violated.

Paradoxically, the supreme power that in principle remains with the community only becomes real when the government's overreaching brings about its own dissolution. In the normal run of affairs, the legislature is supreme during its time in office. So long as it fulfills the contract, no justification exists for removing it. In the final two chapters of the

Second Treatise, Locke, thinking no doubt of his own political times, analyzes the conditions in which power reverts to the community. Chapter 18 poses the question of tyranny, which is defined in the classical manner as arbitrary action undertaken without authority. In Locke's modern formulation, "where-ever law ends, tyranny begins."[30] Tyrannical action returns society to the state of nature, creating the possibility of opposing force to force. Rebellion against subordinate officers who act without authority or who overstep the limits of their charge is not difficult to justify. But what is to be done when a king commits such acts?

Locke knew that he had to weigh his answer. He was aware of the debates set off by Calvin's followers.[31] What if the wrong blamed on the monarch is imaginary? Who is qualified to judge the ruler? Just as violations by lesser magistrates can be appealed to higher authorities, so too the first recourse against tyrannical actions by the monarch must be an appeal to the law. If that fails, however, and force has to be opposed to force, then the state of nature has returned, and the result will depend on what Locke calls an "appeal to heaven." Returning to the question in his consideration of tyranny, Locke admits that "if a long train of actions shew[s] the councils all tending that way," there can be no doubt a need for action.[32] But he does not say what kind of action should be taken or who should undertake it. He concludes simply that the illicit actions themselves have condemned the regime to dissolution due to its lack of legitimacy.

These considerations lead to the final and longest chapter in the *Second Treatise*. This analysis of "the dissolution of government" is addressed primarily to the rulers rather than to the community that is called on to "act" when its rulers violate its trust. Locke warns the rulers that they are in fact rebels whose use of arbitrary force rather than the rule by law justifies their removal. He offers two illustrations of his argument that clarify the implications of his political thought. In the first, it is the executive who, by several different tactics, violates the authority of the legislature. The second points to the possibility that either branch, the executive or the legislative, can overreach its legitimate powers. This second example shows why Locke's antiabsolutist defense of popular sovereignty does not lead to a theory of popular democracy. As with Hobbes, but with different arguments, the rights that Locke wants to protect are the private rights of modern liberalism.

In Locke's first illustration of the dissolution of government, the monarch alters the status of the legislature in a way that prevents it from playing its role as umpire because it no longer expresses the will of the majority. In a healthy political society, the parliamentary majority produces unity out of diversity; and because unity is the soul of the commonwealth, its destruction entails the death or dissolution of the authority to govern. The constitution of the legislature was the political society's first act, so the claim by another body (such as the executive) to make binding laws in the legislature's place is a usurpation that dispenses with the people's obligation to obey and frees them to constitute a new legislative power that will not give up its rightful power to an overreaching executive. Although Locke doesn't stress the point,. this reassertion of popular sovereignty need not result from an act of violence; after the "long train" of violations, when the monarch has lost his ability to rule because he is despised, his legitimacy is not recognized, his authority is lost, and the legislature must reassert is role as representative by establishing a new executive power (as did the Whig leaders of the Glorious Revolution in 1689).

Imagine, says Locke, a legislature like that of England, which is made up of three distinct persons: a hereditary monarch who can convoke or dissolve the other two branches; a hereditary noble assembly; and a representative assembly chosen for a fixed term by the people. Such a mixed constitution permits four possible violations. The prince may set his arbitrary will in the place of laws declared by the legislature, which is executive usurpation. Second, the prince may prevent the legislature from meeting or may prorogue its sessions, or he may prevent it from fulfilling freely its function by withholding information it needs for deliberation, or he may refuse to pay the members. Any of these acts changes the legislature, which is not just a convocation of delegates, but a place where free debate and deliberation are necessary. Third, the prince may alter the mode of election for the legislature, changing the qualification of electors or the periodicity of elections, which changes the representative nature of the assembly, whose illegitimacy then prevents it from playing its neutral role. Finally, the ruler may deliver the people to a foreign power—for example, by an unfavorable alliance that serves his personal religious convictions. Although Locke describes general conditions, his readers knew well that each of these violations referred to recent events in British history.

In each of these cases, Locke insists that the responsibility for dissolution sits directly on the head of the prince who has persuaded himself—or been persuaded by the friends of absolutism—that his power is unlimited. Locke adds that a prince may also destroy the legitimacy of the legislature by refusing to execute the laws that it has made. In this case, it is clear that the legislature should name a new executive who does indeed express the will of the majority—as it did when William and Mary came to the English throne in 1689 after accepting Parliament's understanding of the social contract as expressed by the Bill of Rights.[33]

Although Locke wrote his *Second Treatise* in part to justify what became the Glorious Revolution, his second illustration of the dissolution of government has broader political implications. The need for a second illustration was suggested by the conclusion to the first example of dissolution. Locke remarks that "the state of mankind is not so miserable that they are not capable of using this remedy [to create a new legislature], till it is too late to look for any."[34] Although he does not develop the implication that, for example, the rights of free speech and of an energetic public sphere are necessary for the protection of freedom, it is implicit in his insistence that it is wrong to wait until oppression has become unbearable or a foreign power is at the gates before telling people that they must defend their freedom. The only way to be secure against tyranny is to avoid it before it is too late. The rights needed to prevent tyranny are therefore more far-reaching than simply the right to demand a new government once tyranny has appeared. But Locke does not explain how a popular form of antityrannical politics might work. His concern is only to protect liberty (as he has defined it) by remaining alert to the possibility that a tyranny emerges when the monarch or the legislature violates its obligation to protect "life, liberty, and estate."

At the conclusion of this second example, Locke admits that it may appear that he is defending the power of the people in spite of the traditional view that "to lay the foundation of government in the unsteady opinion and uncertain humor of the people is to expose it to certain ruin." He presents three replies to the objection that his theory of popular sovereignty encourages frequent rebellion. The first of these replies expresses his confidence, like Machiavelli's, that the people want above all else to protect their freedom. When they feel the yoke of arbitrary power, they will not be deceived by their rulers' proclamations of good intentions and will be ready to seize any occasion to lift their burdens.

Second, revolutions do not result from minor mismanagement, which will be always born with patience. "But if a long train of abuses, prevarications and artifices, all tending the same way, make the design visible to the people . . . it is not to be wondered, that they should then rouse themselves and endeavor to put rule into hands that will secure to them the ends for which government is enacted."[35] But Locke goes no further than to suggest that this doctrine of the power of the people is the best "fence" against rebellion and the most likely means to prevent its occurrence. Locke's argument warns those who are tempted to violate constitutional laws that they are the ones who are in fact rebels by using force to oppose the legitimacy of the law. With this claim, Locke has defended popular sovereignty, but its only function is to protect private rights and freedoms. That is why Locke's theory is antipolitical.

◆

Locke's critique of absolutism is telling as a defense of liberal rights. His stress on the natural diversity produced by human freedom reinforces his political argument. Because he assumes that men are naturally social, he sees no need to explain how they will come together to preserve their rights before the tyrant appears on the scene. This resistance to tyranny brings the people to the stage, but as a reaction to the violation of natural rights rather than as a process through which rights are preserved by enriching them—for example, by adding a civic republican complement to liberal individualism. This weakness appears in the penultimate paragraph of the *Second Treatise,* which returns to a dilemma that had appeared already in the state of nature. Locke explains here, as he did in chapter 3, that when there can be "no appeal to a judge on earth, [men are] properly in a state of war, wherein the appeal lies only to heaven." Locke and his Whig allies of course had another option; they appealed to the Dutch armies of William and Mary to overthrow the tyrant. Liberals were not always so fortunate, which is why others tried to apply classical republican theory to the imperatives of modern individualism.

ROUSSEAU'S DEFENSIVE REPUBLICANISM

In the eighteenth century, the question of political obligation took a new form as the spirit of scientific progress that had encouraged material progress was applied to the search for social betterment. Although English liberals enjoyed a period of peace and prosperity, the international movement called the Enlightenment spread from Paris under the leadership of thinkers known as "philosophes." These individuals (in this case, both men and women) were not professional philosophers or academics; they were engaged, public intellectuals. The goal of the Enlightenment, as its name indicates, was to cast the light of reason into the dark spaces ruled by blind, unthinking tradition. By unveiling what the dominant powers sought to hide, the philosophes intended to further the cause of human progress. Nothing was sacred in their eyes. Booksellers who distributed their illegal works did not hesitate to sell pornographic literature alongside other products of the Enlightenment under the heading "philosophy."[36] Similarly, the infamous Marquis de Sade would write not only *Les 120 journées de Sodome* (One Hundred Twenty Days of Sodom), but also *La philosophie dans le boudoir* (Philosophy in the Bedroom). After all, what is pornography if not the crudest of materialism, stripping away the illusions of love and the fantasy of romance to reveal the simple mechanical actions that are their real foundation?

The great collective realization of the Enlightenment project was the *Encyclopedia*, edited by Denis Diderot and Jean le Rond d'Alembert, whose thirty-five volumes were proposed to subscribers in 1751 and delivered over the next two decades. The knowledge it conveyed was in part practical know-how, as indicated by the many intricate plates that depicted the newly introduced tools and machines whose efficient virtues the project encouraged. This practical information was supplemented by theoretical essays that elaborated the Enlightenment's critique of unthinking tradition. Although the royal censors banned the *Encyclopedia* in 1759, claiming that its materialist premises were a threat to religion, the support of some influential aristocrats with access to the court permitted publication to continue. The philosophes did not realize that this support was an early sign of a rift within the ruling strata of French society that would crack wide open in 1789, when members of the aristocracy deserted the monarchy to form an alliance with the rising commercial and industrial bourgeoisie. No one expected, imagined, or perhaps even desired revolution. Insofar as the philosophes sought political influence, their model was an updated Platonic dream called "enlightened despotism" or, more politely, "enlightened absolutism." Diderot was only one of a number of the philosophes who joined the court of Catherine the

Great in Russia, and Voltaire was the best known of the philosophes drawn to the court of Frederick the Great in Prussia.

Although Voltaire was no doubt the emblematic figure of the Enlightenment, he was among its more moderate political thinkers.[37] Master of prose and poetic diction, historian and philosopher, playwright and pamphleteer, popularizer of Newtonian physics and British philosophy, Voltaire was above all a civil libertarian and apostle of religious toleration; the unity of his life is expressed by the famous injunction "écrasez l'infâme" (crush the infamy) with which he signed many of his letters. He was often in trouble with the authorities, who had him imprisoned in the Bastille, later constrained him to exile in England, and forced him to live his last years at his estate at Ferney, just outside of Geneva, to which he was prepared to flee if his freedom was threatened in France. A month before his death in 1778, the aged Voltaire met publicly in Paris with Benjamin Franklin, the ambassador of the newly independent United States, a symbolic gesture that contemporaries described as "the embrace of Solon and Sophocles." This phrase expresses the age's ambivalence toward the ideal of individual freedom. Whereas some looked back to these classical models, others adhered to a modern materialism typified by Claude Adrien Helvétius's international best-seller *De l'esprit* (On Mind, 1751), which reduced mind to matter, freedom to self-interest, and virtue to utility.

◆

Jean-Jacques Rousseau (1712–1778) stood apart in his theories and his life. He was an autodidact who left his native Geneva at sixteen, invented a system of musical notation, and had an opera performed at the royal court before becoming friends with the Parisian philosophes. On his way to visit Diderot, who had been jailed for the antireligious implications of his materialist *Letter on the Blind,* Rousseau had a vision that dominated the rest of his work: although man is naturally good, the unhappy condition of contemporary men is the paradoxical result of society's constant pursuit of self-perfection. The dialectic between society's progress and the harm that progress inflicts on humanity became the basis of his prize-winning essays the *Discourse on the Arts and Sciences* (1750) and especially the *Discourse on the Origins of Inequality among Men* (1755), known respectively as the *First Discourse* and the *Second Discourse*. This insight is developed differently in Rousseau's widely read epistolary novel *Julie, or the New Heloïse* (1761),[38] which portrays its heroine's fateful attempt to preserve her virtue in spite of the influence of the immorality of her times. His *Émile, or On Education* (1762) sought to show how men can be educated in a way that maintains their goodness in the face of ever-present social temptations. The same year saw the publication of the book for which Rousseau is most remembered today, *The Social Contract*. Although this essay was the least read of his works during his lifetime, it would soon be treated as the bible of the French Revolution.

After these initial successes, Rousseau's life began to imitate his work. The French authorities condemned his *Émile*, forcing him to flee to Geneva, where *The Social Contract* was in turn condemned. He was protected for a time by Frederick the Great; then he accepted an invitation to England by the philosopher David Hume, with whom he soon quarreled. Returning to France under a false name and avoiding the Parisian society that he scorned, he earned a bare living transcribing musical scores. His autobiographical *Confessions*, begun during this time, were published only posthumously. One interpretation of his later work is that he was making yet another attempt to prove his theory of a natural human goodness, in this case his own, that is constantly threatened by the demands of society. Although his former friends thought that he had become paranoid, his late works can be seen as a manifestation of the instability of the modern subject, which was turning increasingly inward as its separation from the public sphere grew. Rousseau had anticipated this dilemma and had sought political means to defend against it, especially in *The Social Contract*, whose first draft was subtitled "An Essay on the Form of the Republic." But what could republicanism mean in modern times? The republican ideal was identified with the virtues of Rome, whose grandeur had brought with it a fatal decadence, a forerunner of the modern dialectical linkage of progress with decline.[39] How could a modern republic defend against this inevitable fatal fall? Rousseau's answer set him apart from his age.

Insofar as the critical philosophes opposed reason to privilege, equality to hierarchy, and natural man to artificial convention, Rousseau was one of them. But their project could be cold, hard, and abstract in its materialism, and their concern with the utility of knowledge clashed with

Rousseau's sentimentality, his setting of the heart above the head, and his faith in men's natural goodness. Reforms leading to compromises with "enlightened despotism" were alien to his independent spirit. He was a materialist only in the sense that he opposed the goodness of nature (and natural man) to the artificial conventions of civilization. In *Discourse on the Origin of Inequality*, for example, he insists that pity is a "natural sentiment" that is "the cause of the repugnance every man would feel in doing evil." He denounces the philosopher who is concerned with universal truths, worrying about "dangers to the entire society," even while "his fellow-man can be murdered with impunity right under his window."[40] But Rousseau could be carried away by his own rhetoric. As Voltaire wittily commented in a letter, "I have received your new book against the human race, and thank you for it. Never was such a cleverness used in the design of making us all stupid. One longs, in reading your book, to walk on all fours. But as I have lost that habit for more than sixty years, I feel unhappily the impossibility of resuming it."[41] But Rousseau knew that it is impossible to return to a prelapsarian state. Political theory can use the state of nature only as a norm that explains the conditions of legitimate obedience.

The book that Voltaire dismissed was *The Social Contract*. Rousseau explains in the *Confessions* that he had begun working on this project when he was secretary to the French ambassador to Venice. He came to understand that "everything is fundamentally bound together by politics" and that the best possible government was the one that "would be fit to form the most virtuous people, the most enlightened, the wisest and, in the largest sense, the best."[42] He explains that for more than five years he made little progress in his projected study, to be called "Political Institutions"; it was only after he developed the vision he had on the road to Diderot's prison in the *Discourse on the Origin of Inequality* (the *Second Discourse*) that a breakthrough occurred. That essay, he explained, already "contains everything bold and daring in *The Social Contract*."[43] In fact, the two works complement one another. The project of the *Second Discourse* has to be understood in political terms; Rousseau's question is not simply how inequality came into being, but what makes it legitimate and why, therefore, it is accepted by those who suffer from it. For its part, *The Social Contract* seeks to invent political institutions that can avoid the loss of freedom that comes with the social subordination that, for a republican, constitutes the essential nature of inequality, whose roots are political and not based simply in material exploitation.

The shared political perspective of Rousseau's two texts is evident in the formulation of their initial question. The first chapter of *The Social Contract* points to the paradox of political legitimacy. "Man is born free, yet everywhere he is in chains. One who believes himself the master of others is nonetheless a greater slave than they. How did this change occur? I do not know. What can make it legitimate? I believe I can answer this question."[44] "Slavery" for a republican is the loss of freedom. Rousseau's master who is in fact a slave is identical with the man who was born free and yet finds himself in chains. His slavery is not the result of external force; the chains are self-imposed; they are the unintended by-product of the quest for mastery, which is itself the result of the misapplication of naturally given freedom. How this self-enslavement took place is an historical question to which a particular answer would be needed. But Rousseau claims to be able to explain how this alienation of natural freedom became legitimate because that is a normative problem to which a universally valid, rational solution must be found. This is the task of *Discourse on the Origin of Inequality,* whose normative concern is clear in its first command: "Let us therefore begin by setting all the facts aside, for they do not affect the question."[45]

This concern with norms has a paradoxical consequence in both essays. Natural freedom makes each person the equal of all others, but this universal equality means that no one has the right to assert his particular freedom because that would create differences among men. Yet freedom, if it is not to be illusory, must manifest itself in the world. When it does so, it becomes particular, making itself different from the others. Locke and his liberal followers would deny that this naturally occurring difference is a form of inequality that affects the citizen's political freedom. For a republican such as Rousseau, however, it threatens social unity, which is based on all citizens' equal liberty. Before we look more closely at Rousseau's account of the origin of inequality, we need to consider the broad outline of his republican theory as presented in *The Social Contract* in order to explain what kind of inequality concerns Rousseau and what he proposes to do to avoid its effects.

Rousseau's starting point is not natural law, but human freedom, which he defines simply as the absence of subordination to any other person. The social contract that preserves this essential freedom has the form of any other contract: something is given up or "alienated" in exchange for something that is both different from it and yet of equal value to it. Rousseau does not shy away from the paradox in his explanation of how his social contract becomes legitimate. Each person must alienate the rights that he had as a free person; as a result, each person has nothing—no thing or possession—that is particular to himself. In this way, all have now made themselves equal in a normative political rather than a natural or material sense. No one now has any private interest, and because no one can make particular claims on the basis of particular needs, no one has an interest in being burdensome on others or taking advantage of them. This universal alienation by which the contract comes into being does not erect a third party, like a Hobbesian sovereign, because that would create political inequality by making freedom someone else's possession. The only possible solution is that each person abandons his particular freedom to the law, whose universality makes it applicable without prejudice to everyone, preserving the freedom of all by preventing their subordination to any particular person or interest.

This paradoxical logic in which freedom is preserved by means of its universal alienation explains the next step in Rousseau's demonstration. Although all are subject to the law, they are not identical in every aspect of their existence. Diversity exists in the private and social spheres, whereas unity is ensured by the citizens' political action. This unity is manifested by what Rousseau calls the "General Will" (*volonté générale*) as opposed to the particular wills whose individual actions together add up to the "Will of All" (*volonté de tous*) (for simplicity, I use the lowercase forms of both the English and the French terms from this point). Participation in the general will transforms the particular and therefore limited and private freedom realized by the individual in the state of nature into a general and universal freedom achieved within the republic. In chapter 6 of book I of *The Social Contract*, Rousseau describes this alchemy as transforming the private person into a member of a "moral and collective body" that is a sort of secular church. He then explains in chapter 8 that the member of the civil state that results from this republican project is "substituting justice for instinct . . . and giving his actions a morality that they previously lacked [in their natural state]." Particular concerns are left behind as men become citizens of a republic. "Only then, when the voice of duty replaces physical impulse and right replaces appetite, does man, who until that time only considered himself, find himself forced to act upon other principles and to consult his reason before heeding his inclinations." This political achievement brings the "moral freedom, which alone makes man truly a master of himself."[46] Only as universal, as citizens, are men free from subordination to any others.

The key to Rousseau's argument lies in the distinction of the *volonté générale* from the *volonté de tous*. The will of all is simply the gathering together of the individual wills of all of the particular members of the society; it expresses their particularity rather than the universality of the freedom that makes them all equal citizens of the republic. This *volonté de tous* expresses the diversity of society; it is a snapshot of the present concerns and the different interests and desires of the people who live within the frontiers of the state at a given moment. Although the general will also emerges from all of the particular individuals, it is the expression of their will as citizens, and its concern is the good of the whole—which, Rousseau adds, is precisely their own true good. Because the *volonté générale* is political, it leaves no place for particularity and has no room for difference. If it were riven by faction or conflict, it would be unable to will. For the same reason, it is inalienable; a will cannot will if it has delegated its powers to someone else, be it a monarch or a representative government. As if carried away by his own logic, Rousseau adds that the general will cannot err because, for the same reason that a person always wants what is good for himself, the people in a republic will seek always their true good.

The fact that the citizens as individuals express both the general will and the will of all can lead to confusion. Even when the will of all members of society is taken into account, the result is not "general." The crucial distinction is that in one case each individual is expressing his particular concerns, whereas in the other he is acting as a citizen concerned with the good of the whole. Rousseau suggests two ways of dealing with the possible confusion of the two types of will. He knows that what he calls "partial associations" or "factions" may put their particular interests before the good of the whole. In that case, he suggests that "their number must be multiplied and their inequality prevented . . . to ensure that the general will is always enlightened and that the people is not deceived." He adds that in the process through which the general will emerges, "the citizens [are] to have no communication among themselves." If they did, he explains, the result would express only the will of all as produced by negotiation among interests. The implication is that the universality of the general will has an intuitive, prereflective quality that is distinct from the result of deliberation among representatives of different interests. But the universality that excludes particular interests from the formation of the general will also ensures the protection of those interests because the only objects on which that will is exercised are those that have a universal character. The general will, Rousseau insists, "cannot pass judgment on either a man or a fact."[47] It is not a referee to whom men appeal to settle their petty private quarrels over property rights and personal liberties; its function is to guarantee republican freedom and civic virtue in the public domain.

Rousseau distinguishes the universality of the general will and its pronouncements from government, the nation from its temporary rulers. The general will makes laws; the government then applies them to particular cases. For example, in chapter 6 of book II of *The Social Contract,* Rousseau explains that "the law can very well enact that there will be privileges, but it cannot confer them on anyone by name. . . . It can establish a royal government and hereditary succession, but it cannot elect a king or name a royal family. In short, any function that relates to an individual object does not belong to the legislative power."[48] That is where government enters the picture. It mediates between the sovereign people's universal will and the particular citizens who are subject to the law in specific cases. The fact that the general will cannot be alienated implies that the government remains always subordinate to its dictates.

The general will's sovereignty does not mean that Rousseau's republic depends on all citizens' active democratic participation in all decisions. He does at first appear to argue for direct democracy when he explains that because the general will cannot be alienated, it cannot be represented by the government. His rejection of representative government is most pointed in chapter 15 of book III, which mocks the English, who think they are free when in fact they "are free only during the election of the members of Parliament. As soon as they are elected, [the English people] is a slave, it is nothing."[49] But earlier, in chapter 4 of book III, he had argued against direct democracy and in favor of the separation of powers. If the body that makes the laws has also the charge of executing them, it will necessarily focus on particular concerns and lose its concern with the general good. For that reason, Rousseau argues that abuse of laws by the executive is less dangerous in a republic than is the corruption of the legislator that would result from his becoming involved in the competition among interests.[50] Such corruption appears to be inevitable in a democracy, where those who make the laws are to take into account the diverse interests of all the people. Rousseau thus concludes that "if there were a people of Gods, it would govern itself democratically. Such a perfect government is not suited to men."[51] Gods are concerned with the universal; men are unavoidably involved with both particular interests as well as with the general interest. Rousseau's republicanism seeks to protect the common good that alone can preserve the natural goodness of free men.

Rousseau's critique of direct and representative democracy makes his republicanism seem defensive. His careful separation of the domain of the general will from particular interest in order to assure that its absolute power is not destructive of private interests makes the political sphere into a sort of secular church reserved for the elect. Among these virtuous citizens, the inequalities created by private interests are irrelevant. But these inequalities are not simply material, nor does their origin lie solely in the social sphere. Rousseau's fear of factions or "partial associations" reflects a recognition that the republic will have to be on guard against the return of inequalities that can deflect the general will from its universal goal by paralyzing its ability to express a unitary will. From this point of view, it is political inequality that explains why (and which) forms of material inequality become salient; for example, when the republic becomes the instrument of a faction, it will favor one or another particular social interest, which results in others becoming unequal. This is the source of the questions raised at the outset of *The Social Contract*: How and why do free-born, natural men impose chains upon themselves? Why do they seek to become masters, and how does this attempt in fact enslave them? These questions dominate the *Discourse on the Origin of Inequality*. Its account of the natural origin of inequality explains why *The Social Contract* has a defensive character, which the revolutionaries who took Rousseau's theory as a positive program for erecting a modern democratic republic fatefully failed to recognize.

The inequality with which Rousseau is concerned in the *Second Discourse* is not natural, but rather conventional, which means that it depends on (tacit or explicit) consent. Its essence consists in privileges, which by definition are given to some at the expense of others. Although force may have been involved at the outset, the replacement of violence by law transforms the possession of privilege into a legitimate property. Such privilege is the source of inequality. According to Rousseau, philosophers who have tried to understand its origins by returning to a state of nature have only projected onto that natural state the values of their own society—assuming, for example, the existence of innate ideas of what is just and unjust, invoking a natural right to property, or attributing to human nature qualities such as need or greed, oppression or pride. That is why Rousseau earlier proposed "setting all the facts aside, for they do not affect the question."[52] It is not possible to deduce universal norms from particular facts. Rousseau proposes instead to ask what would have been the case if man had remained in a state of nature? "Nature" signifies here the opposite of civilization, which is founded on a basic hypocrisy that Rousseau contrasts repeatedly to individual authenticity. Natural man is self-sufficient and content to live in the present with no concern for his future. The universality that Rousseau attributes to this natural man anticipates the purity of the general will in his republican political theory.

Beginning with physical man, Rousseau encounters a biped with human hands, looking out upon nature and contemplating the vastness of the heavens. He is an animal like others, weaker than some, less agile than others, but well organized. His advantage over other animals is that he can subsist on all sorts of nourishment, whereas they are limited. Rousseau does not yet stress this incipient universality, preferring to develop the first of a series of ironic comparisons of natural and civilized conditions. Primitive man is a robust fellow whose children are born healthy and develop naturally; if weak offspring die naturally, this occurrence contrasts with conventional society, where the state, by making children a burden, kills them off indiscriminately before birth. In the natural state, man's body is his only instrument; he uses it for a multiplicity of purposes, many of which have been forgotten by civilized man, who has lost the force and agility of his natural ancestor due to of the benefits of industry. Because he has an ax, his wrists are not strong enough to break branches; because he has a slingshot, he cannot throw stones so well; because he has a ladder, he no longer can climb trees. "In becoming sociable and a slave he becomes weak, fearful, servile; and his soft and effeminate way of life completes the enervation of both his strength and his courage."[53] In short, progress has hidden costs. But why do men value it, then?

Rousseau turns next to man's "metaphysical and moral side." The difference between man and other animals is that "nature alone does everything in the operations of a beast, whereas man contributes to his operations by being a free agent." One works by instinct; the other uses its freedom. The fact that Rousseau stresses human freedom rather than presuppose that men are rational prepares a new set of dialectical ironies. The animal cannot deviate from the rule of nature even when that would be advantageous to its survival, whereas humans enjoy a freedom that can be used, but also abused. As opposed to the animal, which after a few months has become what it will remain all its life, man is capable of self-perfection. Yet, asks Rousseau, "why is man alone subject to becoming an imbecile?"[54] His answer is that the perfectibility that draws man from his innocent natural state toward an enlightenment can also produce error; it is a virtue that can also generate vice. The use of freedom in the quest for self-perfection makes possible the abuse of nature and the self-abuse of human nature.

Meanwhile, the natural man who lives simply, willing or abstaining, desiring or fearing, encounters new conditions. As a result, more complicated ideas replace the old habits. But the dialectical irony reappears: the more man knows, the more he fears and the more he then desires in order to overcome his fears. Whereas natural man fears only pain and hunger, the man who has begun to think learns to fear death and its terrors. Language is necessary in order to fix the fleeting data of experience—to think. Natural man, living independently, has no need for thought or language; he has naturally "the passions which inclined them to provide for his needs." Imagine, says Rousseau, that natural man sees lightning kindle wood. How will he come to know that he himself can initiate the same process? "The more one meditates on this subject, the more the distance from pure sensations to the simplest knowledge increases in our eyes." This points to a wider question: "Which was most necessary, previously formed society for the institution of language; or previously invented languages for the establishment of society?"[55] Is language an innate ability that makes men naturally social, or are the moderns correct to see that it is the result of conventions among members of a society of individuals?

If language did not exist prior to the assembly of men, why did they come together? Those who attribute this reunion to need or to the desire to escape from misery are guilty of importing assumptions from their own society into the picture of natural society. What could misery mean to natural man? Misery exists only relative to an idea of perfection. Can a free, healthy being truly be called miserable? After all, it is civilized people who complain of their lot, going so far even to kill themselves, which savages do not. And although the natural state knows no virtue, it also knows no vices. Hobbes is said to have seen correctly that men cannot be supposed to be naturally virtuous or sociable, but he erred by projecting onto the natural state passions typical of his own civilization. This projection blinded him to the one natural virtue that precedes reflection: the pity that binds men together. Even the apostle of economic egoism, Bernard Mandeville, "departing from his cold and subtle style" was "forced to recognize man as a compassionate and sensitive being" and to admit that "men would never have been anything but monsters if nature had not given them pity to assist their reason."[56] The basic human sentiment of pity, a passion that is not expressed with words but by human tears, is the foundation of the virtues of generosity, mercy, benevolence, and friendship. It is this pity—not fear or misery, language or desire—that naturally leads men to wish for the company of others.

If pity is an innate human passion that unites men, and if the freedom that permits the perfection of the species is natural, the emergence of reason must now be explained. Rousseau introduces the distinction between self-love (*amour de soi*), which is natural, and vanity (*amour propre*), which is artificial. Reason is produced by and contributes to vanity. The person who is vain separates himself from himself in order to look upon himself with the eyes of another; he seeks to perfect himself, but only in the eyes of the other. The reasoning subject in fact separates himself from the object of thought; he is interested in the thought rather than in the object that gave rise to the thought—even when that object is another human. As a result, reason is prudent; it keeps its distance from the world and its passions. Unlike the "market women" who intervene without thinking in a brawl to "prevent honest people from murdering each other," reason is calculating and utilitarian.[57] Self-absorbed reason overrules natural pity. Although a Socrates might be able to achieve virtue through reason, concludes Rousseau, humanity would have disappeared long ago if it depended on the dry, abstract, and ultimately inhumane force of reason and the vanity from which it springs.

Rousseau concludes this phase of his account of the state of nature by insisting that it excludes the possibility of inequality. "Wandering in the forests, without industry, without speech, without domicile, without war and without liaisons, with no need of his fellow-men, likewise with no desire to harm them . . . savage man, subject to few passions and self-sufficient, had only the sentiments and intellect suitable to that state; he felt only his true needs, saw only what he believed he had an interest to see, and his intelligence made no more progress than his vanity." These "true needs" based on self-love are opposed to the false needs that spring from vanity, which produces the social conventions that permit inequality to emerge. That is how the perfection of individual reason leads to the deterioration of the species. In the state of nature, some may be healthy of body, others of mind. This difference makes no difference. The idea that the strong (of body or mind) oppress the weak is meaningless. "Is there a man whose strength is sufficiently superior to mine and who is, in addition, depraved enough, lazy enough, and wild enough to force me to provide for his subsistence while he remains idle?" If he does so, as soon as his vigilance relaxes, "I take twenty steps in the forest, my chains are broken, and he never in his life sees me again."[58] Slavery, a condition of dependence, does not and cannot exist in the state of nature. Privilege and inequality are nothing but civilized slavery. The *Second Discourse* goes on now to explain how self-enslavement became both possible and legitimate.

Rousseau frames his new problem with an aphorism: "The first person who, having fenced off a plot of ground, took it into his head to say *this is mine* and found people simple enough to believe him, was the true founder of civil society."[59] If only someone had denounced this preposterous claim, humanity would have been spared wars, crimes, murders, and miseries. Yet the existence of private property, in spite of its ill effects, is not arbitrary, nor is it the result of violence or conquest. Rousseau sets out to explain how it could have arisen legitimately in the process of leaving the state of nature. There are really two questions here. Why, in a state of nature, would someone claim something as "mine"? To say something belongs to him assumes that it does not belong to someone else who might have a justified right to it. This question poses the further question, Why would others be ready to believe him?

Returning to the genealogy of humanity's fall from its natural equality, natural man now confronts some problems that he must overcome. For example, fruits may hang high on trees, and man is not the only animal competing for them. As a result, he has to develop his body; he eventually has to learn to use branches or stones to bring down the desired object. Progress has now begun. Success permits the population to grow; the race spreads to new climates, where it must learn to adapt to seasonal changes. Perhaps long winters or fallow years can be overcome by the invention of the hook and line for fishing or the bow and arrow for hunting. Animal skins become clothing. The use of fire is discovered. With this thickening of relations, the origin of language can be seen. At first, repeated relations are described with simple words such as *large* or *small, strong* or *weak, fast* or *slow.* The use of even such general terms introduces reflection in the place of natural man's instinctual action in the world. This reflection makes men aware of the universality of thought, which stands above and apart from the particulars of immediate experience. This awareness explains the prudence that Rousseau criticized in the first part of the *Second Discourse.* Although prudence increases man's superiority over other animals, it also makes him aware of and proud of his difference from them. It is the source of the vanity that produces the egoism whose pernicious effects Rousseau now proceeds to trace.

These first steps create the conditions for further progress. As the mind is increasingly enlightened, men begin to perfect their material lives. They no longer sleep under a tree or in a cave; they find instruments to cut wood, dig soil, and make huts from branches that they cover with clay. With these steps comes what Rousseau calls a "first revolution, which produced the establishment and differentiation of families, and which introduced a sort of property." Although this primitive property could lead to quarrels, it was first acquired by the strong, who could defend it and who did not have the need (or the occasion) to despoil their neighbors (who, for that reason, were "simple enough" not to denounce "this preposterous claim"). Property also brings an unintended benefit for humanity when "the first developments of the heart" unite the members of the family. But, as always, there are costs, because the lifestyle of the sexes also changes. Women become sedentary, and their softness makes them unfit for the hunt. But a shared sentiment now unites the couple, and the use of the new, more efficient tools permits the family to enjoy leisure time, which allows them to produce previously unknown conveniences. Another inversion occurs, making the "first yoke they imposed on themselves without thinking about it, and the first source of the evils they prepared for their descendants."[60] These conveniences not only further soften body and mind, but also become new needs, ends rather than means of human satisfaction. People are soon more unhappy about losing them than they were satisfied to possess them. This self-imposed "yoke" leads to a new series of dialectical paradoxes in which progress and regress make up a single, unbreakable chain.

As the population grows, social relations thicken further, becoming still more dense. People are now make comparisons among the objects each possesses, which leads to the formation of preferences that are justified by attributions of beauty or merit. Seeing one another more frequently, people come to feel a need for one another, but these bonds of tenderness can also lead to a jealousy that hardens into discord. Nonetheless, sociality increases; people come together to sing and dance, transforming leisure time into amusement for idle men and women. This sociability has the further effect that each begins to look at the other, and, for the same reason, each wants to be looked at. Public esteem—recognition as the best singer or dancer, for example—becomes a value, but with it emerges a step toward inequality and toward vice. The desire to be admired by others encourages vanity and contempt on the one hand, shame and envy on the other. But now a positive dialectical rebound occurs. The same attempt to be esteemed by others leads each individual to demand to be respected, and this demand for equal respect gives rise to the idea that people owe one another the duties of civility. This demand for respect by others increases one's own self-respect. The positive brings with it a negative, however, because now what in nature would have been an accidental wrong appears to be an intentional harm that is felt as expressing contempt. As a result, punishment no longer seeks reparation for real harm done; now it must be proportional to the victim's self-esteem (for example, nobles demand different penalties than commoners).

The ground has now been prepared for a new stage, whose result is that "all subsequent progress has been in appearance so many steps toward the perfection of the individual, and in fact toward the decrepitude of the species."[61] With the coming of metallurgy and the development of agriculture (which Rousseau calls a "fatal accident"), the nature of property changes. These two types of production force men to reflect on the future benefit they can gain by sacrificing something in the present, a calculation that would not have occurred to natural man. This cultivation of land and the forging of ore also brings a recognition that nature can be modified. Now, finally, the legitimacy of private property can be explained.

Why would others accept the claim of private ownership made by the first person to fence in land for cultivation? The simple answer is that they, too, want their possession of their own terrain to be legitimate. This possession was already based on their own labor "because one can not see what man can add, other than his own labor, in order to appropriate things he has not made." When a possession is recognized as property, justice comes to be defined as a right that each person has to what is his. Things would have remained at this stage, says Rousseau, if talents were equal among men, but those who are strongest do more work, and those who are clever learn to shorten their labor time. Material inequality now begins to be transformed into social inequality; the differences among men become more salient and more permanent. "Things having reached this point," concludes Rousseau, "it is easy to imagine the rest."[62] Progress in the arts, language, and talent goes together with inequality of fortune and the use and abuse of wealth.

Rousseau does not criticize material inequalities as such; despite his praise of pity, he is not an advocate of the downtrodden, but a republican worried about the classical symptoms of corruption. He worries when faculties that develop in the species, such as imagination or memory, are put to use by vain individuals to advance particular purposes. The fate of men no longer depends on the material goods they possess or even their ability to harm others; now qualities such as intelligence or beauty, skill or talent, cement one person's artificial power over another person. Although socially sanctioned privilege may appear preferable to the rule of pure force, its political influence is far more corrosive because free men can always at least attempt to resist unjust force. The new relations that depend on rank and reputation oblige everyone to develop these artificial qualities or at least to pretend to have them. Men must show themselves as something other than they truly are; they are forced to become inauthentic because their value lies outside themselves.[63] The distinction between being and appearing opens the way for deception, ostentation, and the vices that accompany them.

Rousseau's criticism is animated by his republican fears. In a remark that recalls the introduction to *The Social Contract,* he points out that civilized men are no longer truly free and independent; they have become slaves to the very process by which they seek to become masters. When rich, they need the services of the poor; if poor, they depend on the help of the rich. Each has to interest the other in his fate, appealing to their vanity to make them think that they will benefit by benefiting others. Hypocrisy flourishes. Ambition leads men to want to increase their fortune not as a result of material need, but in order to distinguish themselves from others. All this, concludes Rousseau, is the result of the fact that private property is accepted as legitimate.

The situation worsens. Prior to the invention of "representative signs of wealth," men possessed only land and livestock. As a result, wealth was limited. In the new conditions, because some have now grown wealthy beyond physical limits, others will become poor in spite of the fact that the amount of their possessions has not diminished. The resulting change in people's character has political consequences. Modes of behavior expressing domination or servitude are now accented. The result is the emergence of the two types of men Machiavelli described: those who want to dominate and those who want to avoid domination. The rich use their old slaves (their workers) to gain new ones; they are like "famished wolves which, having once tasted human flesh, refuse all other food and thenceforth want only to devour men."[64] Natural equality is destroyed, and disorder follows as the rich increase their usurpation and the poor turn to brigandage. This state of war is not natural, but the result of the "yoke" of private property. The conflict that in Rome had enriched the republican spirit of liberty thus has a different, less happy result in Rousseau's modern individualist republic.

Rich and poor want to escape the consequences of their implacable opposition. The rich see the problem more clearly because they have the most to lose from the struggle. They claim that their labor justifies their wealth, but they know that natural man will ask them, "By virtue of what do you presume to be paid at our expense for work we did not impose on you? Do you not know that a multitude of your brethren die or suffer from need of what you have in excess?"[65] This question leads to the crucial step in Rousseau's argument that unveils the unspoken economic implications of social contract theories.[66] To counter the threat to their property, the wealthy have "conceived the most deliberate project that ever entered the human mind":[67] they use the force of their adversaries against themselves. They turn their enemies into their defenders by proposing a contract that calls on everyone to join together to protect the weak and restrain the ambitious, thus assuring for the poor as well as for the rich security in their possessions. These rules of justice are to be valid for all members of the society, admitting no exceptions. In this way, the division of the rich from the poor is made legitimate by laws that are universal. Natural or material inequality that had no significance becomes the source of political privilege that in turn becomes the basis of social inequality.

Rousseau concludes that "such was, or must have been, the origin of society and laws, which gave new fetters to the weak and new forces to the rich, destroyed natural freedom for all time, established forever the law of property and inequality, changed a clever usurpation into an irrevocable right, and for the profit of a few ambitious men henceforth subjected the whole human race to work, servitude and misery." Why does this deception work? Rousseau's answer illustrates again the defensive character of his republicanism. Inequality has corrupted human nature: "Crude, easily seduced men, who in addition had too many disputes to straighten out among themselves to be able to do without arbiters, and too much avarice and ambition to be able to do without masters for long," were led to think that they were securing their freedom when they were in fact chaining themselves by this contract. As a result, people are now more concerned to dominate those below them than they are afraid to lose their independence to those above them. They forget the basic lesson of republican theory, that "it is very difficult to reduce to obedience one who does not seek command; and the most adroit politician would never succeed in subjecting men who wanted only to be free."[68]

Pursuing the pessimistic logic of his defensive republican theory, Rousseau argues that despotism is "the ultimate stage of inequality, and the extreme point which closes the circle and touches the point from which we started. Here all individuals become equals again because they are nothing . . . subjects no longer having any law except the will of the master. . . . Here everything is brought back to the sole law of the stronger, and consequently to a new state of nature different from the one with which we began, in that the one was the state of nature in its purity, and this last is the fruit of an excess of corruption." In the first phase of inequality, the status of the rich and the poor are legitimated; in the second phase, the domination of the powerful over the weak is affirmed; now, the relation of master to slave expresses "the last degree of inequality and the limit to which all the others finally lead." But this ultimate phase of inequality implies also that when revolt does occur, "since the contract of government is so completely dissolved by despotism . . . as soon as [the despot] can be driven out, he cannot protest against violence. . . . Force alone maintained him, force alone overthrows him."[69] But Rousseau is no advocate of political force. Like Locke, he wants to ensure that the slide toward tyranny is avoided.

The *Second Discourse* concludes with a reaffirmation of the dialectic of inequality that opposed savage man, who sought tranquility and freedom, to social man, who is always active, in a sweat, agitated, and self-tormenting, working until he dies, paying court to the powerful, whom he hates, and to the rich, whom he scorns. The savage, who doesn't understand the meaning of the words *power* and *reputation*, cannot understand how someone can be happy on the basis of someone else's opinion rather than his own experience. This savage is the voice of Rousseau, but Rousseau is no longer speaking from within a genealogical process whose fatal downslide he has described. He is looking backward rather than forward. It is not hard to understand how the French revolutionaries would try to transform the logic of his theory into a vision of progress. The idea here is appealing: the radical overthrow of social inequality by a naturally good humanity that would return virtue to a republic that was corrupted by aristocratic court society. But that was not Rousseau's thesis when he turned from the *Discourse on the Origin of Inequality* to political theory in *The Social Contract*. Like most republicans, Rousseau was a pessimist; only revolutionaries are eternal optimists.

Rousseau seems to leave his reader with three options. The first lies with the hope for moral rather than political renewal. The critique presented in the *Discourse on the Origin of Inequality* is broadened and deepened in *Julie, ou La nouvelle Heloïse* and in *Émile,* which were popular presentations of the way in which the spark of natural goodness remains at the heart of all humans in spite of the obstacles created by modern society. But the virtue defended by Julie's sacrifices in the novel is a domestic virtue. Rousseau's intuition anticipated the future in which the classical republican virtue would be privatized and feminized. In *Émile,* he recognized that public life was no longer able to fulfill its classical function of integrating the young into the life of the society. The idea that a proper education can teach youth how to avoid the snares of social temptation seemed to be the only available alternative. Rousseau was the first in a long line of modern thinkers who have hoped to achieve political reform by inventing a theory of education to replace political engagement. Karl Marx later underlined the difficulty faced by such projects when he asked in his *Theses on Feuerbach* (1845), "Who will educate the educator?" In a society of free and equal individuals, what gives some of them the authority to teach others?

The second option is presented in the concluding chapter of *The Social Contract* (chapter 8 of book IV), where Rousseau explains the need for a public or "civil religion" to reinforce the spirit of republican liberty. He argues, "Men at first had no other kings than the Gods, nor any other government than theocracy." The reason was that they could not accept another man who was their equal as a master. As a result, all classical founders of states claimed a religious justification for their political creations. Christianity, however, "far from attaching the citizens' hearts to the State . . . detaches them from it as from all worldly things." Indeed, "a society of true Christians would no longer be a society of men. . . . By dint of *being* perfect, it would lack cohesion; its destroying vice would lie in its very perfection." The diversity of civil society can be unified only by the development of a "purely civil profession of faith." Rather than a dogma imposed by heaven, it must be the expression of the "sentiments of sociability without which it is impossible to be a good citizen or a faithful subject." Its articles of faith "ought to be simple, few in number, stated with precision, without explanations or commentaries." Rousseau proposes a short list of these beliefs: "The existence of a powerful, intelligent, beneficent, foresighted, and providential divinity; the afterlife; the happiness of the just; the punishment of the wicked; the sanctity of the social contract and the laws."[70] To these commands he adds one interdict—intolerance. Tolerance will ensure that diversity within society is preserved at the same time that the society's unity is maintained.

The theoretical foundation of this modern civil religion is the general will; the civil religion is its practical expression, transforming the daily experience of private members of society by giving it a shared universal legitimacy. Civil religion rekindles civic virtue when the corruption that results from the existence of political inequality deforms its expression. But this classical republican theme, which Rousseau stresses in his analysis of the nature and function of "the legislator" (in book II, chapter 7, of *The Social Contract*), supposes that some founder introduced the civil religion at the same time that he instituted the new republican institutions. Where will modern societies find their Moses, Lycurgus, or Theseus? As with the hope that a proper education can preserve the individual from the temptations of society, however, the hope that a new civil religion can save the modern world from self-created traps is unrealizable. The reign of equality leaves no room for a founding father. Civic celebrations mobilizing artists, poets, and musicians are inferior substitutes for the public virtue, vigilance, and self-confidence lost by a privatized citizenry.

The third option is that Rousseau's reader becomes an actor, rising against the tyranny of inequality in the name of humanity's natural goodness. Although this option misreads the normative character of Rousseau's argument, it was the option taken by French revolutionaries who did not recognize or did not want to recognize the defensive character of Rousseau's republicanism. As a result, in the words of French historian François Furet, "Between 1789 and 9 Thermidor 1794, revolutionary France used the paradox of democracy, explored by Rousseau, as the sole source of power. Society and the State were fused in the discourse of the people's will; and the ultimate manifestations of that obsession with legitimacy were the Terror and the war, both of which were inherent in the ever-escalating rhetoric of the various groups competing for the exclusive right to embody the democratic principle. The Terror refashioned, in a revolutionary mode, a kind of divine right of public authority."[71] Each of the factions that succeeded (by eliminating) one another as the revolution was radicalized claimed to be the incarnation of the general will. Its opponents could object that their claims were a usurpation because the general will is inalienable. But those in power could in their turn answer that the general will excludes the particularity of interests and that their opponents represented a "faction" that threatened the very unity of the revolution. The group that won the battle could then affirm that because the general will is incapable of error, they obviously had the correct understanding of its dictates.

The same theoretical misunderstanding of the defensive and normative character of Rousseau's theory explains why, in spite of his critique of democracy, he is often considered a radical democrat. The association of his name with the revolution reinforces this impression. The successive radicalizations that led to the institution (by law) of the Terror were essential to a process by which the parasitical, artificial, and privileged interests described in the *Discourse on the Origin of Inequality* were eliminated. Once these sources of inequality had been eliminated, it could be assumed that the general will would emerge automatically from a society of equal citizens. At that point, Rousseau's objections to democracy would no longer have any basis; the particular interest and the general interest would be identical, just as *The Social Contract* had prescribed. So it was that the Committee on Public Safety that administered the Terror was in fact composed of men who were convinced that their virtue ensured that these measures, however extreme, were necessary to effect the revolutionary victory. Indeed, at the height of the Terror, when Maximilien Robespierre created the "Fête de l'être supreme" (Festival of the Supreme Being), he seemed to be following Rousseau's suggestion that the founders of a republic must also institute a civil religion.

Rousseau cannot be blamed for the excesses of the French Revolution. Its leaders thought that they were founding a democratic republic, but their understanding of democracy as the institution by state action of social and economic equality was incompatible with a republican political framework. A social democracy cannot escape from the particular constraints of (economic) necessity, which are a threat to the universal republican liberty that is the presupposition of such a democracy.[72] It becomes an absolutism that slides inevitably toward tyranny because nothing can limit the general will in its forward rush to destroy social diversity, which appears to it as a threatening sign of inequality that must be overcome. This sign, however, is a misunderstanding of the distinction between the *volonté générale* and the *volonté de tous*. As the representative of republican freedom, the general will can make only laws, whose universal nature protects the rights of the private individual, which are particular. The will of all, in contrast, represents the sum total of all of these particular interests. As such, it is variable and subject to accident and error. Without the general will, those particular rights that constitute the will of all would be threatened, ephemeral, and uncertain. Rousseau's defensive republicanism protects the individual's particular rights by guaranteeing the citizen's liberty. That is all it can do.

◆

The plausibility of the revolutionary interpretation of Rousseau suggests the existence a need increasingly felt within modern societies to go beyond defensive normative theories of obligation to find a new, real, and practical basis for political theory. The political had to be brought down to earth. On the one hand, the practical materialism of the Enlightenment suggested that economic interest provides the glue uniting a society of individuals. Not yet ready to abandon the classical idea of politics, pragmatic philosophes and Scottish allies such as Adam Smith began to develop the new science of political economy. Unity would be discovered within the diversity of the new and rapidly changing world of commerce and industry. On the other hand, the destruction of the political unity of the ancien régime led the radical heirs of the Enlightenment to try to impose a new unity on a society that seemed unable to cope with the reality of its uncharted freedoms. The individualism unleashed by the overthrow of monarchical absolutism seemed to demand a return to classical virtue if society was to be stabilized. Robespierre and the Jacobins were willing to impose ruthlessly the politics of virtue that they had learned from histories of classical republicanism. The future unity of a society of equals justified the attempt in the present to eradicate all signs of the past.[73]

The reaction to this thoughtlessly blind and heedlessly bold attempt to begin the world anew was the invention of conservative thought. Although in retrospect it is possible to identify conservative thinkers in earlier periods, it was only when the French Revolution claimed to open a limitless horizon to an indefinite future that it became necessary to insist not only on the values inherited from tradition, but also on the value of the past as such. The most perceptive of these newly minted conservatives was Edmund Burke. The fact that he had supported American independence and criticized British colonial predations in India shows that conservative thought did not have to be antiliberal, although it often was. The more significant fact is that Burke supported the Americans as defenders of the traditional "rights of an Englishman," whereas Adam Smith saw their revolt as the result of the economic irrationality of the mercantile system. For the Americans, their revolution produced something new and unintended: a republican democracy that, at least for a time, combined the virtues and avoided the vices of both republican and democratic thought.

№ 6
THE END OF POLITICAL PHILOSOPHY?

THIS CHAPTER BEGINS and ends with a question. No longer an undercurrent that threatens the autonomy of political thought, antipolitics has increasingly replaced political thought since the end of the eighteenth century. This trend is seen first of all in the role that what was once called "political economy" and now is simply referred to as "economics" has played in the political self-understanding of society. How did labor in the quest for wealth, which was classically relegated to the *oikos* and was considered by Christians to be the result of original sin, become the source of the political legitimacy of social relations? Adam Smith's *The Wealth of Nations* was published in 1776, the year of the American Declaration of Independence. Those who criticized emerging capitalist social relations could also look to it, or to another revolution for inspiration, this one breaking out in 1789. Its goal was to use the power of the state to eliminate inequality in society by creating a democratic republic. Its radical protagonists, the Jacobins, led by Maximilien Robespierre, instituted the Terror in 1793 in order to realize their project, but its failure did not diminish its attractiveness to later generations, who called it by the gentler name of "socialism." What came to be known as conservative political thought was formulated first by Edmund Burke in reaction to the French Revolution. His appeal to the wisdom of tradition and to the quasi-religious bonds of political unity was a challenge to the theorists of political economy as well. A fourth type of political thought, which I have called "republican democracy," emerged during this same period in the new United States. It escaped, at least for a moment, from the antipolitical temptation. Whether it can continue to do so is the question with which this chapter concludes.

◆

At the outset of this study, I described Plato's political theory as an "antipolitics." His ideal republic was ruled by philosopher-Guardians whose task was to put an end to political division by replacing diversity with unity, particularity with universality, appearance and opinion with reality and truth. But Plato's analysis of the cycle of regime changes showed that he was aware of the practical difficulty of realizing his theory. Although he recognized that philosophy cannot replace politics, he could never free himself from its appeal. In *The Statesman,* for example, he compares the politician-ruler to a doctor whose knowledge has constantly to adapt to the patient's particular condition, considering the variability of human life. But this concession to finitude is temporary and tactical. The doctor's knowledge is superior to the patient's, whose consent is not needed to legitimate the doctor's intervention. What should the patient do, asks Plato, if his condition changes, but the doctor is away? Should he accept remedies proposed by others of whose qualifications he cannot be sure? No; he should stick with the certainty of the old prescription rather than leave his fate to chance. For the same reason, the law-governed society in *The Laws* is the best that can be hoped for. Although its laws are explicitly conventional (*nomoi*), Plato attributes their origin to a divine source, which means that they cannot be challenged.

The representatives of the antipolitical strain in political thought, like Plato, knew that their normative theory could never be fully realized, but Augustine, Luther, and Hobbes refused to abandon the search for a source of legitimation that is absolute, independent of society, and unaffected by citizen participation. Augustine criticized the heretics because they assumed that the creature can know or affect the Creator; Luther, faced with his own heretics, exchanged the grace of God for the power of the prince; and Hobbes conquered the fear haunting the state of nature by giving absolute power to the sovereign. But none of these antipolitical philosophies succeeded in eliminating politics. For Augustine, the tension between the City of God and the City of Man, for example, leads him to formulate a theory of just war. In Luther's case, the power of the secular ruler that protects invisible church does not eliminate evil, which the believer must suffer patiently even while joining the ruler in secular combat against it. Hobbes's absolutism ensures peace and welfare in society while protecting liberal freedom in private life. The importance of politics is reduced in each of these cases, but its possibility is not excluded. Even antipolitical thought cannot put an end to politics.

Social and historical contexts help to explain when and why antipolitical thought emerges and recedes. Periods of conflict awaken a yearning for unity, whereas epochs of stability and growth encourage exploration and experimentation. Historical conditions do not alone explain political thought, however. For all of their differences, Plato and Aristotle were Greeks; Augustine and Thomas were Catholics; Luther and Calvin were Protestants; and Hobbes and Locke were seventeenth-century Englishmen. These proximities suggest that the Aristotelian strain in the history of political thought in turn is not exempt from the antipolitical temptation. The stress on diversity and particularity is not a protection against antipolitics. This is evident, for example, in Aristotle's appeal to the middle class to ensure stability in a mixed society, in Thomas's faith that divine law could both limit and supplement the fallible forms of human law, in Calvin's legitimation of resistance only if led by the legitimate holder of office, and in Locke's limitation of government to the function of neutral referee against whose misdeeds only an "appeal to heaven" is possible. In each case, social diversity depends on an unchallenged vision of power that guarantees political unity. That is why politics cannot replace political thought without risking an antipolitical deviation. If politics becomes simply the contest for power, the tension between the real and the ideal that gives rise to political thought is lost.

There is an apparent exception to the antipolitical temptation. The republican tradition that began in Rome and was developed by Machiavelli stressed a kind of unity that social conflict *strengthened* rather than weakened. The example of Rousseau, who had read the Romans as well as Machiavelli, indicates, however, that the antipolitical tendency can appear in this tradition as well. His distinction of the general will from the will of all, his refusal of representative government, and his concern to create a civil religion that could rekindle the classic virtues destroyed by inequality point to an antipolitical temptation in his theory. The general will is not the result of the conflict of different interests; its unity is mystical and otherworldly. Rousseau himself recognizes that the liberty that he refuses to alienate to representative government is incompatible with the clash of interests in a self-governing democracy. And the shared civil religion to which the proud citizen of Geneva appeals finally guarantees unity at the price of diversity. The fact that antipolitics can appear even in republican political thought does not mean that it must. Nonetheless, conflict is no more an unmitigated political good than is harmony, stability, or well-wrought unity.

This brief recall of an undercurrent that has silently accompanied the political history studied here becomes more important in this final chapter, but there is a crucial difference between the classical and the modern forms of antipolitics. The antipolitical philosophy that began with Plato opposed an ideal world to the real one. Whether in Plato's Ideas, Augustine's City of God, Luther's Christian prince, or Hobbes's absolute monarchy, there was always a gap between the fact and the norm, the particular and the universal, the real and the ideal. A similar distinction was present in those aspects of the Aristotelian tradition that were at times tempted by antipolitics. Classical antipolitics was philosophical; whether Platonic or Aristotelian, it enclosed the particular within the universal. As modern individualism became the shared premise of citizens and philosophers alike, a change occurred. Now all of the sources of antipolitics are found within the world itself. Classical transcendence is replaced by modern immanence. As a result, modern antipolitics is antiphilosophical; it tries to universalize the particular, to absolutize the individual, and to value tradition over reason. The invention of political economy, the revolutionary overthrow of the ancien régime, and the emergence of conservative thought as a reaction to those two transformations may have brought political thought to the end of its possibilities. The tension between the norm and the empirical reality that were the warp and the woof of political life is overcome; the real has become the rational, and the rational is to be found in the real. That is the simple but implicit claim of the new antipolitics.

The apparent triumph of this antipolitics will be no more permanent in modern times than it was in the past, but the antipolitical temptation may be more evident now than it was. The three modern antipolitical theories studied in this chapter were developed at the end of the eighteenth century. Others followed in the next centuries, but their basic form has remained constant, as will be seen in this study's brief concluding chapter. Before turning here to the analysis of these three basic forms of modern antipolitics, I should stress that antipolitics does not always succeed. Although the temptation is always present, not every society succumbs to it. That is the reason why this chapter concludes with an account of the republican democracy developed in the founding experience of the United States.

A POLITICAL ECONOMY?

Among the French philosophes were a group called the Physiocrats, who are often considered the first to stress the importance of production for the creation and circulation of national wealth. Although this stress on production seems self-evident to contemporary ears, the dominant economic theory of the times was mercantilism, which asserted that to maintain and increase national power, a country had to achieve a positive balance of trade, which meant that it had to export more than it imported. To achieve this goal, production had to be subsidized in order to provide cheap exports, monopolies had to be accorded to favored manufacturers, and agricultural prices (and thus wages, which assured a basic subsistence) had to be kept to a minimum. The legitimation of the mercantile system was political; a positive trade balance meant that the nation was not dependent on others because the surplus permitted the rulers to undertake political projects of their own choosing. Meanwhile, the effects of these policies on the population was of no concern to the governments, for whom power in international relations rather than national wealth and its citizens' well-being was the main concern.

The Physiocrats, whose name combines the Greek words *physis* (nature) and *kratos* (rule), accepted the general idea that only labor can produce wealth; they argued, however, that truly productive labor occurs only in agriculture, where the development from seed to fruition not only is evident, but also is unaffected by transitory phenomena such as inflation or deflation. Appealing to the distinction between natural and positive law, the Physiocrats criticized the state interference supported by mercantilist theory; from their point of view, the natural law of productive labor implied that agricultural prices should be kept high, artificial industrial monopolies should be eliminated, and artisans and commerce should be left to their own devices. This view led them to adopt the idea of laissez-faire, which had appeared somewhat earlier, as the essential implication of their theory of natural law. National power would depend on flourishing fields that could feed a growing population, not on a stock of inert gold and silver coins used to pay mercenary armies.

François Quesnay (1694–1774), who also was physician to the French king, drew the broadest picture of the physiocratic theory in his 1759 *Tableau économique,* which traced the distribution of the net product of agriculture (which made up roughly 80 percent of the French national production) to the three classes that constituted the nation: the agricultural class, who produce wealth and pay rent; the landed proprietors, who use that rent to support themselves by purchasing food and manufactured goods; and the so-called barren class employed in nonagricultural sectors, who spend their wages for self-maintenance and the purchase of raw materials to produce goods sold to the other two classes. Because only the agricultural class is productive, its surplus will determine the wealth of the other classes in society. If the government needs additional revenues to deal with emergencies, a "single tax" should be levied on land rent (because the rent is used for consumption rather than to increase productivity).

Despite the fact that their natural-law theory stressed the contribution of productive human (agricultural) labor, and despite their laissez-faire criticism of governmental support for monopolies, the Physiocrats were no friends of popular participation in political life. They placed their hope on an enlightened despotism. This political orientation made more sense in the most populous and most centralized nation of Europe, where agriculture was a mainstay of economic life, than it did in the less densely inhabited, parliamentary British Isles, where industrialization had begun. Although the Physiocrats had some success in influencing the monarchy, kings bestowed their favors for arbitrary and frequently changing reasons. The Physiocrats' influence on practical politics was thus only temporary and limited.

In 1776, the year that Turgot, the physiocratic chief minister to Louis XVI, fell from power, Adam Smith (1723–1790) coincidentally published *An Inquiry into the Nature and Causes of the Wealth of Nations.* The book was an instant best-seller. Smith was a professor of moral philosophy at the University of Glasgow whose respected *Theory of Moral Sentiments* had appeared in 1759. Although he agreed with the Physiocrats' critique of mercantilism and their insistence on laissez-faire, he discovered a different source of the productivity that creates national power and wealth: the division of labor. He had focused attention on the social and moral foundations of this phenomenon in his earlier book, drawing positive implications from the kind of dialectical paradoxes that Rousseau analyzed in the *Discourse on the Origins of Inequality*. In order to understand the political implications of Smith's economic theory, it will be useful to look briefly at his *Theory of Moral Sentiments*.

How, asked Smith, are men able to formulate legitimate moral judgments? If they are self-seeking beings who prize their own interest above all else, why would they care about the welfare of others? They gain nothing from it, save perhaps the pleasure of observing the happiness of another. Smith's answer begins from the existence of an "original passion," which he calls "sympathy" or "empathy." Certain types of behavior, which appear to be appropriate to the occasion, awaken this passion, which, like Rousseau's idea of pity, makes men into social beings. This insight made sense in a society where traditionally valid norms of behavior had begun to conflict with emerging individualist society. Behavior that is "appropriate" no longer conforms to preexisting traditions; it now creates new standards, norms that everyone can accept. The shared sympathy or empathy offers the basis for a new morality in an individualist society.

Everyone, asserts Smith, has had the spontaneous experience of sympathizing with behavior that seems appropriate (although he may not know why it seems so). This sympathy forms the basis for moral action. Each person tries to attract the sympathy of others by acting in a way that he thinks they also would act— or would like to think they would act—in the same circumstances. Although angry, the individual controls himself. When successful at something, he does not brag; if defeated, he praises the victor's skills. Where Rousseau saw an alienation of the authentic *amour de soi* in a vain quest for the approval of others, Smith sees instead the emergence of new norms that regulate social behavior. His idea is that each person will act in a way that he thinks will be appreciated by others, and the result will be the emergence of norms of reciprocity. In society as a whole, people seeking the sympathy of others contribute unintentionally to the emergence of an ideal, impartial spectator who judges what counts as the appropriate behavior in a given situation. This spectator poses the norm, which each member of the society then internalizes as the standard of behavior worthy of being praised according to the norms that regulate the society as a whole.

Smith is aware that there are problems with his idea of "moral sentiments." His account of the creation of behavioral norms resembles a Calvinism without predestination. The socially appropriate forms of behavior are decided by the conscience of the individual who has internalized the expectation that all of his actions are constantly observed and judged by an invisible but omnipresent spectator. But how can he be certain that conscience will compel the morally correct behavior? A famous example illustrates the conflict of normative theory with actual practice. Smith imagines a man of truly humane disposition who must react to two catastrophic events: an earthquake in China and the threat of losing a part of his little finger. It would seem that self-interest and self-love will command him to take whatever measures are necessary to save that finger from the personal pain that he will suffer instead of dealing with the far greater harm to human beings that he only abstractly knows is suffered in China. The idea of sympathy cannot explain why the man of conscience would do the moral deed, abandoning his little finger to bring aid to the Chinese victims; he cannot know what counts as appropriate behavior in China because he has never been to China or met a Chinese. As a result of this moral dilemma, the amount of aid given to the Chinese victims will prove insufficient to alleviate their suffering.

To deal with the moral problem illustrated by his Chinese example, Smith introduces an early version of his famous theory of an "Invisible Hand" working behind individuals' backs to produce a collective good that they themselves have not sought. Bernard Mandeville had already introduced in *Fable of the Bees* (first published in 1714) this idea of a harmony that is the unintended consequence of self-seeking actions. In Smith's version, human reason, which cannot know the consequences of men's actions, is supplemented by passions that are unconscious. One of these passions, the passion for wealth, has an unintended and ironic consequence. The poor person who thinks that wealth will make him happier works hard to amass increasing amounts of it. But once he becomes successful, he realizes that he has worn out his body in exchange for baubles that bring only a transitory satisfaction. Although the individual has once again been misled by his reason, which identified happiness and wealth, the labor that he now sees as wasted has unintentionally benefited society as a whole by inventing new industries, cultivating fallow land, and producing better-quality goods more economically. Although Smith admits that the rich gain more than the poor in this circumstance, he praises the Invisible Hand that has used the private passions for the public good. But this theory does not solve the moral problem of aid to China, which may be one reason why Smith constantly revised *The Theory of Moral Sentiments*, publishing a sixth edition in 1790, shortly before his death.

◆

Can the production of economic wealth solve moral problems? Smith doesn't ask that question directly in *The Wealth of Nations*.[1] Although the book contributed to economic theory, its demonstration of the superiority of "commercial society" over feudalism or mercantilism is not based solely on the commercial society's ability to produce greater wealth. Smith produced his economic theory, which legitimates an emerging capitalist society (although he does not use the term *capitalist*), also with a political intent. In the introduction to book IV, he makes explicit what has been clear to the reader from the outset: political economy is "a branch of the science of a statesman or legislator . . . [that] proposes to enrich both the people and the sovereign."[2] *Wealth* is a synonym for power. It is not an absolute quality, but one that varies in changing conditions. Just as the same sum of money can buy more or less goods depending on conditions of abundance or scarcity in society, so too the power that wealth can mobilize is variable. A nomadic tribal leader may command vast amounts of labor, but his fortune is tiny compared to the commercial wealth of a British magnate who controls directly only a small number of workers. What, then, is "the wealth of nations"? How does it affect the nation's citizens? And does economics replace politics?

At the outset of *The Wealth of Nations*, Smith defines wealth as the nation's annual labor. Contrary to the prevailing mercantilist doctrines of the time, a nation is obviously better off and more powerful when there is more of this labor. Although national wealth depends also on variations of soil, climate, and the like, these variables cannot be affected by political or economic choices. The variations that can affect national wealth are the skill, dexterity, and judgment of the workforce and the proportion of those doing useful labor to those who are idle. The analysis of both factors shows the superiority of the emerging commercial society over its feudal or mercantile predecessors. Such a society gives more people useful work, and workers are more productive. In what Smith calls "civilized nations," the working class is better off than members of savage societies where everyone works, yet the society remains "miserably poor." The difference is due both to the cultivation of the workers rather than of just the land, which increases their skills and dexterity, as well as to development of the machinery and materials with which they work. Both of these developments take place in the emerging urban and commercial cultures rather than in traditional agricultural nations. The increased quantity and quality of the capital employed is due to the fact that some of what is produced is not consumed but instead invested with an eye to the future. That choice has political implications. How is it made?

The attainment of the good life depends on the ability to maintain life itself, and so the first chapter of book I in *The Wealth of Nations* begins with the famous analysis of production in a modern pin factory. Smith wants to show how the division of labor increases the nation's productivity by improving the workers' skill and dexterity. When each individual worker produces the entirety of a pin, an average worker can make some twenty in the course of a day. When the operation is broken down into distinct but partial tasks—eighteen of them in this case, which Smith says he himself observed, some of which are performed by the same person—ten laborers are able to produce forty-eight thousand pins in a working day. The result is that each worker produces 240 times as many pins as he would have made by working alone. This remarkable increase in productivity must be explained.

Three distinct causes, each representing a further refinement of the division of labor, are responsible for the increased production. The first is that pin making is now a particular branch or specialty rather than a part of a larger productive process. As a result, making pins becomes an end rather than an accessory means to a greater goal. This first specialization leads to a second as the particular tools used in the now independent branch are refined and specialized because each operation within the new specialization has in turn become an end for which new tools will become the now adequate means. This process by which means are transformed into ends ensures continual progress in the invention of tools that are more precise and less wasteful of raw materials and human effort. Finally, a third specialization occurs as workers themselves become masters of one or another particular task; the polyvalent worker is replaced by a specialist at a single operation. In this process, the worker is no longer a means of production, but an end whose perfection increases the productivity of the whole.[3] What takes place in the pin factory spreads throughout commercial society as other industries apply the same technique, breaking down jobs into distinct operations assigned to specific workers working with more precise tools. The result is a "universal opulence" that, insists Smith, extends to the lowest ranks of society.

Although the benefits of the division of labor explain the spread of this method, they do not explain its origin, which Smith in chapter 2 calls the "principle" that gives rise to it. He knows that for most of human history and in most human societies, the quest for opulence was not the chief motivation of men's behavior. He is aware that just because a result has been produced (increased wealth or its opposite in the case of a nation that wagers on war as the source of wealth), that result is not necessarily what was originally intended. Smith looks for some aspect of human nature that is capable of explaining the "principle" of the division of labor. He finds it in the human "propensity to truck, barter, and exchange one thing for another."[4] He admits that he is not certain if this tendency is built into the physical nature of man or whether, as Aristotle argued, it is the result of the faculties of reason and speech. What is crucial is that it is found in all men—but not in any other animal race. Two hounds running down a hare, for example, may seem to cooperate, but this apparent coordination results simply from the fact that their passions are directed at the same object. Smith used a similar argument in the *Theory of Moral Sentiments* to explain the sympathy that made men social animals. His consideration of this propensity's role in creating the principle of the division of labor now becomes the foundation for an economic theory that is also political insofar as it explains what makes the new commercial social relations legitimate.

Smith goes on to add a new element to his theory. Dogs on the hunt are unable to coordinate their efforts in the chase for the same reason that they do not exchange bones with one another: they don't have a notion of property, which means that they have nothing to trade. As a result, when an animal wants something from a man or from another animal, it seeks favor: the puppy fawns, says Smith, and the spaniel seeks its master's attention in order to be fed. Smith admits that men do indeed sometimes seek the favor of others by base supplication—doing so was an essential element of feudal society—but this method is inefficient because scarcity of time makes it impossible to do so on all occasions when a person needs the help or simply the cooperation of others. There are too many people in society and too many occasions for encountering them; an entire lifetime scarcely suffices to gain the direct and personal friendship of a few men. What is more, whereas other animals reach their full maturity without the help of others, men are in constant need of their fellows' aid as they grow toward independence. At first, individuals are not aware of this need for one another; each seeks only his personal good, the increase of his private property. Behind his back, however, reason, or the "Invisible Hand," continues to work.

The emergence of the idea of the division of labor that spreads from the pin factory to the whole of society is the unintended result of the individual pursuit of self-interest. Smith insists that there is no reason to expect the help of others as a product of human benevolence or the teachings of the Gospel. Successful cooperation can be ensured most simply and directly by appeal to the self-love of others. A person who expects to benefit by helping others can be counted on to fulfill his commitments. To make a bargain or to enter into a contract is to say to the other party, "Give me what I want, and I will give you what you desire." Egoism thus leads to cooperation; private vices become public virtues. So it is, continues Smith, that the butcher, the brewer, and the baker do not contribute to my dinner because I have appealed to their humanity; I don't talk to them about my needs but show them their own advantage, knowing full well that they can be counted on to act from self-love. Even the beggar, who appears to depend on others' benevolence, knows how to make use of this human propensity: when he doesn't receive the specific things that he needs, he knows how to barter the surplus that he doesn't need in order to satisfy the necessities of the moment. In such cases, both parties benefit from the exchange; although they benefit differently, they benefit equally. If this were not the case, the exchange would not be legitimate.

This disposition to truck and barter presents the occasion that is crystallized as the "principle" of the division of labor. Over a period of time, in even the most primitive of conditions, it becomes clear that one person is more skilled than another at a given task. The person who is able to produce more bows or arrows more quickly than others comes to recognize not only that he can exchange them for meat that others have hunted down, but also that he is a less efficient hunter than some others and that by spending more time making the tools of the hunt and less time looking for game, he is able to feed himself not only more efficiently, but more sufficiently overall. As a result, the process of specialization begins. It will spread, Smith explains in chapter 3, with the expansion of the market. Simple barter is replaced by specialization when producers know that there will be purchasers for their products. In this way, the "principle" of the division of labor is fixed as the kind of norm that Smith analyzed earlier in the *Theory of Moral Sentiments*.

At first glance, this analysis does not seem original; Plato used a similar illustration in book II of *The Republic* to explain what he called the city of pigs. For Smith, however, the division of labor is not natural; it is the result of a deliberate choice to increase the wealth of the nation. This idea transforms an economic demonstration that the technical division of labor in the production process increases productivity into a political claim that legitimates the social division of labor and therefore the relative power of different strata of society. At times, Smith recognizes implicitly what he has done. For example, he admits that the difference among the natural talents of different men in a market society may be in reality far less than it appears to the outside observer because their differences are not the cause but the effect of the division of labor. In Plato's simple example, natural differences lead to specialization; in Smith's picture, it is the "principle" of the division of labor that constrains men to specialize in order to increase their wealth. That is why Smith admits in chapter 2 that the difference between a philosopher and a common street porter is due less to nature than to habit, custom, and education. His economic theory has in effect become a political theory that legitimates the social relations imposed by the new commercial society.

The political implications of Smith's economic theory are apparent at the end of his study, when he looks at the duties of the sovereign, by which he means the government. He is aware that the constantly refined specialization has made the worker into a tool of his tools and that, because a means has become an end, there is no limit to the expansion of the technical division of labor. But this apparently neutral process has social costs.

Thus, for example, when Smith considers the "institutions for the education of youth" in book V, chapter 1, he recognizes that "a man whose whole life is spent in performing a few simple operations . . . has no occasion to exert his understanding, or to exercise his invention in finding out expedients for removing difficulties which never occur." Such a man becomes "as stupid and ignorant as it is possible for a human creature to become." This stultification has political consequences because "he is altogether incapable of judging [the great and extensive interests of his country]; and . . . he is equally incapable of defending his country at war." Indeed, "his dexterity at his own particular trade seems, in this manner, to be acquired at the expense of his intellectual, social and martial virtues." In this way, the technical principle that Smith explained at the outset of *The Wealth of Nations* not only works to the disadvantage of what he calls "the common people," but also produces harmful political effects that must be ameliorated by the support of education, which will make them "less apt to be misled into any wanton or unnecessary opposition to the measures of government."[5]

In order to legitimate the emerging commercial society of his time, Smith had to show that the production of wealth by the new economy was not only beneficial but also just. His premises are those of liberal individualism. His explanation of the source of legitimate profit distinguishes what he calls the real from the nominal price of commodities. The real price is the amount of labor from all of the different producers whose work went into the production of the good, whereas its nominal price is the money it takes to purchase that commodity on the market. The real price is thus the amount of labor that a person can save himself from having to do by purchasing the commodity. This same social relation can be expressed politically by saying that the real price is the amount of labor that the purchaser can impose on others, who have to work to make the product for him. The nominal price is simply the amount of money needed to buy the product. As a result, an individual's wealth is relative; in different conditions, the same nominal monetary value can purchase goods that incorporate more or less actual labor. This distinction permits Smith to explain how profit is produced legitimately in a contractual exchange of apparent equals. Profit, for the liberal individualist and for Smith, is not the by-product of the quest for a higher good, as in Aquinas; it is an end in itself.

How can it be said that the exchange of real value for nominal value is an exchange of equals? Some products result from labor that is more intense or that demands more skill; an hour's work by a highly trained person may "contain" more labor than two hours of simple physical exertion by a "hired hand." Nonetheless, says Smith, the "higgling and bargaining of the market" will produce what he calls a "rough equality" sufficient for carrying out the exchanges that are needed in everyday life. Smith doesn't explain how this process works (nor does he invoke an invisible hand in this context).[6] The situation is complicated by the fact that commodities are not usually exchanged for other commodities; the butcher who wants bread first sells his meat for money and then takes that money to the baker to purchase his daily bread. This process is one source of profit. The value of gold and silver, like that of any commodity, varies with the amount of labor that it takes to produce them. As mines wear out, demanding more labor to dig their riches, the real value of their product—the amount of labor that it can command or that it replaces—changes. For example, at the time Smith was writing, the discovery of South American gold mines reduced the nominal value of existing gold and silver to roughly one-third of its previous value. Thus, although equal quantities of labor have the same real value for the individual who does the work, and although the same quantity of labor is required to produce the given commodity, the variations in the price of money affect its purchasing power. The nominal value of the labor that can be purchased at any given time can thus also rise or fall. The buyer of labor can purchase more or less labor with his money, and the seller of labor can purchase more or fewer commodities with his wage. But this variation results from accidental conditions outside of the production process; it does not yet explain the ultimate source and legitimacy of wealth—or of poverty.

The crucial variable in the new relations of production—the real source of profit—is the wages paid to the laborer, to which Smith devotes a separate chapter (book I, chapter 8). In the state of nature, the entirety of the product that a worker created belonged to him. Had this state continued, real wages—the amount of goods that labor can buy—would have increased as productivity grew due to the improvements brought by the division of labor. The increase in productivity would have made all goods cheaper because it takes a smaller amount of that more efficient labor to produce them in the first place. The problem is that the original state of nature did not last; land was appropriated privately, and capital stock fell into the hands of individuals. Smith's concern is not to explain how this new inequality emerged; it is an accidental factor that lies outside the production process. His task is to explain its economic consequences in order to judge the legitimation of the new social relations. Once private lands are appropriated, the landlord can justly demand a share of their product in the form of rent. The farmer, who is rarely able to maintain himself until the harvest, will ask for an advance from the stock of the landlord, who has no interest in employing the farmer unless he gets a share of his profit. This share is a second, perfectly fair deduction from the working farmer's share. In the case of industrial production, the employer advances to the workers the materials they work on, the tools with which to work, and even the wages needed to live prior to the sale of the product. For each of these reasons, the industrialist also legitimately gains a profit on his investment.

Smith is aware that his economic theory justifies the social relations of the new commercial society. At several points in the rather long chapter on wages, he is at pains to argue that although the workers are in a subordinate and unequal position, the increased productivity resulting from the division of labor makes their lot better than that of their ancestors. "The real recompence of labor, the real quantity of the necessaries and conveniencies of life which it can procure to the laborer, has, during the course of the present century, increased perhaps in a still greater proportion than has its money price." The "industrious poor" benefit not only from cheaper grain, but from access to a wider variety of foodstuffs; the cost of potatoes and other vegetables has decreased by half; the quality of cloth has risen as its price decreased, permitting them to dress more agreeably; household furniture is more easily purchased; and so on. It is only just, insists Smith, that workers, "who make up the far greater part of every great political society," benefit along with the rest of society because "they who also feed, clothe, and lodge the whole body of the people, should have such a share of the produce of their own labor as to be themselves tolerably well fed, clothed and lodged."[7] That is why, Smith implies, wealth has replaced political liberty and equality as the criterion defining the Good Life. As a result, the economic theory of its production has thereby replaced political theory.

Despite this irenic vision of an unequal but harmonious commercial society, Smith is aware that all is not as it seems. The market that ensures that the "higgling and bargaining" produces fair prices for the goods being exchanged also regulates the wages paid for labor. Like all exchanges, wages are contractual, but in this case the two parties have diametrically opposed aims—the one seeking higher wages, the other lower costs. Smith is well aware of who will win in this contest. The masters are fewer; they can join forces more easily; and the law that forbids "combinations" (i.e., trade unions) of the workers does not affect the masters. Although they need the workers, they can hold out against strikes by living on accumulated stocks. Smith is not only lucid; he is harshly realistic. "We rarely hear, it has been said, of the combinations of masters, though frequently of those of workmen. But whoever imagines, upon this account that masters rarely combine, is as ignorant of the world as of the subject." There is "a sort of tacit, but constant and uniform combination, not to raise the wages of labor above their actual rate." Still more, because they know that lowering wages will be unpopular, they combine to form a plan, keep it secret, and then spring it suddenly. The workers may resist, but they know that they cannot hold out for long, which may lead them to become violent, acting "with the folly and extravagance of desperate men, who must either starve or frighten their masters into an immediate compliance with their demands."[8] The masters will call out the law; violence is quickly subdued, and the ringleaders are ruined.

This example shows that the free market does not set prices for all products; if a "combination" of industrialists can fix the prices of wages, what is to prevent them from doing so for other items in the national economy? The market is not a neutral referee, nor does it fix norms that regulate economic actors' "moral sentiments." The government's role in Smith's account is not just to wield the weapon of the law against workers' strikes. As in the case of public education, government exists also to compensate for the undesirable effects of the division of labor that produces a society that knows no limit to its own expansion and to social division. Smith specifies three tasks for government: national defense; the creation and maintenance of public works that no private interest would provide since profit would not justify these works despite their benefit to society as a whole; and the protection of citizens from injustice "as far as possible" by ensuring the administration of justice. These three functions, in effect, make the society safe for the new economy by counteracting the dysfunctional effects of the social division of labor.

It is not necessary to look at the detail of Smith's analysis of how government carries out its obligations; his recognition that neither the market nor the division of labor nor the increased production of social wealth is self-sufficient proves that the new economy cannot by itself replace the need for politics. But he cannot explain the positive principles on which political action would be based. His explanation of the reason that the state must assume the costs of national defense illustrates the economic reductionism of his political theory. In a commercial society, those who join the army cannot pay their own expenses, as did classical republican citizen-soldiers. Because an industrial worker who has to go to war will have no source of revenue for himself and his family, soldiers must become professionals who are paid by the state. This provision is, of course, just another new step in the division of labor, which in turn changes the nature of war itself, making weaponry more costly while permitting the development of more sophisticated types of maneuvers, the creation of specialized units within the army, and longer campaigns. Smith neglects the fact that this professionalization will have the same numbing effects as the division of labor in the factory, and the state will presumably once again have to take over the costs of this dysfunction. But the taking of that step, too, can be seen as an expansion of the social division of labor. In short, the political has become simply another element in the social division of labor; it is no longer the highest principle charged with organizing and legitimating social relations as a whole.

Smith's justification of the need for the state to finance public works seems for a moment to forget the limits imposed by his laissez-faire theory, but the historical examples of private persons' refusal to finance public goods imply that it was in fact the market that made this decision because no investment was forthcoming. The market recognized the lack, and its partner, the state, has to correct it. This act is political, but its justification comes from the market. This case shows again the antipolitical logic that underlies Smith's theory of political economy in spite of the role he gives the state in regulating social relations. The legitimacy of the state's action depends on its contribution to the production of material wealth.

The antipolitical logic is present also in Smith's account of the state's third function—the establishment, "as far as possible," of the administration of justice. He presents a hypothetical history of the different reasons for which men have accepted the authority of law, concluding, however, that none of them is fully adequate. His own explanation is that the law establishes a concord of interests between the rich, who want to preserve their power, and the men of mediocre fortune, who want to protect what they have. The result is only apparently an arrangement for the mutual benefit of both classes. Civil government, "so far as it is instituted for the security of property, is in reality instituted for the defense of the rich against the poor, or of those who have some property against those who have none at all."[9] This unabashed admission that the state's task is to legitimate the exploitation of the poor, who were the victim of the "combinations" by which their wages were driven to a minimum, makes clear the lack of autonomy of politics in the new commercial society. Although Smith's account recalls Rousseau's denunciation of the social contract in the *Second Discourse* as "the most deliberate project that ever entered the human mind," he makes no attempt elsewhere, as did Rousseau in *The Social Contract*, to discover a satisfactory theory of politics.

◆

Although *The Wealth of Nations* is rich in historical comparisons and political accounts of the past, Smith's insight into the uniqueness of commercial society leads him to an antipolitical theory. The confusion of the technical division of labor with the social division of labor is a telling flaw. At times, he avoids this conflation of two different types of argument, especially when he admits the human costs of the technical division of labor. Although he sees the inequality protected by the economic system that he legitimates, his theory can offer only such palliatives as the state's intervention in education or its role in meeting out formally equal but in reality substantively unequal justice. Smith, however, is not the apologist for pure laissez-faire capitalism that his modern disciples have made him; he at times sounds more like a social reformer than a died-in-the-wool free marketer. His crucial contribution to the history of political thought is his recognition that in modern society the economy has become political, replacing what historically was the domain of politics and political thought. The unity of modern society emerges "behind the backs" of the plurality of economic interests that compose it, leaving no place for political action. It is antipolitical.

THE FRENCH REVOLUTION AND THE AMBIGUITIES OF A DEMOCRATIC REPUBLIC

As opposed to the Glorious Revolution, which instituted a constitutional monarchy in Great Britain, the French Revolution a century later replaced the absolutism of the monarchy with an antipolitical absolutism that claimed to incarnate the will of the sovereign nation.[10] This outcome was not the original intent of the early revolutionary leaders, who looked at first to the English model. The dilemma that drove the French constantly to radicalize their politics had deep roots in the particular history of that highly centralized nation. Royal absolutism was legitimated by the French Catholic doctrine of "Gallicanism," which supported the power of the monarchy that liberated it from the ecclesial domination of the papacy. As the French state emerged from the era of religious war, the chief ministers to King Louis XIII were Cardinals Armand Jean de Richelieu and Jules Mazarin, who served, respectively, from 1624 to1642 and from 1642 to1661. The Gallican monarch's legitimacy was both theological and political; he was the anointed representative of God as well as the incarnation of the nation. In both capacities, as sacred and as secular, he was a placeholder for a higher power. The famous cry "The king is dead, long live the king!" that greeted his death signified that although a particular king had died, the kingship is never vacant because neither God nor Nation ever dies. As a result, there was no place for any intermediary bodies between the king and God or between the king and his nation; royal sovereignty was absolute and undivided. Although the revolutionaries wanted to break with the past, they could not escape the weight of this French history.

◆

Royal absolutism brought with it a vulnerability that came to a head in the years before 1789. The French monarch was responsible for all of society and even for the natural world. A series of bad harvests, a debt resulting from costly support for the American Revolution and worrying commercial interests, and the discredit of the court by rumor-mongering philosophes together forced Louis XVI to call a meeting of the Estates General for the first time in more than a century. In the run-up to this meeting, a pamphlet produced a spark that fell on dry timber. "What is the third estate?" asked Abbé Emmanuel Joseph Sieyès in the title of the pamphlet. The literal answer was that it is the nonecclesiastical and non-noble part of the nation, which was its vast majority. Sieyès's political answer lay in the absolutist tradition: "it is the nothing that should become everything." Although the third estate was excluded from power, it represented the nation's living forces. What, therefore, could justify its political exclusion? When the Estates General met, its deputies adopted the title of "National Assembly," in effect claiming to be "everything" and thus challenging the monarch's absolutism. Less then a week before the seizure of the Bastille on July 14, 1789, the delegates of the third estate and representatives of the other two estates joined together and called themselves the Constituent National Assembly, defining their goal as the creation of a new constitution for the realm. Anticipating the radicalization to follow, on the night of August 4, 1789, the nobility officially abandoned its feudal privileges. The long march of egalitarian antipolitics had begun.

It is in this context that the Constituent Assembly wrote and approved the Declaration of the Rights of Man and of the Citizen. Most delegates saw this document as leading toward the creation of a constitutional monarchy, but its antipolitical logic had more radical implications. It differed from the American Declaration of Independence, which had no constitutional function despite its ringing affirmation of natural rights that "we hold . . . to be self-evident." It differed also from the American Bill of Rights (composed of the first ten amendments to the U.S. Constitution), which was explicitly not a philosophical claim because its authors feared that might prevent the recognition of new rights that might be needed later to fit a changed world. It differed also from the English Bill of Rights, which defined neither the rights of man nor those of the citizen, but only proclaimed the rights belonging to Parliament. The French declaration proposed to define the basic principles on which the new constitution would be built; it sought to articulate the natural-law basis on which the positive laws of the nation were to be based.

The preamble to the Declaration of the Rights of Man is a typical statement of Enlightenment principles, whose practical implications it then radicalized. It asserts that "ignorance, forgetfulness or contempt of the rights of man, are the sole causes of the public miseries and of the corruption of governments."[11] Once the light of truth has dissipated the shadows of darkness and the follies of vanity, natural rights, which are inalienable and sacred, would inevitably return. Because not everyone is capable of discovering for themselves these natural truths, the declaration proposes to set them forth, promulgating them to ensure that all members of society will be aware of their rights as men and of their duties as citizens. The radical implication of these premises comes from the fact that this statement is a critical standard against which citizens are to judge the acts of government, comparing them "at every moment" to the goal of all political institutions, which is the protection of these universal natural rights. In this way, the preamble concludes, the citizens' demands will be founded on simple incontestable principles that will maintain both the Constitution and the general welfare. The authors do not explicitly charge the citizens with the democratic role that is implied in this final statement, but it is easy to see why many people would read it as an invitation at least to resistance if not to full participation in the making of the laws.

The positive presentation of the rights of man and of the citizen in the seventeen brief articles that follow the preamble ignores rather than solves the classic question of the relation between the good man and the good citizen. Although the first sentence of the first article proclaims that "men are born and remain free and equal in rights," the second adds that social distinctions are justified if they are based on "public utility." This second phrase justifies an inequality that the first rules out; as a result, the harmony of the two claims is not self-evident. The same problem returns in the final article, which explains that property is a "sacred and inviolable right," but adds that it can be taken if a "legally established public necessity exists and compensation is paid." The problem is that public utility and public necessity are determined by political decisions, which can be challenged, as the preamble promises, by citizens' appeal to their natural rights if the resulting inequality does not seem to them to be justified.

The second article explains that the "political association" exists to protect the natural rights of man, which are defined as "liberty, property, security, and resistance to oppression." The first three of these rights were not controversial at the time; such triadic definitions of basic rights were frequent. But the idea of a right to resistance had troubled political thinkers over the centuries. Who can resist? What threats can be justly resisted? As opposed to passive, private disobedience, resistance is active.

Although this right of resistance is a restatement of the purposes set out in the preamble, its assertion in the body of the declaration is not justified, nor are its modalities explained.

The inconsistencies of the declaration become apparent when the third article defines the nation as the source of sovereignty, insisting that no body or individual can exercise an authority that does not directly emanate from it. This statement implies that right of resistance must belong to the nation as a whole. It seems to explain why the sixth article insists that law is the "expression of the general will," but it goes on to declare that "all citizens have the right to take part personally, or by their representatives, in its [the law's] formation," which increases the confusion. The problem is that the general will or the nation or the people or perhaps even individual resisting citizens are in effect replacing the absolute monarch. Like the actual physical king, however, they can never be more than the temporary incarnation of the general will or the nation or the people; they can never be fully identical to it. That means that inequalities accepted at one time as publicly useful may be rejected later, when conditions change. The attempt to overcome the difference between the principle of sovereignty and its political manifestation became the motor driving the revolution from one phase to the next. At each radicalization, the idea of public utility that was generally accepted was criticized as having represented only the particular interests of one or another faction whose will had replaced the general will, thus violating natural law and calling for popular resistance.

The internal contradictions that would haunt the revolutionary process are manifested in another aspect of the declaration. In 1789, monarchical absolutism was rejected because of its arbitrariness and because of the third estate's demand to participate in the nation's political life. The Constituent Assembly thus had to establish the universal rule of law at the same time that participation in political life was (in principle) opened to all citizens.[12] The rule of law would come to be identified with the republic; the desire for participation, if carried to its logical end, would result in democracy. The revolution would founder on the attempt to reconcile the two by creating a democratic republic. This dilemma was anticipated by another classical problem that the authors of the declaration ignored: the sharp distinction between the virtuous republican citizen working for the public good and the private man caring only for his individual interest. The overthrow of the ancien régime not only opened the doors to public life for members of the third estate, but also created new economic possibilities for individual entrepreneurs from that social class as well. Would their private economic interests introduce inequality into the republican political life of the nation? What effect would this inequality have on the liberty that was also a natural right?

After establishing equality as a basic natural right, the declaration defines liberty in Article 4 as the power to do whatever one wills so long as it does not harm others. And, the article continues, what harms others can be determined only by law. Article 5 then explains that the law can only forbid action that is harmful to society, adding with regard to the individual that whatever is not forbidden by law is in effect permitted. These two articles assume that what harms others and what harms society must be identical, but they do not explain how this comes to be the case. Thinking perhaps of Rousseau's *Social Contract,* the Constituent Assembly assumed that private freedom is protected because the law, as the expression of the general will, cannot interfere with particular affairs. Yet this same article also stipulates that "all citizens" have the right to participate in the formation of the law, which must be the same for all of them. And, it adds, because all citizens are equal, they all have a right to public employment that is limited only by their ability. This stipulation leaves unanswered the question whether the liberty that is protected is private or public, expressing the general will or protecting the will of all. Are the rights that are protected those of *l'homme* or those of *le citoyen*? The declaration's constant concern is to ensure the rule of law, but the theoretical difference between the general will and the will of all is reflected in the practical distinction between laws protecting private rights and the freedoms needed for public participation in making those laws.

The tension between the rights of man and the rights of the citizen takes the form of a conflict between equality and liberty. As the catalog of rights is made more specific, it appears that freedom must be assured in order to protect the reign of equality. For example, Article 7 protects against arbitrary arrest, and Article 9 establishes the presumption of innocence. The power of these protections is reinforced in Articles 10 and 11, which not only guarantee freedom of opinion, but add an important qualification without which that freedom would be meaningless: the right to the free communication of ideas in writing, speech, and print. Liberty here clearly means political freedom. Although Article 13 returns to the theme of equality, affirming that taxation (proportional to the ability to pay) must be equal for all citizens, Article 14 then explains that this equality in taxation can be guaranteed only by the exercise of political freedom in the form of consent to this taxation and the right to survey the use of this revenue. In Article 15, "society" is curiously now given the right to demand that every public agent account for his actions. But the political nature of this society is made explicit in Article 16, which asserts that any society that guarantees neither rights nor the separation of powers has no constitution. The addition of the separation of powers to the rights being established is meant to protect against the return of absolutism. Unfortunately, this clause was not heeded as the revolutionaries applied the logic of the final article, that "public necessity" can justly limit even the "sacred" right of property.

The Constituent Assembly continued to meet until, in September 1791, it produced a constitution that both the monarch and the Assembly approved. It was now time to elect a Legislative Assembly to make the positive laws that would govern society. In fact, as the inconsistencies in the declaration suggest, the Constituent Assembly had begun the process of social transformation. Its measures tended constantly toward the elimination of privilege and the establishment of the kind of equality symbolized by the gesture of August 4, 1789, when the nobility gave up its privileges. Symbolic of the new egalitarian *esprit*, the guillotine would eliminate the traditional privilege of nobles, who were beheaded, whereas commoners were hanged. Monasteries were eliminated, church properties seized, and the clergy were made employees of the state; civil marriage was instituted, and primogeniture eliminated; the aristocratic *parlements* were replaced by elected judges; laissez-faire became the rule in economic relations, and internal tolls and tariffs separating provinces were abolished; all remaining restrictions on Protestants were lifted, and, at the very end of its term, the Constituent Assembly accorded citizenship rights to Jews. The quest for equality affected other aspects of life. The map of France was redrawn in order to eliminate distinctions among the provinces, ignoring geographical differences in order to ensure electoral constituencies that were quantitatively equal. The work that produced the universal units of measure that became the metric system was begun. The antipolitical temptation that underlay all these measures was expressed in the Le Chapelier law, which forbade the creation of artisan guilds on the grounds that such "partial associations" threatened the republic's unity.[13]

The Legislative Assembly continued its predecessor's leveling work, but there remained a major obstacle in the new constitution. The monarch was guaranteed the veto, which created a conflict with the principle of popular sovereignty that came to a head when the royal family attempted to flee to join the aristocratic forces and their foreign allies who threatened to invade France. Their capture at Varennes, followed by the glorious military victory at Valmy, destroyed any remaining trust in the principles of monarchy while reinforcing the revolutionary nation's self-confidence. Events accelerated; in August 1792, a popular rising called for a convention to write a truly republican constitution. In the meanwhile, the revolutionary work continued. A new calendar, renaming the traditional months, was created; new holidays were invented to replace traditional religious festivities; and the date of the proclamation of the republic, September 22, 1792, was declared the beginning of the Year One. Royalty was of course abolished; the king was tried, condemned, and executed. Meanwhile, the monarchies of Europe trembled at the threat of the new revolutionary politics whose spread they were determined to avoid.

In spite of the rejection of intermediary bodies between the sovereign popular will and its political representatives, voluntary associations and the newspapers maintained an active public sphere. The existence of political clubs, such as the Jacobins and the Girondins, were justified by the declaration's command to remind the citizens "of their rights and their duties, in order that the acts of the legislative power and those of the executive power may be each moment compared with the aim of every political institution" (preamble). Members of the clubs were acting as citizens concerned with the good of the whole; their projects and programs always spoke in the name of the general will, but they differed among themselves in interpreting that will because they looked at it from the perspective of their own interests and experience. As a result, each one's claim to represent the nation as a whole meant that it could not compromise with its opponents, but instead, in the last resort, had to eliminate them. This antipolitical logic led to a series of purges that pitted former comrades against each other. The Girondins were accused of supporting federalism to the detriment of national unity; Jacques Hébert and the *enragé* leaders of the Paris Commune were condemned for their excess of zeal; the former Jacobins Georges Danton and Camille Desmoulins were convicted of "indulgence" because they sought to stop the slaughter. Even the "indifferent," concerned to stay out of the public eye, were denounced as a threat to national unity because their lack of revolutionary enthusiasm led France's monarchical enemies to believe that support for the revolution had weakened. In this process, the rights of the individual came to be subordinated to the rights of the citizen, which were identified with those of the nation itself.

The antipolitical logic by which the revolution devoured its children was dictated by each faction's attempt to claim that it, rather than those who previously had been in power, spoke for the nation, expressed the general will, and was the true defender of the revolution (which became an end in itself rather than a means to ensure the rights of man and those of the citizen). The convention elected to write a constitution for the new republic completed its work in 1793, but it decreed that this constitution would be placed in a sacred arc, where it would remain until peace was achieved. Meanwhile, the Jacobin-controlled Committee on Public Safety (Comité de salut public) governed the revolutionary nation. Although the declaration's Article 16 had insisted on the separation of powers, the Jacobin-lead committee exercised both legislative and executive power. Calling itself "revolutionary government," it held an absolute power that was the culmination of an ineluctable radicalization whose only end could be a democratic republic in which universal equality left no place for distinctions either among the citizens or between the government and the people. But the successful elimination of all opposition paradoxically made the Jacobins, led by Robespierre and Louis de Saint-Just, as vulnerable as the absolute monarchy had been a scant four years earlier. Their furious attempts to destroy diversity paradoxically made them appear to be only another particular interest that was usurping power that truly belonged to the nation (or to the revolution).

Not only were the radical revolutionaries trapped between the universality of the general will and the particularity of its manifestations, but they were also caught between the past and the future, bound all the more tightly by their own reverence for political history. They had read Cicero and Livy as well as Machiavelli; they were certain that a republic can endure only if virtue is preserved. They also knew Rousseau's reply to his own question: "Do you want to realize the general will? Then make sure that all particular wills relate to it. And since virtue is nothing but the agreement of the particular wills to the general will, the point can be made simple: ensure that virtue reigns."[14] When they tried to apply the classical republican model, they had to find a way to protect also the rights of the individual, an idea that was foreign to the ancients. Their problem was recognized later, in 1816, in a famous lecture titled "The Liberty of Ancients Compared with That of Moderns."[15] In it, Benjamin Constant distinguished classical liberty, which meant the freedom to take part in public life, from its modern form, which is confined to the private sphere, where each is free to develop as he sees fit. Understanding the revolutionaries' confusion of these two types of liberty helps to clarify both the revolution's radicalization and its inevitable failure to impose the classical republican vision on modern men who were defending their particular, individual rights.

Robespierre may have sensed this dilemma without being able to articulate its modern form. In June 1794, less than two months before the overthrow of the Committee on Public Safety, he created the Festival of the Supreme Being. It was an attempt to invent a civic religion to uphold the republican spirit in a society where individual interest had been unleashed. Although the episode ended in failure, it nevertheless indicates that Robespierre's politics were built on the classical model. Recalling Cicero's claim in *On the Commonwealth* that there is no republic without morality and no morality without a republic, Robespierre proposed in a ringing speech to define "the principles of political morality that should guide the National Convention in the domestic administration of the republic."[16] Although he does not mention Cicero's denunciation of violations of the republican spirit as "capital crimes," his speech is an explicit justification of the Terror instituted by the Jacobin-led Committee on Public Safety. It also encapsulates the logic that led the revolution toward an antipolitical and therefore unstable democratic republic.

The revolution, asserts Robespierre, has been based on an instinctive love of the good and of the nation. Now that its enemies have been defeated, there is time for it to develop a precise theory of its political goals and its rules of conduct. Its goal is the reign of eternal justice, which is found "in the hearts of all men—including those of the slave who forgets this justice and the tyrant who denies it." He explicates the meaning of eternal justice by a long series of equivalences, all of which seek to transform subjective dispositions into republican ideals, beginning with the creation of laws that ensure the replacement of cruel passions by generous ones. Personal ambition will become the desire to gain glory by serving the country because "every soul grows greater through the continual flow of republican sentiments." Commerce must become "the source of public wealth rather than solely the monstrous opulence of a few families." Morality will overcome egotism, personal integrity will replace formal codes of honor, principles will acquire priority over customs, and the rule of reason will triumph over the tyranny of fashion. Merit will replace intrigue; self-respect and greatness of soul will be prized over insolence and vanity. Furthermore, there will be an "exchange of truth for glamour, the charm of happiness for sensuous boredom, the greatness of man for the pettiness of the great." In sum, the revolution's aim is "to fulfill nature's wishes, to further the destinies of humanity, to keep the promises of philosophy, to absolve providence of the long reign of crime and tyranny." This is the irenic future envisioned by a philosophe in power.

To realize these wonders, continues Robespierre, "a democratic or republican government" is required. A republic is distinguished from the particular rule of monarchy or aristocracy because it rules by universal laws. A democracy is "a state in which the sovereign people, guided by laws which are of their own making, do for themselves all that they can do well, and by their delegates do all that they cannot do for themselves." The leader of the Committee on Public Safety does not explain how to distinguish what the people can do from what their delegates must do in their place because, he says, that question presupposes that tyranny has been overcome. For the moment, winning that victory is the task of the "revolutionary system," which is based on the public virtue that "worked so many wonders in Greece and Rome . . . [and] ought to produce even more astonishing things in republican France." The basis of the revolutionary system is the love of the nation and the nation's laws, a sentiment that is impossible for the private man who is a "slave of avarice or ambition." The revolution has made possible "real democracy" whose basis is equality and full rights of citizenship, which is why tyrants have joined to fight it—their enmity stands as proof of the purity of revolutionary intentions.

The practical consequence of these revolutionary principles is that all political action must seek to maintain equality and develop virtue. To achieve these goals, the laws must strengthen patriotism, develop and protect morals, and direct the passions toward the public interest. The legislator must avoid measures that reward selfishness or encourage petty rather than great deeds. Weakness, vices, and prejudices must be avoided because "that which is immoral is impolitic, [and] that which is corrupting is counterrevolutionary." The threat to the republic does not come from excessive zeal against those marks of "the path of royalty," but results rather from a "fear of our own courage." Robespierre is warning former allies such as Danton and Desmoulins, called the Indulgents, who criticized the Terror as a betrayal of the revolution's principles. Their arrest and death are foretold when Robespierre in effect accuses them of treason: "Indulgence for the royalists, cry certain people. . . . Are not the enemies within the allies of the enemy without?"

A second implication of the principles of virtue and equality is that their enemies can never be defeated once and for all. This lesson is taught in the decline of Sparta, Athens, and Rome. Robespierre's argument is epitomized in a single phrase: "What matter that Brutus has slain the tyrant? Tyranny lives on in human hearts, and Rome exists only in Brutus." It is necessary to root out tyranny repeatedly because even when its external carrier is destroyed, it may live on in "human hearts." It is therefore not sufficient to compare constantly the action of government to the principle of egalitarian virtue, as the preamble to the Declaration of the Rights of Man and of the Citizen insists. The members of society must themselves be made virtuous if the universality of principle is to overcome the particularity of its temporary realization. This is the way to create a "real democracy" that will in effect be the realization of philosophy and the replacement of politics by "political morality."

The practical consequence of these democratic republican principles is that "the character of popular government is to be trusting towards the people and severe with itself." This imperative justifies the continual purges that characterize the revolutionary process: the enemies of the revolution exist within as well as without. The strength of the revolution that arises from its defense of truth and of the rights of the public over private interests can become a source of weakness when vicious men who fear liberty and seek to despoil the people in order to satisfy their ambition and greed take advantage of its naïveté. France has become the "theater" of a mighty struggle between the friends of tyranny and the forces of the democratic republic. The policy that must be followed in these conditions is to "lead the people by reason and the people's enemies by terror." This tactic assumes that the friends of liberty and equality will listen to reason, whereas their enemies can be moved only by force. The former, of course, are Robespierre's allies; the latter are opponents who must be eliminated in order to reaffirm the unity of the democratic republic.

These tactical considerations lead Robespierre to his fundamental thesis: no virtue without terror, but no terror without virtue. In peacetime, a government of the people is animated by virtue, but in times of revolution such a democratic government must combine virtue and terror: "virtue without which terror is disastrous, terror without which virtue is powerless." Robespierre immediately defines terror as "nothing but prompt, severe, inflexible justice," which is "therefore an emanation of virtue." The implication is that terror is not a special principle, but simply the rigorous application of the general principle of democracy to the needs of the moment. Historical examples of republican virtue repeat the lesson that tyranny must be opposed at all costs. Robespierre knows that terror has traditionally been the method of despots, but he insists that if the revolutionary government appears despotic, it is the "despotism of liberty against tyranny." Why do people think that the use of force protects only crime? Can it not serve also to strike the evil-doer? Does not nature herself impose the obligation of self-preservation not only on physical beings, but also on moral ones, such as the revolutionary government? If tyranny is left to rule for even a single day, it will snuff out the friends of liberty, who must remain vigilant and avoid "false sensitivity" that may protect the wicked from "the avenging blade of national justice."

The final third of Robespierre's speech is a masterful application of political rhetoric to divide his enemies into two factions, one of which "pushes us toward weakness, the other toward excess." His criticism is based on the assertion that by dividing the revolutionary government and misleading the people, these factions are aiding an omnipresent enemy who is always waiting for an occasion to destroy the revolution. This enemy is not limited to the real armies of Europe's monarchies; it includes especially those within who oppose radical revolutionary measures to ensure equality and virtue. These domestic enemies sow division at a time when unity is necessary. For example, those Indulgents who "regard a few victories won by patriotism as the end of all our dangers" do not see that vigilance is more necessary than ever, precisely because the malicious enemy that lurks in "human hearts" is dividing and thus weakening the revolution's will. Equally dangerous are those who seek "to rally all the Republic's enemies by reviving the spirit of party" as a result of their excessive zeal. Robespierre's claim is that he and his politics are the incarnation of the revolution, the spirit of the nation, and the voice of the people. He praises himself for having the courage to practice the terror of virtue that is the expression of the general will because only the virtue of the Terror can actualize the principles that are the foundation of the democratic republic. What Robespierre has described in this speech, however, is in fact the reality of antipolitics.

Robespierre's "Discourse on the Principles of Political Morality" represented the culmination of the logic that had been the implicit guiding thread of the revolution since the Declaration of the Rights of Man and of the Citizen. From the outset, in the French absolutist tradition, the power of the state was used not to create privilege, but to abolish it, to establish equality, and to (try to) create virtuous citizens.[17] Robespierre did not shy away from the fact that this project depended on the use of force. The Terror guided by virtue that he defended was legitimated by the result that it claimed to realize; it was a means rather than an end. But when Robespierre demonstrated that the republic and democracy were synonymous, he revealed the secret, antipolitical principle that motivated the revolutionaries. A democratic society of equal citizens who themselves make laws that are applied universally to all citizens would eliminate the distinction between *l'homme* and *le citoyen*. But this is not possible, in fact or in principle. That is why Robespierre always found new threats to the unity of the general will, the nation, and the revolution itself. He claimed to incarnate an absolute and unitary revolutionary will that maintained its republican spirit by finding ever again new traces of particularity that it had to denounce as threats that reinforced its real or imagined enemies. If these threats were truly and radically eliminated, the unitary will would have nothing left to will. As Robespierre claimed at the outset of his great speech, it would have kept "the promises of philosophy." In so doing, however, it would leave no place for politics. That is why the Terror illustrates brutally the dangers of a philosophical politics whose goal is to put an end to politics.

◆

The defeat of royal absolutism in France led finally to the invention of a new type of absolutism, the democratic republic in which the all-powerful, sovereign will of the people could tolerate no resistance. This project was never realized, no more than was the absolute monarchy, but it has haunted the modern political imagination. In French history, it is called Jacobinism, the name of the club led by Robespierre. In politics, it implies that the state is charged with understanding, interpreting, and realizing the popular good. More generally, it means that philosophy, with its concern for universality, comes to replace politics, which is always involved with the particular. The promise of a future harmony comes to be more important than the present, which is always found lacking. This future-oriented politics of will leaves no room for political judgment in the always particular conditions of the present. Rather than solve the problems inherited from the revolution, nineteenth-century political thinkers sought to transcend them by appealing to the logic of history. The problems of today become necessary stages on the path through which human history will reveal its rational structure. Hegel and Marx are, from this perspective, the true heirs of 1789,[18] but so, too, is a new vision of the task of political thought: conservatism. This new vision also appeals to history, past history, to justify its antipolitics.

THE LEGITIMACY OF CONSERVATISM?

Edmund Burke (1729–1797), the intellectual father of modern conservatism, was a supporter of the American Revolution as well as a persistent prosecutor of misdeeds in British colonial relations and a supporter of Irish independence. These facts point to the need to avoid the reduction of the antipolitical logic of conservatism to the simple defense of existing relations of power and wealth. Conservatism is not a justification of the status quo; it does not accept the world as it is or refuse to consider how it ought to be. Conservatism is not opposed to all change, nor does it abandon the right to criticize existing conditions. Despite its respect for past experience, it is not bound by the idea of returning to it, as if past history can be erased and force can restore the ancien régime under the pretence that nothing changed between its overthrow and its renewal. If that were the meaning of conservatism, the French Revolution's infatuation with an ideal Roman republic would de facto have enrolled it into the conservative cause. More than a response to changed historical conditions, conservative political thought has to be considered as a type of political thought in its own right.

◆

In one sense, all political philosophy is conservative insofar as it tries to understand how to maintain social unity and warns against dangers that may lead to regime change. But the concept of conservatism emerges only when paired with the idea of revolution. It makes no sense to ask whether Plato was more or less conservative than Aristotle, Augustine than Aquinas. Their worlds were teleological, not historical. The Renaissance marks a shift—for example, when Machiavelli criticizes his humanist contemporaries for treating the past like "a statue" to be admired rather than imitated. The Reformation was indeed a revolution, and the Anabaptists who radicalized its message forced Luther and Calvin to stress the politically conservative aspects of their reforms. At the same time, the Catholic Church launched the Counter-Reformation at the Council of Trent in 1564. The Counter-Reformation's reassertion of the church's authority was accompanied by a renewal of the old institutions. The following century of religious war exhausted the parties and devastated Europe. It was only the Whig triumph in 1689 that gave rise to a specific response that can be called modern conservatism.

The Tory opposition to Whig domination of British politics was given its theoretical foundation in a short essay by David Hume (1711–1776) titled "On the Original Contract." Hume points out that the validity of the promise on which the Lockean social contract is based presupposes an earlier contract ensuring that the promise can be enforced; this earlier contract, in its turn, presupposes yet another contract, giving rise to an endless regress that can never discover an original contract by which men agreed to leave the inconveniences of the state of nature. Hume makes explicit the difference between his Tory vision and that of the Whigs in his final remarks. "The only passage I meet with in antiquity," he writes, "where the obligation to obedience to government is ascribed to a promise, is in Plato's *Crito*: where Socrates refuses to escape from prison, because he had tacitly promised to obey the laws. Thus he builds a *tory* consequence of passive obedience on a *whig* foundation of the original contract."[19] What Hume calls "Tory" legitimation of obedience is based on loyalty to the country's tradition, whereas the "Whig" foundation of the contract is individual participants' consent. Hume accepts the legitimacy of the former but rejects the latter's binding force. As a result, his political theory is both antimodern in rejecting the legitimacy of individual consent and antipolitical in its fixation on the authority of the past.

Although Burke was a member of the Whig Party, he moved to its conservative wing in reaction to its more liberal members' support of the French Revolution, which they imagined as the first step to the creation of a parliamentary monarchy like their own. His *Reflections on the Revolution in France* was published in November 1790, before the successive radicalizations of the revolution began. The book's prediction of many of the revolutionary failures was based on three conservative claims. The first rejects the priority that individualism accords to rights over duties. Like Hume, Burke insists that the community molds individual character. The second criticizes the idea that politics can resolve the age-old problems that are the price of living together with one's fellows. Political judgment is necessary because, although there is no single best, wholly rational, and uniquely moral solution to political problems, some actions and institutions are better than others. The third claim denounces rationalist (or materialist) philosophy that denies the mystery of life while claiming that science can replace the comfort that religion once provided. This recognition of complication underlines the need for political prudence and rejects the appeal of abstract principles that hide the messy details of a diverse reality and that replace the need for social experience, practical judgment, and political prudence with the unitary sovereign will to impose a priori truths on a world without depth that has forgotten its own history and cannot resist a determined individual or collective will.

These three conservative principles appear to be warnings against political action rather than guidelines for its realization. If the excesses of the French Revolution were the result of revolutionary antipolitics, the conservative critique had to avoid the danger of becoming a different variant of the antipolitical spirit of the age. Burke had previously explained his understanding of politics in a famous campaign speech in Bristol in 1774. Although a member of Parliament must take seriously his constituents' wishes, consult with them, and prefer their interest to his own, "his unbiased opinion, his mature judgment, his enlightened conscience, he ought not to sacrifice to you, to any man, or to any set of men living. These he does not derive from your pleasure; no, nor from the law and the constitution. . . . Your representative owes you, not his industry only, but his judgment; and he betrays, instead of serving you, if he sacrifices it to your opinion."[20] Obedient to his own particular judgment, the politician takes the measure of the uniqueness of the present and of the past from which it emerged. As Burke recognizes at the outset of the *Reflections on the Revolution in France*, however, the politician cannot let the past dominate the present or block the future: "A state without the means of some change is without the means of its own conservation." But, he adds, true change is possible only if one does not get "entangled in the mazes of metaphysic sophistry."[21]

Burke not only favors (ordered) change, but also declares himself a friend of liberty. Prudent judgment cannot ignore changed circumstances, however. A decade ago, he says, he might himself have criticized French absolutism. "Can I now congratulate the same nation upon its freedom? Is it because liberty in the abstract may be classed amongst the blessings of mankind, that I am seriously to felicitate a madman, who has escaped from the protecting restraint and wholesome darkness of his cell, on his restoration to the enjoyment of light and liberty?" Liberty is not just an abstract principle; political freedom has to be "combined with government; with public force; with the discipline and obedience of armies; with the collection of an effective and well-distributed revenue; with morality and religion; with the solidity of property; with peace and order; with civil and social manners."[22] All are good things without which liberty will neither bring benefits nor be long-lasting. The philosophers forget that there is a difference between a principle and its expression in society; the one is simple, the other complex.

Burke's critique is telling, but his appeal to complexity may divert attention from the simple principle of liberty, so that his critique becomes antipolitical in spite of itself. As Benjamin Constant, a liberal critic of revolutionary antipolitics, pointed out, "To say that abstract principles are only vain and inapplicable theories is itself an abstract principle. . . . If there are no principles, nothing can be fixed; there are only circumstances and each is free to judge them."[23] Legitimate political action is impossible without shared principles. The critique of revolutionary antipolitics does not suffice to develop a conservative politics.

At times, Burke seems aware of the difficulty, but he is unable to escape it. For example, after declaring his approval of another metaphysical abstraction, the idea of the rights of man, he repeats his argument that rights must be "combined with government" in order to exist in society. "Government is not made in virtue of natural rights, which may and do exist in total independence of it; and [they] exist in much greater clearness, and in a much greater degree of abstract perfection; but their abstract perfection is their practical defect." He favors a government in which the realization of rights is made possible by the renunciation of their absolute claims in order to make them compatible with the rights of others. The creation of government depends on the "science of constructing a commonwealth, or renovating it, or reforming it." Such a science, "like every other experimental science, [is] not to be taught *a priori*." Its basis is past experience because no single individual, "however sagacious and observing he may be," can acquire sufficient experience to learn this science, even in the course of a whole lifetime. The revolutionaries instead "chose to act as if [they] had never been moulded into civil society, and had every thing to begin anew." As Burke puts it pithily, they have "set up [their] trade without a capital."[24] This "capital" is the lessons of history, ignored by the tenors of pure principle and radical beginnings. As a result, rights "which may and do exist" outside of government become abstract formalities.

In *Reflections on the Revolution*, Burke draws on his own historical capital to criticize the revolutionary appeal to naked reason. His example may surprise the contemporary reader. He recalls his last visit to the queen of France, praising her splendor and dignity as a sign of the tradition of honor that characterized the "age of chivalry [that] is gone."[25] The phrase is striking and can lead to misunderstanding. Burke is not proposing a return to the past; rather, as a modern conservative, he is using the example of the past to criticize the present. The distinction is important in order to understand that conservatism is a philosophy, not just a social attitude.

Burke's critique is directed also at the materialism illustrated by the pornographic Enlightenment, which ignores the fact that man's historical "capital" distinguishes him from other animals. This materialism is an expression of the abstractness of the revolutionary principles, which dissolve the past by means of a "new conquering empire of light and reason." The "decent drapery of life is to be rudely torn off," leaving men unable to "cover the defects of our naked shivering nature, and to raise it to dignity in our own estimation." "On this scheme of things," the diatribe goes on, "a king is but a man; a queen is but a woman; a woman is but an animal; and an animal not of the highest order." All that is left is a stark world of "sophisters, oeconomists, and calculators" whose materialist individualism produces a "barbarous philosophy, which is the offspring of cold hearts and muddy understandings."[26] Laws are now obeyed only from fear or because they serve private interests. As opposed to this "mechanic philosophy" based on public force and private self-interest, Burke's former "age of chivalry" offered political legitimacy that made "power gentle, and obedience liberal." His vision of that past may be romantic, but it discloses as well the revolutionaries' self-deceptions.

Despite his historical idealism, Burke admits that "a certain *quantum* of power must always exist in the community, in some hands, under some appellation." The question that needs to be answered is that of its legitimacy. Power in the hands of the people, unchecked by the reciprocal duties that bound together traditional societies, will lead to plots and conspiracies by those who feel excluded; for the same reason, those in power will opt for preemptive action. The result will be instability. If the revolutionaries gave political power to the people, suggests Burke, it was because their philosophical individualism led them to think that the state is based on a contract by which rational men seek to preserve their lives, liberties, and estates. They ignored the fact that the state precedes the individual, who does not choose to join it but is born into it. The state is not "a partnership agreement in a trade of pepper and coffee, calico or tobacco, or some other such low concern, to be taken up for temporary interest, and to be dissolved at the fancy of the parties.".[27] It is a partnership in all science and art, one that encompasses every virtue and perfection; it brings together not just the living, but also the dead and those who are yet to be born. The "mechanic philosophy" of the revolutionaries does not understand that, although the state can be reformed, we "must bear with [its] infirmities until they fester into crimes." Or, as Burke puts it later, criticism should address the state's "conduct" rather than its constitution.[28]

Just as it is an illusion to think that individuals can make their own history—when it is history that has made them who they are—so it is an illusion to think that men can simply destroy the existing state, whose existence is the presupposition of their own lives, in order to begin history anew by creating a tabula rasa. In the place of the illusory power of reason, Burke stresses the value of what he calls "prejudice." This concept (which has taken a different coloration today) refers to those prejudgments that have become habits or instinctive values passed to the present by means of tradition and custom. "We are not the converts of Rousseau; we are not the disciples of Voltaire; Helvetius has made no progress among us," insists Burke.[29] "We know that we have made no discoveries; and we think that no discoveries are to be made, in morality; nor many in the great principles of government, nor in the ideas of liberty, which were understood long before we were born." As opposed to abstract reason, which has no content and is therefore liable to overreach, prejudice is neither blind nor without limits. "Prejudice is of ready application in the emergency; it previously engages the mind in a steady course of wisdom and virtue, and does not leave the man hesitating in the moment of decision."[30] The prejudice shared by the community replaces fear or self-interest as the legitimation of political obedience.

In the place of the prejudice that binds the individual to the state and to its history, the revolution gives power to the philosophes, says Burke, who joined with the men of money to ride the revolution in their own interest. The newly rich, freed from customary restraint and social obligations by the overthrow of the ancien régime and by the adoption of laissez-faire economics, are not industrialists or landed nobility; their fortunes are based on speculation on state bonds issued to finance the expense of placating the different interests among the people on whose support power now rested. They are the natural allies of the men of letters, whose critique of the traditional prejudices swept away the interdictions that limited their self-engrossing activity. The alliance also works because the philosophes, who had long ago fallen from royal favor, form their own countersociety, which Burke calls a literary cabal that with religious zeal seeks the abolition of religion. They appeal to the new weight of public opinion, winning literary fame with the support of the new men of money. This alliance succeeds also by directing popular frustrations at the old, aristocratic landed wealth and the priesthood. When the clergy are made elected state officials, "philosophical fanatics" are encouraged to demand the replacement of religion by "civic education" because nothing should be allowed to remain outside of the popular will. How else, asks Burke, could something so unnatural as the payment of government debts by the confiscation of church properties that had stood for ages be understood?[31]

The destructive power of abstract reason is founded on its simplicity, which induces a rashness that replaces the need for prudent judgment with faith in the power of a resolute will that takes no account of the complexity of reality. The revolutionaries seek constantly "to evade and slip aside from *difficulty* . . . [that] severe instructor, set over us by the supreme ordinance of a parental guardian and legislator, who knows us better than we know ourselves, and loves us better too." Difficulty teaches circumspection; it warns against facile shortcuts; it imposes limits. It requires no skill, but only brute force for a mob to destroy the product of centuries. That is why caution and prudence are "a part of duty too, when the subject of our demolition is not brick and timber, but sentient human beings." The philosophically trained revolutionaries do not understand that politics demands "not an excellence in simplicity, but one far superior, an excellence in composition."[32] For example, their attempt to apply mathematical principles to the problem of political representation, the redrawing of the map of France in order to create an abstract equality among citizens, is doomed to failure. Philosophy cannot impose prudence joined with prejudice, tradition alongside history, and duties that create reciprocity. The conservative must recognize that these values preexisted the arrival of the individual, so cherished by philosophy, into the world.

In the last resort, the political reign of "philosophy" will produce an effect opposed to its intention. The revolutionaries are "so taken up with the rights of man, that they have totally forgot his nature," which is to be a part of a history larger than himself. As a result, because this "man" is protected by no social attachments, a government that wants to ensure his rights must have vast powers, leaving no room for the civic associations that provide the protections that the church or the workingmen's guilds had previously offered. At the same time, however, the equality imposed by the revolution robs the government of its authority; because no one is superior to another, those who are in power will always be accused of betraying the popular trust simply because they are in power. The result will be constant competition for power among those who think they can represent more adequately the will of the people. This constant competition will doom hopes for a constitutional monarchy. Burke predicts that it will lead instead to the creation of a grand tribunal for judging crimes against the nation—"that is, against the power of the assembly." In the end, the army will lose respect for the jealous, quarrelsome assembly "until some popular general, who understands the art of conciliating the soldiery, and who possesses the true spirit of command, shall draw the eyes of all men upon himself."[33] Then, Burke concludes presciently, your republic will have a master. It took less than a decade for Napoleon Bonaparte to fulfill this prophecy.

Burke's devastating critique of the French Revolution for replacing political judgment with philosophical abstractions appears at first to call for a renewal of political thought. For example, toward the end of the *Reflections*, he describes the night of August 4, 1789, when the nobility renounced its feudal rights, as "prodigal of light with regard to grievances . . . sparing in the extreme with regard to redress." He goes on to explain that "to make a government requires no great prudence. Settle the seat of power; teach obedience; and the work is done. To give freedom is still more easy. It is not necessary to guide; it only requires to let go the rein. But to form a *free government*; that is, to temper together these opposite elements of liberty and restraint in one consistent work, requires much thought, deep reflection, a sagacious, powerful and combining mind."[34] But he offers no further advice; the series of warnings against the revolutionary form of antipolitics in the *Reflections* presents no political alternative because, in the last resort, conservatism is itself a form of modern antipolitics.

The conservative enters the political arena with the tools of judgment and prudence, instructed by experience, tempered by tradition, and nurtured by history. These political principles incline him toward a new type of antipolitics. If the French Revolution can be said to fall into a Platonic tradition that wants to impose rational norms on reality, Burke's conservatism belongs to the Aristotelian mode, seeking the norm in social experience itself. This search gives rise to a series of unintended consequences. The assumption that traditional community norms underlie individual experience disqualifies differences among people or social groups. The world as it is becomes the world as it ought to be. But if the universal validity of the norm is present in the particular experience of society, what happens when society changes? Was the earlier norm invalid? This possibility that norms may change means that traditional values cannot be assumed to be naturally valid; they have to be imposed by the conservative politician, just as the egalitarian revolutionary tried to do. The result is paradoxical. The traditional norms are said to be imminent to society, even though they are imposed by the politician, so they become absolute values to which nothing can be opposed because—at least for a conservative who accepts the constraints of modernity—there is nothing outside of society. With this conclusion, the descent to antipolitics is complete.

◆

Burke's conservatism differs from classical theories of social order that appeal to a transcendent, often religious source of values to which society must adhere. This difference is what makes his critique of the French Revolution so powerful and astutely predictive. It is not built on a reactionary appeal to "throne and altar." Its recognition that the individual needs to be given reasons to accept the legitimacy of the social relations within his society is modern, but it is a modern theory that rejects modernity and attempts to justify traditional institutions and values in spite of contemporary individualism and rationalism. Nonetheless, like all forms of antipolitics, conservatism is condemned to eventual failure. Just as radical democracy proved to be a danger to itself in the French case, a full-throated conservatism is driven from paradox to paradox in its attempt to demonstrate that the real already is the rational. The fact that modern conservative antipolitics accepts the obligation to provide legitimation for its claims condemns it for still another reason. This concern with legitimacy implies that conservatism recognizes a right to dissent. There will always be individuals who make use of this right, demanding the creation of a republican and democratic politics that renews the quest to make the real ever more rational. This demand may lead to a form of antipolitics, but, by overcoming the conservative version, it ensures that the search for a politics that can renew the republican and democratic traditions will continue.

THE UNITED STATES AS A REPUBLICAN DEMOCRACY

Burke's support for the American colonists' attempt to preserve the rights and freedoms that they were convinced they already possessed was consistent with his conservatism. The course of events that led to independence and the experience gained in the struggle to achieve it convinced the Americans that they needed to invent a new form of self-government. These lessons were not learned easily; the early confederal government that was supposed to bind together the thirteen independent states, each with its own constitution, was so poorly structured that the War for Independence might well have been lost without French help. It became clear that the price of ensuring local diversity was the weakening of national unity. Specially elected conventions in the states had to ratify the new constitution written by delegates to a special convention in Philadelphia in 1787. A national debate followed. Eighty-five brief essays printed in local newspapers under the pseudonym "Publius" and later bound together under the title *The Federalist* played an important role in these deliberations. Reflecting on those essays in 1825, Thomas Jefferson described this work as "the nearly indispensable authority . . . on the state of mind and the opinions of those who prepared as of those who adopted the Constitution of the United States."[35] It retains that status.

◆

The historical context in which the Americans developed their new theory helps to understand the central problem facing the Constitutional Convention. After the British victory in the so-called French and Indian War, the colonists no longer felt threatened by outside enemies, but the British faced the task of organizing their new empire while paying the debts incurred in fighting the war. American commercial interests were no longer willing to pay British taxes and restrictions as the price for protection, justifying their resistance with the Whig argument of "no taxation without representation." What kind of representation did the Americans want? Or were they reacting against British restraints on their existing forms of self-government? The years from 1763 to 1776 were a time for debate and experiment. Two interrelated problems came to dominate discussions: How could America have a truly representative government, and what kind of sovereignty did it enjoy? Failure to solve the first problem within the imperial framework made the second decisive. How could America be free while remaining within the empire? The attempt to realize or successfully to represent popular sovereignty was the motor that drove the Americans forward to invent a republican democracy.

It was not sufficient to declare independence; rather, independence had to be won and then preserved. The primacy placed on the question of sovereignty at first had negative implications insofar as each of the thirteen new states wanted to maintain its own self-government. The attempt to find a means to preserve the diversity of the independent states while protecting the unity of the nation raised anew the previously unresolved but central question of representation. The best-selling pamphlet *Common Sense* by Thomas Paine (1737–1809), published in January 1776, provided the spark that set public opinion to blaze in favor of the final break with Great Britain. Its fierce denunciation of monarchy did not propose representative government as an alternative. Society, declared Paine, is produced by our wants and contributes to our happiness, whereas government, which is the result of our wickedness, serves only to repress our vices. These optimistic beliefs were widely shared; they continued to echo in the debates over the ratification of the new constitution proposed in 1787. The new constitution's critics, called Anti-Federalists, were proponents of a democratic stress on diversity, whereas its defenders, called Federalists, insisted on the need for a republican unity promised by that document.

The authors of *The Federalist*—James Madison, Alexander Hamilton, and John Jay—suggested their intention by their decision to write under the name "Publius" rather than one of the more frequently used classical pseudonyms such as "Brutus," "Cato," or "Agrippa." In Roman history, Publius had two distinct roles. He is remembered as a staunch republican who joined Brutus in the overthrow of the Tarquin monarchy in 509. Later, when he became the sole consul after Brutus's death, his construction of a large house near the Senate led to accusations of self-enrichment. Reaffirming his antimonarchical virtue, he immediately destroyed the building. Publius continued to defend the republic against attempts to restore the monarchy, and when he died, he possessed so little personal wealth that the entire citizenry had to contribute to his funeral. Publius is remembered also as a great lawgiver who, in Plutarch's *Lives of the Noble Greeks and Romans,* is paired with Solon. He is said to have enacted a series of reforms opening the political system to popular participation and to have sponsored measures that not only benefited the plebeians, but increased the penalty on aristocrats who violated the laws. The American "Publius" was thus in effect claiming to be both a virtuous republican and a democratic reformer.

The first paragraph of *Federalist* No. 1 sets a high political goal while defining the theoretical problem to be solved. "It has been frequently remarked that it seems to have been reserved to the people of this country, by their conduct and example, to decide the important question, whether societies of men are really capable or not of establishing good government from reflection and choice, or whether they are forever destined to depend for their political constitutions on accident and force." The second paragraph is clear about the difficulties that the defenders of the Constitution face, while rhetorically putting its enemies on the defensive. "The plan offered to our deliberation affects too many particular interests, innovates upon too many local institutions, not to involve in its discussion a variety of objects foreign to its merits, and of views, passions and prejudices little favorable to the discovery of truth." More concretely, the argument continues, the new constitution threatens "the obvious interest of a certain class of men in every State to resist all changes which may hazard a diminution of the power, emolument, and consequence of the offices they hold under the State establishments; and the perverted ambition of another class of men, who will . . . hope to aggrandize themselves by the confusions of their country."[36] These warnings against the various forms of particular interest that threaten the republic's unity and sovereignty are adumbrated polemically in the next seven papers.

When one reads *The Federalist,* it is important to remember that Publius is taking part in a political debate whose thrust and parry affects the way in which the theory that underlies the new constitution is presented. At the end of the first paper, Publius promises to treat a series of clearly delineated questions: "The utility of the UNION to your political prosperity; The insufficiency of the present Confederation to preserve that

Union; The necessity of a government at least equally energetic with the one proposed, to the attainment of this object; The conformity of the proposed constitution to the true principles of republican government; Its analogy to your own state constitution; and lastly, The additional security, which its adoption will afford to the preservation of that species of government, to liberty, and to property." This framework, imposed by the imperatives of the political debate, downplays *The Federalist*'s central theoretical concern, which is to ensure the sovereignty of the people while limiting the self-destructive potential that Publius evokes at the outset of *Federalist* No. 9 when he admits that "it is impossible to read the history of the petty Republics of Greece and Italy, without feeling sensations of horror and disgust at the distractions with which they were continually agitated, and the rapid succession of revolutions, by which they were kept in a state of perpetual vibration, between the extremes of tyranny and anarchy." Yet, he continues, these popular governments have produced "momentary rays of glory" that both "dazzle us" and "admonish us to lament" their failure to perdure. The goal of the new constitution is to preserve popular sovereignty while avoiding the "vices" that result from an inability to set limits on its exercise.

In order to clarify the implications of the problematic nature of popular sovereignty, the linear structure proposed in *Federalist* No. 1 as well as the chronological order in which the separate papers were published in the contemporary press have to be ignored. For example, Publius explains in *Federalist* No. 47, which introduces the detailed analysis of the three branches of government and their relations, that the checks and balances among these institutions must avoid two threats: a paralysis that results from the existence of checks without balances, which destroys the autonomy of each branch, or an anarchy that is produced when balances without checks leave each power free to go its own way. Popular sovereignty ensures against the first danger by making its weight felt through its representatives, and it prevents the second by acting like a sort of glue that is present in each of the branches. This relationship is illustrated by the bicameral legislature, which was a practical compromise between the large and the small states, according the latter an equal representation in the Senate while making representation proportional to population in the House. The theoretical foundation of that compromise, Publius shows, is that both legislative chambers are based on popular sovereignty—the former expressing its unity, the latter its plurality—which permits them to complement as well as to compete with one another.

Before we look more closely at the specific ways in which popular sovereignty is represented in the new constitution, the limits on its exercise, which are self-imposed rather than the result of barriers external to the political institutions, need to be stressed. The fact that these limits are primarily judicial constitutes an institutional innovation that resulted from the Americans' attempt to give popular sovereignty its proper political place. These limits are the counterpart to the idea that a modern constitution must offer the possibility of amendment by a procedure that differs from ordinary lawmaking, just as that constitution itself is different from the positive laws made to deal with particular conditions. A constitution that is based on popular sovereignty establishes rules that are general, defining the framework in which the branches of government function. But these rules are not fixed limits on sovereignty; because they are self-imposed, they are open to change.

Why should popular sovereignty be limited if it is the basis of the Constitution? In *Federalist* No. 78, Publius admits that the autonomy of the judiciary is an innovation. "Some perplexity respecting the rights of the courts to pronounce legislative acts void, because contrary to the Constitution, has arisen from an imagination that the doctrine would imply a superiority of the judiciary to the legislative power." But that objection supposes that the three branches of government are completely separated from one another, acting on each other like an external force. It forgets the idea of representation expressed, for example, in *Federalist* No. 47, where Publius reminds his reader that "there is no position which depends on clearer principles than that every act of delegated authority, contrary to the commission under which it is exercised, is void." He implies that when the people elect representatives, they do not give them the right to substitute their own will for that of the people. The alternative, however, is not to insist that the legislator is bound by an imperative mandate, leaving him no room to exercise his own judgment. Rather, says Publius, "it is far more rational to suppose that the courts were designated to be an intermediate body between the people and the legislature in order . . . to keep the latter within the limits assigned to their authority." In other words, the basis for judicial intervention is a distinction between popular sovereignty as constitutive and popular sovereignty as constituted. When judges nullify a legislative or an executive action, they are interpreting the Constitution as the expression of the will of the people manifested in special conventions designated for the general and political purpose of creating a republican constitution. That will is judged to be more general and thus superior to the particular manifestation of the popular will at a given electoral occasion. If this were not the case, the electorate's changing whims would produce instability, which threatens or destroys the national unity. That is why the president and the members of both houses of Congress take an oath to "support and defend" the Constitution rather than, for example, to ensure the safety or well-being of the population.

The popular sovereignty expressed by a constitution that limits popular sovereignty obviously differs from the momentary expression of the electorate's will articulated according to rules established by that constitution. But the U.S. Constitution cannot be simply identified with the will of the sovereign people as expressed in the ratification debates of 1787–1788. On the one hand, it can be amended, although the need for strong majorities of two-thirds and three-quarters of the legislators and states underlines the seriousness of that action. On the other hand, as Publius stresses in the penultimate essay, *Federalist* No. 84, the Constitution remains in living contact with the spirit of the people. Against the critics who denounced the absence of a bill of rights, he explains here that the Constitution's preservation of popular sovereignty makes such a parchment protection unnecessary. Unlike the Magna Carta or the Declaration of Rights that concluded the Glorious Revolution, the government and the people are not two distinct entities bound by a sort of contract. "It is evident, therefore, that . . . [bills of right] have no application to constitutions professedly founded upon the power of the people, and executed by their immediate representatives and servants." The implication is that neither the Constitution nor the courts that interpret it are the final expression of the popular will. In a government by the people, that will is present in all institutions, but none of them can claim to be its unique and authorized expression. As a result, such a government is representative. In a modern society from which all hierarchy is eliminated, however, what is the difference between the president's and a Congress member's representativity? What distinguishes a senator from an elected member of a state assembly? In what way is a judge also a representative?

The problem of the representation of the sovereign people appears most strikingly in the bicameral legislature. After all, in ancient Rome as in contemporary Great Britain, the upper house represented the aristocratic element of society. In *Federalist* No. 63, Publius explains first the historic role of the Senate in republican governments as "an anchor against popular fluctuations." After pointing to similar examples in recent American history, he addresses his reader in a tone typical of *The Federalist*: "To a people as little blinded by prejudice or corrupted by flattery as those whom I address, I shall not scruple to add that such an institution may sometimes be necessary as a defence to the people against their own temporary errors and delusions." How can Publius justify the role of the Senate as limiting the expression of popular sovereignty? He points to the existence of "particular moments in public affairs when the people, stimulated by some irregular passion, or some illicit advantage, or misled by the artful misrepresentations of interested men, may call for measures which they themselves will afterwards be the most ready to lament and condemn." Publius is not alluding only to the critics of the Constitution whom he denounced in *Federalist* No. 1; his argument is more far-reaching, referring, for example, to the "people of Athens," who "might have escaped the indelible reproach of decreeing to the same citizens, the hemlock on one day, and statues on the next" if only they had a Senate composed of a "temperate and respectable body of citizens . . . to check the misguided career and to suspend the blow mediated by the people against themselves, until reason, justice and truth can regain authority over the public mind." But where can such citizens be found in a democratic society of equals? And how will the people, in the grips of "irregular passion" or seeking "some illicit advantage," recognize the Senate's authority?

Publius's explanation of the Senate's legitimacy stresses the distinction between a classical republic and a modern republic. Illustrations from ancient Athens, Carthage, Sparta, and Rome show that these societies knew and used the principle of representation. But, Publius continues in *Federalist* No. 63, using italics to emphasize his central point, "the true distinction between these and the American governments lies *in the total exclusion of the people in their collective capacity*, from any share in the *latter* and not in the *total exclusion of the representatives of the people* from the administration of the former." Publius's point is that the ancient republics did not distinguish the people from their representatives, whom they expected to realize immediately the popular will through a sort of imperative mandate. In doing this, these republics forgot that "liberty may be endangered by the abuses of liberty, as well as by the abuses of power." Or, to use a different vocabulary, they were too democratic; their participatory institutions led to their own self-destruction. The modern American republic avoids the tempting claim that the people "in their collective capacity" can be truly incarnated in its government. Rather, it is the republican constitution that guarantees the free and democratic nature of social relations. Republican unity is compatible with social diversity because the sovereign people's will is expressed in all political institutions but is fully incarnate in none of them. This unity protects and encourages diversity.

Publius's defense of what I have called a "modern republican democracy" is not yet complete. The positive role of social diversity, which traditionally is seen as a threat to republican unity, has to be explained. Diversity is usually criticized for introducing a kind of self-interest that corrupts republican virtue. The first lines of *Federalist* No. 10 face the issue squarely, identifying interest with faction and promising to eliminate the threat. "Among the numerous advantages promised by a well-constructed union, none deserves to be more accurately developed than its tendency to break and control the violence of faction." Publius speaks here of factions as representing either a minority or a majority, but his true concern is centered around the ill-effects of "an interested and overbearing majority" that is harmful "to the rules of justice and the rights of the minor party." It is the minority factions that ensure diversity. Publius's demonstration of their necessity builds from a careful analysis of the possible remedies for the danger of factions that shows that, although a threat, they also have a legitimate function in a republican democracy.

Publius's analysis in *Federalist* No. 10 is a masterful illustration of his political logic. When a person is confronted by a danger, he may either try to eliminate its cause or seek to limit its effects. The elimination of the cause of factions would be self-defeating because their basis is the freedom that is essential to the existence of the republic. For the same reason, a remedy that would inculcate into every citizen the same passions and the same interests has to be rejected as neither desirable nor possible. Liberty and diversity cannot be separated, in spite of what some philosophers might think. Liberty is similar to popular sovereignty, however, insofar as it is a right that must limit itself in order to preserve itself. Liberty is the foundation of the republic, but the republic must also protect liberty by giving it legitimate limits.

Although "the diversity in the faculties of men" is the origin of property rights, property is not an unmitigated good because "the most common source of factions has been the various and unequal distribution of property. Those who hold and those who are without property have ever formed distinct interests in society." But this does not mean that property and economic interest are the sole root of faction, which can also arise from different opinions concerning religion or government as well as from support for different leaders contending for power. "So strong is this propensity of mankind to fall into mutual animosities that where no substantial occasion presents itself the most frivolous and fanciful distinctions have been sufficient to kindle their unfriendly passions and excite their most violent conflicts." In short, faction cannot and should not be eliminated; the only option is to control its effects.

It would appear that the threat posed by faction can be avoided if measures are taken to prevent the creation of a majority seized by a common passion that leads it to infringe on the rights of the minority or even those of a single obstinate individual. Avoiding this outcome, however, will be impossible in what Publius calls a "pure democracy, by which I mean, a society, consisting of a small number of citizens, who assemble and administer the government in person." Such a "democracy," however, differs from the "modern" American republic that *Federalist* No. 63 distinguishes from the classical models. Here, in *Federalist* No. 10, Publius offers two arguments in favor of a representative republic. The first concerns the choice of leaders. Representation serves "to refine and enlarge the public views by passing them through the medium of a chosen body of citizens whose wisdom may best discern the true interest of their country. . . . [T]he public voice, pronounced by the representatives of the people, will be more consonant to the public good than if pronounced by the people themselves, convened for this purpose." The electoral process, assumed to be free and fair, filters the particular, passionate, and irrational character of private interest to produce a general, dispassionate, and rational public expression. In this way, the representative republic preserves the private freedom and diverse interests that are the cause of faction and makes them less of a threat to themselves and to the unity of the republic.

Publius is not naive; he is aware that the private freedom and interests that undergo this filtration process remain a potential threat to national unity. Although his analysis of factions makes clear that their elimination is undesirable, he recognizes the possibility that a demagogue might mobilize popular passions or material interests in order to be elected, but then betray the people's true interest while destroying the rights of the minority who may disagree. This is where the second remedy for the effects of factions comes into the analysis. The reigning opinion of the times was that a republic could be realized only in a small territory. This truism seemed to be illustrated by the decline of the Roman republic following its imperial enlargement. On the contrary, argues Publius, it is precisely the great size of the American republic that will contain the effects of faction. The greater number of electors selecting each representative will make it more difficult to deceive them. In addition, those who stand for election will have to be more worthy if they are to win the admiration of a larger number of their fellow citizens. What is still more, the geographical reach of the republic means that there will arise more diverse interests competing with one another. Not only does this greater diversity lessen the possibility of a single passion becoming dominant, but, as in the case of religious sects, the competition among the factions will teach each of them that they share a common interest in protecting the rights of the minority.[37]

This analysis of faction as both necessary and dangerous to a free republic is often abusively reduced to an exercise in the sociology of interests. If that were the case, there would be no reason to create republican political institutions to protect freedom and popular sovereignty from their own excesses; society would protect itself without any need for the state. That is why Publius returns to the role of an enlarged republic at several crucial junctures. For example, in the discussion of the Senate in *Federalist* No. 63, he notes that "it may be suggested that a people spread over an extensive region cannot, like the crowded inhabitants of a small district, be subject to the infection of violent passions or to the danger of combining in pursuit of unjust measures. I am far from denying that this is a distinction of particular importance. I have, on the contrary, endeavored in a former paper [i.e., *Federalist* No. 10] to show that it is one of the principal recommendations of a confederated republic." But, he adds, "this advantage ought not to be considered as superseding the use of auxiliary precautions." The Senate is only one of these "auxiliary precautions," whose institutional structure is presented most fully in *Federalist* No. 51, which again invokes the threat of faction and the remedy for its potential danger through an enlarged republic: "Whilst all authority in it will be derived from and dependent upon society, the society itself will be broken into so many parts, interests and classes of citizens, that the rights of individuals, or of the minority, will be in little danger from interested combinations of the majority." But geography can no more replace politics than can a sociology of interests. The nature and function of the institutions described in *Federalist* No. 51 have to be analyzed politically. How do they represent popular sovereignty in a manner consistent with the theory of republican democracy?

The principle of popular sovereignty as present everywhere in republican institutions, even though none of them can claim to be its full incarnation, is explained in *Federalist* Nos. 47–50. Publius seeks to answer the objection that the Constitution violates the doctrine of the separation of powers. For example, *Federalist* No. 48 agrees with critics who fear the invasive nature of executive power if the only protection against it depends on parchment documents. But that criticism would be valid only in a monarchy; or, he remarks, in a democracy, "where a multitude of people exercise in person the legislative functions and are continually exposed, by their incapacity for regular deliberation and concerted measures, to the ambitious intrigues of their executive magistrates, tyranny may well be apprehended, on some favorable emergency, to start up in the same quarter." In both the monarchy and the democracy, the source of the danger of executive tyranny is the absence of representative republican institutions that limit the executive "in both the extent and duration of its power." That is why the Constitution creates a legislative power that is exercised by "an assembly which is sufficiently numerous to feel all the passions that actuate a multitude, yet not so numerous as to be incapable of pursuing the objects of its passions by means which reason prescribes." This legislative check on the executive is not mechanical; it depends on the fact that the lawmakers are themselves dependent on popular sovereignty.

The legislative check on the executive can in turn become a threat to popular freedom, however, if the legislature interprets its election as making it the true incarnation of popular sovereignty to which the executive is subordinate. Publius recalls an aphorism from Jefferson's *Notes on the State of Virginia* that "173 despots would surely be as oppressive as one" in order to stress that Americans had not fought to replace an hereditary tyrant with an elective despotism. The threat of legislative tyranny poses again the question of how to represent popular sovereignty. In *Federalist* No. 49, Publius considers Jefferson's proposal that a popular convention be called if two of the three branches of government request it in order to check legislative power by an alliance of the executive and the judiciary. But he fears that calling such a convention would deny to government the "veneration, which time bestows on every thing, and without which perhaps the wisest and freest governments would not possess the requisite stability." This is not a conservative argument in favor of tradition. Publius's point is that because all free government is based on opinion, and because people become more stubborn when they believe that their opinion has mass support, calling for a convention risks the explosion of unreflective popular passion. This explosion would renew the threat posed by a majority faction to the minority. Instead, *Federalist* No. 49 concludes that "it is the reason, alone, of the people, that ought to control and regulate the government. The passions ought to be controlled and regulated by the government." The implication of this proposed triumph of reason over the passions is then drawn in *Federalist* No. 50. "When men exercise their reason coolly and freely on a variety of distinct questions, they inevitably fall into different opinions on some of them. When they are governed by a common passion, their opinions, if they are so to be called, will be the same." For this reason, the social diversity that results from the exercise of reason protects popular sovereignty from being overcome by unitary passions, which is another of the benefits of a republican democracy.

Publius returns to the separation of powers in *Federalist* No. 51. Because none of the methods for representing popular sovereignty presented in the previous essays was sufficient on its own, "the defect must be supplied, by so contriving the interior structure of the government as that its several constituent parts may, by their mutual relations, be the means of keeping each other in their proper places." The "mutual relations" to which Publius refers are both checks and balances, whose function is to prevent any of the branches from pretending to be the incarnation of the popular will. Each branch of government can relate mutually to the others only if all branches are homogeneous so that none can claim a natural superiority over the others. Publius does not explain how this homogenization takes place, but the earlier considerations of the way in which sovereignty is represented in a modern republic suggest that the branches are identical to one another insofar as each of them is a representative of the popular will. This configuration would account for the political "balance" among the branches of government. To ensure the "checks," continues Publius, it is necessary to endow each branch with a will of its own by ensuring that it does not depend on the other branches for the nomination of its staff. This insistence on the autonomy of each branch does not contradict the fact that they all are representatives of the sovereign people; it demonstrates that the modern principle of representation can be extended to other political institutions. If a branch of government becomes too autonomous, losing its representative character, it will pay the price by forfeiting the authority needed to exercise its "checking" function.

Although Publius's concern in *Federalist* No. 51 is to convince his reader that the U.S. Constitution does indeed preserve the separation of powers, he illustrates the reach of his theory of representation in the process of doing so. The independence of each of the powers is ensured by "giving to those who administer each department the necessary constitutional means and personal motives to resist encroachments of the others." More concretely, "ambition must be made to counteract ambition. The interest of the man must be connected to the constitutional rights of the place." This interdependence of political rights and personal interest would shock a classical republican (or a French revolutionary) for whom public virtue is threatened by private interest and personal ambition. But men are not angels; if they were, no government would be necessary; and if angels governed men, there would be no need to control government. "In framing a government which is to be administered by men over men, the great difficulty lies in this: You must first enable the government to control the governed; and in the next place to oblige it to control itself." Although the checks and balances established by the Constitution perform the second function, the first depends on the Constitution's ability to fulfill its role by faithfully representing the sovereign people. Insofar as it is able to perform this task, it provides the government that it establishes with the legitimacy that permits that government to "control the governed" without recourse to force or coercion.

◆

There is no need to pursue further the analysis in *The Federalist*; its twin theories of popular sovereignty and political representation were confirmed with the election of Thomas Jefferson in 1800. That election marked the first peaceful passage of political power from one party to another, opposed political party in history. The historical originality of this event cannot be overstressed. The idea that popular political parties were legitimate was itself new. Jefferson's party was not a parliamentary opposition of the type that opposed Whigs and Tories in Great Britain; it was a democratic party appealing to the people for support. Although its opponents might have seen it as a "faction," *The Federalist* showed the necessity and legitimacy of political factions in a free republic. The idea of representation that Publius forcefully articulated did indeed, as Jefferson said, express "the state of mind and the opinions" of contemporary Americans. But the principle of representation does not work automatically; it needs a motor, which is provided by popular sovereignty. Publius offers a concrete description of this motor's function in *Federalist* No. 51 when he explains the "policy of supplying, by opposite and rival interests, the defect of better motives, [which] might be traced through the whole system of human affairs, private as well as public." This conflictual logic is in a sense typical of republican thought, but its frank acceptance of the role of interest would have surprised a classical republican. Publius is a modern republican, however; his argument is that interest is at one and the same time the principle of popular government and its product. It is the principle that preserves the separation of powers that is essential to a republic, and it is the product of a government that preserves the freedom of the members of society. From this perspective, the passage of power from the Federalists to the Jeffersonians was a consecration of republican democracy.

The participants in the election of 1800 did not see its results in this way, though. The Jeffersonians assumed that they now incarnated the popular will. When outgoing president John Adams used his last evening in office to appoint some partisans to federal offices, the Jeffersonians refused to issue the commissions, which led to the Supreme Court decision in *Marbury v. Madison* in 1803 that ruled against the Jeffersonians, in effect demonstrating that the Constitution, not the temporary will of the people as expressed three years earlier, represented the popular will. This decision confirmed the "modern" republican theory of popular sovereignty expressed by *The Federalist*. Although some would say that the Court was making itself into the Constitution's ultimate mouthpiece, violating the checks and balances among the branches, the force of its decision was to demonstrate that the elected government is only the temporary representative of the popular will. More precisely, *Marbury* implied not only that the republic, as defined by the Constitution, is the framework within which the democracy must function, but that its task is to encourage the maintenance of a democratic society in which the conflict of interests can be played out. It confirmed the theory of republican democracy that underlies Publius's reasoning.

The politicians felt no need to spell out this theory, which came to be the common sense of American political life. But because they did not recognize the need to articulate the political theory that underlies this life, subsequent periods of American history have been marked by antipolitical misunderstandings of the notion of sovereignty and the way in which it is represented. That is another story. It does, however, pose the following question: Can the pragmatic republican democracy that emerged from the first U.S. election of the nineteenth century still cope with the problems of the globalized world of the twenty-first century?

CONCLUSION
Elements for a Democratic Renewal

THE DISTINCTION BETWEEN a republican democracy and a democratic republic is not indelibly fixed and fast. As with the other dichotomies that have marked the history of political thought, a nation can suffer from too much republicanism or too much democracy. The republican institutional framework can rigidify; the abstract universality of its laws becomes incapable of recognizing particular conditions to which they ought to adapt, and the identification of the republic with the nation blinds it to the diversity among its citizens. In such cases, the community's apparent good overrides the citizens' individuality, and concern with equality becomes an egalitarianism that leaves no place for liberty. Conversely, too much democratic participation may introduce instability into a body politic when its laws change constantly as circumstances alter, or its stress on popular sovereignty may leave no room for a dissenting minority. In these cases, the attempt to satisfy the needs of every individual interest neglects the general welfare of the community as a whole; the concern with liberty becomes a libertarianism that ignores the inequalities that this concern with liberty may unintentionally encourage. Democracy ideally sets a limit to republican legalism, which, from its side, limits the excesses of democratic populism. In reality, the idyll is short-lived, as it was in American history, but the ideal remains, and it can still inspire political renewal.

Although republican and democratic politics are members of a common family, they may at times find themselves at odds with one another. It may then be necessary for each to add some water to the heady wine of political purity, producing a compromise similar to the types of "social democracy" discussed briefly in the introduction to this volume. This compromise solution has taken many forms in twentieth-century history, from the American and European versions of the welfare state to the attempts to create forms of democratic socialism. But we are living at the beginning of a new century, and we need to invent new political forms. We are not gods, though, nor are we classical lawgivers or revolutionaries who think that we can or must abolish the existing order root and branch. We have to work with the materials at hand and within the history that brought us to our present. We can learn from the past some of the false paths to avoid, but the questions guiding our thinking have to be rooted in the present as well.

This book has shown that the "family" to which republican politics and democratic politics belong is larger than either of them. They both are species of the genus called "the political," and the history reconstructed in this book makes it clear that both species are rare and possibly not fit for long-term survival. If they disappear and then reappear at different times and places, it is because their existence depends first of all on their genus's being reproduced. It is the apparent disappearance of the political rather than some genetic flaw in republican or democratic politics that is the cause of their demise. But the political does not truly disappear; its mode of existence merely changes, making it difficult for members of society to recognize it. It may weaken, surviving only in the margins, forgotten or forsaken in the quest for other goals or gods. But if, as we have seen, the older democratic and republican species reappear in new guise, it is because the political has regained its central place in the relations among men and women. Most of the thinkers studied here did not aspire to create republican or democratic forms of political life. What they saw, however, whether they were premodern or modern, theological or secular, was the necessity of politics and therefore of political thought. That has been the guiding thread through more than two millennia of the story told here. Politics and political thought were necessary in order to transform the brute facts of human coexistence into legitimate social relations. A renewal of democratic and republican theory and practice will have to occur within this framework once again in our twenty-first century.

The appearance of modern antipolitics at the end of the eighteenth century announced a new epoch in political thought. But even these antipolitical thinkers shared the recognition that politics is necessary, although their goal was to deny its autonomy and to reject its centrality to human affairs. They succeeded all too well. Despite such exceptions as the string of revolutions that spread across Europe in 1848, keeping political hope alive, their successors in the nineteenth century took the antipolitical project still farther. A variety of methods were used to reduce the political to the necessities of the economy, to dissolve it into the logic of historical progress, to deny that human reason can solve the eternal problems of the ages, or to raise the inventors of new technologies to the status of modern-day Guardians, only to see their heroes denounced as soulless bureaucrats running a machine whose only product is its own reproduction. The nineteenth century was rich in variants on these basic themes; their competition made this period apparently one of the most exciting in political history. But the century of peace that followed the crushing of French revolutionary imperialism concluded with the folly of world war and bloody mass death in 1914. That sad conclusion challenges the illusory politics of the century that preceded it.

As for the short twentieth century, which truly began only after the senseless slaughter of a world war, the political life that was for a brief moment illuminated by the hope of revolutionary renewal in 1917 became increasingly a contest between liberalism and variants of totalitarianism (fascism and communism). Liberalism developed a normative self-justification based on the priority of individual procedural rights over the attainment of any particular social good. In some variants, it also made democracy a norm. When internal rot destroyed communism, however, after fascism had been defeated in a suicidal war of its own choosing, liberalism was the victor only by default. The triumph of liberalism is threatened by an economic globalization (accompanied by the economic vision of men as calculating rational actors) that rolls forward regardless of liberals' normative criticism of its effects on the foundations of its political institutions. Neither the republican framework that protects private freedom nor the democratic participation in the decisions that affect social life is protected from the ravages of the global economy and the ecological threats that go with it. The result is political disenchantment.

The necessity of politics has not disappeared in our twenty-first century. Politics is an inescapable part of the human condition because men and women are creatures who need to have meaning in their lives and who demand that their social relations be legitimate. This essential characteristic of all social relations may be called moral, religious, or just plain philosophical. It deserves the name "political" because it expresses the highest organizing principle of the way people explain to themselves and to others the legitimacy of their diverse social relations. In this sense, even antipolitics is political, as is the choice to locate the highest values in another domain—for example, in religion, morality, or even self-interest. Men and women are not solipsists; they live in society, and their social relations are not simply the result of their own free and private individual choice. They have to find overarching values that give their lives a stability and a legitimacy that are not arbitrary.

The presuppositions and the justifications offered by the theorists studied here differ from our own. Yet, in spite of these differences, all of these theories share some elements, some problems, and some questions posed but not always answered satisfactorily. These shared elements, problems, and questions do not make up a cookbook from which recipes for a democratic renewal in the twenty-first century can be extracted. A spoonful of Plato, a pinch of Aquinas, and a dash of Rousseau, heated by the flames of an Augustinian just war, will no more provide the required nourishment than would an updated version of any of the single, internally coherent theories studied here. The elements for a renewal of a modern republican democracy are not found in a historical collection of old recipes, but the study of the past can free us from illusions about both the possibilities and the limits of the present. Above all, that study makes clear the impossibility of eliminating the political. As a result, it encourages the search for the modern form that the political might adopt (which, unfortunately, might be an antipolitical form, as in the ideology of global free markets or the renewed populism and nationalism that claim to bring politics back to the people). The new politics will not emerge in a single moment, nor will it come into being fully formed, accompanied by an instruction manual for its proper operation.

If politics is indeed essential to being human, the task today is not so much to invent its new forms but to learn to avoid the various ways in which the political is hidden, misused, or reified. If such evasions are avoided, it seems possible that a renewed democracy may perhaps reemerge. But one of the lessons taught by the contrast of the American and the French revolutions is that a self-sufficient democracy cannot exist without a republican framework that prevents democracy's excesses. Such a republican framework sets self-imposed constitutional limits on the practice of a democratic society. Insofar as a republican democracy succeeds, members of society consider these limits legitimate because they are not imposed by force, although they may take into account external necessities imposed by geography or by economics or simply by the fact that power cannot be abolished in human societies. This republican limit on democracy does not mean, for example, that the skillful use of ideological propaganda cannot convince the population that it is necessary, say, for economic globalization to become legitimate and for democracy to flourish where it currently does not. The fact that both Nazi and Communist totalitarianism initially had strong popular support underlines the fact that not everything that the members of a democratic society perceive as legitimate is necessarily a political good. One lesson of this study is that political legitimacy does not depend on social unity achieved at the cost of diversity and difference. Conflict is also a source of legitimacy insofar as it contributes to the vigilant health of self-government.

I cannot foretell the shape that a twenty-first century republican democracy will adopt. What I can say, however, is that its precondition is the rediscovery of the political as the framework of meaning that makes room for the legitimate conflict between the proponents of unity and diversity, the universality of the law and the particular conditions of its application, and that includes more generally the coexistence of the good person and the good citizen. In this way, the political creates the possibility of legitimate politics. All of the oppositions encountered in this book acquired their legitimacy from their (often implicit) assumptions about the nature of the political, which the book's commentary and historical contextualization have highlighted. Both sides of these dichotomies must appeal to a shared source of meaning; otherwise, they would not conflict with one another, but instead would remain indifferent to their challenger. Neither of them can ever become fully identified with that shared political horizon, however. The political is a third party that stands apart from two competing players, each of whom in his own way tries to win the favor of the outside judge. Two results are possible. Because both contestants accept the judge's values, but neither can become the judge himself, it is their competition that creates legitimacy. If one or the other player were to succeed in imposing on the judge his interpretation of the values the two players share, creating a synthesis that incorporates both positions, the result of that "victory" would in fact destroy the judge's ability to play his political role because he would have become identical to the victorious player, thus losing the ability to create the meaningful framework within which political competition occurs. The victory would turn out to be a "defeat" that opens the road to antipolitics. At that point, the search for a new understanding of the political has to begin, sooner or perhaps later.

This is where we stand today, two decades after the unexpected end of the Cold War between the forms of liberalism and totalitarianism, neither of which was immune to the allure of antipolitics. We need to learn once again the art of political thought, which is founded on judgment rather than on normative reason or the purity of unitary will. There are two kinds of judgment. The first, called *subsumptive judgment,* is modeled on the scientific or judicial process; laws exist, facts are established by a jury of peers, and the judge determines whether those facts can be subsumed under the existing laws. This mode of thought, which tends toward the universalist Platonic model of antipolitics, needs to be complemented by a second form of judgment, called *reflexive judgment* and modeled on aesthetic appreciation; it tends toward the pluralist Aristotelian model. It begins from the particular source of pleasure that is called beautiful and tries to find the general qualities that make the judgment of its beauty valid for all those who experience that particular phenomenon.

Political thought is similar to aesthetic or reflexive judgment. It is deliberative, dialogic, and self-reflexive because it has learned to think in the place of the other whose otherness it accepts as legitimate. Just as I try to convince you, all of you, of the validity of my aesthetic claim even though I did not produce the work of art and cannot experience it in your place, so it is in politics: a person has an experience (positive or negative) that appears to offer a lesson to teach that is not merely private or subjective. This person must then mobilize an argumentative framework in which a shared process of deliberation and learning can occur. There are two steps to this procedure: the first is to create a political framework within which everyone can see the uniqueness of the experience; the second is to animate a debate in which ever more participants come to agree with the political judgment that was advanced. The first step creates the political; the second opens the field of politics. This "aesthetic" model of politics is democratic; it is also representative, and, insofar as the new form of the political should be more than a fleeting moment of agreement based on the passions, it will need to assume a republican form to maintain itself and legitimate the political debate that gave rise to it.[1]

Just as my aesthetic pleasure comes from my experience of something that I did not make, so too the experience of political renewal cannot be willed by a single person or a single interest. And just as I may find that the aesthetic pleasure that I thought was the result of a certain object was in fact caused by my particular passions, my immaturity, or my misjudgment, the same errors are possible in the world of politics. Bad experience is no reason, however, to refuse all new experience, either in art or in political life. We cannot know what will renew our sense of the political. We can only be certain that the various forms of antipolitics will prevent that renewal when the occasion finally presents itself. Knowing what the political has been and what it is not hones our senses to recognize it when it finally reappears. Although the antipolitical temptation cannot be eliminated, study of the history of political thought alerts us to the danger it poses to the creation of a twenty-first century republican democracy.

NOTES

1. THE RISE AND FALL OF ATHENIAN DEMOCRACY

1. Philosophy, which concerns the whole of the universe and not just the whole of society, ranks still higher. But the philosopher can only *contemplate* that totality; the political actor can also intervene in the world—for Plato, by becoming a "philosopher-king," and for Aristotle, as a participant in the quest for the good life.
2. Homer, *The Iliad*, translated by Robert Fagles (New York: Penguin Books, 1990), book II, ll. 247–255.
3. Hesiod, *Works and Days*, translated by Stanley Lombardo (Indianapolis, Ind.: Hackett, 1993), pp. 300–305, 235–245.
4. Ibid., pp. 355, 329–335.
5. An anecdote expresses well the Spartan ethos. Aristodemus, who had survived the battle of Thermopylae, found himself scorned at home because he had preferred life to a warrior's death. A year later, at the decisive battle of Plataea, he fought, says Herodotus, "with the fury of a madman in his desire to be killed before his comrades' eyes." Yet the Spartans refused to accord him public honors because he had fought and died "merely to retrieve his lost honor," reflecting an individualism contrary to the collective ethos. Herodotus, *The Histories*, translated by Aubrey de Sélincourt (New York: Penguin Classics, 1961), book VII, pp. 494–495 and 580–581.
6. The translation of *tyrannos* as "tyrant" carries the unfortunate suggestion that such a ruler will be cruel and despotic, which may be the case because his power is unlimited, but need not be so if his power depends on popular support.
7. Ostracism can of course be abused. Indeed, some historians speculate that—because nothing is known of Cleisthenes' fate after his reforms—he may himself have suffered ostracism.

8. The circumstances that led to the outbreak of this conflict are not important in the present context. Its stakes are expressed in Pericles' funeral oration, and its fatal results are suggested by the democratic leader's final warning to the Athenians.
9. Thucydides, *History of the Peloponnesian War,* edited and translated by Sir Richard Livingstone (New York: Oxford University Press, 1960); the funeral oration is in book II, pp. 34–46, and the second speech is in book II, pp. 60–64.
10. "City" is a translation of the Greek word *polis,* which is the root of the Western concept of the political.
11. Thucydides, *History of the Peloponnesian War,* book II, p. 60.
12. Ibid.
13. Ibid., book II, p. 63.
14. Although Thucydides' remarkable history is usually interpreted as the foundational text of realpolitik, it can also be read as an account of the self-destruction of Athenian democracy in these three stages.
15. Thucydides, *History of the Peloponnesian War,* book II, p. 66.
16. Plato mordantly criticizes Pericles' funeral oration in an early dialogue, the *Menenexus,* which he wrote prior to the dialogues relating Socrates' trial and death.
17. Ironically, this same charge was raised against Socrates, whom Plato presents as the true lover of wisdom.
18. For purposes of exposition, I treat Plato's Socrates and Plato himself as identical, unless otherwise specified, in spite of the fact that it is possible to interpret Socrates as more favorable to democratic politics than was his disciple.
19. For *The Apology,* I have used the translation by Thomas C. Brickhouse and Nicholas D. Smith in their useful book *The Trial and Execution of Socrates: Sources and Controversies* (New York: Oxford University Press, 2002), 32a.
20. Ibid., 39c.
21. I follow *The Republic* in the sequence in which it is given and for the most part paraphrase it, giving specific citations in the standard Stephanus form only when I quote and want to point to specific sections. I have used the translation by G. M. A. Grube, revised by C. D. C. Reeve (Indianapolis, Ind.: Hackett, 1992), as well as that of Paul Shorey, which is found in *The Collected Dialogues of Plato,* edited by Edith Hamilton and Huntington Cairns (New York: Pantheon Books, 1961).
22. Ibid., 338c.
23. Ibid., 344c.
24. Ibid., 431c.
25. Ibid., 416c, cf. 382.
26. Ibid., 509d–511c.

27. Ibid., 520e.
28. Ibid., 557e.
29. Ibid., 564a.
30. I return to these claims briefly at the beginning of chapter 6.
31. This reconstruction of Aristotle's political theory makes use of his two major works of practical philosophy, the *Politics* and the *Nicomachean Ethics*. For the sake of the reader who will want to consult the original texts, I have followed the presentation of the *Politics* as often as possible, giving the standard pagination for direct citations or indicating the book and chapter for more general references. For the *Politics*, I used *The Basic Works of Aristotle*, edited by Richard McKeon, from the definitive Oxford translation (New York: Random House, 1941). The quotation here is from book II, chap. 3, 1262a 13–14.
32. Ibid., book II, chap. 3, 1263b 13–14.
33. Aristotle, *Metaphysics*, in *The Basic Works of Aristotle*, book I, chap. 6.
34. Ibid., book I, chap. 9.
35. The fragments, not discovered until 1890, were published as *The Constitution of Athens* (New York: Hafner, 1950). This title is somewhat misleading because, although Athens had written laws, it had a constitution only in the sense that a person has a "robust or feeble constitution." The modern understanding of a constitution emerges only at the time of the American and French revolutions.
36. *Politics*, book I, chap. 2, 1253b 19–22.
37. In book I, chapter 4, of the *Politics*, Aristotle comments that "if each tool could perform its task on command . . . such that shuttles wove cloth by themselves . . . a master craftsman would not need assistants, and masters would not need slaves" (1253b 34–38). Karl Marx would later cite this passage as fundamental to his vision of the communist future in which work and the subordination that goes with it would be abolished.
38. Ibid., book I, chap. 6, 1256b 25–26.
39. Ibid., book VII, chap. 10, 1330a 20.
40. Ibid., book I, chap. 7, 1255b 33, 1256b 31–32.
41. Cf. ibid., book VII, chap. 1, 1323b 7–9.
42. Ibid., book III, chap. 1, 1275b 18–19.
43. *Nicomachean Ethics*, translated by J. A. K. Thompson (New York: Penguin Books, 1953), book I, chap. 2, 1094b 8–9.
44. Ibid., book I, chap. 5, 1094b 24–6.
45. *Politics*, book III, chap. 4, 1277b 29–30.
46. Ibid., book VII, chap. 15, 1334b 10.

47. *Nicomachean Ethics,* book II, chap. 1, 1103a 18, 1103b 1–2.
48. Ibid., book II, chap. 3, 1104a 34–36; book V, chap. 9, 1137a 7–8.
49. Ibid., book VII, chap. 10, 1152a 31.
50. The Greek term for "polity" is *politeia,* which is the same word that serves as the title of Plato's *Republic.* The common English version of the title comes from Cicero's Latin translation of Plato. Translators of Aristotle often use the notion of a "polity" to make clear that he has in mind a specific kind of regime.
51. *Politics,* book IV, chap. 2, and book V, chap. 12.
52. Ibid., book III, chap. 6, 1278b 8–11.
53. *Nicomachean Ethics,* book II, chap. 6, 1265b 26–28.
54. John K. Davies, *Democracy and Classical Greece,* 2d ed. (Cambridge, Mass.: Harvard University Press, 1993), p. 234.
55. *Politics,* book II, chap. 2, 1261a 22–28.
56. Diogenes Laertius, *Lives of Eminent Philosophers,* book 6, chap. 54.
57. A close cousin to the cynical attitude would emerge somewhat later in the form of *skepticism,* which denounces all philosophies as dogmatic while arguing that absolute truth can never be achieved. This position is associated with Carneades (214–129), who for a time was the leader of Plato's Academy, which continued to function after the philosopher's death. It was closed in 529 CE by the Emperor Justinian.

2. THE RISE AND FALL OF ROMAN REPUBLICANISM

1. Polybius, *The Rise of the Roman Empire,* translated by Ian Scott-Kilvert, edited by F. W. Walbank (New York: Penguin, 1979), book I, chap. 1, p. 41, and chap. 63, p. 109.
2. "Punic" is derived from the Roman name for the Carthaginians: "Punici." The first Punic War lasted from 264 to 241 BCE; the second took place between 218 and 201; and the third was rapidly resolved between 149 and 146, concluding with the total destruction of Carthage by the Roman army led by Scipio Aemilianus.
3. Cicero, *On the Commonwealth,* in *On the Commonwealth and On the Laws,* edited by James E. G. Zetzel (Cambridge, U.K.: Cambridge University Press, 1999), book II, p. 41, and book IV, p. 80. The title of the dialogue is sometimes translated as *On the Republic* (or anachronistically as *On the State*). Its Latin title is *De republica.*
4. The manuscript was lost sometime after 600 CE and partially rediscovered only in 1819. Many elements of Cicero's argument were known from his other works. Saint Augustine also copied long passages for use in *City of God,* as will be seen in chapter 3.
5. Cicero, *On the Commonwealth,* book VI, pp. 96, 101.
6. Livy's *History of Rome from the Foundation* originally contained 142 books, of which only 35 still exist. *The Early History of Rome* contains books 1 to 10; *The War with*

Hannibal contains books 21 to 30; and *Rome and the Mediterranean* contains books 31 to 45.

7. Livy, *The Early History of Rome*, translated by Aubrey de Sélincourt (New York: Penguin, 1960), book 1, chap. 1, p. 18.
8. Rome's claim to be the heir of Troy, founded by Aeneas, was given its fullest literary form in Virgil's *Aeneid*, which glorified the new reign of Emperor Augustus.
9. Livy, *The Early History of Rome*, book 1, chap. 8, p. 26.
10. Book 1, chap. 48, p. 72.
11. Book 1, chap. 58, p. 84.
12. Book 2, chap. 1, p. 89.
13. Book 2, chap. 5, p. 94.
14. Book 2, chap. 12, p. 103.
15. Book 2, chap. 15, p. 106.
16. Book 2, chap. 23, p. 113.
17. Book 2, chap. 33, p. 126.
18. Book 2, chaps. 55–58, pp. 154–155, and chaps. 59–63, pp. 156–161.
19. Book 2, chap. 51, p. 150.
20. Book 3, chap. 9, pp. 176 and 177.
21. Book 3, chap. 10, p. 178.
22. Book 3, chap. 21, pp. 191–192.
23. This institution, created after the elimination of the monarchy, was carefully circumscribed to fit a specific task and was never to last for longer than six months. It expressed the need for a republic to be able to confront a state of exception when the laws alone are unable to do so. It was to deal with a particular threat to the whole, just as the tribunes had an extralegal power to deal with a particular threat to a part of the whole, the individual citizen. Many modern constitutions make room for what are called "laws of exception."
24. Livy, *The Early History of Rome*, book 3, chap. 26, p. 197.
25. Book 3, chap. 31, pp. 202 and 203, and chap. 33, p. 203.
26. Book 3, chap. 35, p. 206, and chap. 36, pp. 207–208.
27. Book 3, chap. 66, p. 241.
28. Book 3, chap. 66, p. 242, and chaps. 68–69, pp. 242–245.
29. I follow Polybius's tightly argued text closely, paraphrasing mostly, quoting occasionally, and commenting for the sake of emphasis, so I do not give page numbers for citations after this point. I quote from the Scott-Kilvert translation of *The Rise of the Roman Empire* (cited fully in note 1), and the quote here is from book VI, chap. 7, p. 306.

30. In the funeral oration, Pericles makes a similar argument about the function of the "restraint of reverence." Both democratic and republican political life value individual honor while fearing disgrace above all.
31. Polybius appears to have coined the Greek term *ochlocracy* to make clear that it is a form of rule, as opposed to the classical idea of anarchy, which implies the absence of any rule.
32. These passages are given in Cicero, *Selected Political Speeches*, edited by Michael Grant (New York: Penguin, 1969), p. 28.
33. Cicero, *On the Commonwealth*, book I, pp. 2, 3.
34. These two passages, although originally separated, are reprinted in ibid., book II, p. 57.
35. Ibid., book V, p. 87. This passage was lost; the editor has inserted it from Saint Augustine's citation in *The City of God*, translated by Marcus Dods, with an introduction by Thomas Merton (New York: Modern Library, 1950), p. 62. In the next chapter, I discuss why this claim seemed so important to Augustine.
36. Robespierre would advocate political punishment for such "crimes" during the French Revolution. His justification of the Terror was in many ways similar to Cicero's claims for the moral politician.
37. *On the Laws*, in the Zetzel edition *On the Commonwealth and On the Laws*, book I, p. 111.
38. *On the Commonwealth*, book III, pp. 71, 72.
39. *On the Laws*, book I, pp. 112, 117.
40. Ibid., book I, p. 120. The Latin language distinguishes between *lex*, positive or statute law concerning the relations among private persons, and *ius* (or *jus*), which points to justice in the broader sense of the term. Cicero writes, for example, that "there is only one justice, which constitutes the bond among humans, and which was established by the one law, which is right reason in commands and prohibitions." And he continues with the second step of the argument: "The person who does not know it is unjust, whether the law has been written anywhere or not." Ibid., p. 120.
41. Ibid., book II, p. 132.
42. Ibid., book III, p. 157.
43. Ibid., book III, p. 167.
44. Ibid., book I, p. 113. Cicero clarifies the reference to a celestial order, divine mind, and all-powerful god when he points out that "since all things endowed with reason are superior to those which lack reason, and since it is wrong to say that anything is

superior to the natural universe, it must be admitted that the universe has reason." Ibid., book II, p. 135.

45. Tacitus, *Agricola,* translated by H. Mattingly, revised by S. A. Handford (New York: Penguin, 1970), chap. 30, p. 81. The "desert" in question is literally a "solitude": "atque ubi solitudinem faciunt pacem appelant." Mattingly calls it a "desolation" in his translation.

3. THE CONFLICT OF THE SACRED AND THE SECULAR

1. For convenience's sake, and because this account is a secular one, I refer to "Augustine" or "Thomas" rather than to "Saint Augustine" or "Saint Thomas."
2. The entire passage from Cicero's *On the Commonwealth* is cited in chapter 2; it is taken from Augustine, *City of God,* translated by Marcus Dods, with an introduction by Thomas Merton (New York: Modern Library, 1950), book XXI, chap. 2, p. 62.
3. Augustine, *Confessions,* translated by Henry Chadwick (New York: Oxford University Press, 1991), book I, chap. xiv, p. 23; subsequent citations are given in the following form: I.xiv, p. 23.
4. Ibid., II.iv, p. 9; III.i, p. 1; III.ii, p. 2; III.iii, p. 6; III.iv, p. 7. Manichaeism offers a solution to the basic problem for any monotheistic religion: If God is both good and all powerful, how can evil exist in the world? The Manichaean solution explains that the principles of good and evil compete with one another, as do the flesh and the spirit. The evil principle can triumph at various moments. What is characteristic of Manichaeism is not that men have the option between black and white, but that there is no shade of gray. (Augustine's eventual solution to the problem is Platonic: he denies that God creates evil because evil is only the absence of good, not something that actually exists.)
5. Ibid., Vi.vi, p. 9; Vi.xv, p. 25; Viii.xi, p. 27.
6. Augustine cites Genesis 11:1–9 in chapter 4 of *The City of God.* He may have been thinking also of Plato's idea of *pleonexis,* overreaching.
7. Augustine, *The City of God,* book XIX, chap. 7, p. 683; subsequent citations are given in the following form: XIX.7, p. 683.
8. Ibid., XIX.12, pp. 687–688; XIX.17, pp. 695–697.
9. Ibid., II.21, p. 60, and XIX.21, p. 699.
10. Ibid., II.22, p. 63; XIX.21, p. 699.
11. Ibid., both quotes from XIX.21, p. 700.
12. In North Africa, where Augustine was bishop of Hippo, many sympathized with the Donatists as critics of a church that had become the ally of the Roman oppressors. In

their eyes, native officials were not only political opportunists, but a Latin-speaking elite that dominated the native population. The similarity with many so-called revolutionary groups over the centuries is obvious.

13. This interpretation contrasts with the Western interpretation established by the Nicene Creed, introduced by Constantine at the Council of Nicea in 321, according to which Christ had to assume a human form for his sacrifice to have its salvific effect. As a result, the sacred and the secular are not only distinct from each other, but each can claim soteriological legitimacy. This conflict of legitimacies is one of the sources of the dynamics of Western society.
14. By the mid–seventeenth century, the Benedictine monastery at Cluny stood at the head of 314 subordinate branches spread across what are now France, Germany, and England. Its abbot wielded a secular power and controlled worldly wealth that would have dismayed Benedict. But because the vow of poverty taken by the monks applied only to personal wealth, the members of the wealthy order could still benefit from the collective wealth.
15. St. Thomas Aquinas, *On Kingship*, in *St. Thomas Aquinas on Politics and Ethics*, edited by Paul E. Sigmund (New York: Norton, 1988); all three quotes are found in chap. 14, p. 28.
16. The name was popularized by Charles Homer Haskins's *The Renaissance of the 12th Century* (Cleveland: Meridian Books, 1958, orig. pub. 1927).
17. For Thomas Aquinas's *Summa theologica*, I used Aquinas, *On Law, Morality, and Politics*, edited by William P. Baumgarth and Richard J. Regan , translated by Richard J. Regan (Indianapolis, Ind.: Hackett, 1988), question 90, article 3, p. 15. Although Thomas is a monarchist, there is no reason why his argument cannot apply to a representative legislature. *On Kingship*, which insists that the monarch is subordinate to the papacy, contains a long discussion of the dangers of tyranny, after which Thomas (like Aristotle) suggests that mixed government would be preferable.
18. Thomas Aquinas, *Summa theologica*, question 91, article 3, p. 21.
19. Thomas devotes a separate question (number 97) to the problem of legal change. He argues first that it is to be expected that humans will move toward greater perfection, but he goes on to suggest that laws should be changed only in dire conditions because frequent change will weaken the binding power of the law that is encouraged by habitual behavior. He makes this point differently when he asserts that custom can attain the force of law, "for when a thing is done again and again, it seems to proceed from a deliberate judgment of reason," (*Summa theologica*, question 97, article 3, p. 80). Although Thomas's use of the dynamic interaction of natu-

ral and human law has a conservative orientation, later thinkers will draw more radical conclusions from his analysis.

20. Ibid., question 66, article 2, pp. 178–179. My reconstruction of his argument is intended to illustrate the relation between natural law and human law, although that was not Thomas's declared intent in this discussion.
21. Ibid., question 66, article 7, p. 186.
22. Ibid., question 77, article 4, pp. 196–197.
23. Ibid., question 92, article 1, and replies to objections 2 and 4, pp. 29–31.
24. See also question 152, article 2, on whether virginity is lawful. A similar argument concerns priestly celibacy as opposed to marriage, where Thomas recalls Saint Paul's famous remark, "But if they do not contain themselves, let them marry. For it is better to marry than to be burnt" (I Corinthians 7:9).
25. Alexandre Koyré, *From the Closed World to the Infinite Universe* (Baltimore: Johns Hopkins University Press, 1957).

4. FACING THE CHALLENGE OF MODERNITY

1. Martin Luther, *Luther's Works*, 55 vols., various translators (Minneapolis and St. Louis: Fortress Press and Concordia, 1957–1986); in 2002, Fortress published a CD-ROM version of all fifty-five volumes, edited by Jaroslav Pelikan and Helmut T. Lehman.
2. This famous peroration is cited, in sometimes slightly varying forms, in nearly all histories of the Reformation. This version is the English translation found in Richard Friedenthal, *Luther: His Life and Times*, translated by John Nowell (New York: Harcourt, Brace, Jovanovich, 1967), p. 269.
3. Luther preserved only communion, penance, and baptism. He did not go so far as Jan Hus, who proposed that the congregation share among themselves the communal cup rather than have it administered by a priest. However, the Lutheran priest does face the congregation rather than the altar.
4. For this reason, these peasant rebels were called "Anabaptists," —that is, "Rebaptizers" (the Greek term *ana* means "again").
5. Martin Luther, *Against the Robbing and Murdering Hordes of Peasants*, in *Selected Writings of Martin Luther, 1529–1546*, edited by Theodore G. Tappert (Minneapolis: Fortress Press, 1967), p. 353.
6. Martin Luther, *An Open Letter on the Hard Book Against the Peasants—Introduction*, in Tappert, ed., *Selected Writings of Martin Luther, 1529–1546*, p. 367, 382, 389.
7. This title is used in Harro Höpfl, ed., *Luther and Calvin on Secular Authority*, Cambridge Texts in the History of Political Thought (Cambridge, U.K.: Cambridge

University Press, 1991). The page numbers given in citations to *On Secular Authority* refer to this volume. This edition also contains Calvin's *On Civil Government*, to which we come shortly. The title of the translation for *On Secular Authority* given in *Luther's Works*, vol. 45, is *Temporal Authority: To What Extent It Should Be Obeyed*.

8. *On Secular Authority* explains the need to honor secular authorities, "not because it makes people virtuous in the sight of God, but because it does ensure that the virtuous have outward peace and protection and that the wicked cannot do evil without fear and in undisturbed peace" (p. 20).
9. *On Secular Authority*, p. 29. Luther considers but rejects Augustine's claim that he did not compel the Donatists to believe rightly but simply showed them the external consequences of their false faith. The government must stay out of the spiritual domain; if God's Word cannot triumph, why should we think that secular power can do so?
10. Ibid., p. 35.
11. Ibid., p. 39. At the outset of part two of *On Secular Authority*, Luther argues against severity of punishment because "it is always better that a villain should live than that a just man should be killed. There always are, and always must be, villains in the world, but there are few just men" (p. 23).
12. Ibid., pp. 6, 40.
13. As was the case with the Investiture Struggle, Luther's defense of the autonomy of the sacred had the unintended effect of liberating the secular from any obligation to higher laws. The state was left without a soul.
14. John Calvin, *On Civil Government*, in Höpfl, ed., *Luther and Calvin on Secular Authority*, p. 58; all citations to this work refer to this edition. *On Civil Government* is book IV, chapter 20, of Calvin's *Institutes of the Christian Religion*.
15. A discussion of Max Weber's justly renowned study *The Protestant Ethic and the Spirit of Capitalism* (originally published in 1904–1905, book form in 1921) would take us too far from our present concerns, but suffice it to say that Weber was reacting against the economic determinism of the nineteenth-century Marxists. I treat the birth of capitalism briefly at the outset of chapter 5 and systematically in the discussion of Adam Smith (who spoke of "commercial" rather than capitalist society) in chapter 6.
16. Calvin, *On Civil Government*, p. 49.
17. Ibid., p. 50.
18. Calvin's theory of the church's ideal internal organization builds from the model of mixed government. The church leadership is made up of four distinct groups: pastors, teachers, elders, and deacons. These groups in turn are mixed together to ensure

that diversity is represented. Relations among Calvinist churches have a similar mixed structure, with synods representing different regions first meeting, then sending delegates to the next higher level of deliberation. In both cases, this approach contrasts with the imposition of unity from above by Lutheran bishops selected by the secular princes.

19. Calvin, *On Civil Government*, pp. 56, 55, 57.
20. Ibid., pp. 59, 62. As Höpfl recalls, the young Calvin translated Seneca's *On Clemency*, which was addressed to the emperor Nero.
21. Ibid., pp. 67, 68.
22. Ibid., p. 74.
23. Ibid., p. 80.
24. Ibid., pp. 76, 80, 81.
25. Ibid., p. 81.
26. Ibid., pp. 82, 83. As will be seen in the discussion of John Locke in chapter 5, this idea was the basis of the theoretical justification of the Glorious Revolution of 1689 in England.
27. Machiavelli's Livy is the same Livy discussed in chapter 2. Machiavelli apparently began to write *The Discourses* shortly before he wrote *The Prince* but did not complete it until 1517, about four years after *The Prince*. Both works were not published until after Machiavelli's death, although they circulated as manuscripts. In addition, Machiavelli wrote *The Art of War* in 1521 and *History of Florence* in 1525. His humanist education is evident in his nonpolitical works, which include the play *Mandragola*, which was first performed in 1520 for Pope Leo X and has continued to be performed, most recently in New York City in 2007.
28. This ruler is a "prince." The term does not refer to an individual; Machiavelli's political thought applies generically to any ruler—royal, aristocratic, or popular.
29. I quote from Peter Bondanella and Mark Musa's translation of *The Prince* in their useful edition *The Portable Machiavelli* (New York: Penguin Books, 1979). Because the chapters are short and readers may wish to refer to other translations more handy to them, in my text I cite chapters rather than specific pages in this edition.
30. Although Machiavelli speaks of "the prince," he is in fact referring to government more generally.
31. Their relation is in fact more complicated; misfortune occurs when *fortuna* is not met by *virtù*. That is why these terms are better defined in context, in particular the notion of *virtù*, which is often rendered by the English *virtue*. Mark Musa's introduction to his bilingual edition of *The Prince* (New York: Saint Martins, 1964) points out that the term *virtù* occurs fifty-nine times in that text and is coupled seventeen

times with the notion of *fortuna,* which itself appears fifty-one times. Musa lists some of these contexts on pages xi–xv.

32. I quote from Leslie Walker's translation in Bernard Crick's edition of *The Discourses* (New York: Penguin Books, 1970). As with *The Prince,* I cite books and chapters rather than pages so that readers may use other translations if they are more easily available.
33. In order to avoid anachronistic debate, I have elided Machiavelli's remark that because fortune is a woman, "it is necessary, in order to keep her down, to beat her and to struggle with her."
34. The similarities between the two works can be seen in some of the chapter titles in book I. For example, chapter 16 explains that "a people accustomed to live under a prince, should they by some eventuality become free, will with difficulty maintain their freedom." Chapter 26 asserts that "in a city or province which he has seized, a new prince should make everything new." The politics of opinion is introduced in chapter 51: "a republic or a prince should ostensibly do out of generosity what necessity constrains them to do."

5. MODERN INDIVIDUALISM AND POLITICAL OBLIGATION

1. The textual basis from which I have developed this interpretation can be found in David Wooton's introduction to his useful collection of contemporary texts, *Divine Right and Democracy: An Anthology of Political Writing in Stuart England* (New York: Penguin Books, 1986).
2. Thomas Hobbes, *Leviathan: With Selected Variations from the Latin Edition of 1688,* edited by Edward Curley (Indianapolis, Ind.: Hackett, 1994), chap. 31, p. 243.
3. Ibid., introduction, pp. 4–5.
4. Ibid., chap. 6, pp. 28–29.
5. Ibid., chap. 13, p. 75. Indeed, as Hobbes notes at the end of this chapter, alluding to the possible reasons for his return to England in 1651, the formal institutions of a state may lack a "power able to over-awe them all," in which case the state of nature has de facto returned.
6. Ibid., chap. 13, pp. 76, 78.
7. Ibid., chap. 27, p. 106.
8. Ibid., chap. 17, p. 109. Hobbes frequently repeats the qualification "or upon an assembly of men"; his theory does not necessarily entail a monarchical regime. As he points out in chapter 19, aristocracy, democracy, and monarchy are legitimate regimes, whereas their opposites entail a return to the state of nature because they are not able to ensure social unity. The choice of one or the other form of govern-

ment depends on the conditions in which they are instituted. This distinction may help to explain Hobbes's choice to return to England in 1651.

9. Ibid.
10. The rights that are protected are those that belong to the private sphere. This is the basis of the distinction between modern liberalism and classical democratic politics. The shadow of antipolitics lurks over liberalism, whether in Hobbes's formulation or Locke's, as will be seen shortly.
11. Hobbes, *Leviathan*, chap. 29, p. 210.
12. Ibid., chap. 29, p. 218.
13. John Locke, *An Essay Concerning Human Understanding* (New York: Prometheus Books, 1995), p. xvi.
14. Even *The Two Treatises on Government* was published anonymously. It is only because Locke mentioned it in his will that his authorship of this work was verified.
15. The English Bill of Rights differs in this way from the American Declaration of Independence (which begins with a statement of "self-evident" truths as its natural-law foundation) and the French Declaration of the Rights of Man and of the Citizen (which attributes rights to men as men).
16. A convenient condensation of the *First Treatise* is found in John Locke, *The Selected Political Writings of John Locke*, edited by Paul E. Sigmund (New York: Norton, 2005). This quotation is found on page 5. This volume also contains the entire *Second Treatise* as well as selections from some of the "sources" from which Locke drew and contemporary commentary on his work. In citing the *Second Treatise*, I refer to Locke's own paragraphing as well as to the pagination in Sigmund's edition.
17. Locke, *Second Treatise*, chap. 1, para. 2, p. 17.
18. Ibid., chap. 2, para. 4, p. 18.
19. Ibid., chap. 2, para. 6, p. 19.
20. Ibid., chap. 2, para. 13, p. 22, and para. 14, p. 23.
21. Ibid., chap. 3, para. 16, p. 24. Locke later calls this "a long train of abuses" (*Second Treatise*, chap. 19, para. 225, p. 116), a phrase that reappears in the U.S. Declaration of Independence.
22. Ibid., chap. 5, para. 27, pp. 28–29.
23. Ibid.
24. Ibid., chap. 5, para. 35, p. 31, and para. 36, p. 32.
25. Ibid., chap. 5, para. 37, p. 33, and para. 49, p. 38.
26. Ibid., chap. 9, para. 123, p. 72.
27. Although England became a constitutional monarchy, it had—and has—no written constitution. That is why, when Locke discusses the legislative power in chapter 11

of the *Second Treatise,* his first sentence stresses that "the first and fundamental positive law of all common-wealths is the establishing of the legislative power." He returns to the issue from another angle in chapter 13, "Of the Subordination of the Powers of the Commonwealth."

28. Locke, *Second Treatise,* chap. 9, para. 134, p. 75.
29. Ibid., chap. 13, para. 149, p. 82.
30. Ibid., chap. 18, para. 202, p. 106.
31. The Edict of Nantes, which had granted freedom of worship to French Calvinists, was revoked in 1685, the year that the ascension of James II to the English throne created the tensions that led to the Glorious Revolution.
32. Locke, *Second Treatise,* chap. 14, para. 168, p. 91, and chap. 18, para. 210, p. 109.
33. Locke's influence on the Declaration of Rights, which begins with a long list of James II's misdeeds, is evident. By committing these misdeeds, he is said to have de facto abdicated his rightful powers. As a result, the declaration continues, a new convocation of the delegates of the diverse authorities of the land has met to formulate this declaration, which will state "the best means for . . . vindicating and asserting their ancient rights and liberties."
34. Locke, *Second Treatise,* chap. 19, para. 220, p. 113.
35. Ibid., chap. 19, para. 223, p. 115, and para . 225, p. 116.
36. See Robert Darnton, *Forbidden Bestsellers of Pre-revolutionary France* (New York: Norton, 1996).
37. For all his contemporary political influence, Voltaire's legacy to the history of political thought is best understood as falling into the Socratic tradition, provoking his contemporaries rather than offering institutional remedies. The other icon of the enlightenment, Charles de Secondat, Baron de Montesquieu, is remembered for his institutional proposals rather than for his active participation in political life. Although Montesquieu contributed his *Essay on Taste* to the *Encyclopedia* and participated in the general spirit of the Enlightenment (for example, in his *Considerations on the Causes of the Greatness of the Romans and Their Decline*), he was an outsider who was older and did not participate in the intense social life of Paris. The political thought that he developed in his *Spirit of the Laws* was indebted to the English historical model, which may explain its greater influence on the American revolutionaries than on his French countrymen.
38. "Heloïse" was the name of the lover of Peter Abelard, the great twelfth-century nominalist logician; when their affair was discovered, he was castrated, and she was banished to a nunnery. Rousseau's "Julie" preserves her virtue, at great cost.

39. Montesquieu had elaborated this problem in his *Considerations on the Causes of the Greatness of the Romans and Their Decline* (1734). *The Spirit of the Laws* (1748) can be read as his attempt to avoid its difficulties.
40. Jean-Jacques Rousseau, *The First and Second Discourses,* edited by Roger D. Masters, translated by Judith R. Masters (New York: St. Martin's Press, 1964), pp. 132–133.
41. The often cited Voltaire quote comes from Voltaire's letter to Rousseau dated September 12, 1756. I take this citation from James Miller, *Rousseau: Dreamer of Democracy* (New Haven, Conn.: Yale University Press, 1984), p. 53.
42. Jean-Jacques Rousseau, *Confessions* (Paris: Édition de la Pléiade, 1959), vol. I, book IX, pp. 404–405; the translation is modified from *Confessions,* translated by Angela Scholar (New York: Oxford University Press, 2000), p. 395.
43. Ibid., p. 407; translation modified from the Scholar translation, p. 397.
44. Jean-Jacques Rousseau, *The Social Contract, with the Geneva Manuscript and Political Economy,* edited by Roger D. Masters, translated by Judith R. Masters (New York: St. Martin's Press, 1978), p. 46.
45. Rousseau, *First and Second Discourses,* p. 103.
46. Rousseau, *The Social Contract,* pp. 55–56.
47. Ibid., pp. 61, 63.
48. Ibid., p. 66.
49. Ibid., p. 102.
50. Ibid., p. 85.
51. It should be recalled that "corruption" is a concept that belongs to the classical republican theory of politics. It does not refer to the kind of personal criminality that it has come to imply in contemporary liberal democracies.
52. Rousseau, *First and Second Discourses,* p. 103.
53. Ibid., p. 111.
54. Ibid., pp. 113, 115.
55. Ibid., pp. 116, 117, 126.
56. Ibid., pp. 130, 131. Rousseau is alluding to Mandeville's *The Fable of the Bees* (1714), whose subtitle is *Private Vices, Public Benefits.* A modern formulation of Mandeville's thesis is that "a rising tide lifts all boats." Even the poor are said to benefit as the rich get richer!
57. Rousseau, *First and Second Discourses,* p. 132.
58. Ibid., pp. 137, 139.
59. Ibid., p. 141, emphasis in the original.

60. Ibid., pp. 146, 147.
61. Ibid., p. 151.
62. Ibid., pp. 154, 155.
63. Rousseau adds a bit later that "to this ardor to be talked about, to this furor to distinguish oneself, which nearly always keeps us outside of ourselves, we owe what is best and worst among men, our virtues and our vices, our sciences and our errors, our conquerors and our philosophers—that is to say, a multitude of bad things as against a small number of good ones" (ibid., p. 175). The same thesis returns in the concluding lines of the *Second Discourse*.
64. Ibid., p. 157.
65. Ibid., 158.
66. The Marxist, for whom the laws are simply a formal "superstructure" that masks the reality of economic exploitation that is the material "infrastructure" on which society rests, would make a similar claim but for different theoretical reasons.
67. Rousseau, *First and Second Discourses*, p. 158.
68. Ibid., pp. 160, 159, 173.
69. Ibid., pp. 177, 172.
70. Rousseau, *The Social Contract*, pp. 124, 128–129, 130, 131.
71. François Furet, *Interpreting the French Revolution*, translated by Elborg Forster (Cambridge, U.K.: Cambridge University Press, 1981), p. 77.
72. The notions of a social democracy and, even more so, those of a democratic republic are associated with the socialist and Communist movements of the nineteenth and twentieth centuries. From their perspective, the social revolution that began in 1789 and reached its high point in 1793 before being temporarily stopped by the Thermidorian reaction was reborn briefly in 1830 and spread widely in 1848 and briefly in Paris in 1871; it then left French territory for Russia, where it was realized by the Bolshevik Revolution of 1917 before embarking on a new expansion in the wake of World War II and in the successful struggles against colonialism after the war. I return to this vision of social revolution briefly in my conclusion.
73. The revolutionaries did not argue that history would absolve them or justify their action in the present by appeal to historical necessity. Their claims remained normative. The historicist argument would emerge only in the nineteenth century, partially to answer the conservatives' appeal to tradition as a justification of their political choices.

6. THE END OF POLITICAL PHILOSOPHY?

1. Smith did ask that question in his *Theory of Moral Sentiments*. He begins chapter 3 of part I with the assertion that the "disposition to admire, and almost to worship,

the rich and the powerful, and to despise, or, at least, to neglect persons of poor and mean condition, though necessary both to establish and to maintain the distinction of ranks and the order of society, is, at the same time, the great and most universal cause of the corruption of our moral sentiments." In *The Essential Adam Smith*, edited by Robert Heilbroner (New York: Norton, 1986), p. 86.

2. Adam Smith, *An Inquiry into the Nature and Causes of the Wealth of Nations*, abridged ed., edited by Richard F. Teichgraeber III (New York: Modern Library, 1985), p. 197.
3. Smith is aware of the paradoxical dialectic involved particularly in this latter process. Not only does the ever more specialized tool define the labor that the worker must do, but the worker, who is an end insofar as he must be trained as a specialist, remains a means of production who is no different from the other tools used in the process. From this latter perspective, the worker has become what Aristotle called a slave—namely, an "animate instrument of labor."
4. Smith, *Wealth of Nations*, p. 15.
5. Ibid., pp. 445–446, 452.
6. Although Smith alludes frequently to its effects, the Invisible Hand is explicitly present only in chapter 2 of book IV, "Restraints upon the Importation from Foreign Countries of such Goods as can be Produced at Home."
7. Smith, *Wealth of Nations*, pp. 79–80.
8. Ibid., pp. 68, 69.
9. Ibid., p. 380.
10. Historians disagree about the duration of the revolution. For some, it lasted until the restoration of the monarchy after the defeat of Napoleon Bonaparte at Waterloo in 1815. For others, it lasted until the coup d'état on the eighteenth of Brumaire, 1799, or until Bonaparte's proclamation as emperor of the French in 1804. For our purposes, the revolution ended with the overthrow of the Terror, which was the high point of revolutionary antipolitics, on Thermidor 9, 1794.
11. My translation. For a published edition of the Constitution, see *Les constitutions de la france depuis 1789* (Paris: Garnier-Flammarion, 1970). The declaration itself is the preamble to the Constitution of 1791, but it has a preamble as well. In this edition, it is found on pages 33–35. The Constitution was adopted on August 26, 1789.
12. Marie-Olympe de Gouges, for example, denounced the exclusion of women in her Declaration of the Rights of Women and Citizens, published in 1791. Servants were also excluded because they lacked the autonomy necessary for political participation. But this exclusion proved to be a slippery slope when the Constitution of 1791 established a distinction between active and passive citizens on the basis of wealth.

13. The Le Chapelier law is often treated as a measure limiting workers' rights. In fact, the guilds were made up of privileged workers who controlled and limited free access to the professions.
14. Jean-Jacques Rousseau, *Discours sur l'économie politique,* originally published in the *Encyclopédie,* translation modified from *Discourse on Political Economy and the Social Contract,* translated by Christopher Betts (Oxford, U.K.: Oxford University Press, 1999), p. 14.
15. Constant's brief lecture, which contains the germ of many of his later works, can be found in Benjamin Constant, *Constant: Political Writings,* edited by Biancamaria Fontana (Cambridge, U.K.: Cambridge University Press, 1988), pp. 309–328.
16. All quotations from this speech come from Maximilien Robespierre, "Discourse on the Principles of Political Morality That Should Guide the National Convention in the Domestic Administration of the Republic," in *Robespierre: Virtue and Terror,* edited by Slavoj Zizek, translated by John Howe, pp. 108–125 (New York: Verso, 2007).
17. Alexis de Tocqueville emphasized this point in the introduction to his classic study *Democracy in America,* published in 1835. He further developed his insight in his study *The Ancien Régime and the Revolution,* published in 1856.
18. Hegel's philosophy can be summed up in the concise phrase found in his preface to *The Philosophy of Right,* "The real is the rational and the rational is the real," by which he means that nothing can be truly and fully rational if it is not also real, and anything that is not truly and fully rational is not truly and fully real, but exists only as an appearance. Marx transformed Hegel's claim into a practical imperative in his *Critique of Hegel's "Philosophy of Right"*: "The real should be rational, and the rational should be real," by which he means that the world should be made rational and that the guideline for doing so is a rationality that is to be imposed on the real. Marx's claim can be seen as a development of Jacobin politics, whereas Hegel's can be fitted—although with difficulty—into the conservative ideology that was a repudiation of the revolution. See Dick Howard, *From Marx to Kant,* 2d ed. (New York: St. Martin's Press, 1993).
19. David Hume, "On the Original Contract," in *Political Essays,* edited by Charles W. Hendel (Indianapolis, Ind.: Bobbs-Merrill, 1959), pp. 60–61.
20. Edmund Burke, "Speech at Mr. Burke's Arrival in Bristol," in *The Portable Edmund Burke,* edited by Isaac Kramnick (New York: Penguin Books, 1999), p. 156.
21. For Burke's essay, I used Edmund Burke and Thomas Paine, *Reflections on the Revolution in France and The Rights of Man* (Garden City, N.Y.: Doubleday, 1973), p. 33. All citations of *Reflections* refer to this edition; the italics in quotations are Burke's. Well-taken polemical replies to Burke, such as Thomas Paine's *Common Sense*

(1776), which I discuss later in this chapter in the context of the American republic, do not help us to understand why Burke's conservatism has had such staying power. Paine's hugely popular pamphlet had a political impact on his American readers that was comparable to Emmanuel-Joseph Sieyès's *What Is the Third Estate?* His rapier thrusts remain worth reading, but they do not offer a political theory that justifies the French Revolution (in which he nearly became a victim of the Terror).

22. Burke, *Reflections*, pp. 19, 20.
23. Benjamin Constant, *De la force du gouverenmont actuel de la France et la nécessité de s'y rallier: Des réreactions politiques; Des effets de la Terreur* (Paris: Flammarion, 1988), chap. 8, p. 138, my translation.
24. Burke, *Reflections*, pp. 72, 73, 74, 48.
25. Ibid., p. 89.
26. Ibid., p. 90.
27. Ibid., pp. 156, 91, 110. Burke's criticism can be extended to apply to the claims of economic theory to explain the political organization and goals of society. Conservatism wants to make sure that the economy remains in its place.
28. Ibid., pp. 159, 265.
29. Helvetius was the best-selling author of *De l'esprit* (1758), a proto-utilitarian and starkly materialist treatise that both the court and the church condemned even while it was being translated and widely discussed (for that reason) throughout Europe.
30. Burke, *Reflections*, pp. 99, 101.
31. Ibid., pp. 163, 126.
32. Ibid., pp. 182, 184, 185.
33. Ibid., pp. 77, 219, 226, 236.
34. Ibid., pp. 239, 263.
35. Those who wish to follow the debates on the U.S. Constitution as they took place in real time can consult Bernard Bailyn, ed., *The Debate on the Constitution: Federalist and Antifederalist Speeches, Articles and Letters During the Struggle over Ratification*, 2 vols. (New York: Library of America, 1993). The citation from Jefferson is found in his report of March 4, 1825, to the Board of Overseers of the University of Virginia, reprinted in *The Complete Jefferson*, arranged and assembled by Saul K. Padover (New York: Tudor, 1943), p. 1112.
36. I treat *The Federalist* as if it is the work of a single author, but I also refer clearly to each paper under discussion by its specific number. Because Madison and Hamilton, the principle authors, later joined separate political parties, historians have tried, in vain, to find the roots of their differences in the papers written by one or

the other. For quotes, I used *The Federalist*, edited and with introduction and notes by Jacob E. Cooke (Middletown, Conn.: Wesleyan University Press, 1961). The interpretator offered here a developed in Dick Howard, *Aux origines de la pensée politique américaine* (Paris: Hachette-Pluriel, 2004).

37. For obvious political reasons, Publius does not mention the possibility that this multiplication of interests might expand to the point that the unity of the republic is threatened, as Madison had feared in an earlier letter to Jefferson (October 24, 1788).

CONCLUSION

1. This paragraph draws on the thesis that I developed in *From Marx to Kant*, 2d ed. (New York: Saint Martin's Press, 1993). That study focuses on what I would now call the antipolitics of Hegel and Marx, certainly the most powerful of the great nineteenth-century political thinkers. It was their predecessor, Kant, who developed the theory of judgment that I consider fundamental to political thought. The book claims that Kant provided the conceptual framework needed to realize Marx's political goals (as I interpret them).

GLOSSARY

AGONISTIC: From the Greek *agon*, which means "struggle" or "competition."

AGORA: An open-air marketplace in ancient Greek cities that also served as a public meeting place. Socrates publicly questioned prominent citizens about their beliefs in the Athenian agora.

ALEXANDER THE GREAT (356–323 BCE): King of Macedonia, son of Phillip II, and one-time pupil of Aristotle. During his brief reign (from 336 BCE until his death), he conquered most of the known world, including Greece. His rapidly established empire fell apart just as quickly upon his early death when none of his generals was able to establish himself as a legitimate ruler.

ANABAPTISM: A Reformation movement whose name, which means "rebaptism," is derived from their insistence on adult baptism. The Anabaptist movement, one of the more radical of the Reformation, insisted on a literal interpretation of the Sermon on the Mount, rejected participation in church government, and led a revolt among the peasantry across Europe in the sixteenth century.

ANTHONY (SAINT, C. 251–356): Founder of eremitic monasticism. After withdrawing to the desert in order to live an ascetic life, Anthony gained a reputation for wisdom and holiness that attracted pilgrims begging him for instruction. The conflict this situation created between his responsibility to his fellow Christians and his quest for a holy life of solitude drove him farther into the desert.

ANTONY, MARK (MARCUS ANTONIUS, 83–30 BCE): Roman general and politician. After Caesar's death, Mark Antony allied with Octavian and Lepidus to form the Second Triumvirate to rule the Roman Empire. After defeating Brutus, this alliance quickly disintegrated, and civil war erupted between Antony and Octavian. Cicero expressed his disdain for Mark Antony in a series of invective speeches to the Senate collectively referred to as "the philippics" (after Demosthenes' similar attacks on

Philip of Macedonia). After Cicero made these speeches, Antony had him assassinated and his hands and head displayed in the forum.

A POSTERIORI: Knowable only after empirical investigation.

APPIUS (CLAUDIUS CRASSUS): Roman patrician, consul, and decemvir. After a history of disdain for the plebs, Appius ran a populist campaign for election as a member of the decemvirs. He quickly came to lead this group and, after a year of friendly relations with the plebs, was reelected for second year, during which he ruled as a tyrant until his rape of the plebian Verginia caused public outrage that led to political change.

A PRIORI: Knowable prior to (and consequently without) empirical investigation.

ARISTOCRACY: From the Greek *aristos* for "best" and *arche* for "rule." Rule of the best, frequently determined by wealth or birth.

ARISTOTLE (384–322 BCE): Greek philosopher, Alexander the Great's tutor, and Plato's student. Aristotle studied at Plato's Academy for twenty years. After leaving, despite his admiration for his former teacher, he criticized platonic thought for emphasizing unity over diversity, giving priority to the rational over the empirical, and sacrificing the real good for the ideal best. His works, which cover all domains of thought, from physics to metaphysics, biology to psychology, include *The Politics* and *The Nicomachean Ethics*.

ARTICLES OF CONFEDERATION (1776, RATIFIED 1781): The first constitution of the United States. The Articles of Confederation were replaced in 1788 by the U.S. Constitution, which remains in use today.

***AUCTORITAS*:** Latin for "authority." In Roman law, the Senate possessed *auctoritas*, whereas the people possessed *potestas*, or "power." Pope Gelasius I would later use this distinction to claim the supremacy of the Catholic Church, which possessed *auctoritas*, over the state.

AUGUSTINE (SAINT, 354–430 CE): Bishop and Father of the Latin Church. Augustine was extremely influential in establishing Catholic theology. He brought the conceptual arguments of Plato and Cicero to bear upon the problems facing the church in his time. His writings both emphasize the universal aspect of Christianity and vociferously argue against competing beliefs, such as Donatism and Pelegianism, which were declared heretical after his critiques of them. His *City of God*, in which he intended to refute claims that Christianity was responsible for Rome's fall, was the first attempt to interpret the relation of Christianity and politics. This text develops also the first just war theory. His autobiographical *Confessions* establish faith as a gift of grace rather than an act accomplished by the efforts of the will, which is already corrupted by original sin.

AUTARCHIC: From the Greek *autos* for "self" and *arche* for "rule." Self-sufficient.

AUTONOMY: From the Greek *autos* for "self" and *nomos* for "law." Self-governing.

BENEDICT OF NURSIA (SAINT, 480–547): Founder of cenobitic monasticism. After experiencing the dangers of extreme asceticism, Benedict founded a monastery at Monte Cassino for monks to live a communal spiritual life. The Benedictine monks' daily life was rigidly ordered and governed by a strict code of discipline and authority.

BENEDICTINE ORDER: First of the four great monastic orders. After realizing the dangers of ascetic monasticism, Saint Benedict established a cenobitic or communal monastery in the early sixth century. The Benedictine Order is known for the black robes worn by its monks, whose days were rigidly structured according to its founder's prescription. One consequence of the disciplined lifestyle practiced in the monasteries was a greater influence in the affairs outside the monastery, which often undermined the monks intentional withdrawal from the world.

BRUTUS (LUCIUS JUNIUS): Founder of the Roman republic and first consul. After hearing of his sister Lucretia's rape by the son of then king Tarquin, Brutus led a revolt that expelled the monarchy forever. He was elected first consul of the new Roman republic and died defending Rome from the Tarquins.

BRUTUS (MARCUS JUNIUS, 85–42 BCE): Roman senator. Brutus sided with the Senate against the First Triumvirate and then with Pompey against Caesar. He was a member of the group of senators who assassinated him on the Ides of March. Exiled as an enemy of the state, he waged war against the Second Triumvirate and committed suicide upon defeat in this war.

BURKE, EDMUND (1729–1797): English conservative politician. Burke was an Irish member of the Whig Party in the British Parliament. He supported both Irish independence and the American Revolution, but he is best known for his criticism of the French Revolution. He rejected both the Enlightenment individualism and the "abstract principles" that ground the revolution in favor of respect for the wisdom of tradition.

BYZANTINE EMPIRE: When the Roman Empire split into eastern and western territories, the Eastern Empire, whose capital was Constantinople, came to be known as the Byzantine Empire. Because the emperor was considered to be God's earthly representative, he was treated as both the source and the interpreter of law by the Justinian Code, the empire's primary legal structure.

CAESAR, JULIUS (100–44 BCE): Roman general, politician, and later dictator. As a supporter of the agrarian land reform and a victorious general, Caesar was popular among the plebs and feared by the ruling classes. Recalled to Rome, he instead led his army across the Rubicon into the territory of Rome proper, which prompted a civil war pitting Caesar against his former ally Pompey and the Senate. Victorious, Caesar was appointed dictator in perpetuity, thus threatening the Roman republic. A group of senators led by Brutus assassinated him on the Ides of March.

CALVIN, JOHN (1509–1564): Lawyer, humanist, and theologian. Calvin is perhaps most well known for his belief in the doctrine of double predestination. His ecclesiological focus led him to champion not only the church's autonomy, but also the state's subordination to ecclesiastical power. His claim that obedience to the laws must not conflict with one's obligations to God posed the question of a political right to resistance.

CARTHAGE: Ancient Mediterranean civilization located in North Africa. Carthage engaged in several wars with Rome from 264 to 146 BCE, known as the Punic Wars after the Latin *punicus*, meaning "Carthaginian." Rome ultimately destroyed Carthage in the Third Punic War.

CATALINE (LUCIUS SERGIUS CATALINA,108–62 BCE): Roman politician and conspirator. In 63 BCE, he attempted to assassinate powerful senators and to lead an army into Rome to seize power, an event known as the "Cataline conspiracy." Cicero, a consul at the time, exposed this conspiracy to the Senate.

CENOBITIC MONK: From the Latin for "common life." Coenobitic monks lived holy lives together in monasteries, withdrawn from the world's corrupting influence. The first Roman Catholic cenobitic monastery was created by Saint Benedict at Monte Cassino.

CHARLEMAGNE (CHARLES THE GREAT, 742–814): First Carolingian monarch. The grandson of Charles Martel, who halted the Islamic invasion of Europe at the battle of Tours in 732, Charlemagne legitimated his military power through an appeal to spiritual authority. Pope Leo III crowned him *imperator romanorum* on Christmas Day in 800.

CHARLES I (1600–1649): English monarch and defender of divine right. After fourteen years of absolute rule, Charles was unable to put down a Scottish Protestant rebellion in 1639 and thus was forced to call on Parliament for new taxation. He dismissed the first parliamentary meeting (the Short Parliament) after a month, but had to call another one (the Long Parliament) when he was unable to secure funds through other means. The conflict led to civil war. Taken prisoner and put on trial, Charles continued to assert his divine place above all worldly authority and was condemned to be beheaded.

CHARLES II (1630–1685): English monarch. Son of Charles I, he was exiled to France during the English Civil War. After the death of Lord Protector Oliver Cromwell, the monarchy was restored when Charles was called back from exile in 1661. During his exile, Thomas Hobbes was his tutor. His son James II was overthrown by the Glorious Revolution.

CHARLES V (1500–1558): Habsburg Holy Roman emperor who as a young ruler presided over the Diet of Worms at which Martin Luther was forced to respond to a papal bull threatening excommunication if he did not renounce or revise his views. When Luther refused to do so, Charles issued the Edict of Worms, calling for Luther's capture and forbidding anyone from aiding him. This political moment was decisive for a very young ruler, even in comparison to his later glories.

CHARLES MARTEL (C. 688–741): French ruler and grandfather of Charlemagne. His victory in the battle of Tours (732) prevented the further expansion into Europe of the Muslim army that had conquered much of the Iberian Peninsula.

CICERO (106–43 BCE): Roman Stoic philosopher, orator, lawyer, politician, and "new man." Marcus Tullius Cicero had made a name for himself as a lawyer and was elected consul. During his service, he exposed a conspiracy, headed by Cataline, to usurp power in Rome. As a senator during the civil war, he sided with Pompey against Caesar and was ultimately assassinated by Mark Antony, who ordered that Cicero's hands and head be displayed in the forum. In addition to his publication of legal briefs and stoic moral treatises, Cicero is the author of *On the Laws* and *On the Commonwealth.*

CINCINNATUS (LUCIUS QUINCTUIS, 519–C. 430 BCE): Roman consul and dictator. Although as consul he was an opponent of the plebs, he was also a sharp critic of the patricians for the contempt they showed Roman tradition. After retiring from politics, Cincinnatus was elected dictator in 458 BCE in order to lead Rome in its war against the neighboring Sabines and the Aequians. After quickly defeating Rome's adversaries. he resigned his dictatorship just sixteen days after it began.

CLEISTHENES: Prominent Athenian and democratic reformer. Cleisthenes' reforms in 508 or 507 BCE aimed to establish isonomy by allowing a universal code of laws to take into account differences in particular application. These reforms include the establishment of ten *demes* (population groups) and a reorganization of both the law-giving body (the Boule) and court system that ensured each was more equally representative.

CONCILIARISM: A movement within the Catholic Church asserting the authority of a general church council over the pope.

CONSTANT, BENJAMIN (1767–1830): French intellectual and politician. Following his activity in the latter half of the French Revolution, which he would strongly criticize, Constant became one of the first thinkers to identify himself as a "liberal." In his "The Liberty of the Ancients Compared with That of the Moderns," he distinguished between the more public classical liberty and the private liberty of modern times.

CONSTANTINE (C. 272–337): Eastern emperor and founder of Constantinople. After founding Constantinople, which would become the capital of the Byzantine Empire, Constantine legalized Christianity, to which he had converted. When a council of bishops he convened in 325 to resolve a dispute about the nature of the Trinity failed to produce a unified doctrine, he imposed the doctrine still found today in the Nicene Creed. This act began the long dispute between secular and church authority in spiritual matters.

CONSTANTINOPLE: Center of the Eastern Roman Empire and later the Byzantine Empire. Founded by Emperor Constantine in 330 on the trade route between Europe and Asia, Constantinople became the head of the wealthier and more civilized Eastern Empire. Its location and strong defense shielded Europe from Muslim invasions until the city fell to the Ottomans in 1453.

CONSTITUENT NATIONAL ASSEMBLY (1789–1791): A representative body composed of the French third estate and liberal members of the first and second estates. Formed from the meeting of the Estates General, it was charged with writing a new national constitution. This body produced both the Declaration of the Rights of Man and the Constitution of 1791, after which it disbanded.

CONSUL: Roman political office. After the expulsion of the Tarquins, the powers of the monarch were split between two consuls who were elected for one-year intervals. Consulship was limited to the patrician class until 367 BCE, when qualifications were widened.

COSMOPOLIS: From the Greek *cosmos* for "world" and *polis* for "city." This stoic conception interpreted the world as a lawfully ordered whole in which all persons share membership.

COUNCIL OF CONSTANCE (1414–1418): A Catholic Church council. Convened in order unify the schismatic papacy, the council declared conciliar superiority over the papacy and required the pope to convene similar councils at regular intervals. This declaration is often cited as the first formulation of constitutional rule.

COUNCIL OF TRENT (1545–1563): Convened by the Catholic Church to respond to the Reformation and to condemn Protestant heresies, the Council of Trent reaffirmed traditional Catholic doctrine, ending the hope for a reconciliation between reformers and the church and beginning the Catholic Counter-Reformation.

CROMWELL, OLIVER (1599–1658): English military and political leader. During the English Civil War (1641–1651), Cromwell led purges of the Long Parliament, which reduced its membership to only seventy-five (then known as the Rump Parliament). In 1653, he dissolved the Rump Parliament and declared himself Lord Protector of the Commonwealth of England, a position he held until his death in 1658.

DARIUS (C. 549–486 BCE): King of Persia during the Greco-Persian War and father of Xerxes. His attempt to expand the Persian Empire into Greece was stopped by a defeat at the battle of Marathon in 490 BCE.

DECEMVIR: A member of a Roman law-giving body. Created in 458 BCE, a council of ten men was formed to codify Roman law. As the final authority on the law, members of the decimvirate were considered above the law. After this group completed ten tablets the first year, a new group was appointed to finish the job the following year. Appius, the only member to serve both terms, convinced the second group not to relinquish power after their task, but to rule as tyrants instead.

DECLARATION OF RIGHTS OR BILL OF RIGHTS (ENGLISH, 1689): Unlike its later American counterpart, the English Bill of Rights is a declaration of the rights of Parliament and not of the citizenry. The bill identifies Parliament as the source of the law to which even the Crown is subject.

DECLARATION OF THE RIGHTS OF MAN AND OF THE CITIZEN (FRENCH, 1789): Adopted by the Constituent National Assembly during the French Revolution, this declaration established philosophical principles on which the French Constitution was to be based. This document, in accord with its Enlightenment source, ignores the distinction between the good man and the good citizen and seeks to eliminate all particularity for the sake of unity. It remains the preamble to the French Constitution that was adopted in 1958.

DELIAN LEAGUE: A military alliance among Greek cities founded in 478 BCE after the Greco-Persian War. Athens prevented smaller member states that were unable to supply military aid from withdrawing from the league and forced them to make payment instead. As a result, the league quickly became a resented symbol of Athenian empire, paving the way for the Peloponnesian War.

DIET OF WORMS (1521): At this imperial diet, Martin Luther was summoned to respond to a papal bull threatening excommunication if he refused to revise or renounce his views about the current state of the Catholic Church. He refused, stating, "Here I stand; I can do no other," which resulted in his excommunication.

DIOGENES OF SINOPE (C. 412/404–323 BCE): Ancient Greek Cynic. He is most famous for teaching that custom is detrimental to happiness and praising the natural life of animals as better than the customary life of humans.

DOMINICAN ORDER: A mendicant order. Founded in 1216, the Dominican Order focused on the need for proper learning in religion and soon came to dominate the universities, especially in Paris. Influential members include Albert the Great and his student Saint Thomas Aquinas, who attempted to reconcile church dogma with Aristotle's rational philosophy.

DONATISM: Catholic heresy. Donatus Magnus, namesake of this heresy, insisted on a clergy free from all compromise with the secular world. Augustine criticized Donatus's position on the grounds that it implied one can earn salvation through one's action rather than entirely through God's grace and that it undermined the universality of the church. The position was declared heretical in 409.

DRACO (ALSO DRACON): Chief archon and first legislator of Athens. In order to eliminate factional feuding within Athens, Draco established a public code of law (c. 621 BCE) to which all citizens were subject. In addition to their universality, these laws were known for being extremely severe, mandating death for most offenses.

DUNS SCOTUS, JOHN (C. 1266–1308): Franciscan nominalist logician and theologian. Scotus attacked Saint Thomas Aquinas's Scholastic rationalism, especially his doctrine of the eternal law, which Scotus claimed limited God's freedom.

ECCLESIOLOGY: From the Greek word for "church." The study of theological doctrines as they pertain to the establishment, composition, and governance of the church.

EDICT OF NANTES: This edict, issued by Henry IV of France in 1598, granted substantial rights to the Calvinist minority in Catholic France in the name of national unity. It was repealed in 1685.

EMPIRICISM: A modern philosophical tradition with Aristotelian roots. The empiricist, in contrast to the rationalist, begins with observations of the particular case and then derives general laws from those observations. This Aristotelian emphasis on the primacy of the particular is balanced by an anti-Aristotelian rejection of teleological explanations.

ENGLISH CIVIL WAR (1641–1651): This conflict was both religious and political. It was fought between the royalist Cavaliers and the Protestant Roundheads over the extent of the authority held by Parliament (then in the Protestants' hands) over the Catholic monarch Charles I.

EPICTETUS (C. 55–135): Roman slave and Stoic philosopher. Epictetus taught that happiness, equally attainable to slave or master, is gained by accepting one's role as given by fate.

EPICURUS (341–270 BCE): Hellenistic philosopher. Epicurus's philosophical teachings, known as epicureanism, extol the virtue of personal pleasure as opposed to political gain. The Epicurean is to avoid politics and seek a state of *ataraxia*, or freedom, from all cares, which will allow him to enjoy an inner peace despite his outer circumstances.

ERASMUS OF ROTTERDAM (1466–1536): Augustinian monk and humanist. Erasmus is the author of *In Praise of Folly* and editor-translator of a Bible presenting side by side the Greek version, the Latin version known as the Vulgate, and his own commentaries. His secular interests were coupled with a deep commitment to the church. Although he saw the need for reform and was originally sympathetic toward Martin Luther, he refused to support the reform's more radical development and engaged in a public dispute with Luther about the nature of human freedom.

EREMITIC MONASTICISM: From the Latin term for "hermit." Eremitic monks live solitary and ascetic lives. Saint Anthony and the desert fathers are among their ranks.

ESTATES GENERAL (1789): A meeting of representatives of the three classes of France, called for the first time in more than a century by Louis XVI. The third estate met separately from the other two as the National Assembly. This self-legitimating act inaugurated the French Revolution.

***THE FEDERALIST* (1787–1788):** Written under the pseudonym "Publius" by James Madison, Alexander Hamilton, and John Jay, this collection of eighty-five short essays argues for the ratification of the 1787 U.S. Constitution. The theoretical argument for a republican democracy seeks to make a benefit out of the factional strife inevitable in a state without succumbing to the tyrannical majority always possible in a pure democracy.

FREDERICK THE WISE (1463–1525): Saxon prince and elector of the Holy Roman Empire. Frederick III, seeing benefit to secular power in a strong church reformer, was an early defender of Martin Luther. After the condemnation of Luther at the Diet of Worms, Frederick protected him while he translated the Bible into German.

GALLICANISM: A doctrine of the independent French Catholic Church that accepted the absolute power of the French state in exchange for its own independence from Rome.

GELASIUS I (D. 496): Pope from 492 to 496 and church supremacist. In an attempt to prevent state interference in church affairs, Gelasius I appealed to the Roman distinction between *auctoritas* and *potestas* to establish the supremacy of the church over the state. This argument would become a mainstay of the church's theological arguments against secular power over the years.

GIRONDINS: A political club during the French Revolution. At the outset of the National Assembly, the Girondins were more revolutionary than the predominantly royalist assembly members, although they later refused to support many of the Jacobins' extreme measures. They were eventually subject to purges under the accusation that they supported federalism to the detriment of national unity.

GLORIOUS REVOLUTION (1688): English revolution in which an act of Parliament replaced reigning Catholic monarch James II with Dutch Protestant William of Orange. This revolution, marked by a peaceful passage of power, made England a constitutional monarchy. Much of the theory behind this revolution can be found in the works of John Locke.

GRACCHUS, GAIUS (154–121 BCE): Roman tribune and supporter of land reform. Like his older brother, Tiberius, Gaius supported far-reaching popular reforms, only to die at the hands of his political opponents.

GRACCHUS, TIBERIUS (168–133 BCE): Roman tribune and supporter of land reform. Tiberius pushed for agrarian legislation that would limit the amount of land one citizen could own and allow purchase of conquered lands by plebeians. This effort, which sowed the seeds of civil war, had the more immediate consequence of Tiberius's murder at the hands of his aristocrat opponents.

GREGORY VII (C. 1015/1029–1085): Reformist pope. Upon election to the papacy in 1073, Gregory used the newly rediscovered Justinian Code to initiate a number of reforms centralizing church authority in the papacy. In a clash with Holy Roman emperor Henry IV, known as the Investiture Struggle, Gregory established the church's autonomy in its own affairs.

HANNIBAL (248–183/182 BCE): Carthaginian general. During the Second Punic War, he led the Carthaginian army across the Alps and into Italy. After years of battle on Roman territory, he was forced to return home to defend Carthage from a countersiege, where he was defeated by Roman consul Scipio Aemilianus.

HENRY IV (C. 1050–1106): Holy Roman emperor. After Henry relinquished to Pope Gregory VII the right to choose church officials, in a clash known as the Investiture Struggle, both church and state began to be seen as autonomous in their own affairs.

HENRY VIII (1491–1547): English monarch and first head of the Church of England. When he could not secure from Rome an annulment for his marriage in 1533, Henry declared the English church autonomous, with himself as its head. He put to death for treason those clergymen who remained loyal to Rome, including longtime friend Thomas More, who refused to annul Henry's marriage. This move had the further consequence of giving the Crown ownership of a great deal of land formerly held by the church.

HERETIC: One who, professing faith in Christ, rejects any Catholic Church dogma is considered a heretic. The sentence for obstinate heresy (a heresy that the person maintains is true even after twice being admonished for it) is excommunication. Important heretics include Pelegius and Donatus, for whom the Pelegian and Donatist heresies are named.

HESIOD (LATTER HALF OF EIGHTH CENTURY BCE): Ancient Greek poet. With Homer, Hesiod is a source of much of our knowledge of ancient Greek life and religion. His two most famous works are *Works and Days* and *Theogony*.

HOBBES, THOMAS (1588–1679): Rationalist English philosopher. Hobbes began his life as a classicist and became a materialist-rationalist political philosopher after discovering Euclid's *Elements*. Exiled during the English Civil War, he wrote his major political work *Leviathan*, which introduces the concepts of a "state of nature" and a "social contract" and argues from natural law for the renunciation of each individual's right as the only means of attaining physical safety and lasting private liberty.

HOMER: Legendary blind Greek poet. Homer is the author of the *Iliad*, an account of the Greek siege of the city of Troy, and the *Odyssey*, an account Odysseus's decade-long journey home after the war. With Hesiod, he is a source of much of our knowledge of ancient Greek life and religion.

HUMANISM: A Renaissance movement that rejected scholasticism and saw humanity as of central significance in the universe. It was propelled largely by the rediscovery of Latin and Greek texts. As a result of their pagan inspiration, many humanists, such as Erasmus and Sir Thomas More, had an uneasy relationship with both the Catholic Church and the Reformation.

HUME, DAVID (1711–1776): Scottish philosopher, essayist, and historian. His essay "On the Original Contract" provided the English Tory Party with its theoretical foundation based on the authority of past traditions.

HUS, JAN (1369–1415): Czech priest and educational reformer. His criticism of the church hierarchy was coupled with a defense of the supremacy of the state over the church, which led to the Council of Constance decree that he be burned at the stake as a heretic.

IDES OF MARCH: March 15 in the Roman calendar. Julius Caesar was assassinated on this day in 44 BCE.

INDULGENCE: The Catholic Church's granting of a reduction of the time one is to spend in purgatory. Martin Luther criticized the Catholic Church's sale of indulgences to finance both military and architectural endeavors, arguing that salvation can be found only through faith and Scripture.

INVESTITURE STRUGGLE (C. 1077): A conflict between Holy Roman emperor Henry IV and Pope Gregory VII over who had authority to appoint bishops of the Roman Catholic Church (investiture). When Henry would not withdraw his nominee for the bishop of Milan, Gregory excommunicated him. Hoping to overturn his excommunication, Henry traveled to Canossa to beg forgiveness, which he received in exchange for relinquishing his right to lay investiture. The church and the state were subsequently considered free to govern their own affairs.

ISOCRATES (436–338 BCE): A student of Socrates who called for the formation of an all-Greek federative unity that he called a *sympoliteia* to combat the threat of Macedonia under Philip II, the father of Alexander the Great.

ISONOMY: From the Greek *iso* for "equality" and *nomos* for "law." Equality before the law.

JACOBINS: Members of an influential political club during the French Revolution whose radical wing, led by Maximilien Robespierre and Louis de Saint-Just, dominated the Committee on Public Safety (Comité salut public), which administered the Reign of Terror.

JUSTINIAN (483–585): Eastern Roman emperor and legal reformer. He is best known for his legal reforms, the Justinian Code, that consolidated power in the emperor by claiming him to be God's representative on earth and the legitimate source and interpreter of law.

JUSTINIAN CODE: Legal code of the Byzantine Empire. Because the Eastern Empire treated the emperor as God's earthly representative, the Justinian Code treated him as both the source and interpreter of law. This emphasis on a centralized authority made the code useful later for justifying legal reforms in both the Roman Catholic Church, which consolidated the power of the papacy, and the state, which consolidated power in the ruler.

LE CHAPELIER LAW: This law, voted on by the Constituent National Assembly in France, forbade the creation of trade unions and guilds on the ground that such "partial associations" threatened the unity of the republic.

LIVY (TITUS LIVIUS, 64/59 BCE–17 CE): Roman historian. Livy is best known for his influential 128-volume *History of Rome from the Foundation,* most volumes of which are lost today. This work chronicling Roman history from the emigration of the Trojans through the start of Augustus's rule was the subject of one of Machiavelli's most famous works and served as an inspiration to American founder fathers and French revolutionaries alike.

LOCKE, JOHN (1632–1704): Medical doctor and empiricist English philosopher. Locke, the author of *An Essay Concerning Human Understanding* and *Two Treatises on Government,* was an active participant in the events leading to the Glorious Revolution. Working within the contractarian framework, Locke argues for a more tolerant, pluralist government. Its citizens have a right to resist if it no longer serves its function, which is the impartial arbitration of disputes and the protection of private property, which he claims exists in nature when a person mixes his labor in a thing to improve it.

LONG PARLIAMENT: Called by Charles I of England in order to raise tax revenue in 1640 (after the failed Short Parliament), the Long Parliament passed the Triennial Act and the vote of Grand Remonstrance, which began the English Civil War, during which Charles would be beheaded.

LOUIS XVI (1754–1793): French king. Louis XVI called the first meeting of the Estates General in more than a century, which would set into motion the French Revolution in 1789. He was later arrested after a failed attempt to flee France, found guilty of treason, and guillotined.

LOYOLA, IGNATIUS (SAINT, 1491–1556): Founder of the Jesuit Order. One of the leading intellectuals of the Counter-Reformation, Loyola founded the Jesuit Order in 1540 to lead the fight against the Reformation.

LUCRETIA: Roman noblewoman and sister of Lucius Junius Brutus. She committed suicide after being raped by the son of then king Tarquin. This act prompted a revolution in 509 BCE, led by her brother Brutus, that expelled the Tarquins and ended the Roman monarchy.

LUTHER, MARTIN (1483–1546): Augustinian monk, Protestant reformer, and church founder. Luther's attempt to reform the Catholic Church began when he nailed to the door of his church *The Ninety-five Theses* criticizing the church's sale of indulgences. At the Diet of Worms, he radicalized his views that salvation is found only through faith and Scripture, for which he was excommunicated. While under the protection of Frederick the Wise, he translated the Bible into German. When peasant rebels further radicalized his reforms, Luther wrote a tract in 1525 strongly denouncing their action and lending support to the secular rulers.

LYCURGUS (C. 700–630 BCE): Legendary creator of the Spartan Constitution. The strength and longevity of the Spartan Constitution, which encouraged an ascetic, militaristic way of life, are due largely to the myths surrounding its creator.

MACHIAVELLI, NICCOLÒ(469–1527): Italian politician and political theorist. Exiled from Florence after the republican government was overthrown, Machiavelli began writing his great political works *The Prince* and the *Discourses on the First Ten Books of Livy*. His theories have been praised as well as denounced for his explicit separation of politics from ethics, his "economic" description of the use of violence, and his use of (self-)interest as a means of calculating others' behavior when one is trying to obtain political power.

MANDEVILLE, BERNARD (1670–1733): English philosopher and economist. Mandeville's *Fable of the Bees* argued that public benefit can derive from private vice, anticipating Adam Smith's later theory of political economy.

MANICHEANISM: Gnostic religion. Manicheans asserted the existence of two primary substances—one good, one evil, with no gray zone between them. Augustine, a Manichean himself in his early life, dedicated much of his writing to refuting them.

***MARBURY V. MADISON* (1803):** This U.S. Supreme Court case established the sovereignty of the Constitution rather than of the presently ruling party.

MARCUS AURELIUS (121–180): Roman emperor, Stoic author, and the last of the "five good emperors" identified by Machiavelli. His *Meditations* demonstrate how Stoic philosophy can be adapted to the powerful as well as to the enslaved.

MARSILLIUS OF PADUA (C. 1275–C. 1342): Author of *Defender of the Peace*. An exile in Bavaria along with William of Ockham, Marsillius argued that imperial legislation (*regnum*) should be limited by the fact that laws must be the expression of the popular will (*civitas*). His argument that laws derive their legitimacy from the procedure used to create them rather than from knowledge of the good or the divine will is known today as *proceduralism*.

MEDICI, LORENZO DI (1449–1492): De facto ruler of Florence after its republican government was overthrown. Machiavelli dedicated *The Prince* to him.

MELANCHTON, PHILIP (1497–1560): Professor and theologian. Philip became a major follower of Luther and supporter of the Reformation.

MENDICANT: From the Latin *mendicans*, meaning "begging." Mendicant orders required their monks to take a vow of poverty and depend on charity for their livelihood. The Dominican and Franciscan orders in the Roman Catholic Church are mendicant orders.

MERCANTILISM: An early economic-political theory that took a positive balance of trade to be the only source of national wealth. The mercantile system employed subsidized production and strong monopolies with little concern for the condition of the laborer.

MORE, SIR THOMAS (1478–1535): English politician, humanist, and author. A high-ranking politician to whom Erasmus dedicated *In Praise of Folly*, More was a devout Catholic who refused to swear allegiance to the English Church when Henry VIII declared it independent of Rome. On this account, he was beheaded for treason. More's humanist classic *Utopia* gave rise to the concept of "utopianism."

MÜNTZER, THOMAS (C. 1488–1525): Revolutionary and Anabaptist. Although an early supporter of Martin Luther, Müntzer soon criticized him for being too timid. He became an Anabaptist and the leader of the Peasant Revolt, which was based on radicalized versions of Luther's arguments and which Luther would strongly denounce.

MYCENAE: Home to the ancient Greek civilization that was the source of classical Greek religion. Its agonistic culture is portrayed in Homer's account of the Trojan War, begun when Agamemnon, king of Mycenae, sent the Greeks to war with the Troy.

NEW MAN (*NOVUS HOMO*): The designation of a Roman born outside of the patrician class who becomes the first in his family to be elected consul or appointed senator. Famous new men include Cato the Elder, Cicero, Pompey, and Tacitus.

NEW MODEL ARMY: Parliamentary (and Protestant) army during the English Civil War (1641–1651).

NICEAN CREED: Doctrine establishing the nature of the Trinity that Emperor Constantine imposed on the church in order to maintain both a unified church and a unified empire.

NOMINALISM: The theory, articulated most forcefully by William of Ockham, that there are no universal entities, but only specific ones. Any general laws or universalisms stem from the agreement among humans that a general pattern is present among specific things. In addition to providing the grounds for modern science, nominalism, when translated into political thought, rules out the idea of a natural law to which political relations must ultimately conform.

***NOMOS*:** Greek for "law" or "convention."

OCTAVIAN (AUGUSTUS, 63 BCE–14 CE): First Roman emperor. Julius Caesar adopted Octavian at the age of eighteen. After Caesar's assassination, Octavian joined with Mark Antony in ruling Rome before their rivalry erupted into a second civil war. After defeating Mark Antony, he ruled Rome as its first emperor under the title "Augustus."

ODYSSEUS: King of Ithaca and Greek soldier in the Trojan War. He is remembered for his intellect, exemplified by devising the Trojan horse strategy, which eventually won the war, as well as for his decade-long journey home after the war, which is the primary subject of Homer's *Odyssey.*

OLIGARCHY: From the Greek *oligos* for "few" and *arche* for "rule." Although technically meaning "rule of the few," the term is often used to mean "rule of the wealthy."

ORACLE OF DELPHI: The most important of the Greek oracles. It was located in a temple of Apollo above which the phrases "know thyself" and "nothing in excess" were carved. Chaerephon famously asked the oracle who the smartest in Athens was, only to be informed that "none [in Athens] is smarter than Socrates."

PAINE, THOMAS (1737–1809): American political philosopher. His best-selling pamphlet *Common Sense,* published in January 1776 and strongly urging a declaration of independence, provided the Americans with the impetus for the final break with Great Britain. Paine later participated in the French Revolution and in 1791 published a polemical reply, *The Rights of Man,* to Edmund Burke's critique of the revolution.

PATRISTIC: From the Latin *pater* for "father." The term *patristic* refers to the early Christian writers whose work shaped Catholic doctrine. Notable patristic authors include Ambrose, Augustine, Jerome, Gregory the Great, and Tertullian.

PAUL (SAINT, DIED C. 64–65 CE): Roman citizen, early Christian missionary, saint. Paul, formerly called "Saul," was a Jew and persecutor of Christians until a vision of Jesus led him to change both his faith and his name. His missionary work came to be influential on early church doctrine through his letters to new congregations.

PAX ROMANA (27 BCE–180 CE): Latin for "Roman Peace." Augustus's rule initiated two centuries of relative peace and stability for Rome, although one based on war and imperial domination. Of this peace, Tacitus famously remarked that the Romans "make a desert and call it peace."

PEISISTRATOS (C. 600–527/28 BCE): Military leader of Athens and then tyrant from 546 until his death in 527 BCE.

PELEGIANISM: Catholic heresy. This heresy, named for Pelagius (c. 354–420/440), asserts that original sin does not prevent one's earning salvation through the exercise of free will. Saint Augustine opposed it, teaching that salvation depended on God's grace, and the Council of Carthage condemned it in 418.

PELOPONNESIAN WAR (431–404 BCE): War between Athens and Sparta for dominance in Greece. This long war ended in a crushing loss for Athens.

PERICLES (495–429 BCE): Athenian orator, general, and statesman. Pericles led Athens at the height of its military influence, often called the "Periclean Age," during which time he expanded its democratic institutions. Thucydides memorialized him in *History of the Peloponnesian War,* calling him "first citizen of Athens."

PHILIP II (382–336 BCE): King of Macedonia and father of Alexander the Great. Phillip's expansion of Macedonian territory during his reign from 382 to 336 BCE ended Athenian autonomy. Many Greeks hated him, and Demothenes' vitriolic speeches against him gave rise to the term *philippic.*

PHILIPPICS: A series of speeches against Mark Anthony that Cicero gave to the Roman Senate in 44 and 43 BCE. He modeled these vitriolic speeches after those given by Demosthenes against Philip of Macedonia, from which they take their name.

PHILOSOPHES: Eighteenth-century French intellectuals (including Voltaire, Claude Helvétius, Denis Diderot, and Jean d'Alembert) who tasked themselves with spreading the teaching of the Enlightenment throughout society for the sake of progress. They attacked the church's political power but preferred an enlightened despotism to democratic government. The *Encyclopedia* was one of their crowning achievements.

PHYSIOCRATS: Members of an eighteenth-century movement for political reform (involving philosophes such as Françs Quesnay and Anne Robert Jacques Turgot). The Physiocrats were the first political reformers to emphasize production rather than trade as a source of national wealth. To counter then prevailing mercantilism, they argued that productive labor (specifically agriculture) is the only source of wealth generation and consequently that governments ought to adopt a laissez-faire approach to trade.

***PHYSIS*:** Greek for "nature."

PLATO (428/27–348/47 BCE): Greek philosopher, Socrates' student, Aristotle's teacher, and founder of the Academy. After the Athenians sentenced Socrates to death, Plato founded the Academy outside the walls of Athens. In *The Republic,* he teaches that only a city ruled by philosopher-kings will be a good city because only they can know the good and can order the city in a way that will properly attain the good.

PLEBS (PLEBIAN): The Roman lower class. These Roman citizens who were not members of the patrician class made up the majority of the Roman army. During the early republican period, membership in high offices was strictly forbidden to the plebs. However, after centuries of struggle, they were given their own office, the tribune, and were eventually permitted to be consuls and senators.

POLIS: Greek for "city." The primary political organization of ancient Greece was the autonomous city. As the domain of free and political action, it is distinguished in Greek thought from the *oikos*, or household, which is the domain of necessity. The two most dominant poleis were Sparta and Athens.

POLYBIUS (C. 203–120 BCE): Greek politician and historian. In his *Histories,* which includes a political history of Rome from 220 to 167 BCE, Polybius develops a theory of mixed government that includes checks and balances.

POMPEY (GNAEUS POMPIUS MAGNUS, 106–48 BCE): Roman general, politician, and new man. As an adept general, Pompey quickly climbed the military ranks. He allied himself with onetime rivals Marcus Crassus and Julius Caesar to form the First Triumvirate. When this alliance disintegrated, he sided with the Senate against Caesar during the civil war. He lost this war and was assassinated in Egypt.

***POTESTAS*:** Latin for "power." In Roman law, the people possessed *potestas,* whereas the Senate possessed *auctoritas,* "authority." Pope Gelasius I would later use this distinction to claim the supremacy of the church, which possessed *auctoritas,* over the state.

PUNIC WARS (264–146 BCE): A series of three wars between Rome and Carthage. In the first war, expansionist Rome conquered Carthaginian Sicily. The second war saw Hannibal lead the Carthaginian army across the Alps and into Italy from the north, where they won several major battles but were ultimately forced home when a Roman army threatened Carthage. The third and final war ended with the complete destruction of Carthage by the Roman forces lead by Scipio Aemilianus.

QUESNAY, FRANÇS (1694–1774): Physiocrat and physician to the French king. Quesnay's *Tableau énomique* (1758) argues against taxes on the agricultural class because their labor is considered to be the only productive labor.

RATIONALISM: A modern philosophical tradition with Platonic roots. Major tenants of rationalism include the application of mathematical techniques to a world conceived of as neutral bodies in motion without any inherent ends. In distinction from his empiricist counterpart, the rationalist proceeds by formulating general laws, to which the particular case is then shown to conform.

REFORMATION (C. 1517–1648): A movement to reform the Catholic Church that led to the establishment Protestantism. The Reformation is generally considered to have begun with Martin Luther's nailing of his *Ninety-five Theses* to his church door and to have ended with the Peace of Westphalia in 1648, which recognized each ruler's right (first enunciated in the Peace of Augsburg in 1555) to determine the religion of his realm. In addition to the establishment of several Protestant churches, the Reformation contributed to changes within the Catholic Church, changes in the relationship between church and state, and the establishment of the modern state.

ROBESPIERRE, MAXIMILIEN (1758–1794): Jacobin head of the Committee on Public Safety (Comité salut public). Robespierre's attempt to create a truly virtuous republic led to the Reign of Terror, in which any signs of particularity were harshly punished. He outlined the principles of his "revolutionary government" in "Discourse on the Principles of Morality," asserting the dual principles of virtue and terror: "virtue without which terror is disastrous, terror without which virtue is powerless." He was eventually executed for his revolutionary excess.

ROMAN DICTATOR: Roman political office. In order to address extreme crises, absolute power was given to a single person for a short period of time (usually six months). In early (republican) Roman history, it was considered a sign of honor to relinquish the dictatorship as soon as the crisis was dealt with, as Cincinnatus did.

ROMULUS AND REMUS: Legendary founders of Rome. The twins were said to have been fathered by Mars, the Roman god of war, and suckled by a she-wolf. After they founded Rome, Romulus killed Remus in a fight over who would rule the new city. In order to ensure Rome's survival, Romulus then arranged for the forced marriage of many Sabine women to the young Romans, an act known as the Rape of the Sabine Women.

ROUSSEAU, JEAN-JACQUES (1712–1778): Social contract theorist. Rousseau sought to combine social contract theory with classical republicanism. His claims about the mutability of man's nature forced him to find a justification for social contract outside of the "state of nature." He sought this justification in a society's general will as opposed to the will of all. His major works include *The First* and *Second Discourses*; *Julie, or the New Heloïse*; *Émile, or On Education*; and *The Social Contract*, which would later become the "bible of the French Revolution."

SCAEVOLA (GAIUS MUCIUS): Legendary Roman soldier of the early republic. During an Etruscan siege of Rome (c. 509 BCE), he infiltrated the enemy camp and attempted to assassinate the Etruscan king. After being discovered, he thrust his right hand into the fire to demonstrate Roman valor. The king rewarded Gaius's virtuous disdain for his own well-being by freeing him and calling off the siege. For this act, Gaius was given the name "Scaevola," which means "left-handed."

SCHOLASTICISM: Based on the Latin word for "schoolmen." Scholasticism is a medieval style of thought that sought to reconcile Greek philosophy with Christian teaching. Thomas Aquinas's *Summa theologica* is exemplary of scholastic reasoning in its attempt to face up to and overcome apparent contradictions.

SCIPIO AEMILIANUS (SCIPIO AFRICANUS) (185–129 BCE): Roman aristocrat and Republican consul. Cicero used Scipio, much revered for his victory in the Third Punic War and opponent of the Gracchi land reform, as his mouthpiece in *On the Commonwealth.*

SHORT PARLIAMENT (1640): Charles I of England called the Short Parliament to raise tax revenue but dismissed this first meeting of Parliament in more than a decade after only a month, during which it refused his request.

SIEYÈS ABBÉ EMMANUEL-JOSEPH (1748–1836): French clergymen and political pamphleteer. Sieyès famously answered the question of his 1789 pamphlet *What Is the Third Estate?* with "it is the nothing that should become everything." He was one of the few original revolutionaries to have survived the torments of the entire revolutionary period.

SMITH, ADAM (1723–1790): Scottish moral philosopher and political economist. Following the Physiocrats in their understanding that political economy is an aspect of statesmanship, Smith supported a commercial society over a mercantile and feudal one. His publications include *The Theory of Moral Sentiments* and *An Inquiry into the Causes and Nature of the Wealth of Nations,* which includes his famous discussion of the division of labor and the market's "Invisible Hand."

SOLON (C. 638–558 BCE): Athenian politician and lawmaker. His establishment of four classes based on property ownership (rather than on kinship relations) and elimination of debt bondage laid the foundation for the subsequent democratic reforms in Athens.

SOPHIST: From the Greek *sophos,* meaning "wise one." Much impugned by Plato and most subsequent philosophers and accused of abandoning truth for appearance, the Sophists taught rhetoric to those willing to pay. This skill was particularly useful in Athens, where one was expected to defend oneself before one's peers if sued.

SOTERIOLOGICAL: From the Greek *soterion* for "salvation." This term is used to describe those theological doctrines that, like many of Martin Luther's, are focused exclusively on the quest for salvation.

SPARTA: Competitor with Athens for dominance over Greece. Its inhabitants, also known as Lacedaemonians, are famous for the development of the phalanx and for their militaristic, sparse, and almost ascetic way of life. Famous episodes in Sparta's history include the creation of its constitution by Lycurgus, stalling the invading Persian army in the battle of Thermopylae, and its conquest of Athens in the second Peloponnesian War.

TARQUIN THE PROUD (?–496 BCE): Last king of Rome. When his son raped Lucretia, her kinsman Marcus Junius Brutus started a revolt that expelled Tarquin and the monarchy from Rome. After his expulsion, Tarquin convinced the neighboring Etruscans to attack Rome in order to stop the spread of republicanism. The assault on Rome failed, and the Tarquins died in exile.

***TELOS*:** Greek for "end" or "purpose." In ancient Greek thought, a thing's telos is commonly used to understand what it is.

TERTULLIAN (C. 160–C. 220): Early church father. Tertullian's famous assertion "Credo quia absurdum" means "I believe it because it is absurd." This religious ideal led him to ask, "What has Athens to do with Jerusalem?" a perennial question about the relationship between religion and philosophy.

THEODOSIUS (347–395): Last emperor of a united Rome. After reuniting the eastern and western empires, Theodosius declared Christianity the official religion of the Roman Empire in 391. This declaration led people who had once rejected the church to return for political reasons, against which the Donatist position of insisting on the purity of the clergy (unsullied by politics or heresy) was aimed.

THERSITES: A common Greek soldier during the Trojan War. Homer portrays him as ugly, vulgar, and dull-witted.

THIRTY TYRANTS: An oligarchy sympathetic to Sparta that was installed in Athens after Athens's defeat in Peloponnesian in 404 BCE. Among its members were Plato's uncle and a friends of Socrates, who nevertheless refused their order to arrest an innocent man.

THOMAS AQUINAS (SAINT, 1225–1274): Dominican monk and Scholastic teacher. He taught at the University of Paris, where he worked to synthesize church doctrine with the recently translated works of Aristotle. He authored many works, including *On Kingship,* numerous commentaries on Aristotelian writings, and the *Summa theologica.*

THUCYDIDES (C. 460–395 BCE): Greek historian. Thucydides' *History of the Peloponnesian War* was famous for its "political realism" and its brilliant reconstruction of the speeches of the contending parties. Among these speeches is his celebration of Pericles as the "first citizen of Athens" and his reconstruction of Pericles' funeral oration during the war.

THYMIC: From the Greek *thymos,* which is commonly translated as "spiritedness" and means "a desire," especially for recognition. *Thymos* is one of the three parts of the division of the human soul (*psyche*) found in Plato's dialogues *Phaedrus* and *The Republic.*

TIMOCRACY: From the Greek *time* for "honor" and *arche* for "rule." Rule of the honored.

TORY PARTY: English political party. Successor to the Cavaliers of the English Civil War, Tories thought that because community molds individual character, deference is owed to the authority of tradition. Its members included David Hume, whose "On the Original Contract" provided the party with its theoretical foundation.

TRIBUNE OF THE PLEBS: Roman office. Because of long-standing political grievances, the plebian soldiers seceded from Rome and refused to go to war in 494 BCE. In response, the Senate created the tribuneship, which was responsible for preventing patrician abuse of the consulship. Among his powers, the tribune had the authority to veto any act of the Senate.

TRIENNIAL ACT: Passed by the English Long Parliament in 1641, this act affirmed that Parliament, not the monarchy, would determine when it met.

TRIUMPH: The highest honor a Roman citizen could receive. The Senate awarded the triumph most often to honor a general returning victorious from a major war, which gave this body great power in emphasizing or minimizing the deeds of a particular general.

TWO SWORDS: Catholic doctrine of legitimate authority. There are numerous sources for this doctrine in the New Testament, which suggests that the relationship between secular and sacred authority as well as between the spirit and the letter of the law is analogous to the relationship between two swords, each of which God uses to rule man and the world. This doctrine, subject to multiple interpretations, was later used to support the Gelasian doctrine of papal authority and to legitimate Charlemagne's reign.

VIRGIL (70–19 BCE): Roman poet. Virgil's most famous works include the *Bucolics,* the *Georgics,* and the *Aeneid,* an incomplete epic poem chronicling the history of Rome from the time of Aeneas's escape from Troy to the creation of the empire.

WHIG PARTY: English political party. The liberal Whig Party of Parliament supported a constitutional rather than an absolutist monarchy. In order to secure the rights of English citizens, the party passed the Habeas Corpus Act of 1679. Its members included Locke's patron, Anthony Ashley Cooper (the earl of Shaftsbury).

WILLIAM OF OCKHAM (C. 1288–C. 1348): Franciscan logician and theologian. Ockham radicalized Duns Scotus's teaching on God's absolute freedom into a nominalist logic that emphasized the limits of human rationality by denying the reality of universals. He is most recognized today for his claim, known as Ockham's razor, that explanations ought not postulate unnecessary entities. This logic, which came to be taught at the *via moderna,* laid the groundwork for modern science.

WYCLIFFE, JOHN (C. 1320–1384): Wycliffe produced the first vernacular translation of the Bible (into English) in 1382. This translation broke up the church monopoly on the sacred text and was then used to justify many of the peasant revolts of the period.

XERXES (519–465 BCE): King of Persia during the Greco-Persian War. His army suffered significant losses at the battles of Salamis, Plataea, and Mycale, which forced it into retreat.

ZENO OF CITTIUM (334–262 BCE): Hellenistic philosopher and founder of the Stoic school of thought. A younger contemporary of Epicurus, Zeno emphasized each person's membership in the community of humanity and their consequent subjection to the laws of nature. This subjugation to the same set of laws implies an equality among all, which grounds any claims about universal human rights and obligations.

INDEX